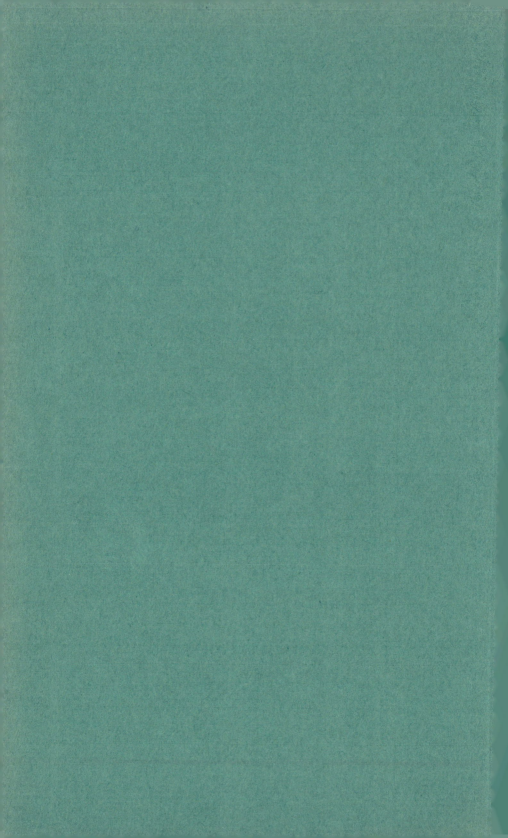

Slavery's Borderland

EARLY AMERICAN STUDIES

Series editors:
Daniel K. Richter, Kathleen M. Brown,
Max Cavitch, and David Waldstreicher

Exploring neglected aspects of our colonial, revolutionary, and early national history and culture, Early American Studies reinterprets familiar themes and events in fresh ways. Interdisciplinary in character, and with a special emphasis on the period from about 1600 to 1850, the series is published in partnership with the McNeil Center for Early American Studies.

A complete list of books in the series
is available from the publisher.

SLAVERY'S BORDERLAND

Freedom and Bondage along the Ohio River

MATTHEW SALAFIA

PENN

UNIVERSITY OF PENNSYLVANIA PRESS

PHILADELPHIA

Published by
University of Pennsylvania Press
Philadelphia, Pennsylvania 19104-4112
www.upenn.edu/pennpress

Printed in the United States of America on acid-free paper
10 9 8 7 6 5 4 3 2 1

Library of Congress Cataloging-in-Publication Data
Salafia, Matthew.
  Slavery's borderland : freedom and bondage along the Ohio River /
Matthew Salafia. — 1st ed.
      p.   cm. — (Early American studies)
  Includes bibliographical references and index.
  ISBN 978-0-8122-4521-9 (hardcover : alk. paper)
  1. Slavery—Kentucky.   2. Slavery—Indiana.   3. Slavery—Ohio.
4. Ohio River Valley—History—18th century.   5. Ohio River Valley—
History—19th century.   I. Title.   II. Series: Early American studies.
E445.K5S25   2013
306.3'620977—dc23

                                                      2012049856

To Beth

CONTENTS

Introduction: Listening to the River   1

Chapter 1. Origins of the Border between Slavery and Freedom   15

Chapter 2. Crossing the Line   43

Chapter 3. Slaveholding Liberators   70

Chapter 4. Steamboats and the Transformation of the Borderland   108

Chapter 5. Politics of Unity and Difference   137

Chapter 6. Fugitive Slaves and the Borderland   165

Chapter 7. The Nature of Antislavery in the Borderland   185

Chapter 8. The Borderland and the Civil War   215

Notes   251

Index   315

Acknowledgments   319

Listening to the River

In *Uncle Tom's Cabin*, Eliza Harris clasped her child as she darted toward the river's edge. Then "with one wild cry and flying leap, she vaulted sheer over the turbid current by the shore on to the raft of ice beyond . . . she leaped to another and another; stumbling, leaping, slipping, springing upwards again. . . . She saw nothing, felt nothing, till dimly, as in a dream, she saw the Ohio side, and a man helping her up the bank." Eliza risking her life to cross the Ohio River personified the sentiment "liberty or death." On the southern bank slave catchers tried to pull Eliza back to slavery; on the northern bank someone helped her toward freedom. However, without the ice sheets the Ohio River would have been impassable. Eliza leaped across a solid, albeit unstable, divide between slavery and freedom.[1]

Yet Harriet Beecher Stowe's border was fleeting because Eliza leaped across chunks of ice that disappeared from under her feet. Indeed outside of fiction the Ohio River remained an unstable divide between slavery and freedom throughout the antebellum period. In 1787 the Northwest Ordinance made the Ohio River the dividing line between slavery and freedom in the West; yet when the Civil War broke the country in two in 1861, this region failed to split at this seam. This book traces the history of the Ohio River borderland from its natural and human origins, through its political definition in the early republic, to maturation during the antebellum period, and to its surprising resilience during the sectional crisis. As residents on both sides of the river struggled to accommodate it as at once a dividing line and a unifying economic force, they defined this borderland by its inherent contradictions. Rather than marking a line that slavery could not penetrate, the Ohio River muddied distinctions, and residents used that ambiguity to try to hold the region together even against the threat of civil war.

*   *   *

The Ohio River Valley was a peculiar place in antebellum America. North of the Ohio River, southern migration and economic connections with the southern economy gave the region a southern bent, and cultural historians often put the cultural division between North and South somewhere north of the Ohio River. Historians of slavery have demonstrated that slavery at the top of the South was different from that of the Deep South. As a result white Kentuckians' lukewarm commitment to the institution became a source of conflict with their more southerly neighbors. In 1861 as northerners and southerners alike geared for war, Kentuckians refused to secede and actually declared their neutrality. In this book these stories are brought together to demonstrate that while the lower North was uniquely southern and the upper South was uniquely northern, the result was a region defined by its blend of influences.[2]

So that the peculiarities of this region can be understood, this study historicizes the border itself. Placing the areas north and south along the river at the center of the interpretation contributes to a new history of the Ohio River Valley that looks for regional coherence across state borders. Historians, political scientists, and cultural and literary critics have argued that where geographical borders fail to contain and define human interactions, residents create a unique third country in between called borderlands. Out of their interactions, residents of these borderlands create regions defined by their hybridity. Studies have demonstrated that borderlands are complicated zones of cultural and physical confrontation and accommodation where interactions shape policies. When national leaders made the Ohio River the boundary between slavery and freedom, they reshaped residents' movements and interactions in the region. The movements encouraged by this river border informed local residents' understanding of the region and their place in it. Movement was normative in the Ohio River Valley, and as a result it was a place where dichotomies could not apply; instead residents defined the region as a borderland.[3]

In most historical treatments, the rise of the new American nation was the beginning of the end for the Ohio River Valley borderland. But historians base this argument on a historically specific definition that ties the borderland to the colonial period. By this definition, borderlands were "the contested boundaries between colonial domains," and the creation of nationally recognized state borders turned borderlands into "bordered lands." In the case of the Ohio River Valley, however, this definition overstates the ability of borders to divide. Americans on both sides of the Ohio River shared common social and cultural backgrounds, and yet a border divided them. Residents and settlers had to accommodate that division, and in so doing they created social and cultural differences between free and slave states. But the reality was that the interaction between the flow of the river and residents' attempts to define it as a border made the geographical divide between slavery and freedom an abstraction that was both decisive and elusive.[4]

I have tried to follow the contours of residents' mental mapping of the region. I have not made the history of this region fit my model of a borderland; quite to the contrary, this region was a borderland because residents defined it that way. When first created in 1787, the northern and southern limits of this borderland extended into the interiors of the states. Over the course of the antebellum period, economic and social changes shrank the borderland to the counties that bordered the Ohio River, because those who lived along the river continued to define themselves by their relationship to this border. While they may not have seen themselves as very different in 1800, by 1861 Ohioans and Indianans believed that they were quite different from their slaveholding neighbors in Kentucky. If they imagined themselves as different from one another, borderlanders also defined their region as unique from the rest of the country. By the 1850s sectional conflict pushed northerners and southerners apart, but residents of the Ohio River borderland denounced sectionalism on both sides and emphasized their own ability to coexist across a divisive border. This was not a region without conflict, but residents never gave up on the idea of living half slave and half free. It was a place where confrontation coexisted with accommodation, and where disunity highlighted similarities. This simultaneous existence of contradictory impulses characterized the Ohio River borderland.[5]

In this study I have limited my definition of the Ohio River borderland to areas of Kentucky, Indiana, and Ohio. While there are comparisons to the border between Pennsylvania and Maryland where appropriate, this is not a study of the entire border between slave and free states in America. The Mason-Dixon Line surely shared some characteristics with the Ohio River border, but just as certainly they were not identical. Perhaps most important, Ohio, Indiana, and Kentucky were divided by a river rather than a line of latitude. The fact that these states shared access to the Ohio River and with it a lane of commerce that connected the region with markets as far south as New Orleans made residents more likely, and perhaps more willing, to foster harmonious relations with their neighbors across the slave/ free border. Illinois is also absent from this study, but not because Illinois did not share similar characteristics with its free-state neighbors. Much excellent work has been done on Illinois's history with slavery, while less has been done linking the stories of Ohio and Indiana with those of its slaveholding neighbor.[6]

Interpreting this region as a borderland helps explain peculiarities about the lower North and the upper South by drawing them into the same narrative. First, this book explains why and how the Ohio River, an artery of trade, became the dividing line between slavery and freedom in the early American West. The natural history of the Ohio River made it a meeting place for the people who settled the Ohio Valley. The river defined hunting grounds for Ohio Indians, marked one edge of the French and English empires, and became the border between the American backcountry and Indian territory, all before it became the legal boundary between slavery and freedom in the United States. When members of Congress approved article 6 of the Northwest Ordinance, which banned slavery north of the Ohio River, they wrote a new definition onto an old border and left it up to local residents to interpret the meaning of that border.[7]

As white Americans moved into the region, slaveholding Kentucky became a place where emancipation seemed possible, and the Northwest Territory, the first region with free-soil origins, had a disguised form of slavery. The role of the Ohio River border in the settlement process sheds light on this apparent contradiction as well. Some settlers heading west hoped to make Kentucky a model of America's antislavery future. But Virginia's land claims extended north to the Ohio River, and so Kentucky was under the jurisdiction of Virginia. Settlers capitalized on enslaved labor to break the land and set up their homesteads. The enslaved population grew so rapidly that gradual compensated emancipation became impossible and immediate emancipation threatened social disruption. In addition the Ohio River border was a safety valve, because those who were disappointed with their opportunities in Kentucky moved across the river. The migration of white settlers across the river, in turn, both gave them access to bound labor and led them to reject chattel slavery. By making careful distinctions between servitude and slavery northern residents defined the Ohio River as the northern limit of the chattel principle, but they retained a system of bound labor.[8]

In the antebellum period, slavery expanded in Kentucky while the bound labor system in Ohio and Indiana rapidly disintegrated, but the region's peculiarity remained. The perceived "mildness" of slavery in Kentucky and the virulence of racism in Ohio and Indiana set these states apart from their respective regions. However, these peculiarities were closely related to the Ohio River border. The relatively small number of slaves in Kentucky led to assumptions that slavery there was weaker and milder than plantation slavery farther south. The ostensible "mildness" of Kentucky slavery carried over into historical perspectives. The turn in the historiography of slavery, beginning with Kenneth Stampp's *Peculiar Institution* in 1956, destroyed the image of slavery as a benevolent institution. Yet in their effort to capture the brutal essence of slavery, historians focused primarily on Deep South plantations, while the issue of "mildness" continued to plague historians of Kentucky. Marion B. Lucas uncovered the unique social configuration of slavery in Kentucky, including small slaveholdings and the prevalence of slave-hiring. The very uniqueness of slavery in Kentucky led Lucas to conclude that slavery in Kentucky was not mild. Lucas argued, "Slavery in Kentucky may not have been, typically, as harsh as in the Deep South states. Yet the examples of abuse in the Commonwealth doom the system to condemnation, demonstrating what an awful thing slavery was."[9]

Rather than letting the mildness debate frame the argument, this study places the lived experience of slavery in a borderland context, demonstrating the role of location, power, and politics in the institution of slavery. In this case the peripheral location of slavery and its close ties with free labor in the region gave the institution vitality and strength despite the modest numbers of enslaved African Americans. Following Ira Berlin's lead, historians have demonstrated that the conditions of slavery in the upper South differed from those in the cotton plantations of the Deep South. More recently historians have pointed to the ways in which the proximity of slavery influenced the laboring lives of free African Americans, particularly in Maryland. Following in this tradition but extending it across state lines, this project demonstrates that the borderland context created a unique labor system for both free and enslaved African Americans on both sides of the Ohio River.[10]

Slavery along the Ohio River was unique, not only because it was at the top of the South but also because the Ohio River economy linked borderland slavery with borderland free labor. African Americans' ability to cross the border as runaways and travel along the river as workers highlighted the similarity between bound labor and wage labor along the river. In fact, one of the stunning anomalies of the Ohio River Valley was the similarity between the work regime of racial slavery and that of wage labor on the borderland. In reality, in antebellum America, African Americans could be capital, labor power, and laborers, and the Ohio River brought them all into juxtaposition. Enslaved and free African Americans experienced characteristics representative of both slavery and freedom, as along the Ohio River wage labor and chattel slavery became points on a capitalist continuum rather than mutually exclusive categories for African Americans.[11]

The mobility inherent in this borderland labor system contributed to the persistence of virulent racism in Indiana and Ohio. Historians have argued that white racism in the old Northwest was a legacy of migration by upland southerners. But while origin can explain the initial racism of white settlers, it fails to account for the persistence of white racism throughout the antebellum period. White Indianans and Ohioans put their racism on display because it served a specific social and political function along the border. White residents of the borderland learned that the border between slavery and freedom was nearly impossible to police, whereas racial boundaries were easier to enforce. Thus politicians legislated, and residents enforced, racial boundaries to mask the similarities between free and slave states.[12]

This obfuscation of the geographical division between free and slave states for African Americans lent stability to the region because the link between race and status followed African Americans across the Ohio River border. For example, enslaved blacks viewed the region as a borderland where racial barriers to freedom and the similarity between work regimes on both sides of the river served as reasons not to risk an escape attempt. Beyond simple opportunity, fugitive slaves from Kentucky recalled that they determined the desirability of escape through a reasoned evaluation of how a potential change affected their lives. The very factors that prompted former slaves to escape also allowed them to endure their bondage. In this way white Americans' subversion of the freedoms of African Americans limited the conflict between white neighbors across the border.[13]

The link between race and the division between slavery and freedom helps explain the final, and perhaps most vexing, peculiarity of the borderland: Kentucky's failure to join the Confederacy. Despite the fact that the Ohio River divided slave and free territories, when hostilities erupted in

1861, the region failed to split at its seam. The nature of antislavery and proslavery thought along the Ohio River underlay the resilience of the borderland. The social conditions of the borderland, specifically the domestic slave trade, informed both white and black Americans' antislavery actions. In response to the dominance of the slave trade, free and enslaved African Americans tried to protect themselves from commodification. In contrast, white Americans moved along and across the river in order to take advantage of both legitimate and illicit river commerce. Their freedom of movement encouraged a diversity of opinion on the border, because, unlike black Americans, they did not face an imminent threat to their personal safety. White northerners attempted to defend their states from intrusions by outsiders but recognized Kentuckians' legal right of reclamation. Kentuckians defended their rights to reclamation but imagined that a gradual and peaceful process of emancipation would eventually free them from the necessary evil of slavery. White residents clashed, often violently, over how to control African Americans' movements, but they agreed that the border regulated the movement of free and enslaved African Americans by limiting it. Thus the border became increasingly politically important throughout the 1830s and 1840s but at the same time limited the appeal of disruptive radical antislavery sentiment.[14]

By 1850 white and black abolitionists became convinced that the fluidity of the border between free and slave states undermined their causes and therefore aimed to polarize the river's borders. As white abolitionists spoke of disunion and black abolitionists of collective resistance, conservative antislavery prevailed along the border. Similarly the radical sectionalism espoused by the fire-eaters of the Deep South found little traction in Kentucky, because Kentuckians believed that an unstable border between states within a union was better than a hostile border between enemy nations. Thus the logic of sectionalism, whether from a pro- or an antislavery perspective, simply did not make sense to residents who had long defined their region by the presence of the border between northern free soil and southern slavery.[15]

But the absence of radical pro- and antislavery ideas does not alone explain the power of unionism along the border. As the country careened toward civil war in the 1850s, residents along this border denounced radicalism and actively worked to continue the region's tradition of compromise and accommodation. In the 1850s local residents and politicians increasingly celebrated the uniqueness of the borderland. Perhaps more than anything else, local residents' definition of the Ohio River Valley as a borderland helped hold the region together. The border gave them a shared sense of purpose because it linked their futures. They did not ignore conflicts with their cross-river neighbors, nor did they seek to paper over their differences. Instead they stressed that their conflicts yielded accommodations, and their ability to coexist despite their differences set them apart from the rest of the country. Their Ohio River borderland was not a third country in between; it was the ultimate representation of the American Union. Thus when the Civil War erupted, the majority of white residents remained firmly committed to maintaining the river border because they believed it best protected their freedom.[16]

* * *

The Ohio River border made the social and political aspects of slavery inseparable, and so neither a strictly social nor a strictly political history can explain this region's many peculiarities. This study, therefore, focuses on moments when the social and political history of the region intersected. For example, the region's failure to split in 1861 suggests that only the combination of social and political forces was sufficient to propel residents toward civil war. The historiography on the Civil War causation divides between social and political explanations. Historians who favor political explanations, most prominently Michael Holt, define the Civil War as a politicians' war. While admitting that slavery caused tensions, they suggest that without the political disruptions of the 1850s the Civil War would not have occurred when it did. In contrast, historians who favor social explanations, such as Eric Foner and more recently Bruce Levine, make the argument that the differences between the North's free-labor society and the South's slave-labor society made war inevitable. Kentucky's failure to join the Confederacy and the opposition to Lincoln in the southern counties of Ohio and Indiana demonstrate that war was neither inevitable nor the result of the breakdown of the two-party system. Instead, along the Ohio River, social and economic accommodations defined the limits of political differences even over slavery.[17]

The argument that conflicts over slavery, even violent ones, fostered a tradition of compromise and accommodation ostensibly puts this narrative at odds with other histories of slavery violence in the antebellum period. Historians of southern culture have argued that violence suffused southern society and was essential to southerners' sense of honor. John Ashworth argued that the differences between the North and the South were rooted in the inherent violence of the master-slave relationship as opposed to the boss-worker relationship. Similarly William Freehling argued that southerners' belief that a powerful minority can, and should, dominate the majority set them at odds with northerners. Arguably these differences should be most pronounced along the border, where Kentucky slaveholders repeatedly attempted to bend Ohioans and Indianans to their will. Indeed borderlanders repeatedly clashed, especially over fugitive reclamation and the kidnapping of free African Americans. Yet these conflicts never descended into war. Was there armed conflict? Yes, certainly there was. Ohioans went to war with Michiganders over their state border, but they never did so with Kentuckians. Both sides blustered a lot, but the casualty list was relatively low, especially when compared with appropriately named "Bleeding Kansas." Thus repeated examples of violent conflict that did not result in outright interstate war or national intervention allowed borderlanders to make their history an example of coexistence.[18]

Recently the historian Stanley Harrold argued that years of conflict over the border between slavery and freedom propelled Americans toward the Civil War. Similar to David Grimsted's argument for the oppositional systems of violence that developed in the North and the South, Harrold cited violence as the key to heightened sectional tensions in the 1850s. The fighting, according to Harrold, convinced northerners that they had to defend their freedom from intrusions and convinced southerners that slavery was under attack. These real and perceived threats erupted in the Kansas Territory in the 1850s, as the border war transitioned into a civil war.[19]

While Harrold argued that constant conflict made accommodation impossible, I argue that constant conflict made accommodation necessary. Residents had to find a way to curb their differences because of the centrality of the Ohio River to the local economy and social stability. The diverse mixture of free and slave labor in their state left white Kentuckians less vulnerable and defensive than cotton planters in the Deep South and convinced them that slavery was somehow milder in their state than farther south. Their belief in the mildness of slavery in Kentucky led antislavery northerners along the river to view Kentucky as a state where gradual and peaceful emancipation was possible. Perhaps because they continued to define themselves in relation to the border, neither Ohioans nor Indianans nor Kentuckians ever stopped looking to the federal government as the last resort to resolve interstate conflicts. In contrast, South Carolinians lost faith in the federal government and indeed looked at the Lincoln administration as the problem. Therefore the Union was a threat to their unique sectional interests. Ohioans, Indianans, and perhaps especially Kentuckians believed that the Union best served their interests. Thus they could fight over slavery, but they never lost faith in the Union.

My primary entry into the social and political history of borderland slavery was through the words and actions of fugitive slaves. Fugitive slaves were not representative of the enslaved population, because so few slaves actually made the escape. However, fugitive slaves had to transform themselves from slaves into free persons, and in so doing they crossed shared social boundaries between slavery and freedom. After the passage of the Northwest Ordinance, enslaved blacks tried to use the Ohio River as a pathway to freedom and tested the limits of free soil in the early West. As these cases repeatedly came before the courts, they forced white residents to articulate the meaning of the border by making distinctions between servitude and slavery. During the antebellum period, advertisements for fugitive slaves revealed the changes wrought by the emerging steamboat economy. These advertisements explained enslaved African Americans' strategies of escape, which involved blending into the existing free-black population. White residents north of the Ohio repeatedly expressed their concern that they were being inundated with fugitive slaves from Kentucky, and white politicians repeatedly tried to control the legal and illegal immigration of African Americans. Their fears and actions originated in fugitive slaves' ability to transgress the geographical and visual boundary between slavery and freedom. On this borderland the actions of the enslaved powerfully undermined politicians' attempts to maintain interstate harmony. In turn, the politics of border-making shaped African Americans' lived experience of slavery.[20]

Narratives of Kentucky slaves provided another vital source base. Former slaves used their narratives to secure their freedom, which forced each to construct a popular and unambiguous story. The slaves' desire for freedom was the foundational convention of the narratives. There was not any room for ambiguity because creating a dichotomy between slavery and freedom confirmed the righteousness of freedom over slavery. Rhetorically separating slavery and freedom turned the narratives into epic battles for liberty. The form of a narrative allowed the narrator to mute the emotions associated with bondage. In their narratives former slaves used the slave/ free dichotomy to control their anger, fear, apprehension, love, and attachment and turn them into indictments of slavery.[21]

I approached these narratives looking for breakdowns of the slave/free dichotomy. Those moments reveal enslaved African Americans' perceptions of the complexity of human bondage in the diverse labor system of the borderland. Three challenges to the slave/free dichotomy recur in the fugitive slave narratives. First, former slaves forcefully argued that racial prejudice in the North undermined their freedom. Writers made this link explicitly in order to advocate for blacks' civil rights. Testimonies from free African Americans, as well as court records, confirmed the racial limitations of freedom. These descriptions of racial barriers in the narratives suggest that enslaved and free African Americans in the borderland believed that race limited their experience of freedom in America.

Fugitive slaves' descriptions of the interchangeability of slave labor and free labor along the border was the second challenge to the slave/free dichotomy. Enslaved ministers traveled into free states, barbers lived on their own in Louisville, and fugitives worked toward freedom as hired laborers in free states. In their narratives, formerly enslaved blacks indirectly critiqued the limitations of the emerging free-labor economy by making slave labor and free labor virtually indistinguishable. Their ability to slip between free labor and slave labor revealed the interconnected Ohio River economy and how race influenced economic opportunity. Even free labor was not truly free.

Fugitive slaves built on the themes of racial limitations to freedom and the blending of slave labor and free labor to make their third critique of the slave/free dichotomy. Often fugitives described moments when they had opportunities to escape but ultimately decided to remain where they were. Their specific reasons varied, and in some cases they may have overstated their chances to escape. However, this theme of standing at the precipice of freedom recurred in virtually every narrative by a Kentucky slave. Taken as a whole, they demonstrated that former slaves weighed the benefits of freedom against its limitations before they fled. They perceived the practical differences between slavery and freedom, and in so doing they critiqued freedom in the borderland, because freedom was not always worth the risk. Not only that, but the insecurity of freedom in the borderland meant that they could not leave the chains of bondage on the Kentucky bank.[22]

The centrality of fugitive slaves to the history of the borderland high-lights the relationship between border crossing and border creation. Theo-rists have argued that people on the margins have challenged the legitimacy and power of borders by crossing them. Their ability to cross the border, they suggest, highlights the inherent hybridity of borderlands, and cultural hybridity is the natural antithesis to the unnatural, imposed political bor-der. Some theorists, such as Gloria Anzaldua, argue that national borders subvert preexisting, primordial cultural identities; therefore the way out of oppression is to embrace multiculturalism.[23] According to this understand-ing, the hybridity found in borderlands makes them fundamentally more tolerant than other cultural paradigms. While I embrace the theory that borders are areas of cultural creativity, this interpretation of borderlands replaces one understanding of difference (national) with another (multicul-tural) without exploring the process involved in the creation of cultural differences, in particular the nature of border crossing.

Borderlands are not utopias of accommodation and hybridity. Residents have to adapt their definitions of the border to facilitate coexistence. Along the Ohio River, coexistence involved the regulation of border crossing. The Ohio River economy required mobile labor to function. Free and enslaved African American laborers worked on steamboats plying the river; enslaved blacks worked among free laborers in free states on yearly contracts; and others simply ran errands across the river on a regular basis. Fugitive slaves worked amid this world of mobility and thus challenged the power of the border. However, in response, white residents of the borderland policed racial boundaries to control the inherent instability of the slave/free border. They used culturally constructed racial boundaries to remap the border between slavery and freedom. Thus the dynamic interplay among nature, social relations, and local politics made this region a borderland defined by both creativity and intolerance.[24]

*   *   *

This narrative of the Ohio River borderland is broken into three sections. The first three chapters detail the origins and creation of the Ohio River border. Before humans began settling in the area, the drainage, soil, and climate of the Ohio River Valley defined the physical landscape as a coher-ent region, drawn together by the flowing waters of the river. Drawing the natural history of the river and colonial history into the narrative of the creation of the American republic, the first chapter explains why the American Confederation made the Ohio River the dividing line between slavery and freedom. Chapter 2 is an examination of how western settlers accommodated the new federal border on a river that remained an artery of movement between empires. As opportunity for advancement evaporated in Kentucky, white settlers pushed across the river and brought their bound laborers with them, but the federal government refused to interfere with slavery in the newly created Northwest Territory. As a result, Americans who crossed the Ohio River after 1787 crossed a border, but not all had the same idea of what that meant. As the southern Northwest Territory became the states of Ohio and Indiana in the first two decades of the nineteenth century, the steady stream of migration across the Ohio River forced Americans to articulate how the river served as a divide. In Chapter 3 I argue that the establishment of the states of Ohio and Indiana made the Ohio River a divide between servitude and slavery, rather than between freedom and slavery.

Chapters 4, 5, and 6 explain how white and black residents learned to accommodate the border amid rapid economic change. Chapter 4 traces the economic and social transformation of the region in the third decade of the nineteenth century. In the 1820s Americans' efforts to harness and capitalize on the economic potential of the Ohio River undermined the existing distinctions between slavery and freedom and led to closer associations between race and status. Chapter 5 links the social and economic changes wrought by the river economy with political conflicts over slavery. After the Missouri Crisis laid bare the divisiveness of the slavery issue, politicians promoted commerce and legislated race to quiet conflict along the Ohio River. The rise of politically, legally, and socially defined racial barriers led enslaved African Americans to interpret the region as a borderland. Based on this, Chapter 6 is an analysis of escape from slavery along the Ohio River. While it is true that more slaves escaped from the upper South than from anywhere else in the country, considering the proximity of free soil, their numbers remained small throughout the antebellum period. Enslaved blacks saw both racial barriers to freedom and the similarities between free and slave labor along the river as reasons not to risk an escape attempt because the stigma of bondage followed them into free territory.[25]

Chapters 7 and 8 outline the limits of antislavery and proslavery radicalism and the resulting resilience of the borderland during the sectional conflict that led to the outbreak of the Civil War. Chapter 7 links the development of pro- and antislavery sentiment with the movement induced by the Ohio River border. Because white residents stressed the importance of the border in regulating the movement of African Americans, they had little patience for radical pro- and antislavery views. In contrast, this regulation of border crossing radicalized abolitionists, both blacks and whites. Chapter 8 explains that borderlanders reacted against local and national radicalism by stressing their ability to coexist across a divisive border. While they disagreed and clashed, often violently, over the best means of regulating the border, white Americans on both sides of the river defined themselves by their relationship to the border. As a result they viewed their borderland as a reasonable and rational alternative to the growing sectional conflict elsewhere in the country. Despite being on the precipice of war in 1860, the region had cross-river social and economic connections that remained strong. When war finally came, the region split but not along the Ohio River. Kentucky split in two when the southwestern part of the state became part of the Confederacy, but the Ohio River borderland remained intact.

The Ohio River was there before the border between slavery and freedom was drawn, and the river remained after the border's destruction following the Civil War. Therefore, perhaps as much as anything else, this narrative follows the Ohio River. Norman Maclean wrote that a "river . . . has so many things to say that it is hard to know what it says to each of us." This book is my effort to listen to the story of the Ohio River.[26]

CHAPTER ONE

Origins of the Border between
Slavery and Freedom

The Ohio River has two intertwined histories: one that follows the twists and turns of the river's natural course and one that crosses the river's flow. The Ohio River is a conduit of energy, propelling life downstream as the flowing water seeks the most efficient and uniform expenditure of energy. This river constantly adjusts, compensating for events that affect it. In this sense, the Ohio is a product of its own past history. Humans have given another set of meanings to the river in their effort to utilize and ultimately master it. Mastery of the river involved the ability to harness the river's energy as a means of transportation and to remake the river into border. As Euro-Americans moved in they transformed the Ohio River's current into a barrier to settlement and expressed their control over the river's history with maps and labels that appeared to hold the moving water in place. If nature defined the river by movement, humans defined it by stasis even as they used it to move through the valley. In effect, the impossibility of making the Ohio River stand still locked these two histories in conflict.[1]

The Ohio River is the confluence of two rivers, the Allegheny and the Monongahela in western Pennsylvania, which flow in opposite directions. Along its thousand-mile course to the Mississippi River eighteen major tributaries, among them the Muskingum, the Scioto, the Miami, the Kentucky, the Wabash, and the Cumberland, empty into the Ohio from both northern and southern sources. The Ohio Valley borders the main stream of the river in the states of Pennsylvania, West Virginia, Ohio, Kentucky, Indiana, and Illinois. However, the drainage basin of the Ohio River covers over two hundred thousand square miles and reaches fourteen states, including Alabama, Georgia, Maryland, Mississippi, New York, North Carolina, Tennessee, and Virginia.[2]

While the drainage of the Ohio united the northern and southern banks for thousands of miles, beginning in the eighteenth century humans repeatedly engaged the river as a means of division. The river defined hunting grounds for Ohio Indians, marked one edge of the French and British Empires, separated "Indian Country" from the colonial backcountry, and eventually divided slavery and freedom in the United States. With each succession of settlement the river was both an artery of movement that forged connections throughout the region and a boundary that divided settlement. With the Northwest Ordinance of 1787, the legislated division between slavery and freedom became the newest manifestation of the Ohio River Valley borderland, this time within the new American nation, but the combination of natural and human forces defined the Ohio River Valley as a borderland long before Americans fixed their label on the river. In a way, Americans inherited a borderland that had existed for decades, and they simply relabeled it. In the eighteenth century, border making propelled the long and winding history of the Ohio River Valley.

*   *   *

The drainage, soil, and climate of the Ohio Valley defy any effort to fix the Ohio River as a coherent border. Before the formation of the Ohio River, the Teays River drained the region for two million years. Beginning in western North Carolina, the Teays flowed northward across Virginia and West Virginia, northwest through Ohio, and west across Indiana and Illinois before emptying into an embayment of the ocean. Between fifty thousand and ten thousand years ago, a succession of at least six glaciers destroyed the Teays river system and rearranged the topography of the land west of the Appalachian Mountains. When the glaciers advanced southward, they created a massive dam that blocked the Teays River and created Lake Tight, which covered seven thousand square miles in present-day southern Ohio and parts of West Virginia and Kentucky. The lake waters eventually breached drainage divides and created new drainage channels. Thus the entire region was a prehistoric floodplain, and as the water moved, it distributed the soil and molded the environment. The overflow of prehistoric lakes and rivers flooded the region, cut into the terrain, and formed new rivers. The formation of this new drainage system marked the beginning of the modern Ohio River drainage system. The drain-off of two early glaciers formed the remaining course of the lower Ohio River. The new rivers combined at the point known as the Falls of the Ohio near modern-day Louisville, Kentucky, to form the Ohio River. This stretch of shallow water, small waterfalls, and rapids connected the upper and lower sections of the Ohio River and also became a jumping-off point for future travelers.[3]

In addition to creating a new drainage system, the expansion of glaciers across the land rearranged the topography of the Ohio River Valley. As the glaciers advanced, they leveled the land, filled valleys, scraped off hilltops, and smoothed uneven surfaces. When the glaciers receded, they melted into the surface, deposited trapped soil, and created three distinct topographical zones that crossed the newly formed river and set the river valley apart from the surrounding regions. The Wisconsin glacier leveled the northern two-thirds of Ohio and Indiana and left behind fertile soil. In contrast, south-central Indiana is hill country because it was never glaciated. This topographical region is part of the eastern uplands and basins, which cross into Kentucky. When the Illinois glacier receded farther west, most of southwestern Indiana, southern Illinois, and a portion of Kentucky became part of the middle western upland plain. Eastern Kentucky and southeastern Ohio are part of the eastern highland division, defined by the Appalachian Mountains. These changes united the region along three separate north-south axes, meaning that southwestern Indiana and northern Kentucky had more in common topographically than southwestern Indiana and south-central Indiana did. These physical subdivisions contributed to the agricultural development of the region.[4]

Climatically the Ohio River marks a transition zone between the frosty North and the warmer South. The average minimum temperatures of the eastern portion of North America, which determine the growth of plant life, meet at the river and create a distinct agricultural zone. North of the river the average minimum temperature quickly drops, and south the climate quickly grows more tropical. The drainage, soil, and climate made this physical landscape a mixture of northern and southern influences, creating a natural borderland region.[5]

*   *   *

Nature's development of the Ohio River Valley shaped human interaction with the environment. When glaciers were reshaping the Ohio River Valley during the Ice Age, roughly between 13,000 and 9000 B.C.E., migrants from Asia crossed a land bridge connecting Siberia and Alaska in pursuit of megafauna. These Asian migrants reached the Great Plains by way of an ice-free corridor and discovered a hunter's paradise filled with big game. The recession of the glaciers and the decline of big game led these Native Americans to farming in order to supplement their diet. As trees and plants replaced the ice sheets in the newly forming Ohio River Valley, Native Americans settled in the area, domesticated corn, and became extremely efficient horticulturalists. By 100 C.E. the Hopewell people had developed an expansive culture in the Ohio River Valley. The Hopewell organized themselves in large villages and set up a trading network based on the great waterways of the continent. This trade network extended from Louisiana to Wisconsin and from the Great Lakes to the Rocky Mountains down to the Gulf of Mexico.[6]

The Hopewell went into precipitous decline by 400 C.E., but on the heels of an agricultural revolution around 1000 C.E., the Mississippian Indians repopulated the Ohio Valley. Cahokia, located on the site of present-day East St. Louis, was an urban center of these Mississippian people, which at its height in the twelfth century was home to more than twenty thousand people. As the population grew, the people of Cahokia, and other Mississippian chiefdoms, relied on widespread trading networks to bring in food from agricultural hamlets along the various rivers of the Ohio River Valley. Located near where the Ohio and Missouri Rivers joined with the Mississippi River, Cahokia received traders from east and west along with those from north and south. The rivers united city and hinterlands in one system of exchange. However, the growth of Cahokia sowed the seeds of its demise. The destruction of forests, the depletion of the animal population, and the accumulation of waste on the outskirts of the city destabilized the region. Then the onset of the "Little Ice Age" in the middle of the fourteenth century sent the Mississippian cities into decline. The decreased agricultural production set off a cycle of war and drought, and the Mississippian people dispersed and settled in villages made up of between five hundred and two thousand people.[7]

Beginning in the seventeenth century, Algonquian-speaking Indians settled in the Ohio River Valley. For the most part each community was independent of the others; however, routes of trade following the rivers survived the decentralization and diversification of Indian country and facilitated interaction between the otherwise independent groups. Those waterine routes of trade ultimately proved destructive to the Algonquian Indians when the powerful Iroquois confederation in western New York descended the Ohio River and raided Algonquian villages. In response to the spread of epidemic diseases brought on by the arrival of Europeans, the Iroquois began raiding the Ohio Valley in the 1670s and 1680s to control hunting in the region and to replenish their numbers with human captives. The Iroquois commonly adopted captives to replace deceased tribal members. These captives became full members of the tribal community through intermarriage and adoption. The practice strengthened Iroquois power while weakening their enemies. However, war losses demanded more captives and more torture, which encouraged Algonquian Indians to move outside of Iroquois influence and to protect themselves against the raids. By the middle of the 1680s, Iroquois war parties met resistance from western Indians and their new French allies, frustrating continued Iroquois, and with it English, dominance in the region. While the Covenant Chain had established an alliance between the Iroquois and the English in the 1670s, the English did not have the resources, or the authority, to directly engage the French. The Iroquois established peace with both the French and the English in the Grand Settlement of 1701, which opened the Ohio Valley to further settlement by Algonquian Indians.[8]

After the Iroquois decimated the Algonquian villages, the push of demographic pressure and the pull of the energy of the Ohio River facilitated the growth of new multiethnic and multilingual villages in the eighteenth century. Repopulation of the Ohio Valley came from every direction. Cherokee moved in from the south, Kickapoo came from the east, and the Miami and the Wyandot came from the north. The combination of demographic pressure generated by European expansion and Iroquois dominance pushed the Shawnee, Lenni Lenape, and Delaware from western Pennsylvania and Virginia into the Ohio Valley.[9]

While the Ohio River had long been a vital artery of exchange, for the first time the emerging Ohio Indian population began to use the river as a barrier. The Shawnee, Delaware, and Miami established permanent villages only north of the glacial line, planting vast communal cornfields on the fertile, flat plains north of the hills (an area that would later become America's Corn Belt). The hill country, left untouched by the glaciers, was not as well suited to agricultural development, and so the Ohio Indians left the hill country largely unsettled. In addition the Shawnee, the Delaware, and the Miami preserved the area south of the Ohio River as a hunting ground.

Large animals, such as bison, followed a game trail that crossed the Illinois country before it veered south of the Ohio River near the falls. During the fall and winter months, Ohio Indian men went on hunting trips lasting for weeks or months and covering long distances. These long hunts brought them across the river in pursuit of game. Long hunts were not solely male events; whole families participated, leaving villages north of the river nearly deserted in winter months. In the spring and summer months, Ohio Indians returned to their settlements north of the river and tended to their crops.[10]

Ohio Indians used the river as a border in order to preserve the abundance of game because their well-being depended on it. Deer meat supplemented their diet, and the skins were valuable commodities to Europeans. Ohio Indians actively worked to maintain the hunting paradise by periodically burning the forests to clear out underbrush and stimulate the growth of grasses in order to nourish herbivores. Anglo-Europeans, using the river as an avenue of trade, failed to recognize the Ohio Indians' seasonal claims to the hunting territory south of the river. Instead Anglo-Europeans viewed that area as empty of humans and filled with wild game; it was prime land for occupation through settlement. In using the Ohio River as a boundary for hunting, Ohio Indians inadvertently furthered Europeans' conceptions of the Ohio River as a boundary.

In the eighteenth century, architects of the French and British Empires sought to carve out their places on the North American continent by defining and establishing spheres of influence. The British Empire was still primarily rooted along the Atlantic coast; however, by the middle of the century settlers were beginning to expand into western Pennsylvania and Virginia. The western edges of the seaboard colonies were ill defined, often in conflict with one another, and made with little knowledge of the size and geography of the North American continent. The charters for some seaboard colonies, such as Virginia, Massachusetts, and Connecticut, established latitudinal claims stretching from sea to sea. Amid these disputed land claims, English traders began tramping westward, often following established trails and major rivers.[11]

The largest population centers of the French Empire were Montreal and Quebec in Canada, but the claims of the empire stretched from Canada down to Louisiana and the Gulf Coast. The Caribbean island of Saint Domingue was the primary southern French port, but New Orleans quickly became the entry point on the North American continent. In order to connect this wide geographical area from New Orleans up to the Great Lakes, the French relied on settlements situated along major rivers. The Mississippi River was the primary artery of trade connecting the northern and southern reaches of the French Empire. Of particular importance was the Illinois country, which was roughly situated along the Ohio River bounded on the east by the Wabash River and the west by the Mississippi River. Kaskaskia, located on the Mississippi River, became the principal French settlement in Illinois country, with other, smaller villages situated on other rivers in the area. By the middle of the eighteenth century, there were nearly 1,400 residents of the Illinois country. Of those, 785 were white settlers, 446 were African slaves, and 149 were Native American slaves. The Illinois settlements became the regional focus of trails and a trading entrepôt, sending farming and mining produce south along the Mississippi River and furs to the east. The growth of the Illinois country settlements heightened the importance of the Ohio River as a major artery connecting the far-flung settlements in the French Empire.[12]

The Shawnee, Delaware, and Miami who moved into the Ohio Valley understood that their villages were situated at the fringe of French, British, and Iroquois dominance. The Iroquois dominated western New York but maintained only limited control over the Ohio Valley. Thus the newly established Ohio Indians were officially under the protection of the Iroquois but far enough away to be outside of direct control. Indeed the Ohio Valley Indians recognized how their location at the fringes of dominant empires gave them a certain measure of autonomy, and they utilized their position in trade and imperial politics. Settlers in these new villages capitalized on the Ohio River to trade with the French in the Illinois country on the Mississippi as well as the British in Virginia and Pennsylvania. European traders primarily sought furs from the Ohio Valley Indians. In particular they collected beaver pelts from the Great Lakes region and deer skins farther south along the Ohio River. By midcentury the notion of the Ohio River as an unofficial boundary between the French and British lands emerged as Ohio Indians used the river to facilitate the movement of goods and peoples between empires. However, the growth of the trade encouraged both British and French traders to follow the Native American migrants into the Ohio Valley, which threatened the fragile peace of the imperial borderland.[13]

The same push of demographic forces and pull of the environment that had defined the history of the Ohio Valley for hundreds of years generated irrepressible tensions among the French, English, and Native American settlers of the region. The French, who had long controlled the fur trade of the early West, found their hegemony threatened by the encroachment of British settlers and traders who increasingly engrossed the trade with Ohio Indians. Ohio Indians, fearing eventual displacement, viewed the movement of British settlers into the region as a mounting threat. British leaders who sought land for settlement and to control trade with the Ohio Indians perceived the French as a threat to their dominance of the valley. These tensions, which ultimately precipitated a worldwide war for empire, established the Ohio River as a border in the minds of both Europeans and Native Americans.[14]

For centuries the Ohio River encouraged the peopling of its lush valleys, but the incessant flow of water defied occupation. However, the process of colonization redefined the landscape as a great chessboard in the game of imperial politics. Europeans' views of the land as something to be controlled, dominated, and exploited generated a new concept of space adapted by Native Americans. By 1749, as global empires clashed, the Ohio River border became fixed in the minds of Europeans and Native Americans alike. That border, however, remained elusive, because just as the water brought human beings to the valley, so it flushed them out.

*   *   *

In 1749 the Ohio Company, made up of a group of wealthy Virginians, received a royal grant from the Virginia House of Burgesses for two hundred thousand acres along the upper Ohio River. According to their petition to the British Parliament, the members of the Ohio Company desired the land for settlements and to extend trade with Native Americans. The Ohio Company rejected French claims to the territory. Positing a Lockean understanding of settlement that land could be claimed only by "seating and cultivating the soil," members of the Ohio Company argued that Britain had to promote settlement of the contested region in order to establish dominance there. The land grant included the headwaters of the Ohio, where the Monongahela and Allegheny Rivers joined, and thus served as a gateway to the trade of the Ohio River Valley. The potential wealth of the western riverine trade lured Virginia speculators to the water's edge, and these speculators brought the British Empire to the edge of war with France.[15]

Unlike his British counterparts, Marquis Duquesne, the governor-general of Canada with the responsibility of securing Indian alliances and retaining control of the Ohio Valley, did not seek to control the Ohio Valley through settlement. French claims in North America depended on outposts and forts connected by waterways throughout the interior of the continent, from which French traders exchanged goods with Native Americans. Trade with Native Americans was France's best means of maintaining its imperial claims. Therefore French leaders were more interested in protecting their waterine trading networks than with planting new settlements. Duquesne authorized the construction of a string of forts from the southern shore of Lake Erie to the headwaters of the Ohio River in order to keep English traders at bay. By the fall of 1753, the French militia had erected three forts and was set to erect the fourth in the spring. This final fort, the linchpin of the French plan, was to be located at the forks of the Ohio, the same area the Ohio Company planned on securing with a fort of its own.[16]

Ohio Indians had been asking British colonial officials in Virginia and Pennsylvania to build a fort at the forks for several years, supply their traders with weapons, and defend them from French-allied Indian raids from the Great Lakes. By the middle of the century, the Iroquois had extended the Covenant Chain to include the Shawnee and the Delaware in the Ohio Valley. But the alliance between the Shawnee and Delaware Indians and the Iroquois was uneasy. The Iroquois did not actually control the Shawnee and Delaware, despite the fact that they often claimed to speak for them. In the rising imperial crisis, Ohio Indians wished to secure the Ohio River and its tributaries as trade routes. The British moved too slowly for Ohio Indians, who watched as the French militia erected its string of forts while the British failed to act. Thus when George Washington marched north through the Ohio country in the fall of 1753, he discovered that the British had little support among Ohio Indians, whose hopes for a fort at the forks remained unfulfilled.[17]

The lack of support among Ohio Indians and French fortifications sufficiently scared the Virginians into action. Upon hearing Washington's grim report, Robert Dinwiddie, governor of Virginia, immediately mobilized a force to begin building a fort at the forks. The Virginians had almost completed the fort in April 1754 when the French forces arrived, took over the fort, and completed its construction. The building of this fort, aptly named

Fort Duquesne, set in motion a series of events that ultimately propelled the French and British Empires to battle for control of the North American continent. It is clear that by the outbreak of this war both Europeans and Native Americans viewed the Ohio River as a border that divided two regions. The French Empire to the north looked and functioned differently than did the British Empire to the south. The French erected forts to protect the border, and the British "violated" French claims by claiming land north of the river. Thus while the Ohio River was the gateway to western trade, it also divided two regions.[18]

The Seven Years' War cemented this division with violence. Between 1755 and 1760 French, British, and Native American forces battled for control of North America. The war raged across the continent and the ocean but had begun in the Ohio River Valley. During the first years of the war, Ohio Indians allied themselves with French forces and handed the British army defeat after defeat. However, in 1756 William Pitt dramatically changed the British war effort. First, Pitt made a financial commitment to the effort; he guaranteed payment for military services and supplies, paid half the cost for colonial armies, and supplied the colonists with arms. Second, Pitt committed a major British fleet to the war effort, which made it increasingly difficult for ships to get to New France. Third, Pitt committed thirty thousand British troops to the conflict. These new troops adapted to the backcountry style of warfare, including a greater appreciation for Indian allies. The British army, with the invaluable help of Native American allies, turned the tide of war. In 1758 the British captured Fort Duquesne, destroyed it, and built Fort Pitt in its place, signaling the shift in power in the Ohio River Valley. The British had ousted the French from North America entirely by 1760.[19]

The withdrawal of the French erased imperial boundaries, which undermined Ohio Indians' leverage in negotiations with British leaders on the continent. Jeffery Amherst, supreme commander of British forces in North America, recognized the shift in power. In 1761 he outlawed gift-giving at western posts and kept Indians "scarce of ammunition." By 1762 Ohio Indians were experiencing famine and disease, and many blamed Amherst's new regulations. Amherst's arrogance angered the Ohio Indians and fueled the resentment that resulted in Pontiac's Rebellion in 1763. Native Americans throughout the western country captured a number of former French outposts at the same time that the British and French were signing the

Treaty of Paris, which effectively handed all French land claims east of the Mississippi over to the British.[20]

In response to the crisis, British leaders sought to erect new borders to pacify disaffected Ohio Indians and control land-hungry colonists. The Proclamation Line of 1763 ran along the spine of the Appalachian Mountains, and all land west of the line was declared off-limits to colonists. In addition the British set up two superintendents of Indian affairs, dividing the jurisdictions along the Ohio River. However, this line ignored the human geography in the interior of the continent. Settlers were already west of the line into the territory south of the Ohio River. If the drawing of the line ignored the reality of the imperial West, it indicated how the arrival of the British signaled a shift in perceptions of difference. The French Empire had relied on traders who were able to cross cultural barriers; indeed the success of the fur trade depended on the blurring of boundaries as these *couriers de bois* often married Native American women, which facilitated the exchange of goods. In contrast, after failing to establish dominance, the English sought to draw a line between white colonists and Native Americans. The Proclamation Line may have been nothing more than a declaration of principle, but it revealed the English method of dealing with conflict: separation by race.[21]

Much to the chagrin of English officials, the Proclamation Line encouraged colonial excursions beyond the Appalachian Mountains by sparking curiosity. Settlers primarily moved south of the Ohio River both because it was excellent hunting territory and because it was largely devoid of permanent Native American settlements. In 1768 William Johnson, superintendent of Indian affairs in the north, negotiated with Iroquois leaders the Treaty of Fort Stanwix, which effectively made the Ohio River the boundary between the colonial backcountry to the south and Indian country to the north. The Delaware and the Shawnee, who actually lived in the Ohio Valley, refused to accept the treaty because it gave away their hunting grounds. However, the treaty ostensibly opened the land to settlement, which encouraged more colonial excursion parties to travel the Cumberland Gap into Kentucky. In the end, rather than resolving conflict, the racial border initiated a war between Ohio Indians and Euro-American settlers that ebbed and flowed for thirty years.[22]

In 1774, with the support of frustrated Virginians, Lord Dunmore, the royal governor of the Virginia colony, provoked a war with Ohio Indians without the approval of the British government. Dunmore hoped that a war would remove the threat of the Native Americans who opposed colonial expansion and open the southern Ohio Valley, and all of Virginia's enormous land claims, to settlement. By October 1774 Dunmore's army of Virginians had forced a faction of the Shawnee, who by no means spoke for all Ohio Indians, to cede their hunting grounds to Virginia. However, Dunmore's war failed to end the border war. In fact, the previous June the British Parliament had drawn another line with the Quebec Act, which designated the entire area northwest of the Ohio River part of the Quebec Province. The Quebec Act was largely in recognition of the continued French presence and dominance in Canada and the Great Lakes region. However, the Quebec Act officially quashed all Virginian land claims in the Ohio country, which only created resentment. Instead settlements in the territory remained fortified outposts because the backcountry grew increasingly violent in the coming years.[23]

In the Ohio River Valley, the American Revolution again turned the river into a bloody border. Virginians and Ohio Indians conducted violent raids and counterraids across the river. The fighting had little or nothing to do with the political ideals espoused in Boston or Williamsburg. Virginians wanted to settle on the Ohio River, and Ohio Indians wanted to keep them out. George Rogers Clark was the leader and spokesperson for the Virginians seeking to gain control of the Ohio Valley. Clark claimed that as long as the British promised supplies to the Shawnee, the land south of the Ohio Valley was in danger. In 1778 the Virginian military leader established the post of Lewisville at the Falls of the Ohio. Clark used the post to protect the backcountry and as a springboard for expeditions against the British and Ohio Indians north of the river. In 1782 Clark and his men built Fort Nelson at Lewisville and oversaw the construction of an armed galley to patrol the Ohio River in an attempt to discourage raids on Kentucky.[24]

By 1783 the Ohio was looking less like a river and more like a military boundary. The racially defined border yielded a racial war in the form of a revolution. The brutal, often personal violence of the Revolution effectively turned Native Americans into a racialized "other" in the minds of white settlers arriving in Kentucky. Ohio Indians north of the river looked on the arriving colonists with increasing menace because the war had made white settlers their enemies. Thus during and after the American Revolution, the Ohio River divided hostile parties.[25]

Once again treaties did little to stop the bloodshed, and Ohio Indians and Virginians continued raids after the Treaty of Paris officially ended the war for American independence in 1783. In the treaty the British Empire relinquished control over all land south of the Great Lakes and east of the Mississippi River to the new American Confederation. However, British leaders in the West and Ohio Indians felt betrayed by the treaty because, despite Cornwallis's famous defeat at Yorktown, they did not feel as if they had lost their battle. British Regulars and Ohio Indians continued to occupy Detroit and other western outposts after the treaty. Although the British government remained officially neutral, British agents supplied Ohio Indians with arms and other goods and supported the formation of the Western Confederacy, an Indian coalition with the goal of resisting American expansion north of the river. The Western Confederacy aimed to make the Ohio River the permanent border between America and Indian country.[26]

* * *

In defeating the British and gaining independence, Americans inherited Britain's empire of boundaries. However, the Treaty of Paris wrapped British boundaries in the expansive claims of the new American Confederation. Within the scope of the American Confederation, the Ohio River was essentially both an external and an internal border. On the one hand, Ohio Indians and their British allies struggled to hold the Ohio River as a border between American and Native American empires. So in a very real way, the Ohio River separated violently opposed empires. On the other hand, American settlers, and the American government, claimed the land north of the Ohio River as part of the American Confederation. While the land may have been largely unsettled by whites, and indeed occupied by Native Americans and French settlers, white Americans looked at the land (and the people) as something to be pacified and "civilized." American settlers believed that the Ohio River was a border between open land to the south and unsettled territory to the north. Thus from their perspective it was land that had to be opened to white settlement.

The American Confederation's organization of western lands capitalized on the apparent divisions represented by the Ohio River to control settlement. As part of its original charter, Virginia claimed all of present-day Kentucky and all of the land north of the Ohio. In 1781 the threat of British general Cornwallis's army in Virginia convinced the Virginia government to relinquish land claims in order to facilitate the passing of the Articles of Confederation. Virginia ceded the land north of the Ohio River to the federal government, and the American Confederation granted Virginia authority over its claims south of the river. By 1784 the Ohio River officially divided Virginia to the south from federal territory to the north—well, almost. Two matters complicated this apparently simple designation. First, Virginia set aside large chunks of land to distribute as bounties to soldiers who fought in the American Revolution. These land claims were a product of Virginia's old charter boundaries and therefore failed to recognize the Ohio River as a boundary. Instead Virginia military lands included the southwestern section of the Kentucky Territory and large sections of land north of the river. In addition Virginia claimed the Ohio River as part of its land claims. Thus federal territory did not begin until the low-water mark on the northern bank of the river. Therefore, on the one hand, the Ohio River symbolized the border between two realms of authority, Virginia and federal territory, which significantly influenced the settlement of the region. However, the complications with that border, Virginia's claim on the river and military bounty lands, ensured that from the very start, the Ohio River could not be a hard and fast division.[27]

Old imperial boundaries and rivalries further complicated the American creation of the Ohio River border. Old borders do not fast disappear, even upon the creation of new ones. Therefore in the 1780s the Ohio River still marked the meeting place of the French and British Empires: a middle ground occupied by the Ohio Indians. This was not only the meeting place of multiple empires but also the meeting place of two different concepts of empire: France's empire of commerce and Britain's empire of land. In 1774 the British had recognized the continued presence of French settlers and authority with the Quebec Act. Ten years later the French influence on western territories, especially the Illinois region near the Wabash River, remained strong. Thus their riverine trade routes that connected the Great Lakes with the southern Mississippi Valley remained in place as commodified goods and laborers continued to flow through the region. In contrast, Virginia's claim on land south of the river, and on the river itself, was an extension of the British empire of land. This was a vision based on controlling, occupying, and cultivating land through settlement. The British vision required settlers to control and exploit labor in order to bring land under cultivation. In short, one was a mobile empire that relied on flowing water and the free flow of goods and laborers, and the other was a more static empire based on controlling land and people.[28]

Thus when the American Confederation inherited this region, the question was not whether or not the Ohio River would be a border. Instead the question was what *type* of border it would be, because in 1784 the Ohio River symbolized numerous divisions. On the northern bank, the land was under federal jurisdiction, controlled by British and Ohio Indians, and a remnant of France's empire of commerce, and it consisted of fertile plains flattened by prehistoric glaciers. The southern bank was Virginia territory, settled by intrepid American immigrants, a remnant of Britain's empire of land, and made up of hillier terrain once populated by large game. At the same time, the Ohio River drained the territory on both banks and connected the valley from Pittsburgh to the Mississippi River. In fact, the only stopping point was the Falls of the Ohio, an area occupied and controlled by George Rogers Clark and his armies. Between 1784 and 1787 the American Confederation passed three land ordinances, the last of which was the Northwest Land Ordinance, to assure the swift and orderly settlement of this western land. In part the ordinances, and the borders they created, were products of the region's existing divisions. But the ordinances were also a vision of America's future, its empire of liberty, and they were means of resolving the Ohio River's conflicting past borders.

*   *   *

As part of Virginia, the Kentucky territory was open to settlers. Euro-Americans began settling on the land south of the Ohio River in the 1770s, and the end of the American Revolution along the coast sped western migration. The *Pittsburgh Gazette* counted 177 boats and nearly 2,700 people bound for Kentucky in the winter of 1786 and spring of 1787. As Americans headed west, they realized that the Treaty of Paris had failed to quell the violence in the backcountry. Raids by Ohio Indians successfully slowed the tide of migration and pushed it south of the river. During the violent years of the early 1780s, the threat of a common enemy compelled emigrants to band together. Americans traveled down the Ohio in companies made up of several boats. In 1780 one emigrating family joined a group of 62 boats traveling down the Ohio, hoping for safety in numbers. These large contingents elected leaders and arranged the boats in a defensive position. One man recalled, "The boat which led the way as pilot was well

Figure 1. The Ohio River borderland ca. 1787.

manned and armed, on which sentinels, relieved by turns, kept watch day and night." Migration forced Americans of various backgrounds to cooperate, and once they landed, emigrants settled together and mostly near other settlements for protection.[29]

Hostilities between Ohio Indians and Euro-American settlers slowed the movement of Americans across the Ohio River. Throughout the 1780s American settlers viewed the Ohio River primarily as the border between safe American land and uninhabited and dangerous Indian territory. Travel along the Ohio River was extremely dangerous and limited regional trade. Americans settled in the interior of Kentucky because the chance of being hit with a raid increased closer to the Ohio River. Travelers heading down the Ohio wrote of an "Indian Coast" and a "Virginia shore," suggesting the strength of the Native American presence north of the river.[30]

With the Ohio River serving as an unofficial border between an American territory and Ohio Indian territory, the land south of the river filled up rapidly, while the land north of the river remained sparsely populated by the new Americans. In 1786, already with a substantial population, Kentucky became a territory under the jurisdiction of Virginia. As white migrants sped into Kentucky, many brought enslaved laborers to break ground on their new homesteads. As the territory was a province of Virginia, the only restriction on the spread of slavery was that slaves could not be brought to Kentucky from outside of Virginia without a bond being paid. However, the majority of the Kentucky immigrants came from Virginia, which also happened to be the state with the largest enslaved population. Kentucky attracted yeoman farmers, wealthy Virginia gentlemen, and backcountry settlers; some accepted slavery, some abhorred it, and some were indifferent. Some migrants brought their slaves with them, but others migrated with the hope of finding a fresh start outside the influence of the Virginia gentry. By 1790 the Kentucky Territory had over seventy-three thousand residents, of whom nearly twelve thousand were enslaved.[31]

Settlers north of the Ohio River were officially under the jurisdiction of the federal government. The Ordinance of 1784 called for the division of the West into territories and the admission of a territory as a state as soon as its population equaled the smallest existing state. The Land Ordinance of 1785 required regions to be surveyed before settlement and mandated a grid that divided the land into blocks for sale. This broke with the previous metes and bounds system used in Kentucky, which had created irregular land claims based on natural barriers and landmarks. Seeking to keep the land under the jurisdiction of the American Confederation and in order to maintain order in the settlement of the western territories, the Confederation officially banned settlement north of the Ohio River. However, the existing human geography north of the river and the evolving settlement south of the river complicated this attempt to enforce the border. The war between Ohio Indians and Euro-American settlers along with the rapid, and haphazard, settlement of Kentucky heavily influenced the settlement and labor situation in the territory north of the Ohio and east of the Wabash River. Beginning at the Wabash River and heading west, France's colonial past left an indelible imprint on the land, people, and labor system.[32]

Despite the official ban on settlement, a lack of affordable and available land in Kentucky pushed Americans north of the river. Land titles were a mess in Kentucky in the 1780s. The Virginia Constitution supported squatter rights, which meant that a person could find vacant land and possess it by occupancy. Squatters could then turn occupancy into legal title at a reduced price. The result was a mess of speculation and conflicting titles that ultimately frustrated many settlers who hoped to find economic opportunity and independence in Kentucky. Americans moved across the river to escape.[33]

On the north bank of the Ohio River and east of the Wabash River, Americans found the hill country vacant of permanent settlements, and there were over two thousand Anglo-American families settled north of the Ohio by the spring of 1785. The men and women who moved to the northern bank in the mid-1780s were unwilling to settle in the interior north of the river because of the threat of raids. Ohio Indians remained especially powerful east of the Falls of the Ohio, but their influence extended from the forks in western Pennsylvania to the Wabash River, which limited American migration despite the push from Kentucky. In addition American Confederation troops patrolled the territory and evicted squatters. The troops signified the presence of the American Confederation and forced residents to take notice of the new authority in the West. The army was the new republic's nation-making machine. The combination of Confederation troops and Ohio Indians made settlement north of the river unstable and, for many, undesirable.[34]

These forces held the push for emigration from Kentucky in check but did not stop it completely. Much like those in Kentucky, these early settlers believed that bound labor facilitated expansion and settlement. Clearing land was a difficult and labor-intensive undertaking, and hired labor was not readily available in the West. Some brought slaves with them, and others hired slaves from settlers in the interior of Kentucky. [35]

Farther west, along and west of the Wabash River to the Mississippi River, on land technically under the jurisdiction of the American Confederation, remnants of France's once great commercial empire remained intact. The collapse of imperial authority did not mean that settlers and traders abandoned the West. French settlements along the rivers were home to French settlers and Native Americans who had intermarried. Imperial authorities, especially the French, had granted significant autonomy to settlers in these western outposts. The town of Vincennes on the Wabash River was "a mixture of all nations." The homes were a combination of French and Indian styles. Many French intermarried with Indians, and according to one observer, "whoever knows the Indian dress, knows theirs [the French] also."[36]

Much has been made of the accommodation and interaction between Native Americans and French settlers, but as the historian Brett Rushforth has argued about France's vast empire, "Slavery made the system go." The fact was that both Indian slavery and African slavery were essential to France's empire. Although these were not mutually exclusive systems, they represent two different aspects of the French system. Enslaved Africans from France's Caribbean sugar colonies arrived in Illinois settlements within a few years of the French settlers' arrival. By the middle of the century African slaves made up roughly 32 percent of the population in the Illinois country. Moreover, in Kaskaskia 41 percent of households owned one black slave or more, which was higher than the percentage in the American South in 1860. French settlers typically employed African slaves as agricultural laborers, and the more land one owned, the more African slaves he owned as well. However, French settlers in the Illinois country engaged in a unique type of agricultural production. Land claims in the Illinois country were called "long lots." These were long, narrow blocks of land that had frontage with a major river but did not contain dwellings. Instead settlers fenced these claims in as one common field and engaged in open-field agriculture. Open-field agriculture yielded a different understanding of both production and private property. Certainly, agricultural production was important, as increased landholdings were so closely correlated with increased slaveholdings. However, this was not a plantation system dedicated to the production of a single staple crop. Historians have clearly demonstrated how the plantation complex in sugar colonies and English colonies of Virginia and South Carolina facilitated the rise of a modern form of racialized chattel slavery. Slavery was essential to the French settlements in Illinois, but it differed from plantation slavery in other areas.[37]

Perhaps this difference owes much to the position of the Illinois country in the French empire. In the western trade world, slaves were most valuable as commodities and seem to have been articles of exchange throughout the eighteenth century. In particular, Indian slavery was critical to French imperial relations. The French engaged in the trade in captive bodies to both facilitate relations and breed rivalries among their Native American allies and enemies. Therefore the trade in slaves was just as important to the system as was the use of slaves in agricultural production. For example, Major Francis Bosseron, a merchant from Vincennes with far-flung connections, bought and sold slaves at various posts along the Mississippi River during the 1760s and 1770s. Over time the capture and exchange of African slaves became part of imperial politics, effectively blending Indian and African slavery. Ohio Indians commonly carried off slaves during their raids and then either sold or ransomed them. In 1777 Louis Chavrard paid Bosseron for the expense of sending his clerk to ransom Chavrard's slave from the Indians. In 1782, after George Rogers Clark captured Vincennes, Colonel Legras informed Clark that Indians had carried off a slave and were trying to ransom him in exchange for liquor.[38]

Thus, through agricultural production and imperial warfare and politics, the French developed a thriving slave trade that stretched at least from the Ohio River Valley down to New Orleans. By the 1780s French settlers had a strong attachment to slavery, some for agricultural work and others from this imperial world of exchange. The small-scale slaveholding of the French settlers likely heightened the importance of slaves. Slaves could perform a variety of duties within the household, assist on hunts, facilitate trade, and ultimately be salable commodities. As Bartholomew Tarvideau, a leader in the French community, explained, "many of the inhabitants of these districts have Slaves, and Some have no other property but Slaves." It is unclear exactly what Tarvideau meant by this statement, because most who owned slaves also owned land. Perhaps he referred to a French settler who used slaves for livestock production and therefore did not own any communal farmland. It is also possible that he referred to traders who owned slaves for purposes other than agricultural production. Or perhaps he just misunderstood the French landowning system. In any case, these French traders would have been acutely sensitive to threats to their only form of property.[39]

When Major John Hamtramck led federal troops into Vincennes and established a military post late in 1787, the French and Indian settlers hoped that the "real Americans" had finally arrived. Kentuckians, acting independently of the American Confederation, repeatedly crossed the Ohio River and raided the settlements of the Wabash Indians, until the Indians withdrew to Kaskaskia, on the Mississippi River and the border of the Spanish Empire. From Kaskaskia, Wabash Indians could use the international border to their advantage and cross into Spanish territory for protection against American intrusions. However, the withdrawal of the Wabash Indians left the French settlers of Vincennes without allies and exposed to the superior strength and numbers of the Kentuckians. The French settlers turned to the "real Americans" for protection. These settlers hoped that

Hamtramck and the Confederation troops would limit or at least regulate the Kentuckians' crossing of the Ohio River border.[40]

That is not to say that, prior to the arrival of the Confederation troops, all Americans raided these western settlements and terrorized French and Native Americans in the region. Indeed Americans began settling around Vincennes in the middle of the 1780s, and some settlers coming from Kentucky and Virginia arrived in Vincennes with their slaves in tow and joined the existing slave trade. The Decker clan, including John and Dinah Decker and their eight children, arrived in the territory with their slaves, claimed land, and began farming. John and Dinah's son Luke immediately established himself as a prominent member of the community by forging ties with the French community through trade. He traded slaves and other goods at French posts along the Mississippi River.[41]

To Americans, French settlers, and Native Americans in the early West, the Ohio River was both a border and an artery of movement. The river gave them access to the western country but also marked a boundary of settlement. It was a waterway of opportunity but also a symbol of danger. The river's duality arose from all settlers' inability to control access to the flowing water. White Americans used the river to reach the West, but they could not stop Ohio Indians from using the river to raid settlements. Ohio Indians defended the river as a border, but they could not stop American settlers from capitalizing on the swiftly flowing current to propel them downstream. In addition French settlers relied on the western rivers as trading networks, yet sought to use the Ohio River as a border when unwanted American settlers infringed on their world. The American Confederation sought to impose order on this chaos with the creation of the new Northwest Land Ordinance of 1787.[42]

*   *   *

In the summer of 1787, during the heated debates of the constitutional convention, politicians along the coast imposed a new political designation on the western territory north of the Ohio River. The Northwest Ordinance of 1787 created the territory that eventually became the states of Ohio, Illinois, Indiana, Wisconsin, and Michigan. The passage of the Northwest Ordinance opened an American borderland with article six, which legally excluded slavery north of the Ohio River. Article six of the Northwest Ordinance read: "There shall be neither slavery nor involuntary servitude in the said territory, otherwise than in punishment for crimes, whereof the party shall have been duly convicted: provided always, that any person escaping into the same, from whom labour or service is lawfully claimed in any one of the original states, such fugitive may be lawfully reclaimed, and conveyed to the person claiming his or her labour or service as aforesaid." Congress approved article six with virtually no debate. The creation of the ordinance and article six were linked with the constitutional convention taking place in Philadelphia. In the summer of 1787, delegates in Philadelphia were in the midst of heated debate over the place of slavery in the country's new constitution. These debates threatened to derail the negotiations, as northern delegates complained of slaveholders' undue power and southern delegates fought to protect against any threat to their human property. These debates demonstrated that sectional power could be leveraged in political debates to enhance both personal and regional political standing. Article six and its implied vision for the West helped diffuse tension at the Philadelphia convention.[43]

Southern politicians seemingly accepted article six without a second thought. On the surface southerners' acquiescence to an ostensibly antislavery amendment is puzzling. Indeed historians continue to discuss the connection between constitutional debates over slavery and the passage of the Northwest Ordinance. Some historians contend that southern delegates accepted the antislavery provision of the Northwest Ordinance in exchange for northern support of the fugitive slave clause in the Constitution, while others find the evidence for this connection unconvincing. This is not an argument for or against a direct connection between these two controversial provisions. However, the context of the sectional debates in Philadelphia and the implications of the ordinance for the settlement of the West help explain the cross-sectional appeal of the antislavery provision in the Northwest Ordinance. At the very least, southerners understood that in directly banning slavery north of the river, article six indirectly guaranteed the expansion of slavery to the south. That is not to say that in 1787 southerners necessarily sought the expansion of slavery for its own sake. Rather southerners enjoyed the possibilities that came with the expansion of slavery. In 1787 Virginia was the most populous state, and Virginia slaveholders were exploding into Kentucky, which suggested that slavery was more expansive than free labor. Thus as slaveholders populated the South, the Northwest Territory could support the South rather than compete with it. William Grayson, a congressman from Virginia, explained in a letter to

James Monroe that article six "was agreed to by the Southern members for the purpose of preventing tobacco and indigo from being made on the NW side of the Ohio." Congressmen hoped that article six would draw westerners together by creating complementary rather than competitive sectional interests. Congressmen understood that the river had long been a border but that at the same time the river had the potential to connect various areas. Thus the ordinance split the region, but the river could tie it together in trade.[44]

The design of the Northwest Ordinance suggests that the national government was responsible for enforcing or at least interpreting article six. The ordinance specified that a territory must pass through stages before reaching statehood. Those stages initially limited the autonomy of local settlers and instead gave the national government significant influence over territorial development. In the first stage, Congress appointed a governor and judges to administer the territory. Thus at the first stage the Northwest Territory was in some respects a colony of the national government and subject to its authority. Once the population reached five thousand free adult men, they could pass to the second stage and elect a territorial legislature. Then when the population reached sixty thousand, the legislature could write a constitution and apply to join the American Confederation. As the territory passed through each stage, it gradually separated from the authority of the national government. Citizens exerted more influence over the territory in each stage because the territory gradually became more representative.[45]

While Congress designed the Northwest Ordinance to encourage sectional differentiation, article six, from its inception, was not a straightforward ban on slavery. Perhaps if Congress had drawn a line through completely uninhabited territory the border could have been clearer. But the United States inherited a region that had a written history over one hundred years old, a human history spanning thousands of years, and an environmental history over millions of years. Members of Congress likely understood that the boundary between slavery and freedom was more of an abstract political category than a concrete division. As with Kentucky, Virginia's possession of the Northwest Territory left an imprint on future development. The Virginia law that transferred possession of the territory to the United States protected the property rights of the residents already there. Thus the United States had to protect the property (including human property) of those residents as well. Article six did not, and could not, free slaves already in the territory. In addition the ordinance did not contain an enforcement clause, which left unclear what body of government could take action to end slavery.[46]

Instead the national government imposed purposeful silence on the issue. The presence of slaves in the territory immediately prevented the national government from interference. The notion that the ordinance freed slaves would have set off alarm bells because southerners were sensitive to the issue of federal intervention with regard to slavery. Southerners feared that if the federal government could enforce emancipation in one territory, nothing could stop it from enacting national emancipation. In addition the sanctity of private property severely limited the chance for national intervention. Enforcement of the antislavery article would have required the liquidation of property. Americans were far too dedicated to the protection of private property to allow that to happen. At best the federal government could have interpreted the article as a gradual emancipation clause, one that did not free any existing slaves but prevented the importation of slaves to the territory. This would not have freed existing slaves or even their children, but it would have at least limited the growth of slavery in the region. The problem with even this conservative interpretation is that it still would have required enforcement of the border. Instead Congress said nothing about the matter, as the only concrete interpretation of the ordinance never reached the floor for debate. Thus while Congress drew the border, the residents and newly arriving settlers would have to enact and give the border meaning.[47]

The Northwest Ordinance's combination of idealism and ambivalence most confused, and worried, slaveholders along and west of the Wabash. The ordinance placed under the official jurisdiction and protection of the new United States those outposts on the Wabash River that had been nominally under the control of the French Empire, the British Empire, and the colony of Virginia respectively. Exactly what that change in authority meant to residents of the Northwest Territory was unclear to them. Imperial authorities, especially the French, had granted significant autonomy to settlers in these western outposts. Now the United States Congress and President George Washington had new visions of a rational and orderly settlement of western territories, and part of their vision was a territory free from slavery. But their vision conflicted with westerners' own ideas and the reality that slavery already existed in the territory. The question was, would the transition from imperial colony to national republic be a smooth one?

Would Major John Hamtramck and Confederation troops allow settlers to live as they pleased, or would they be the blunt instruments with which distant members of Congress and the president enacted their vision? When word of the Northwest Ordinance, specifically article six, reached settlers in 1788, slaveholding Vincennsians wondered if protection came at too high a price.[48]

Rumors swirled in these western settlements about the meaning of article six, which simply read, "there shall be neither slavery nor involuntary servitude in the said territory." Settlers wondered if the law applied to slaves already in the territory or just to the importation of new slaves. Vincennes residents worried that with the arrival of the territorial governor, Arthur St. Clair, all slaves would be freed. French settlers appointed Bartholomew Tarvideau as their agent to lobby Congress, and twice in 1788 he petitioned Congress to secure the French settlers' property, both human and landed. While certain members of Congress unofficially assured Tarvideau that the ordinance was not meant to deprive the citizens of their property, Congress failed to adopt an official explanation. Hoping to calm the fears of the citizens, Tarvideau sent a letter to Vincennes explaining Congress's position. Some slaveholders did not wait for news and fled across the Mississippi River into Spanish territory to protect their stake in human property. Major Hamtramck reported to the American Confederation that "a number of people had gone & were about going from the Illinois to the Spanish Side, in consequence of a resolve of Congress respecting negroes." Once Tarvideau's letter reached Vincennes, Hamtramck published this information in hopes of stopping the exodus. Tarvideau quickly dashed off a letter to Governor Arthur St. Clair in the summer of 1789 explaining the situation, hoping that St. Clair could remedy it. St. Clair then explained to the residents of Vincennes that the ordinance was "a prohibition to any future introduction of them [slaves], but not to extend to the liberation of those the People were already possessed of." St. Clair's declaration officially sanctioned the presence of pre-1787 slaves, but it also suggested the government's reticence to enforce any type of ban on slavery. Thus the presence of the new government was not the imminent threat some settlers had previously expected.[49]

St. Clair's declaration likely defused the panic, but it did not offer a guarantee for the future. Slaveholders in Vincennes and the Illinois settlements had legitimate reason to fear the American government. Federal troops had long signified the presence of the Confederation and forced residents to take notice of the new authority in the West, and the Confederation did not have a problem flexing its muscle and confiscating property. The human geography and existing power relations strongly influenced Hamtramck's and St. Clair's decisions to negotiate in the case of the French slaveholders. In particular, Hamtramck and St. Clair were concerned about slaveholders' willingness to flee to the protection of the Spanish Empire. With the country still in its infancy, the immigration of settlers to a foreign country was a genuine threat to national power. In 1787 the Spanish government controlled navigation of the Mississippi River and the port of New Orleans. The primary concerns of Arthur St. Clair and the Continental generals in Vincennes were to secure the loyalty of western peoples, bring them within the realm of the new government, and neutralize foreign threats. Rapid settlement of the western territories was in the best interest of the country.[50]

In addition slaveholders wielded considerable power despite their small numbers out west. Luke Decker, a slaveholder whose family had come to Vincennes just in the 1780s, was appointed justice of the peace and a judge of the Court of Common Pleas and was one of the most prominent citizens of Vincennes by 1792. The influx of American settlers like Decker, who were engaged in the business of slavery and prominent men in the community, strengthened the cause of the French slaveholding settlers. National concern over the protection of human property augmented the power of these few slaveholders in the western territories. Their concerns over even the potential for the confiscation of property resonated with congressmen as far away as South Carolina. The constitutional convention debates and the resulting compromises revealed the importance of the protection of human property in the new nation. At the same time that they inserted article six in the Northwest Ordinance, the framers of the Constitution inserted a fugitive slave clause that read, "No person held to service or labor in one state, under the laws thereof, escaping into another, shall, in consequence of any law or regulation therein, be discharged from such service or labor, but shall be delivered up on claim of party to whom such service or labor may be due." The fugitive clause demonstrates that the framers recognized that the presence of free and slave territories failed to negate claims to property.[51]

The evolution of St. Clair's thinking on the Northwest Ordinance was in response to the events transpiring out west and therefore ratified more than affected the development of the region. On the one hand, St. Clair owed his appointment as territorial governor entirely to the president, and Congress had to approve any declarations that he made. On the other hand, George Washington and congressmen were hundreds of miles away in Philadelphia, and St. Clair had to deal with the inhabitants of the Northwest Territory more directly. While St. Clair was notoriously aloof when it came to the interests of westerners, in this case he seemed content to follow the path of least resistance. Some of the wealthiest and most vocal settlers in Vincennes and the far West were slaveholders, so the protection of their interests benefited St. Clair's self-interest. Thus, rather than imposing a hard and fast restriction, St. Clair approached the matter pragmatically. St. Clair would never condone the unchecked expansion of slavery, because that would alienate him from the federal government. Neither would he enforce the antislavery clause for fear of alienating the residents of the Northwest Territory. Instead St. Clair preferred to let settlers decide the issue for themselves. In 1793 he explained in a letter to Decker that article six was "no more than the declaration of a principle."[52]

St. Clair's ambivalence and the ambivalent legacy of article six of the Northwest Ordinance are well-trodden ground in histories of the Ohio River Valley. However, historians have largely focused on the effectiveness of the ordinance. Whether tracing the spread of slavery across the river or determining at what point in time the border became clear, the focus on efficacy overlooks the importance of the origins of the border. The Northwest Ordinance represented the culmination of a past rooted in border making *and* an imprint for the nation's future. Therefore efficacy is only part of the issue. While article six set the new nation on a path toward sectional differentiation, Congress's decision to divide the West at the Ohio River was owed to previous attempts to use the Ohio River as an unofficial and official boundary.

The land ordinances and the designation of the border between slavery and freedom in the new American nation recognized both real and conceptual divisions that already existed in the region. In the requirement that land be acquired by treaty and then purchased from the federal government, the Ohio River border was recognized as the division between Anglo-American settlers and Ohio Indians; the border gave meaning to the distinction between federal land and Virginia's land; and the border linked the natural landscape with the means and goods of production. In addition the border captured French and British concepts of empire and labor by protecting Virginia's land and property to the south while allowing for the free flow of commerce to the north. The border also satisfied national sectional issues by dividing the West into slaveholding and nonslaveholding regions. The creation of the border was both the culmination and the resolution of a long history of border making in the region. However, the very complications of the past that led to the border's creation also prevented a straightforward resolution. Instead, as they had for hundreds of years, the residents interpreted and enacted the border.[53]

Rather than focusing on how effectively the Northwest Ordinance deterred slavery from developing north of the river or even when the river became a border, this study historicizes the border itself. The federal government's ambivalent embrace of the words of the ordinance forced black and white Americans in the region to define the meaning of the legislated geographical division between slavery and freedom. At the time of the passage of the Northwest Ordinance in 1787, the Ohio River had the potential to unite Americans more than it divided them. The river pulled soil, goods, and people through the valley connecting Pittsburgh with Cincinnati, Cincinnati with Louisville, and Louisville with St. Louis. However, throughout the history of the region, the Ohio River was a boundary and a magnet for settlement; it facilitated trade, carried people into the valley, forced interaction, and brought people into conflict. With each succession of settlement, therefore, the settlers' interactions with the Ohio River shaped the drama of the borderland. While 1787 marked the beginning of the end of the imperial borderland, that year marked just the beginning of the borderland of slavery and freedom.

CHAPTER TWO

Crossing the Line

In 1787 the Ohio River Valley was a region contained by fluid borders. The Mississippi River marked the border between the United States and the Spanish Territory, and within the United States the Ohio River divided slaveholding Virginia from the nominally free Northwest Territory. By 1818 the Louisiana Purchase had erased the Mississippi River border, but along the length of the Ohio River American settlers established the states of Kentucky, Ohio, Indiana, and Illinois, which ensured that the river would form the legislated boundary between freedom and slavery in the region. The federal government created the Ohio River border to facilitate sectional differentiation and cooperation; local residents then used the border to define the limits of slavery and freedom in the region. In the process, the Ohio Valley transitioned from a western territory to a borderland of slavery and freedom made up of four states.

From the outset the Ohio River was both a highway into and a bifurcation of the early West. The river's dual identity as a conduit of movement and a border complicated the settlement of the region. In the 1790s residents fiercely debated the place of slavery in Kentucky's future, which made it far from inevitable that Kentucky would become a slaveholding state. White residents offered a variety of reasons for their opposition to slavery, some of which had little to do with the morality of human bondage. In many cases both pro- and antislavery debaters shared a language of paternalism that condemned slavery for encouraging dependency among African Americans, which in turn threatened the social stability of the state. But from the outset white residents used slave labor to facilitate the settlement of Kentucky, which handicapped the antislavery movement, and residents made Kentucky the first state with a constitution that legally protected slavery. As opportunities for personal advancement evaporated in the new state of Kentucky, the same search for opportunity that pushed settlers west pushed them across the Ohio River.

Exactly what type of opportunity settlers sought differed from person to person. This chapter will examine the motives that compelled Americans to head north across the Ohio River into federal territory that banned slavery. The Ohio River and its tributaries facilitated the mobility of western settlers, which placed significant stress on the relationship between federal authorities, who wanted to regulate border crossing, and settlers who crossed the borders with ease. Whether they were settlers seeking cheap land, morally committed ministers, or speculators primarily concerned with gaining wealth and power, they had to accommodate the federally created boundary between slavery and freedom when they moved to the Northwest Territory. However, in the 1790s the Ohio River remained an artery of movement between empires. Captive exchange born out of international wars allowed some of the newly arrived American settlers to participate in a slave trade that connected French settlers and Native American traders north of the river with settlers throughout the Ohio and Mississippi Valleys. Clashes between eastern authorities and local settlers over the voluntary and coerced movement of human bodies were struggles over the settlement of the Ohio River Valley.

The federal government's ambivalent embrace of the words of the Northwest Ordinance encouraged black and white Americans in the region to constantly define and redefine the meaning of the legislated geographical division between slavery and freedom. Some white Americans defended the antislavery origins of the Northwest Territory, and others brought their slaves across the river. Most white Americans in the Ohio River Valley challenged the boundary between slavery and freedom only when it personally affected them. African Americans discovered that this ambivalence ensured that bondage followed them across the river.

There was a clear lack of consistency in the words and actions of settlers, suggesting that while the Ohio River legally divided slave and free territories, it did not yet constitute a cultural boundary between distinct regions. But the presence of the Ohio River border ensured that, after 1787, Americans consciously and without a second thought enacted their interpretations of the boundary between slavery and freedom as they moved across the Ohio River. It would be easy to use the river border to simplify the motives of white and black Americans in the region, but these individuals' personal experiences with the border were anything but simple. However, what made this region unique was that no matter what motivated a person to cross the border, that movement had political ramifications. In turn, residents politicized movement in their efforts to define the border. Thus this chapter, along with each succeeding chapter, traces this combination of social and political forces that made the Ohio River Valley a borderland.

*   *   *

While the slavery enforced by the French settlers in the Northwest Territory was largely a remnant of its imperial past, south of the river the settlement process encouraged the expansion of large-scale modern American slavery. Because the Kentucky Territory was under the jurisdiction of Virginia, slaves were among the first settlers in Kentucky. By 1790 they numbered roughly twelve thousand, nearly 17 percent of the total population. In 1790 there were slaves in every state in the Union, but only in Georgia, Maryland, North Carolina, South Carolina, and Virginia (all states at least as far south as Kentucky) did slaves make up a higher percentage of the population than in Kentucky. However, half of the counties in Kentucky had slaveholdings of less than 17 percent, meaning that slaveholding was more heavily concentrated in, while not limited to, specific geographic areas, generally the bluegrass region of central Kentucky.[1]

While slavery spread quickly during the settlement of Kentucky, it was not certain that slavery would be a part of Kentucky's future. In fact, during the state constitutional convention in 1792, Kentuckians came close to ending slavery in the state. Historians often link the early social history of Kentucky with the attempt to end slavery at the convention. But while there was some public debate about slavery in the run-up to the state convention, it is difficult to determine the public's feelings about slavery. During the convention, opposition to slavery came primarily from the churches. Seven ministers were convention delegates, and all of the ministers present voted against slavery. Ministers were community leaders at this early period, and perhaps, given their profession, they did not truly represent the larger population. The historian Eva Sheppard Wolf has demonstrated that strong personalities had the greatest impact on the course of emancipation in Virginia during this same period. She argues that in socially and economically similar communities, residents were more likely to free their slaves where ministers led the way by freeing their slaves. Similarly in Kentucky certain congregations expressed strong antislavery convictions, whereas others explicitly rejected an antislavery stance. The ministers likely held strong moral convictions against slavery and may have been the moral beacons of their respective communities. However, while they represented pockets of strong antislavery sentiment, they did not necessarily reflect a statewide movement against the institution. It is entirely possible that the number of antislavery delegates overrepresented antislavery sentiment in the state as a whole.[2]

At the convention the delegates voted twenty-six to sixteen against erasing a constitutional provision that forbade legislative interference with slavery in the state. All of the twenty-six delegates who supported slavery held slaves themselves. More interesting, however, is the fact that only four of the sixteen men who voted against slavery did not own slaves; and five of those men owned more than five slaves, a substantial holding in frontier Kentucky. These numbers reveal just how important slave labor was to the settlement process. Even many of those Kentuckians who opposed slavery still felt compelled to take advantage of enslaved labor to establish their homesteads. The Presbyterian minister David Rice, the most outspoken leader of the antislavery movement, held slaves his entire life, freeing them only upon his death. Thus from the outset the antislavery movement was handicapped by Kentuckians' perception that slavery had been a necessary evil of settlement. While they wanted to eliminate slavery from Kentucky's future, they knew that it had contributed to the region's current growth and presence.[3]

In part, the delegates who owned slaves could support gradual emancipation precisely because they owned slaves. Gradual emancipation allowed them to maintain possession of their enslaved laborers because, under most schemes, African Americans already enslaved remained in bondage for life and their children became free only when they reached adulthood. Thus those delegates who owned slaves in 1792 controlled labor and could pass it on to their children. Their support of gradual emancipation allowed them to satisfy their moral qualms about slavery in a way that was not economically detrimental, which was a position less wealthy Kentuckians did not have the luxury to take.[4]

The best means of understanding the leaders of the antislavery movement is to look at what they said about slavery during the debates for the election of constitutional convention delegates. Despite the heated rhetoric, the differences between pro- and antislavery men were not great. Paralleling the debate at the national level, the debate over slavery in Kentucky was about articulating the legacy of the American Revolution. Political leaders explained their understanding of the meaning of America by debating Kentucky's future. However, political leaders on both sides of the slavery question feared the social disruption that accompanied radical change. Thus their visions of the future could not escape the present. Since many of the antislavery leaders were in fact slaveholders, this certainly influenced their perspective. They declared their moral opposition to slavery, but they generally coupled it with a statement against immediate emancipation. Proslavery leaders similarly declared their moral opposition to slavery, but they argued that emancipation would cause social anarchy.[5]

Thus both pro- and antislavery leaders were slaveholders who were morally opposed to slavery, but they differed primarily on the practicality of gradual emancipation. The antislavery spokesman David Rice wrote that slavery made African Americans "incapable of enjoying and properly using" freedom. Another antislavery writer wrote, "Immediate emancipation would be attended with the most dangerous consequences." The leader of the proslavery men, George Nicholas, wrote, "I never did approve of slavery, but I have thought that the removing of it in a proper manner, would be attended with great difficulties." Both Rice and Nicholas feared the effect that a large free black population would have on the white population of the state. They wanted to secure a stable and virtuous community through the establishment of an independent citizenry. While both Rice and Nicholas supported gradual emancipation, Rice found it practicable but Nicholas did not.[6]

While they held opposing viewpoints about the future of slavery in the state, men on both sides of the emancipation question shared a fear of dependency and social anarchy. White political leaders held independence sacred and harbored paternalistic feelings toward dependents. Proslavery leaders' paternalism clearly crossed the color line and included both enslaved African Americans and landless whites. John Breckenridge, a wealthy slaveholder and the leader of the proslavery contingent in 1799, also sought independence, but he rooted his idea of independence in wealth and property. He wrote in a private letter, "If they can by one experiment emancipate our slaves, the same principle pursued will enable them a second experiment to extinguish our land titles; for both are held by rights equally sacred." In public letters Breckenridge accused antislavery leaders of ultimately striving for wealth redistribution and social leveling because they were lazy.[7]

Antislavery leaders spoke, at least publicly, about African Americans only as dependents in need of guidance. Thus even those laboring against slavery held paternalistic feelings toward the African American population. Harry Innes, a delegate to both the 1792 and 1799 conventions, was a judge and slaveholder in Kentucky who worked both personally and politically to end slavery in the state. Innes held more than twenty slaves, which was a substantial holding in Kentucky. Edmund Lyne freed his slaves in his will and left them in the care of Innes after his death. Lyne wrote that he wanted Innes to "support the freedom" of his young slaves and left him the funds to do so. Innes paid to clothe, board, feed, and educate Lyne's former slaves in order to prepare them for freedom.[8]

White Kentuckians such as Lyne and Innes viewed freedom as more than a legal status; to them, it was a delicate privilege. They worried that if they immediately freed slaves, those newly emancipated would destroy society because they could not handle the responsibility of freedom. Therefore these antislavery leaders decided that only compensated emancipation allowed for the elevation of the African American population through education. The problem was that compensated emancipation was more than most owners or the state could possibly afford. Although some white Kentuckians were ready to denounce the moral evil of slavery, they were not willing to immediately expand the full embrace of liberty to African Americans. Political leaders of the antislavery movement were concerned with the livelihoods of enslaved African Americans insofar as those affected the future of the state in which they lived.[9]

The intentions of antislavery Kentuckians such as Harry Innes and David Rice were rooted in a similar paternalism as that of their political opponents. Both pro- and antislavery writers feared that immediate emancipation would unleash a large, lazy, immoral, and potentially dangerous population of dependent freed slaves, but antislavery men emphasized the effect of slavery on the white population. Antislavery men feared that slavery degraded both slaveholders and nonslaveholders because, "When slavery becomes common, industry sinks into disgrace. To labour, is to slave; to work, is to work like a Negroe: and this is disgraceful." The young Henry Clay wrote that slavery "in the end injures the master . . . by laying waste his lands, and enabling him to live indolently, thus contracting all the vices generated by a state of idleness." Slavery led to vice, ignorance, and laziness for all parties. The freedom to labor was the key to their vision of the future and what set white farmers above black slaves. Slavery threatened to turn whites into dependents, make them more slavelike, and deny their independence.[10]

Ultimately the political debates of the constitutional convention offer a rhetoricized distillation of Kentuckians' views on slavery. Without some antislavery sentiment among the general population, politicians would not have run on an antislavery platform. However, the emancipationists were totally defeated in 1799, electing only three antislavery delegates for the constitutional convention, among them Harry Innes and Samuel Taylor, who were both slaveholders. Whereas politicians wrapped their antislavery arguments in the language of freedom and independence, the general population formed their politics based on their personal experiences.

The antislavery sentiment among the white population in Kentucky often had as much to do with frustrations over the stratification of society as with the unrighteousness of slavery. There were competing visions for Kentucky's future. On the one hand, Breckenridge and other wealthy landowners wanted to use slave labor to diversify their economic ventures, engage in the market, and become wealthy. Yeomen farmers, on the other hand, viewed the thirty-acre farm as the ideal. They still sought profit, but they sought a different means. The drive for profit made neighborliness an insufficient form of labor and increased the value of slave labor. However, many white Kentuckians who were unable to purchase land or slaves resented the slave system. The words of Henry Clay resonated with these farmers because they believed that slavery threatened to turn them into dependents by denying their freedom to labor.[11]

White Kentuckians attacked slavery as a part of the inequality in the state more than slavery specifically. One antislavery writer explained, "The right to appropriate the labor of another to our own use, is equally possessed by all, therefore possessed by none exclusively." He continued, "Slavery impoverishes the country; because it promotes idleness; because wealth is nothing more than a representative of labor." The 1792 constitution disenfranchised tenant farmers who did not own any land. Thus when Kentuckians railed against slavery, they usually coupled it with an argument against property qualifications for suffrage. One broadside from 1799 read, "These men are in favor of emancipation and in favor of free suffrage." White Kentuckians resented their dire economic situation and those in charge who put them in that situation.[12]

The rapid spread of slavery in the 1790s and the increasing number of slaveholders suggest that economic and political inequality had added a sense of urgency to Kentuckians' moral opposition to slavery. Over the course of the 1790s, many white Kentuckians moved into the slaveholding ranks and more hired slaves. Between 1790 and 1800 Kentucky's enslaved population increased to over forty thousand, and as it did, slavery became more geographically dispersed. Whereas in 1792 half of the counties had slaveholdings of 17 percent or less, by 1800 in twenty-six of forty-one counties more than 20 percent of householders owned slaves. This suggests that nonslaveholders purchased slaves and others increased their holdings. For example, in Madison County six households who held zero slaves in 1790 owned slaves by the end of the decade and another twenty-six increased their holdings. Although those numbers appear small, actually those thirty-two households were over two-thirds of the total households in the county. Daniel Drake recalled that among the Jersey men who migrated to Mason County, all except his father became slaveholders. Slaveholdings were fairly small, with an average holding of four slaves and 20 percent of Kentucky slaveholders owning only a single slave. South Carolinians at this time, in contrast, averaged twelve slaves per slaveholding family. Overall by 1800 roughly 25 percent of heads of households in Kentucky held slaves.[13]

However, this number underestimates the extent of slavery's influence. Slaves facilitated the settlement process for whites. Male slaves cleared land, built houses, grew crops, and assisted in the defense of the settlement. Female slaves assisted white women with cooking, spinning, weaving, sewing, laundry, and other household tasks. For those who could not afford to purchase slaves of their own, hiring provided a much needed labor source. Daniel Drake wrote, "Father never purchased a slave for two substantial reasons: *first*, he had not the means; and *second*, was so opposed to slavery that he would not have accepted the best Negro in Kentucky as a gift, provided he would have been compelled to keep him as a slave. Now and then, he hired one, male or female, by the day, from some neighbouring master (white hirelings being scarce), but he or mother never failed to give something to the slave in return for the service." Hiring out turned unfree labor from a competitor into a contributor and broadened the support base for slavery. As Drake's comment suggests, hiring slaves was also easier on the conscience than ownership.[14]

In the 1790s the constitutional debates over slavery and the geographical dispersal of slavery revealed the nature of slavery and antislavery in the developing borderland. While Kentuckians came close to banning slavery in the state, the early antislavery movement was not monolithic. Ministers represented the most powerful antislavery voices during this early period, inspiring their congregations to speak out and act against slavery. As they debated slavery's future in Kentucky, both pro- and antislavery delegates rooted their arguments in their fears of dependency and racial conflict. Outside the convention, many white Kentuckians' attacks on slavery stemmed from their frustration with economic inequality. Over the course of the decade, on a practical level, slavery survived and thrived because of its flexibility, as white residents employed enslaved laborers to perform a variety of tasks associated with establishing a homestead. In fact, once white Kentuckians ceased viewing slavery as an obstacle, many simply accommodated themselves to its presence. This suggests that white Kentuckians' views on slavery defied generalization. Similarly frustration with slavery alone did not drive white settlers across the border. Slavery was not *the* deciding factor; it was just a piece of the puzzle.

*   *   *

Historians place too much emphasis on slavery as a motivating factor for immigration to the Northwest Territory because of the heated debate to end slavery in the state of Kentucky in the 1790s. The antislavery leaders David Rice and Henry Innes never left Kentucky. Henry Clay, who became an outspoken leader of the antislavery contingent at the 1799 convention, also never left the state. Almost immediately after the convention, he married into a slaveholding family and went on to become one of the great compromisers on the issue of slavery. He refrained from speaking in support of gradual emancipation in the state. Apparently their failures in 1792 and 1799 were not enough to convince these leaders of the movement to leave the state.[15]

Ultimately the political debates of the constitutional convention provide only a glimpse of the wide range of motivations for migration and therefore on their own do not offer an adequate explanation for the stream of migration across the Ohio River. There were as many reasons for moving to the Northwest Territory as there were migrants, and it is perhaps impossible to prioritize them. John May, a wealthy merchant, wrote about his choice to settle in Ohio: "Am building from several motives. First, for the benefit of the settlement; second, from a prospect or hope of gain hereafter; third for an asylum for myself and family, should we ever want it; fourth as a place where I can leave my stores and baggage in safety; and lastly, to gratify a foolish ambition, I suppose it is." However, while the specific reasons were innumerable, the search for opportunity was the overarching force driving migration to the Northwest Territory. The move across the river was an extension of the initial migration from the East into the backcountry and then into Kentucky. The hope of sustaining a wife and children compelled American men to pack up and head west to Kentucky. Inspired by booster tracts such as John Filson's *The Discovery and Present State of Kentucke,* eastern farmers hoped to find independence in the Edenic paradise that was Kentucky.[16]

White Americans initially headed to Kentucky to secure economic autonomy for themselves and for their families. However, unless one arrived wealthy there was little chance of becoming so in Kentucky. John Breckenridge, a wealthy Virginian, sent over twenty slaves to establish his homestead and explained that he migrated to "provide good lands here for my children, & insure them from want, which I was not certain of in the old Country." William Christian warned his mother before she joined him in Kentucky, "Unless you can sell in Botetourt to get some good working Negroes & money to bring with you had better remain where you are."[17]

Other farmers, less wealthy than Breckenridge, wanted enough land to achieve a level of autonomy that elevated them above dependents, such as slaves, tenant farmers, propertyless laborers, and women. Small farmers achieved independence by owning their own land and labor. However, the influx of settlers caused land prices to soar out of reach, leaving the majority of Kentucky's new residents landless. Even among those who could afford land, less than half owned thirty acres (the size of a typical family farm). The shift to a high labor-to-land ratio forced many into tenancy with the hope of eventually earning enough cash to purchase land. One visitor wrote that without a fortune one must "at first live low and work hard." The rise of tenancy was unsettling to both tenants and landlords. Tenants viewed their situation as a stepping stone, but many watched as their dreams evaporated before them amid confused land titles and rising prices. As demonstrated in Virginia during Bacon's Rebellion in 1676, young propertyless men were a potentially dangerous population in times of economic hardship. More recently amid the revolutionary ferment, backcountry rebellions against entrenched authorities in places such as North Carolina, and in Massachusetts following the Revolution, made leaders acutely aware of the potential for unrest.[18]

Rather than negotiating with disgruntled and armed tenants, those who could afford it utilized slave labor to put land under cultivation. The spread of slavery into the bluegrass region limited labor opportunities for landless whites, because wealthy landholders preferred slave labor to tenancy, putting landholding even further out of reach for many. Fewer white settlers owned slaves on the fringes of settlement, which was also where land was cheaper. This suggests that those who could afford to purchase land only on the fringes, although they were able to establish small farms, could not afford to purchase slaves and could not afford expensive white tenant labor.

Those whites who were frustrated with the messy land titles and high prices and degraded by laboring for wages alongside African American slaves crossed the river in search of economic opportunity; they hoped to find cheaper land that was agriculturally similar to that in Kentucky. They were not seeking a complete break with their neighbors; they wanted to help themselves and their families. In Marietta, Ohio, for example, Virginians and New Englanders worshipped at the same church. In addition the Marietta settlers depended on Virginians on the southern bank for corn, meat, and medical advice. These white migrants crossed the river because they did not want to live under the thumb of wealthy slaveholders, but they were not necessarily opposed to the use of bound labor, even racialized bound labor. In fact many settlers in southern Ohio hired slaves from Kentucky to work their farms. These migrants resented slaveholders not because they held slaves but because they controlled the social and economic opportunity in Kentucky. The migrants left to take control of their future.[19]

Slavery most directly affected the immigration of antislavery ministers to the Northwest Territory. Ministers led the charge of moral antislavery migrants who, frustrated with the spread and instantiation of slavery in Kentucky, headed to the Northwest Territory to establish themselves in a land free from the slave system. Reverend Obed Denham, for example, was a Baptist leader who took several families with him to Ohio in 1797. Philip and Elizabeth Gatch moved from Virginia to Ohio in 1798; although he freed his own slaves, Phillip wrote that he "could not feel reconciled to die and leave my posterity in a land of slavery." Francis McCormack left Kentucky and established the first Methodist congregation in Ohio. Some ministers headed north for a combination of moral and economic reasons. John Campbell Dean left Kentucky to escape the "curse of slavery" but also to escape from an uncertain land title. Robert Finley, a Presbyterian minister, made it clear that he left Kentucky in search of new lands; however, before making his trek he freed all fourteen of his slaves and led a contingent of antislavery Kentuckians to Ohio in 1795. Perhaps as many as thirty of the migrants were newly freed African Americans. These former slaves built homes for the white settlers but failed to become landowners themselves. These whites' moral opposition to slavery stemmed from their concern over their own salvation. They thus wanted to end their own involvement in the slave system but not necessarily end slavery in the country. This is certainly not to belittle their antislavery convictions but rather only to reveal the limits of antislavery sentiment in the region. At this point for many, opposition to slavery was a personal position but did not necessarily compel them to convince others to follow in their antislavery path.[20]

Some ministers, such as Carter Tarrant and David Barrow, remained in Kentucky and actively worked to convert their fellow Kentuckians to antislavery. Tarrant resigned from his pulpit because his church refused to allow him to preach about emancipation. In northern Kentucky he established his own church, whose constitution declared that slavery was contrary to the gospel. Barrow spoke out against slavery in Southampton County, Virginia, but church leaders forced him to resign in 1798. He was expelled from another church in Kentucky in 1806 for "preaching the doctrines of emancipation." He joined Tarrant in northern Kentucky and established the largest antislavery church in the state. The Baptized Licking Locust Association, Friends of Humanity included eleven ministers and twelve churches totaling three hundred members. No member of this association was allowed to purchase a slave except for the purpose of emancipation. Barrow and Tallant applied their moral opposition to slavery to fighting the spread of slavery within the state of Kentucky.[21]

The spread of slavery into Kentucky clearly encouraged the movement of white Americans across the Ohio River into the Northwest Territory. However, just as with the variety of perspectives within the political antislavery movement, there was significant diversity within this group of antislavery migrants. Some whites who were frustrated with the socioeconomic situation in Kentucky left in search of economic opportunity, while some morally committed ministers left to establish themselves, and sometimes their congregations, on free soil. Each group crossed the river for different reasons, which gave each group a unique understanding of the border they crossed. Ministers and their followers remained morally opposed to slavery and thus viewed the border as a limit to the evils of slavery. In contrast, economically motivated migrants opposed the inequality of the slave system more than slavery itself and thus sought to use the border to control their labor situation. In both cases these migrants escaped from slavery and thus wanted to limit the influence of slavery in the new territory but not interfere with the existence of slavery in Kentucky. Ironically, those who did the most to agitate against slavery, and perhaps were most morally opposed to it, never left slaveholding Kentucky.

*   *   *

The failure of the emancipation movement in Kentucky guaranteed that slavery extended at least as far north as the Ohio River. That guarantee was significant. If Kentuckians had enacted gradual emancipation in their state, there likely would not have been any question about the future of slavery in the Northwest Territory. National leaders expressed millennial hopes for the new American nation, and allowing slavery to spread into an area north of where it had just been banned would have been the opposite of progress. In addition a successful emancipation movement in Kentucky would have made slavery impractical in the Northwest Territory, because Kentucky would have been an island of free territory in a sea of slaveholding states. Instead Kentucky's constitutional protection of slavery influenced the region in an obvious way: it brought enslaved African Americans to the Ohio River Valley. This simple fact increased the ambivalence of Arthur St. Clair, governor of the Northwest Territory, because he did not want to deter immigration to the new territory north of the river by preventing the migration of slaveholders from Kentucky. In turn, his ambivalent position on slavery in the Northwest Territory left the question of how the river border affected the status of enslaved African Americans unanswered.[22]

The Ohio River and old Native American trading paths connected slaveholding Kentucky with Vincennes, the primary settlement in the western part of the Northwest Territory. The Ohio River ran rapidly over a rocky bottom for about two miles and had a roughly four-foot drop that forced travelers to disembark and travel by foot through Louisville. On the northern bank the buffalo trace, a game trail and trading path, connected the Falls of the Ohio with Vincennes along the Wabash River. Traders passed goods through Louisville and Vincennes and proceeded down the Ohio to the Mississippi River. This far-flung trade network was largely a product of the region's imperial past, as it connected Anglo-American backcountry traders, Ohio Indians, French settlers, and Spanish traders in New Orleans in one system of exchange. As such, imperial rivalries and hostilities made captive exchange a part of this trade system. In the early 1790s American generals repeatedly attempted and failed to defeat Ohio Indians and gain control of the Northwest Territory. This made the Ohio River and the buffalo trace dangerous because travelers could be taken captive and moved as exchangeable commodities to Vincennes and potentially down the Mississippi River. At the same time American settlers in Vincennes wanted to acquire enslaved blacks to aid in the settlement of the region. As a result war-time captive exchange and chattel slavery blended together, complicating the Ohio River border.[23]

In the fall of 1793 Peter McNelly and his wife, Queen, escaped from their owner, Anthony Thomson, in Kentucky, crossed the Ohio River, and headed toward Vincennes. The close proximity of free soil was seductive for the enslaved in Kentucky seeking independence from bondage, but those who made the escape quickly realized that slavery did not end at the river. While on the road to Vincennes, Ohio Indians captured the fugitives and detained them for a few weeks. Their captors then took the McNellys to Vincennes and traded them to John Small, a local resident, for rifles and ammunition. Ohio Indians had been exchanging captive bodies for goods since the arrival of Europeans. Captives were particularly valuable in war, and in 1793 Ohio Indians and American settlers were in a state of war. John Small's purchase of the McNellys reveals that some of the newly arrived American settlers embraced this trade in human bodies.[24]

After the McNellys had been in Small's custody for three weeks, Kentuckian Peter Smith traveled to Vincennes and claimed that he had purchased Peter McNelly and his wife from their former owner (Thomson). Small handed the two over to Smith after being reimbursed. Smith kept them confined in the guardhouse of Fort Knox until Henry Vanderburgh, a prominent trader and justice of the peace for Knox County in the Northwest Territory, purchased Peter McNelly and his wife. This exchange reveals a world in transition. Small had traded with the Native Americans for the McNellys, but he willingly handed them over to the Kentuckian, Smith, but not before receiving reimbursement. "Reimbursement" was the word that Peter McNelly used in his deposition, and the meaning is open to speculation. Perhaps Small received his rifles and ammunition back from the Ohio Indians with whom he had initially traded, because McNelly did not say that Small had sold him. In contrast, Peter McNelly specifically stated that the Indians "sold" him to Small and later that Smith "sold" him to Henry Vanderburgh.[25]

According to Peter McNelly, Henry Vanderburgh purchased the two slaves from Smith while they were still in Vincennes. Small had confined the McNellys in the military guardhouse, and Vanderburgh, a military officer and justice of the peace, likely saw the McNellys at Fort Knox and perhaps participated in their confinement. Vanderburgh was a trader with American, French, and Native American connections, which suggests that he was probably familiar with the trade in human bodies. Vanderburgh acquired the slaves from their legal owner, a proper exchange in the American system of chattel slavery, but he did so without a bill of sale. Even if Vanderburgh was just covering his tracks by not creating a bill of sale, his and Smith's willingness to make the transaction without an official bill of sale was peculiar. In effect, it made the transaction a hybrid of imperial captive exchange and the chattel slave trade.[26]

The McNellys' chance for freedom seemed slim as Vanderburgh held them for the next seven months. In May 1794 George Turner, federal judge for the Northwest Territory, arrived in Vincennes, whereupon Peter McNelly approached him in hopes of gaining freedom for his wife and himself. Prior to his appointment as territorial judge, Turner lived in Philadelphia and owed his position to his friendship with George Washington. He, along with the other territorial judges, wanted to impose order in the West and bring the citizens in line with the position of the federal government. Turner tried to enforce the slavery ban because he believed that all slaves were "free by the Constitution of the Territory" and therefore sought to enforce his interpretation of federal law. He did not know, or seem to care much, about the lifestyle of the residents of the West, and his actions immediately cast him as a high-handed outsider.[27]

Turner's interpretation of the Northwest Ordinance as an emancipating document was radical in the context of the federal government's position on fugitives from labor. Although they were in nominally free territory, legally the McNellys were still enslaved. According to both the U.S. Constitution and the then newly passed Federal Fugitive Slave Act of 1793, their master had the legal right to claim them as his own anywhere in the United States. The McNellys' initial decision to escape across the Ohio River possibly indicates that they were aware that slavery was banned north of the Ohio River. Whether they believed that their escape to free soil protected their freedom or that they would have to apply for legal freedom cannot be known. Peter McNelly definitely could not write and quite possibly could not read either, so the information that he had was all hearsay. Yet Peter McNelly sought out Turner and readily admitted that he and his wife were runaway slaves. Perhaps McNelly planned on going to the court when he and his wife made their initial escape. Or maybe the McNellys' experience in Vincennes convinced them that the court was their only hope for gaining freedom; after all, Vanderburgh held the McNellys for seven months with no apparent protest from the residents of Vincennes. Peter McNelly initially consulted Turner informally, before the court officially opened, to learn about his and his wife's chances for freedom.[28]

The informality of legal practice in the western territories actually empowered McNelly because he could consult with Turner despite his enslaved status. One observer described the frontier court in the following way: "On the bank of the Ohio I found squire Ellis seated on a bench under the shade of two locust trees, with a table, pen and ink, and several papers, holding a justice's court, which he does every Saturday. Seven or eight men were sitting on the bench with him, awaiting his awards in their several cases. When he had finished, which was soon after I had taken a seat under the same shade, one of the men invited the squire to drink with them, which he consenting to, some whiskey was provided from landlord Powers, in which all parties made a libation to peace and justice." While enslaved African Americans had no legal standing, in this atmosphere Peter McNelly could approach the federal judge and inquire about the possibility of gaining his and his wife's freedom without much fear of retribution. Turner's answer that "the said writ should issue" must have been music to McNelly's ears.[29]

Applying to Turner was just the beginning of Peter and Queen McNelly's trial to gain their freedom. After Peter McNelly approached Turner, Vanderburgh tried to persuade him and his wife to sign indentures extending their servitude for five years, which, for obvious reasons, they refused to do. Vanderburgh then engaged all of the resources at his disposal to transport the McNellys back to Kentucky by force. The day before the court officially opened, Henry Vanderburgh offered one hundred dollars to Joseph Baird, acting prothonotary of the Court of Common Pleas in Knox County; Nathaniel Ewing, a wealthy trader; and Toussaint Dubois, an "Indian trader," to forcibly remove Peter and Queen McNelly to Kentucky. Vanderburgh told Dubois and Baird that he was taking the McNellys back to Kentucky *because* they had applied for their freedom. Vanderburgh also allegedly told Baird that there would not be any proof that he had purchased the McNellys, adding, "Do not worry, I will make you secure." On the same day Dubois convinced Joseph LaMotte, an Indian interpreter for the United States, to help with the procedure after telling him that the McNellys had applied for their freedom.[30]

The next day Jonas Dutton, a house carpenter employed by Vanderburgh, led Peter McNelly into a field under the pretense of procuring a "load of earth." Once in the field Baird, LaMotte, and Ewing seized McNelly, bound his arms with a rope, tied him to a horse, and dragged him into a thicket. Baird then returned to Vincennes to seize Queen McNelly. Arriving at the home of Dubois, he discovered that Dubois had hired three more persons to help with the task: Henri Renbeau, a French Vincennes resident; Jean Baptiste Constant, a yeoman farmer; and Wild Cat, a Wabash Indian. Henry Vanderburgh and Abner Prior, a captain in the United States Army, arrived at Dubois's home with Queen McNelly, whereupon Baird, Renbeau, Constant, and Wild Cat bound Queen and took her to the thicket where LaMotte and Ewing held her husband.[31]

The diversity of the men involved in the removal of the McNellys reveals much about the early West. Vanderburgh, Ewing, and Dubois were primarily involved in trade. Toussaint Dubois evidently had strong connections with French and Indian residents in town, since he enlisted Renbeau and Wild Cat to help in the affair. Both Vanderburgh and Dubois had trading connections along the Ohio River as well. In fact they probably met Nathaniel Ewing through trade. As a young man, Nathaniel Ewing lived the peripatetic life of a trader. His expeditions took him the length of the Ohio River, from Pittsburgh down to Vincennes, into Kentucky, and even into Maryland. Nathaniel Ewing and his father regularly moved slaves along the river and used slaves to tend to their settlement when absent on trading expeditions. Sometime between 1788 and 1790 Nathaniel Ewing laid down a place of his own in Vincennes, but he continued trading along the length of the Ohio River, as he was described as being "occasionally of Vincennes."[32]

Jonas Dutton was a carpenter, Jean Baptiste Constant a yeoman farmer, Baird a legal clerk, and LaMotte an Indian interpreter. In part, the variety of men involved—a Frenchman, a Wabash Indian, and Anglo-Americans from all over the Ohio Valley—reveals diversity of small western trading settlements and is suggestive of the power of trade to draw people together. However, it also highlights just how important connections were to the livelihood of western settlers. Money seems to have been the primary motive for everyone involved, because all received some sort of compensation for their efforts. But there was more than greed at stake. Vanderburgh and Dubois were powerful and influential men in the region, and helping them could only help one's situation. In the Ohio Valley in the late eighteenth century, trade was a face-to-face enterprise, and networks followed lines of acquaintance. Friendship with Vanderburgh and Dubois therefore offered economic opportunities. Politics was also a face-to-face endeavor. Vanderburgh was the justice of the peace, and his position as a soldier meant that he had connections with the military authority (which was *the* authority) in Vincennes. For the hired hands, the benefits of assisting Vanderburgh and Dubois likely outweighed the risks.[33]

Everyone involved seems to have known that Peter and Queen McNelly had applied for their freedom, which actually seems to have persuaded them to carry the McNellys off to Kentucky. In the eyes of the white men involved, the McNellys were slaves whether they were in the employ of Vanderburgh in the Northwest Territory or another owner in Kentucky. Even Vanderburgh's carpenter, Jonas Dutton, helped in the extradition, which undermines any argument for class camaraderie across racial lines between him and McNelly. Vanderburgh confined the McNellys at Fort Knox with the help from an army captain and the local sheriff, which perhaps is entirely attributable to his personal clout. But it also suggests that white residents of Vincennes were familiar with the mechanisms of control that were part of the system of slavery. At the very least, the men involved believed that it was their responsibility to contain and return fugitive slaves. The regulation of border crossing, therefore, actually brought the white residents and traders together. And the very proximity to freedom that gave the McNellys hope also kept them in bondage.[34]

Once the group had custody of both Peter McNelly and his wife, they moved them to White River Station, a stockade settlement on the White River about twelve miles from Vincennes. Just outside the settlement, Dutton (the carpenter) returned with indenture contracts binding the McNellys to Vanderburgh for five years. Dutton informed the McNellys that if they refused to sign the indentures, then Vanderburgh would take them down to New Orleans and sell them as slaves for life. Peter McNelly later explained that, "terrified at the threat," he agreed to sign the paper and the group proceeded into White River Station to the home of Moses Decker. Moses Decker and his brother Luke Decker, a justice of the peace for Knox

County, owned and traded slaves. Moses Decker knew that the McNellys had applied for their freedom but still housed the fugitives, and he even bore witness to the forced indenture. Moses Decker's most humane action (of which he boasted) was undoing the chains that bound Queen McNelly.[35]

Guarded by Renbeau, Constant, Wild Cat, and Baird, Peter and Queen McNelly remained imprisoned in the home of Moses Decker for ten days. At one point during the imprisonment, Vanderburgh sent word to Baird that George Turner was on his way to White River Station in search of the McNellys. Vanderburgh told Baird to hide the McNellys outside the station until the judge left. The group took the McNellys outside the station and hid them in the prairie until Turner departed, and then they returned to Decker's home. Stockade settlements were not terribly large, and there were fewer than ten enslaved inhabitants of White River Station. The group of four armed men escorting two African Americans, who were bound in ropes and chains, outside the settlement just before the arrival of the judge was probably conspicuous. The settlers would have known that the McNellys were strangers, and perhaps the lack of comment suggests that this type of action was commonplace, or tacitly approved. Either way, Turner's inability to discover the whereabouts of the McNellys suggests complicity, not only from the Deckers but from the residents of White River Station as well.[36]

After ten days of confinement, Peter McNelly made his escape through the roof of Moses Decker's home in the middle of the night, leaving his wife behind. Peter McNelly "presented himself" before Judge Turner the following morning. Meanwhile, upon learning of McNelly's escape, Baird prepared to go to Vincennes to inform Vanderburgh of the situation. Before he left, Richard Levins, constable from Jefferson County, Kentucky, came to Moses Decker's home and told Baird that he wanted to purchase Queen McNelly. How Levins knew about the McNellys is unclear. Levins and Baird went to Vincennes together and met with Vanderburgh in the home of Dubois. Levins and Vanderburgh apparently came to some form of agreement regarding Queen McNelly, because the following night Levins returned to Decker's home and then took Queen McNelly to Kentucky in the middle of the night. Moses Decker claimed that he did not know what had taken place until the next morning when his own slave told him that Levins had taken Queen away during the night.[37]

Meanwhile, Peter McNelly charged Vanderburgh with unlawful and forcible restraint. Turner issued a warrant for the arrest of Joseph Baird and

Joseph LaMotte for participation in the attempted forced removal of the McNellys, which made both Baird and LaMotte nervous. These two did Vanderburgh's dirty work, but they did not have the wealth and influence of Vanderburgh, Dubois, or the Deckers or even the mobility of Ewing. They hoped that Vanderburgh would protect them as he had promised. During the affair Dubois met with Ewing, and together they drew up a paper pledging that, acting for Henry Vanderburgh, they would keep Joseph Baird out of trouble. In addition Dubois told LaMotte that he had a "good paper" from Vanderburgh that would keep him out of harm. Such assurances went only so far, however, and Turner had LaMotte arrested immediately. However, when the sheriff came to arrest Joseph Baird, Baird drew a knife and escaped. A week later he appeared before George Turner and gave his testimony. Baird and LaMotte explained the events surrounding the attempted removal of the McNellys in great detail in their depositions. For the most part, their depositions corroborated the testimony of Peter McNelly, which lends a degree of credibility to their statements. They had no reason to validate the story of Peter McNelly; nor did they even have any way of knowing what Peter McNelly had deposed.[38]

Despite the evidence that Baird, LaMotte, and McNelly provided, the masterminds behind the extradition of the McNellys frustrated the efforts of Turner with their intransigence and clever dishonesty. Moses Decker came forward immediately and gave his deposition before Turner but did little to clarify the situation. In his deposition he referred to Vanderburgh as the McNellys' "reputed master" but made no statement about the legitimacy of Vanderburgh's claim. He also exonerated himself by claiming that he was asleep when Richard Levins took Queen McNelly from his own home back to Kentucky. Dubois, Luke Decker, and Vanderburgh were not deposed until August and September, over two months after the incident. In August, Dubois claimed that as far as he knew, "the prisoners were runaway slaves from Kentucky and that Vanderburgh was sending them back to their master and that he was right in so doing." Luke Decker deposed that at the current time (September) Vanderburgh "had not either directly or indirectly the custody charge or keeping of . . . Queen." This was technically true, of course, but only because Queen McNelly had already been in Kentucky for at least three months![39]

At the end of September, Turner brought Vanderburgh and Peter McNelly into court together. Vanderburgh denied ever having purchased or sold the McNellys and, amazingly, said that he "remembers not employing Toussaint Dubois, Joseph Baird, or any other person to carry away . . . Peter McNelly and Queen his wife." At this point Turner freed Peter McNelly and sent the deputy to Kentucky to locate Queen McNelly. The deputy pursued Richard Levins to Louisville, where he saw him but did not apprehend him because "none of the magistrates there would recognize the warrant." A frustrated Turner jailed Vanderburgh for failing to produce Queen McNelly. The sheriff, however, by his own admission did not watch Vanderburgh closely during his supposed confinement.[40]

Henry Vanderburgh, a man well acquainted with the customs of westerners, complained that it was Turner who held Peter McNelly "contrary to law." While McNelly's freedom was in question, George Turner took custody of Peter McNelly. This only further angered Vanderburgh, who accused Turner of trying to keep Peter McNelly as his own slave. Vanderburgh had a problem with Turner because Turner had acted contrary to *custom*, not contrary to law. In a conversation with Christopher Wyant, the sheriff of Knox County, and Stephen Ashby, a Kentucky farmer, Vanderburgh said, "It is well for you, Mr. Ashby, that you have got no Negroes; if you had you would lose them." Captain Abner Prior, a friend of Vanderburgh, added pejoratively that Turner was a "Negro Judge."[41]

Their incredulity likely stemmed from their experience with the courts in Virginia and Kentucky. African and African American slaves had no rights and very little status in those court systems. Judges ordered the corporeal punishment or even execution of African American slaves for simple crimes such as stealing. Vanderburgh and Captain Prior balked at the prospect of a judge taking the word of a runaway slave over theirs, and they recognized that bondage extended across the river despite the words of the Northwest Ordinance. Vanderburgh planned on taking the McNellys to Kentucky and selling them once outside of Turner's authority. Vanderburgh, therefore, was actually the one who tried to circumvent the law by stealing the McNellys away before the court opened. Turner's attempt to enforce the law violated what Vanderburgh termed the "custom of the country."[42]

Despite Turner's position as territorial judge, his outsider status limited his power in Vincennes. He expressed his frustrations in a letter to territorial governor Arthur St. Clair, complaining, "Certain persons here have lately been guilty of a violent outrage against the laws." In December, St.

Clair wrote to Turner that the ordinance applied only to "slaves who may have been imported since the establishment of that Constitution." He continued, "Had the Constitution the effect to liberate those persons who were slaves by the former laws, as no compensation is provided to their owners, it would be an act of the Government arbitrarily depriving a part of the people of a part of their property." St. Clair admitted that slaves imported into the Northwest Territory after 1787 could sue for their freedom, but he did not apply that to the McNellys' situation. By St. Clair's own construction, Peter and Queen McNelly deserved their freedom because Vanderburgh purchased them and kept them in the Northwest Territory for seven months. However, St. Clair interceded on behalf of Vanderburgh. At the end of his letter to Turner, St. Clair wrote, "I have troubled you with my thoughts upon this subject, because I have heard that there is great agitation among the people respecting it; they should be set at rest, because it was formerly brought before me by some of those people to whom I gave my opinion nearly as I have now stated it to you." St. Clair, more than anything, wanted to end the "great agitation among the people" and basically told Turner to let the matter drop.[43]

A year later, in September 1795, John Cleves Symmes, another federal territorial judge, ordered Vanderburgh's release. Symmes stated that since he did not have custody of Queen McNelly, Vanderburgh could not be held responsible for her failure to appear in court. A month later Vanderburgh created an indenture contract that guaranteed Peter McNelly's freedom in return for two years of service. The contract went unsigned.[44]

George Turner continued his mission undaunted. Following his failure with the McNellys, he tried to liberate other slaves in the territory. However, the residents of the Northwest Territory believed that laws were meant to protect their rights and customs and that the territorial judge was supposed to uphold those laws. Turner however, seemed bent on denying them their rights. His actions infuriated the residents of the Northwest Territory, and they petitioned Congress to remove him from office. In their petition, the residents argued that Turner denied them "the right reserved to us by the constitution of the Territory, to wit, the laws and customs hitherto used in regard to descent and conveyance of property." As the words of the petition suggest, residents regarded the holding and transporting of slaves as a custom that territorial officials had to respect. Their petition for Turner's removal was an attempt to bring the law in line with the customs of the far West. Officials of the federal government evidently agreed, and on the advice of U.S. Attorney General Charles Lee, Congress ordered an interrogation into the conduct of George Turner. Under the threat of impeachment, George Turner resigned from office in 1797.[45]

The aborted extradition of the McNellys, the incarceration of Henry Vanderburgh, and the ultimate resignation of George Turner revealed Americans' contested interpretations of the Ohio River border. The variety of opinions would not have mattered had there been a definitive authority. Without it, the residents clashed over their personal interpretations of article six. The McNellys, with the support of George Turner, attempted to use the Ohio River to gain their legal freedom. Judge George Turner attempted to make the Northwest Ordinance similar to England's Somerset decision, which conferred freedom on any enslaved person who set foot on English soil. Turner, and the McNellys, had to contest federal laws that granted slaveholders the right of retrieval and contend with western settlers defensive of their autonomy. The exchange and sale of bound laborers were common practices among westerners and defended by them as customs of the western country.

While the Ohio River was a border between slave and free territory in the 1790s, the river did not yet constitute a cultural boundary between slavery and freedom. There were fewer than two thousand slaves in the Northwest Territory, which was a relatively small number when compared to the tens of thousands of slaves across the river in Kentucky. Despite the apparent differences between the Northwest Territory and Kentucky, for African Americans, escaping across the border did not immediately confer freedom or even necessarily increase personal opportunities for advancement. Little distinguished white settlers in Kentucky from white settlers in the Northwest Territory, and more important, settlers had little reason to make distinctions.

Rather than emphasizing their differences, white residents west of the Falls of the Ohio forged economic, social, and political connections that crossed the Ohio River. These far westerners emphasized their similarities as white men in a new republic by attempting to control the status of black Americans. While they had to accommodate the border, as evidenced by Vanderburgh's circumvention of Turner's efforts, white settlers ascribed little significance to the Ohio River border. White settlers such as Nathaniel Ewing and Henry Vanderburgh sought to limit the significance of border crossing for African Americans in order to further their own personal advancement. By controlling the movement of African Americans, they could exploit the economic connections with their slaveholding neighbors to the south.

*   *   *

Farther east migrants crossed the river to escape the dominance of slave-holders, but they found a new authority emerging in the Northwest Territory. Settlers only trickled across the Ohio River before the Treaty of Greenville in 1795 because of the constant threat of attack from Ohio Indians. However, speculators proved willing to brave the perilous conditions to establish land claims. As a result, before land belonged to farmers it first passed through the hands of land speculators.

Speculators purchased huge tracts of land for a fraction of the full price and then sold it to other settlers at a price still below the government price. In Ohio many land speculators began as surveyors. Congress had set aside land to be distributed among Virginia's veterans once the "good" lands in Kentucky were claimed. In 1791 the governor of Virginia proposed, and Congress agreed, that good lands were gone in Kentucky and every honorably discharged soldier of Virginia could make a claim to the land in the military district. The applicant's rank and length of service determined the size of the land claim. Veterans hired surveyors to locate military land warrants in Ohio, and the surveyors received one-fifth to one-half of the land as payment. Despite the abundance of land in Ohio, the distribution was far from equal. Few men held huge amounts of land, with roughly 1 percent of landholders in possession of a quarter of the available land. Nathaniel Massie began surveying lands in Ohio in the 1790s, and by 1800 he owned over seventy-five thousand acres. Massie surveyed land in Ohio for the Kentucky political leader John Breckinridge and even for Thomas Jefferson. Through surveying he both acquired a fortune and forged important ties with powerful political leaders in the country. Duncan McArthur, who learned surveying from Nathaniel Massie, acquired over ninety thousand acres of his own.[46]

Land speculators tried to dictate the settlement of western lands in a way that maximized their profit. In 1796 John Edgar and William and Robert Morrison purchased thousands of acres in the southwestern Illinois Territory and hoped to sell it at a profit. However, they found themselves sitting on their purchase as settlers only trickled west. Edgar and the Morrisons blamed the lack of migration on article six of the Northwest Ordinance and petitioned Congress to repeal the ban on slavery. Congress refused on the grounds that the petitioners did not represent the majority of the inhabitants. The petition of Edgar and the Morrisons was a bold move built out of desperation. In the eastern part of the territory, speculators could avoid such moves because they did not have any problems disposing of land. As long as sales were up, there was no need to meddle with the issue of slavery.[47]

In addition to controlling huge amounts of land, the wealthiest settlers exploited bound labor to become the early social and political leaders of Ohio. Because their wealth was largely in land and land sales, there was no need to establish highly productive large-scale plantations such as those found in Virginia or central Kentucky. Instead they overcame the chronic shortage of labor on the frontier by bringing their former slaves with them across the river as indentured servants. Nathaniel Massie brought former slaves from Kentucky into Ohio and bound them as indentures. Henry Massie, Nathaniel's brother, followed another route and simply kept his land and slaves in Kentucky in addition to his huge holdings in Ohio. Fellow land speculator Thomas Worthington established an estate powered by black indentured labor. Edward Tiffin wrote about his relocation to Ohio, "my things and black family could go on as I have a fine young fellow 'Anthony' who I could entrust with my concerns until I overtook them." Tiffin brought his "freed" slaves with him to Ohio and bound others upon his arrival. The servitude that Tiffin and Worthington imposed on their freed slaves was far from voluntary, because the alternative to servitude was sale. For all of these men, connections more than separation were the key to their success.[48]

Dubbed the "Chillicothe Junto" by their political enemies, Massie, Worthington, and his brother-in-law Edward Tiffin parlayed their landed wealth into political prominence in Ohio. They used their power to regulate migration to the territory. The new leaders twice rejected petitions from Virginia soldiers "praying for the toleration to bring their slaves into" Ohio. These former Virginians, familiar with the power of wealthy slaveholders, blocked their entry into Ohio. Preventing the migration of slaveholders with their slaves cemented the power of the "Junto" because they controlled the primary form of wealth (land) and they had laborers to work it. As long as they could take advantage of black indentures, Worthington and Tiffin did not see any reason to introduce chattel slavery to the Ohio Territory.[49]

In preparation for Ohio's impending statehood, Congress divided the Northwest Territory in 1800, splitting the territory of Ohio from the Indiana Territory to the west. The transition to statehood would determine the future of legal slavery within the new state of Ohio. The Ohio land barons did not cross the river with the intention of establishing large-scale slave plantations. Nor did they have a devious plan to create a disguised system of slavery. Actually their motives are quite transparent. They were ambitious young men set on making their fortunes and using those fortunes to become socially and politically powerful. During the debates, the Virginian transplants would have to balance their exploitation of bound labor against their image as political leaders devoted to democracy.

Farther west, with little to stop them following the resignation of George Turner, Anglo-Americans from Kentucky brought long-term indentured servants to Vincennes throughout the 1790s. In 1800 President John Adams appointed Virginian William Henry Harrison as governor of the newly created Indiana Territory. Harrison crossed the Ohio River and arrived in the new territorial capital of Vincennes with his slaves. He cemented his political power by appointing community leaders to political positions. Almost immediately upon his arrival, residents of the Indiana Territory began lobbying Harrison for the legalization of slavery within the territory. In perfect historical irony, Adams appointed Henry Vanderburgh to replace George Turner as one of the three territorial judges of the Indiana Territory in 1800.[50]

*   *   *

Each and every American who crossed the Ohio River after 1787 was crossing a border. Exactly what they hoped to achieve by crossing that border differed greatly. Some white settlers left for moral reasons, and others were in search of new lands; either way the presence of free soil induced some to leave the slaveholding state of Kentucky. However, social and economic ties kept residents on both sides of the Ohio River in regular contact. Thus residents who stayed in Kentucky and those who left drew from the same pool of bound labor, often blurring the line between servitude and slavery. Their commitment to bound labor and paternalism connected white Americans across the legal divide between slavery and freedom. In contrast, black Americans quickly learned that the Ohio River was not the River Jordan and that the strictures of slavery followed them across the river. In some cases the political and social leaders of both the Indiana and Ohio Territories owed their prominence to their slaveholding roots just as much as the political leaders of Kentucky did. In the coming years, statehood movements in Indiana and Ohio brought the issue of slavery into public debate and forced Americans to reckon with their connections to their slaveholding neighbors.

CHAPTER THREE

Slaveholding Liberators

In 1801 Thomas Worthington traveled to the national capital, accompanied by his lawyer and his black servant, to press for the removal of territorial governor Arthur St. Clair. Worthington was a prominent leader in Ohioans' push for statehood, and he hoped his connections with national political leaders from Kentucky and Virginia would help further his cause. Worthington's work as a surveyor in Ohio had brought him in contact with men such as John Breckenridge, a powerful political leader from Kentucky; William Giles from Virginia; Albert Gallatin, secretary of the Treasury; and even the president of the United States, Thomas Jefferson. As he made his case for the corruption of St. Clair and the necessity of statehood, Worthington appealed to these men as a gentleman. It was not a coincidence that many of Worthington's acquaintances were slaveholders. Slaveholding was the mark of the southern gentleman, and despite his residence in Ohio, Worthington styled himself a Virginia gentleman. He established a Virginia-style estate in Ohio powered by bound black labor and traveled with a personal body servant. Although rebuffed by Jefferson initially, Worthington was ultimately successful in his effort, and the president signed the enabling act in April 1802.[1]

*   *   *

Following Worthington's success, the campaign for the Ohio Constitutional Convention became a deeply partisan battle. The debates defined clear divides between the candidates, and few divides were clearer to Americans than the separation between slavery and freedom. Republican correspondence committees interrogated the candidates about their positions on slavery. In print, Worthington and his allies created an image of freedom for the Democratic Republicans by declaring their opposition to the introduction of slavery in the new state. Thomas Worthington, Nathaniel Massie, and Edward Tiffin lambasted the corruption of St. Clair and the Federalists, who they claimed were soft on the issue of slavery.

In actuality, all three young Republican leaders held black indentured servants, but when forced to address the issue of slavery directly, they vehemently proclaimed their antislavery credentials. Worthington explained, "I was decidedly opposed to slavery long before I removed to the territory—the prohibition of slavery in the territory, was one cause of my removal to it." Tiffin wrote in the *Scioto Gazette*, "The introduction of slavery, was it practicable, I should view as the greatest national curse we could entail upon our country." Nathaniel Massie, although admitting the temporary advantages of slavery, still took an antislavery stand. Slavery, Massie wrote, "would ultimately prove injurious to our country; although it might at present, and for some time hence, contribute to improve it." Their words rang true with the new migrants to Ohio, and the Republican leaders rode the tide of antislavery to success, securing twenty-eight of the thirty-five possible positions for the convention. At the state constitutional convention the delegates voted, by a margin of only one vote, to prohibit slavery in the state of Ohio, and the members of the Chillicothe Junto became the seventeenth state's slaveholding liberators.[2]

The relationship between the politics of antislavery in state making and the bound labor systems that developed in the states along the Ohio River forms the core of this chapter. During the first decades of the nineteenth century, white Kentuckians embraced chattel slavery, Ohioans adopted indentured servitude, and Indianans developed a hybrid of the two, which could most appropriately be called chattel servitude. These three systems, all based on the exploitation of African American laborers, developed in relation to one another and appeared similar (especially to observers). However, despite the ostensible similarities, black and white Americans regularly had conflicts over the important and ever so slippery distinction between servitude and slavery. White residents could easily draw on the language of the revolution to draw a sharp dichotomy between slavery and freedom, but distinguishing between the various forms of unfreedom that defined African Americans' experiences in the region proved more challenging.

However clear it appeared on a map, the Ohio River border blurred as white and black Americans crossed it. African American slaves and servants tested the limits of the labor systems that bound them, and their constant movement forced white leaders to articulate how the river served as a divide. With the entrenchment of chattel slavery in Kentucky, politicians in Indiana and Ohio flattened the subtle distinctions between servitude and slavery, in order to stress their antislavery credentials and identify themselves with the cause of freedom. On the surface the political debates over statehood defined the Ohio River as the border between slave and free territories. However, the distinction between slavery and freedom was racially defined, because African Americans in nominally free states failed to receive the full benefits of freedom. Instead African Americans understood that the conflicts and compromises rooted in the distinctions among the three exploitative bound labor systems defined the Ohio River as the limit of the chattel principle only.

*   *   *

Following the 1799 constitutional convention, chattel slavery flourished in Kentucky. There were over 40,000 enslaved African Americans in the state by 1800, over 80,000 by 1810, and over 126,000 by 1820. The desire for slaves was strong and crossed class lines. Skilled workers were in constant demand, and during harvest season farmers always needed extra hands to tend the fields. Even one slave provided much-needed labor during settlement and in the maintenance of a farm. Slaves cleared land, ploughed fields, built homes, planted, tended and harvested crops, built fences, cared for animals, and performed other types of labor. Because of the system's flexibility, many white Kentuckians were desirous of obtaining slaves as a long-term investment.[3]

In the cash-poor economy of frontier Kentucky, slaves were valuable commodities. White Kentuckians offered slaves as collateral for debts, bartered for goods with slaves, gave them as wedding gifts, bequeathed them to their heirs, and sold them for cash. Most white Kentuckians did not establish large-scale plantations, which lessened the "need" for a large body of workers. But slaves were valuable even when owners did not need them for their own use. White Kentuckians engaged in a mixture of slave ownership and slave hiring to meet their labor demands. The high demand for labor on the frontier ensured that someone always needed a laborer, and owners regularly hired slaves out for both short-term and long-term use.[4]

The mixture of slave ownership and slave hiring led to a diverse application of slave labor, which, when combined with the limited number of large-scale plantations and mobility of settlers, led to white Kentuckians' emphasis on the chattel principle in slavery. White Kentuckians' efforts to reduce enslaved African Americans to objects strengthened the slave system. The commodification of African Americans helped spread slavery, which created a common interest in the maintenance of the institution that crossed lines of class. Both slaveholding and nonslaveholding whites actively worked to control the movement of blacks, especially across the Ohio River. While Kentuckians were far from endorsing slavery as a positive good, their efforts to shore up the Ohio River border by controlling the movement of enslaved and free blacks suggests that white Kentuckians viewed slavery as a permanent institution. Men such as Henry Clay would argue that the institution was a necessary evil, but it was an evil that was not going away soon. In addition, even if nonslaveholding Kentuckians chafed under the rule of the emerging slave-holding class, they still understood that the chattel principle made Kentucky different from the Ohio and Indiana Territories. Thus in the first decades of the nineteenth century, Kentucky was quickly transitioning from a western frontier to a frontier of the Old South.[5]

Wealthy Kentuckians' ownership of slaves was essential to their power. Alexander Scott Bullitt settled in Jefferson County near Louisville along the Ohio River in 1787. Bullitt was one of the largest slaveholders in the state, owning between sixty-five and eighty slaves from 1795 to 1814. Bullitt, like many other slaveholders, used his slave capital to increase his overall wealth and extend his influence. Between 1805 and 1815 Bullitt hired out seven or eight slaves to John Anthony Tarascon. Tarascon hired the enslaved workers on two-year contracts to work in his rope walk in Shippingport, Kentucky, along the Ohio River. Each contracted laborer earned Bullitt at least 380 pounds. When Bullitt's responsibilities as a politician and lawyer took him away from his own farm, he hired William Haywood, a white tenant, to manage his plantation for a year. In return Bullitt gave Haywood "a boy called Adam to attend upon his family," which furthered Bullitt's reputation as a powerful and benevolent patriarch. Bullitt continued to acquire slaves even as he was hiring several out, likely from the profits he reaped. He spread the influence of slavery among less wealthy Kentuckians through his use of human investments. Bullitt built his power on a foundation of commodified human labor and therefore was understandably defensive of his property.[6]

There were few settlers of Bullitt's status, but even white settlers without his wealth engaged in a combination of slave ownership and hiring and embraced the chattel principle. One observer said of a Kentucky farmer, "He works himself and employs two negroes. Every thing around him bespoke comfort and moderate wealth. Yet he has cultivated his own land among these hills only 10 years." Some tenant farmers tried to purchase slaves before they owned land. With men such as Bullitt in charge and the constitutional protection of slavery in place, white Kentuckians clearly understood that slave ownership was a road toward upward mobility.[7]

In 1815 Rhode Islander John Corlis purchased land in Kentucky's interior and left his sons, George and Joseph, in charge of establishing a tobacco plantation. However, the reality of establishing a homestead proved more difficult than had been first imagined. Although John Corlis did not own any slaves in Rhode Island, in Kentucky his sons George and Joseph quickly came to the conclusion that slave labor was an absolute necessity. In February 1816 Joseph Corlis wrote to his mother and father about his inability to acquire labor to work on the farm. By March, George had written to his father of the necessity of purchasing a slave: "We find it extremely difficult to obtain help, every one almost being taken up by the raising of tobacco. We have hired one, and are promised another there with one of the above if we purchase will be sufficient." A week after writing to his father, George Corlis purchased a slave named Charles in Lexington for $525. George Corlis proudly wrote to his father that Charles was diligent, honest, and skilled at three trades (shoe making, rope making, and brick making).[8]

George Corlis immediately emphasized the value of his investment, explaining that owners were hiring slaves at "extravagant prices" and thus ownership saved money. In addition George explained to his father that he could sell Charles for $700, more than making up for the price of purchase. George even sought to purchase Charles's wife and son, not out of concern for Charles but as security for his current investment. He wrote to his father of Charles's wife, "It will be far preferable to purchase her and her boy to Charlotte and hers for from what I have seen of Charlotte I am not pleased with her. She is quite lazy and I suspect not very honest—in the mean time I shall if I can hire, Charles's (our negro) wife for I am obliged to let him go to see her every fortnight, which makes it inconvenient." Despite his own personal dislike of slavery, John Corlis praised his son's smart investment in slave property.[9]

One slave could not satisfy the labor needs on the Corlis farm. A month after purchasing Charles, George once again complained about his inability to acquire enough labor, "whether it is owing to our being strangers or that their masters have full employment for them I know not." At the time he employed four hired slaves, two males and two females, in addition to Charles. George actually wrote of his preference for female slaves both to perform domestic duties and to "work among the tobacco," because they were more affordable. He employed male slaves for the construction of his home, especially the skilled work of brick making and molding. Although hired labor was temporarily useful and an absolute necessity, George Corlis lamented his reliance on it. As an employer, George knew that he was still subject to the whim of the slave owner. He was still under the thumb of men such as Alexander Bullitt. When the owner of William, one of George's hired male slaves, took him back and sold him, George clearly understood his position. George was never able to step out of the shadow of the large slaveholder, and he continued to hire slaves on his farm for the next several years. George's ambivalent embrace of the chattel principle offered both opportunities and limitations for the acquisition of labor. It provided access to the labor necessary for settlement and tied him to a slaveholding system controlled by the wealthiest slaveholders' monopoly on the labor pool.[10]

The chattel principle severely restricted the bargaining power of enslaved African Americans, which led many to focus on negotiating within the parameters of the slave system. Charles, although evidently very skilled and "diligent," could only plead with the Corlises to purchase his wife and child, which they never did. Some slaves labored with the promise of future freedom from their owners. Hiring out granted them the hope of self-purchase, but it also curtailed opportunities for community building because of the constant movement involved. Some owners freed their slaves in their wills; however such promises still left slaves largely subject to the whims of their owners. Mrs. Wilmot sold her slave, Will, to Thompson on provision that Thompson would free Will after seven years. When Thompson failed to emancipate him in 1805, Will tried to file for his own freedom, but the court rebuffed his efforts. Mrs. Wilmot appealed to the courts and sued Thompson for damages, and four years after the initial agreement the court granted Will his freedom. Others were not as fortunate.[11]

Part of white Kentuckians' commodification of enslaved African Americans involved controlling the movement of all African Americans. Hiring kept enslaved African Americans mobile but under the direction of whites.

Bullitt happily hired his slaves out and sold others because he totally controlled their movement. In a letter to his father, George Corlis wrote that twelve of his neighbor's hired slaves returned to their owner's home in Virginia. On their own farm, the Corlises regularly hired slaves but did not always hire the same slave twice.

Whites wanted to facilitate the movement of African Americans as capital, but they also wanted to regulate the movement of all black laborers. Kentucky law granted slaveholders the absolute right to retrieve their human property. The slave code of 1798 allowed any citizen to apprehend a "suspected" runaway, and in Kentucky color was prima facie evidence of status. In one case the court declared that "experience teaches, that there is no danger to be apprehended from too great an alacrity, or passionate ardour, in apprehending slaves as runaways, without probable cause." In addition free blacks had to carry proof of their freedom, and the enslaved had to carry passes from their owners. However, Kentuckians had a difficult time putting this law into practice while maintaining basic constitutional rights. In one account, a justice of the peace whipped a free black man for resisting arrest. However, the accused sued the justice of the peace for battery, and the court ruled that "if a justice should inflict the stripes against a free person of color, who lifted his hand to save himself . . . from death or severe bodily harm, all men must pronounce the punishment cruel indeed."[12]

African Americans' movement across the Ohio River proved even more difficult to control. Some enslaved African Americans escaped across the river, some unwillingly migrated with their owners, and others labored across the river only to return to Kentucky. Black Kentuckians challenged white Kentuckians to articulate appropriate versus inappropriate border crossings. Ultimately fugitive slaves had no rights and could be dragged from a free state back into Kentucky by force. The Federal Fugitive Slave Law of 1793 granted slaveholders the right to retrieve their "fugitives from labor" from another state. Escape did not change slaves' status as property. Similarly slaves who temporarily traveled with their owners across the Ohio River or who labored on temporary contracts remained slaves before the law. However, when a slaveholder moved across the river with his/her slaves and established a residence, the slaves became free. Once those slaves became free, legally they could never become slaves again even if they went back to Kentucky.

Two opposing examples make this distinction clear. When his owner sold him in 1798, Joseph was supposed to work for his new owner for four years before obtaining his freedom. But his new owner sold him, and when Joseph filed for his freedom, the Kentucky courts ruled that because "it not appearing that he ever was out of the limits of this state" a promise for freedom did not grant emancipation, making Joseph a slave for life. On the other side of the coin, in 1807 Warrick moved to Indiana with his slaves Flor and her daughter Lydia. Warrick made an agreement with Flor that she would serve him for twenty years. Seven years later Warrick sold Lydia to Miller of Indiana, who in turn sold her to Robert Todd, who brought her back to Kentucky and sold her to Rankin as a slave for life. However, Lydia successfully sued Rankin for her freedom.[13]

In every case white Kentuckians determined what type of border crossing was acceptable because they controlled the law. Their efforts to control and protect their slave property led white Kentuckians to downplay the function of the Ohio River as a border for African Americans. But while they downplayed the border, they did not ignore it altogether. The courts made the distinction between temporary and permanent residence the deciding factor in what gave enslaved African Americans access to freedom. This opening, no matter how minimal, had two effects. First, it meant that potentially enslaved African Americans could hold white Kentuckians subject to a higher power. Rather than being entirely subject to the whims of their owners, enslaved blacks had a legal defense for their freedom. Second, white Kentuckians' recognition of a border, no matter how minimal, helped make it a reality. The court recognized a distinction between free and slave territory and, at times, held white Kentuckians accountable for maintaining that distinction. This offered a legal grounding for what was at this time still only an abstract political border. Significantly it drew the line of community to exclude fugitive slaves entirely. Basically African Americans could cross the border only if white Americans allowed them to do so.

In the first decades of the nineteenth century, white Kentuckians adapted to their position at the top of the South by embracing the chattel principle and limiting the power of the Ohio River border. By combining slave ownership and slave hiring, white Kentuckians capitalized on bound labor and spread the influence of slavery across class lines. Whether they held fifty, five, or zero enslaved blacks, white Kentuckians relied on bound labor to settle and cultivate the land. Thus the institution of slavery thrived in Kentucky despite the relatively small enslaved population. The mobility of enslaved blacks and the long border with free territory forced white Kentuckians to define the geographical border between slavery and freedom.

They developed a border that protected the institution by marginalizing escaped slaves. Both state and national laws dictated that fugitive slaves remained enslaved on both sides of the Ohio River. However, the state court's decision that permanent relocation to free territory freed enslaved African Americans created an important distinction between slave and free territory. Enslaved African Americans continued to test this distinction by crossing the Ohio River border, but they quickly realized that their status followed them across the river.

*   *   *

Enslaved African Americans were among the first Americans to enter Ohio. African American slaves who performed the duties of camp accompanied surveyors who mapped out land claims in Ohio. Although they went from being slaves to becoming servants, materially little changed for the African Americans who accompanied surveyors into Ohio. When Nathaniel Massie threatened him with sale if he refused to sign an indenture contract, Abraham, Massie's former slave, ran away to Cincinnati in the spring of 1801. But once Abraham made it to the city, Charles Willing Byrd, the territorial secretary, imprisoned Abraham and hired him out to perform menial chores until Massie retrieved him.[14]

The story of Abraham was common in the new territory north of the Ohio River. Slaves regularly crossed the river with white migrants and labored on their former owners' settlements. Local court records indicate that African Americans were "brought into Ohio," which suggests that many of Ohio's first black immigrants accompanied their former owners. These migrants repeatedly tried to capitalize on the Ohio River border by exploiting the difference between servitude and slavery. Although Abraham was unsuccessful in his attempt to gain his freedom, other African Americans used the courts and fellow residents' distaste for slavery to put time limits on their servitude and gain freedom. The limitations of the Northwest Ordinance crushed the McNellys' chances in 1793, but as the territory became states, new opportunities opened up for the forced migrants. In fact, just as African Americans sought to distinguish between servitude and slavery, ambitious politicians exploited this distinction for personal gain during the transition to statehood. The difference between slavery and servitude proved a potent political weapon for young white men on the make, even as they tried to minimize the difference between the two in practice.

However, the combination of African Americans' efforts to gain personal freedom and white Americans' celebration of their state's freedom from slavery helped define the Ohio River as a dividing line between slavery and freedom.[15]

While chattel slavery legally stopped at the Ohio River, the demand for labor only increased on the northern bank. As in Kentucky, the lack of available hired free labor made bound labor particularly attractive to settlers moving into the forests of Ohio. However, Ohioans largely turned to contractual bound labor rather than chattel slavery. In 1810 John Cleves Symmes wrote to both of his grandsons about the superior labor situation in Ohio in order to convince them to move out of Kentucky. He wrote, "You cannot live in Kentucky reputably without negroes. Here you will need none." However, he suggested that they make sure their lands in Ohio "are planted with tenants, when after a few years they may become productive and afford considerable rent. But rent will not be sufficient alone to support a family in a style of life that is called decent. You must both have professions of some kind." Symmes celebrated his state's freedom from the need for slave labor, offering instead a vision of workers bound to the land through wage labor.[16]

Charles Short, however, did not agree with his grandfather and remained in Kentucky. Charles believed that the availability of slaves in Kentucky gave him an advantage over his brother John Short in Ohio, where John had to hire his hands. He wrote to his brother John in 1817 that the only way to make money as a farmer was to use slaves to grow cash crops. Charles believed that slave labor was a necessity, and he rationalized the use of slaves to his brother: "As for the use of negroes a person who feeds, clothes, and treats them well should surely require their labour from them without having himself much disturbed." Despite his bold protestations, Charles was only theorizing, and he quickly discovered that the reality of working within the slave system fell short of his expectations. It was John who established a successful homestead in Ohio and Charles who fell on hard times as he was unable to acquire a sufficient number of slaves to work his land. He complained of having to tend his corn with his two hands, Joe and his son Charles. Charles Short held a piece of land in Ohio and asked his brother to sell that piece of land to relieve his debt. Eventually John Short had to bail his brother out of debt. In this case John Short's ability to establish a farm without the aid of slave labor certainly distinguished practices in Ohio from those to the south in Kentucky.[17]

Farmers who migrated to Ohio seemed most concerned with establishing their homesteads and providing enough food for their families. While migrants who did not own numerous slaves in Kentucky did not have the desire or the means to introduce slavery on a large scale into Ohio, they also were accustomed to bound labor. The letters of George Corlis paint a picture of constantly mobile slaves on the Kentucky frontier, and that mobility did not simply stop at the Ohio River. Ohioans hired about two thousand Kentucky slaves on an annual basis during the first decade of the nineteenth century.[18]

The hiring of Kentucky slaves partially satisfied some white settlers' need for labor in Ohio. However, slave hiring still left the employer reliant on wealthy slaveholders, and so some of the immigrants tried to avoid this dependence by maintaining control over their own independent labor sources. A few Ohioans established farms in Ohio while retaining control over their slave plantations in Kentucky and Virginia. More commonly, however, migrants freed their slaves prior to their move under the condition that the former slaves continue to work for them in Ohio. The former slaves of Thomas Worthington labored on Adena, his new estate in Ohio, where Worthington promised each family "a freehold . . . whenever he should judge them capable of preserving the cabin and adjacent acres, which he allowed them by way of probation." None of the families ever received their own land. Although not legally bound to him, the African Americans of Adena had little choice but to remain with Worthington. Thomas Worthington was not alone or unique, and many white residents established plantations in southern Ohio, especially in Ross County, that strongly resembled southern slave plantations.[19]

When convention delegates Nathaniel Massie, Thomas Worthington, and Edward Tiffin crossed the Ohio River, they all brought freed slaves with them to establish their new estates. They therefore wanted to create a constitution that protected the current labor system in the territory. First and foremost the delegates voted not to allow slavery in the new state of Ohio. Delegates then proposed a form of servitude in which male servants could be held until thirty-five years of age and female servants until they were twenty-five years old, but some objected, fearing that the result would be a disguised form of slavery. Rather than entirely rejecting indentured servitude, the delegates instead lowered the age requirements to twenty-one for males and eighteen for females. In addition, according to the constitution, white immigrants could bring their slaves with them and keep them as indentures in the new state for one year. At the end of the year, white residents could retain the services of their former slaves only if those previously bound by slavery entered into indentures "while in a state of perfect freedom."[20]

The indentured servitude allowed in Ohio illuminates the limits of freedom in the new state. The law, first and foremost, reflected the need for labor on the frontier. One-year indentures allowed white Ohio residents to continue the practice of hiring slaves from Kentucky. This practice had begun before statehood, and the delegates, aware of this, inserted the indenture clause to *regulate* rather than restrict the practice. In addition men such as Massie, Worthington, and Tiffin could retain the services of their former slaves and prevent an influx of wealthy slaveholders. Edward Tiffin bound three black children, all under the age of ten, in indentures in 1801 to serve "Edward Tiffin and his heirs" until they reached the age of twenty-one. He also brought "mulatto Bill" with him to the territory in 1798, and Bill in 1822 "was free by virtue of living with him." Under the new constitution nothing changed for Tiffin or his indentured servants.[21]

When Ohio legislators banned slavery in the state constitution, many new Ohioans celebrated the new state's freedom. While residents migrated to Ohio for a variety of reasons, the heated rhetoric they read during the debates for the election of constitutional delegates convinced many that they had settled in Ohio precisely because of their aversion to slavery. However, freedom from slavery did not mean freedom from bound black labor. White Ohioans capitalized on indentured servitude, but they rationalized their freedom from slavery with the belief that their servants chose to remain with them. Nonetheless Ohioans were proud of their freedom from the chattel principle.[22]

Ohioans' celebration of their freedom from chattel slavery linked their settlement of the region with the legacy of the American Revolution by defining the limits of unfreedom. In the first decades of the nineteenth century chattel slavery was rapidly expanding in America. Kentucky became the first state to protect slavery explicitly in its constitution in 1792. However, the development of the cotton gin in 1793, the evacuation of western outposts by the British following the War of 1812, and an expanding population along the coast triggered a massive migration of slaveholders to the new cotton frontier of the then Southwest. In this context white Ohioans' ability to check the expansion of slavery at the Ohio River gained meaning and importance. In addition Ohioans' ability to defeat slavery in the territory fulfilled the ideals of the founders. The founders wrote the North-west Ordinance based on the principle of spreading freedom to the new territory. While the ordinance itself did not exclude slavery, it embodied principles that the pioneers of the West had to fulfill. Over time the ordinance gained importance, but even at this early stage freedom was becoming the regional signifier of the territory north of the Ohio River. Thus keeping the state free from slavery was important to settlers, even settlers who may have utilized black indentured servants.[23]

Although it was minor from a modern perspective, Ohioans believed in the distinction between servitude and slavery, and when new immigrants tried to bring the chattel principle across the river, white Ohioans staunchly defended their freedom from slavery. Robert Patterson participated in the movement to enact gradual emancipation in Kentucky, and his failure convinced him to move to Ohio in 1804. Patterson struggled over what to do with his own slaves. On one hand, he did not want to sell them because that locked them in perpetual bondage, but on the other hand, he did not feel that they were ready for immediate emancipation. So he moved his former slaves with him to Dayton. William Patterson, one of his former slaves, filed for his freedom in the courts, which Robert Patterson did not deny. Others followed suit and registered themselves as free persons in the county court. Robert Patterson seemed to have no problem with granting his slaves freedom as long as they remained to work on his new farm. However, he had trouble with two of his slaves, Ned and Lucy Page, and before he left for Dayton he sold them to William McCalla, although Patterson still took them with him to Dayton. The purpose of the bill of sale was to prevent the Pages from running off and to legitimate their presence on his new farm in Dayton. When approached by the authorities, Patterson simply claimed that the Pages had "absconded from service" and he held them under a one-year contract with McCalla, their legal owner. However, local judges disagreed and ruled that the Pages were free and registered them as such in the record book. When Patterson and McCalla attempted to reclaim the Pages by force, the residents of Dayton defended the Pages and fought off the would-be kidnappers. The actual court cases dragged on for a decade and eventually ended inconclusively, but the Pages were already safe from recapture.[24]

Patterson was surprised to find such a hostile reaction to his attempt to control his former slaves, because Ohioans commonly held former slaves as indentured servants. On three separate occasions in 1812, James Scott took fellow Ohioans to court for holding African Americans in involuntary servitude, and he lost in every case. One visitor to Ohio wrote, "Many persons in this state have coloured people, which they call their property. The mode in which they effect this perpetuation of slavery, in violation of the spirit of the Ohio constitution, is to purchase blacks, and have them apprenticed to them." However, Patterson tried to force servitude on the Pages, which was his first mistake in the eyes of Dayton residents. Thus the judges ruled that the Pages were in fact free, but that did not preclude Patterson from indenturing them. It required only that the contract be made "freely" by all parties.[25]

Robert Patterson's attempt to force the Pages across the river and sell them as slaves for life was his second mistake. According to both Ohio and Kentucky law, once the Pages crossed the Ohio River and settled in Ohio they ceased being chattel slaves. Patterson, however, tried to bring the chattel principle across the river. In theory, chattel servitude reduced persons into things, which gave slaveholders complete power over their human property. White Ohioans were willing to accommodate slaveholders traveling through the state and did not object to others holding slaves in other states, but they objected to bringing the permanency and complete power of chattel slavery to bear on residents of Ohio regardless of skin color. In their eyes servitude was different from slavery, and once a person went from slavery to servitude, movement back across the river could not reduce him/her to slavery.[26]

At times white Ohioans interpreted residence differently from the way the law did. Jane, an African American slave from Virginia, was convicted of stealing four dollars' worth of goods in Virginia and sentenced to death. As a reprieve, Virginia judges decided to sell Jane outside of the United States in place of execution. Jane escaped to Ohio in November 1808 and eventually settled in Marietta. She married, had a child, and was gainfully employed by Abner Lord. Jacob Beeson of Virginia applied for and received a certificate to carry off Jane and her child for himself. Beeson presented his certificate before the justice of the peace in Marietta but failed to reclaim Jane and her child because residents of Marietta had her "secreted and put out of reach of the officer." The governor of Virginia intervened and issued to the governor of Ohio a formal request for Jane as a fugitive from justice. In May 1810 Governor Huntington of Ohio directed a warrant to John Clarke, a Marietta resident, for the arrest of Jane. Clarke successfully reclaimed Jane and delivered her and her child to Beeson, who sold them and gave the money to Virginia's public treasury. Ultimately the law won out in this case, but white Ohioans demonstrated their commitment to defending their state against slavery. While they did not support granting full civil rights to blacks, at the very least white Ohioans recognized African Americans as human beings deserving of the most basic level of liberty.[27]

Although they protected current residents from slavery, legislators also enacted a series of "black laws" that defined African Americans as second-class citizens and stripped them of their rights. By 1807 there was a black code to regulate the black population. The laws restricted voting to white male citizens, restricted military service to white male citizens, excluded blacks from enumeration, required black immigrants to provide proof of their freedom, prevented blacks from testifying against whites, banned black children from schools, and generally denied blacks the rights of white free men in Ohio.[28]

White Ohioans based their efforts to restrict African Americans on their fear of dependency and the vices of dependents. White Americans believed that independence upheld American freedom but dependency threatened the social fabric of the country by undermining virtue and replacing it with self-interested vice. However, in the first decades of the nineteenth century, wage labor was still uncommon, so the achievement of independence was limited to property holders, and the maintenance of independence, ironically, was the responsibility of the community. Thomas Jefferson offered his vision of America as a land of independent farmers; however, that vision failed to translate into reality for all Americans in the Ohio Valley. Instead those needing work bound themselves to others, sometimes working as tenants on farms, as domestic servants in households, or as apprentices in craftsmen's workshops. This status of dependency was supposed to be temporary as workers earned enough to become property holders. Those who fell through the cracks were those who failed to bind themselves to others, and they disrupted the system. Therefore it was in the community's best interest to create ties between all members and expel those who failed to adhere to local standards.

When Ohio became a state, legislators formed the Overseers of the Poor to keep tabs on dependent residents. The specific responsibilities of the Overseers of the Poor included offering financial relief to those who needed it, paying residents for boarding homeless Ohioans, binding children and unemployed men and women to established residents, and expelling unruly paupers from the community. The overall purpose of the Overseers was to maintain the virtue of the community by keeping men and women from becoming charges on the county. Their primary means of accomplishing this goal was to keep everyone working. The records of the Overseers of the Poor for Hamilton County in southern Ohio are filled with receipts for boarding and binding men, women, and children and with notices for constables to expel unwanted residents. The agency itself did not bind or board anyone; they instead paid others for those services. This suggests that white residents believed that it was their responsibility to keep, care for, and control the poorer members of the community.[29]

It was not a coincidence that the group in charge of regulating the African American population was the Overseers of the Poor. Many white Ohioans believed that African Americans, especially those recently loosed from the chains of slavery, were predisposed to lives of dependency. Thus, in the eyes of white Ohioans, the influx of black Americans also meant an increase in dependent citizens who would become liabilities and threaten to break down the social order. Therefore Ohio legislators passed laws to regulate the African American population in the state. One law required free black residents to register with the county court and required each new immigrant to enter into a bond with two or more property holders in the "penal sum" of five hundred dollars to guarantee their good behavior. The Overseers of the Poor had the authority to remove from the state black Ohioans who failed to register. Historians have rightly characterized this as a prohibitive law meant to deter black immigration. White Ohioans feared that their proximity to slave states would bring a stream of former slaves into the state, and they hoped to prevent an influx by forcing all African Americans to register their freedom.[30]

However, the Overseers seldom enforced this law, which did little to deter black immigration. So why would legislators pass a law they had little hope or intention of enforcing? Historians have argued that while the black laws were rarely enforced, they served as a method of enforcement when necessary. However, historians have underestimated the close relationship between the black laws and other attempts to control all dependents. Even the most ardent antislavery advocates supported gradual emancipation because they believed that slaves lacked the proper education and training to enjoy the responsibility of freedom. And those who shared more sympathy for slavery likely also held similar beliefs about blacks' incapacity for freedom. By and large, their experiences with slavery convinced white Ohioans that African Americans, especially former slaves, were destined to become dependents and charges on the state.

Whites viewed blacks' incapacity for freedom as the primary obstacle to emancipation in slave states. This was a problem that white Ohioans wanted to keep in slave states. Ohioans argued that the only way to keep from being overrun with dependent blacks was to keep them out of the state or bind them to established citizens. Whites viewed African Americans as unwanted citizens not simply because they were black but because their skin color marked them as unwanted dependents. The laws were probably seldom enforced because African Americans seldom became charges on the county. There is evidence that financially successful black Ohioans held prominent places in the community and on occasion were marked as white on the census. In addition white Ohioans were willing to protect African Americans once they became residents of the state and ceased to perceive them as an undifferentiated and faceless threat.[31]

Free African Americans in Ohio took advantage of the system to secure their freedom and obtain training as skilled workers. As chattel slaves, African Americans held no legal rights. Even their claims to freedom had to be initiated and supported by white persons. While crossing into Ohio did not elevate African Americans to full membership in society, residency did legally end their status as chattel slaves. White Ohioans intended the registration law to keep unwanted blacks out of the state, but new black immigrants used it as a means of securing their freedom. By entering their status into the court record book they went on record as free persons, which was important because the close proximity to the Ohio River made reenslavement a constant threat. For example, William Pattaway purchased his freedom from his owner before moving to Ohio. However, evidence of his freedom was stolen from his former owner. In order to secure his freedom, Pattaway obtained the support of a white Ohioan and went to court to register his freedom.[32]

In addition to establishing their most basic right to liberty, African Americans used the indenture system to the best of their ability. Some African American parents could offer little in support of their children and had them bound to work for white residents. Young boys, under the age of twelve, went to work on farms, and most young girls worked as domestics, but teenage boys learned skilled trades such as blacksmithing, shoe making, tailoring, and wagon making. The opportunity to indenture one's son to an artisan's shop may have become as much an ideal for many as passing on a tract of good land. While not an ideal situation, African American parents could use the indenture system to free themselves from unmanageable financial burdens and train their children in skilled trades. The indenture system limited African Americans' occupational opportunities because it left African American parents and children dependent on whites for employment. This was far from total freedom. However, indentured servitude still offered hope for the future, something totally absent in chattel slavery. Enslaved African Americans hated their inability to protect their children, and they lamented their children's lifetime of bondage. However, in Ohio parents labored with the hope that their children's lives could be better. Thus, despite the fact that visitors saw little difference between servitude in Ohio and slavery in Kentucky, the difference between indentured servitude and chattel slavery must have been profound for free African Americans in Ohio.[33]

Indentured servitude became a stepping stone for both white and black Ohioans. White Ohioans viewed it as a means of controlling the black population and exploiting their labor without introducing slavery to the state. Indentured servitude in Ohio gave African Americans room to negotiate that was simply not there for chattel slaves in Kentucky. As one observer explained, "black servants will take liberties that are not granted. . . . More dissipated, vile, insolent beings there cannot be. I have been on the point of knocking my shoeblack down twice. I changed him; and but little for the better. It will not do to speak to a Negro as you must to a white man; he assumes upon it immediately." African Americans capitalized on indentured servitude to provide for their children. The adaptation of slave hiring into indentured servitude in Ohio connected white residents on both banks of the Ohio River economically. However, the basic level of liberty that white Ohioans granted to African Americans in defense of Ohio's freedom weakened the system of bound labor. The efforts of African Americans strengthened Ohio's celebrated freedom from slavery by moving the state away from bound labor.[34]

White Ohioans quickly developed self-induced amnesia and convinced themselves that they moved to Ohio because it was free from slavery. One observer noted, "There are some that think the state legislature could pass a law allowing slavery despite the ordinance, but the discussion of this point is of no consequence, as slavery is expressly prohibited by the state constitution; and were the case submitted to the people, I have no doubt but more than nine-tenths of them would be against slavery." Black and white Ohioans differed over what migration to Ohio meant, but everyone worked to ensure that movement from Ohio to Kentucky did not reduce anyone to slavery. This attempt to control movement across the border laid the foundation for conflict between Ohioans and Kentuckians.[35]

*   *   *

While legislators were establishing the indenture system in Ohio, William Henry Harrison and the settlers of the Indiana Territory were struggling to solve their labor shortage farther west. The Land Act of 1800 opened property ownership to a wide population because it allowed for the purchase of federal lands in units as small as 320 acres at a price of two dollars per acre (in contrast to the twelve dollars per acre for land in central Kentucky) and created an installment payment plan requiring only one-fourth of the price as down payment, with the balance to be paid over four years. This situation freed many settlers from speculators because they did not need substantial capital to settle. They could purchase land on credit and let the land pay for itself within a few years. Settlers found little reason to work as tenants when they could become landowners, creating a high land-to-labor ratio. All of this led to a labor shortage. One observer noted, "The farmers of Indiana generally arrive in the country very poor, but somehow they get a great deal of property very soon. They all work, and there are not half so many labourers for hire, as there are farmers."[36]

In Vincennes, the territorial capital and most populous settlement of the Indiana Territory, there was strong support for the introduction of slavery. Settlers around Vincennes already owned slaves and sought legal sanction for what they were already practicing. The 1800 census lists twenty-three slaves in and around Vincennes and five more among the traders on the Wabash River. This number likely underestimated the total, since there were seventy-one persons listed under the category "all other persons except Indians not taxed." Most likely many of these persons were African Americans enslaved in all but name. Those who were there before 1787 were listed as slaves, and those who came afterward fell into the "other" category because their enslavement would have violated the Northwest Ordinance. For men such as Harrison, who had no intention of stepping behind the plow himself, slavery was the easiest solution. For other farmers, who labored on their own land, availability was a motivating factor. Slaves were already in the territory and available in Vincennes because they were commonly traded. Most white settlers owned only one or two slaves, suggesting that slave labor was supplemental. One visitor wrote, "Slavery was originally prohibited, but the law has been relaxed in favour of the new settlers who have slaves."[37]

Settlers confronted Harrison with a petition with 270 signatures in support of repealing article six. Harrison called an election of delegates and assembled a convention in Vincennes in 1802 to petition Congress to resolve the problems of the new territory. Harrison and the delegates asked Congress to suspend article six for ten years to expedite the population of the territory. They argued that article six drove would-be settlers to Spanish territory and was "prejudicial to their interest and welfare." In addition to the suspension, they requested that the children of all slaves brought into the territory remain enslaved for life. Congress denied the request.[38]

Rebuffed, William Henry Harrison and his supporters passed a series of indenture laws that combined elements of chattel slavery and indentured servitude. In 1803 Harrison and the territorial judges (Henry Vanderburgh among them) adopted a Virginia law that required all African Americans who came into the territory under contract to serve that contract. In addition masters could whip those who refused to work and add time to those deemed lazy. However, the most telling aspect of the first law was that masters could sell the contracts or bequeath them to their heirs. In 1805 the legislature elaborated on the indenture code and passed the "Act concerning the introduction of Negroes and Mulattoes into this Territory." This act allowed masters to bring slaves into the Indiana Territory for up to sixty days, and within the first month they had to agree on a contractual arrangement or the slave owner could sell his/her slave to someone in a slave state. The legislature elaborated even further in 1807 with a law that allowed whites to whip "slaves and servants" traveling without passes. One visitor wrote of the indenture system, "the people here are utterly regardless of ordinances, and will take the subject into their own hands," and continued, "Respectable families from Kentucky . . . do all their domestic work, except washing, with their own hands; others indenture negroes for 10 or 15 years."[39]

The indenture laws were clearly an attempt by Harrison and the territorial government to replicate Kentucky slavery in the Indiana Territory. French settlers used bound labor during the colonial period, but the contracts were typically for a reasonable amount of time. The new contracts clearly differed from these contracts. These laws allowed white Indianans to apply the chattel principle to their indenture system, creating chattel servitude in the state. The newspaper editor and printer Elihu Stout sued Peter Jones when Jones refused to return Phebe, an indentured servant, to him. Stout demanded that Jones either return Phebe or pay him $600 in damages. This case demonstrated Stout's attempt to commodify his indentured servant by affixing a value to her body. The language used in the court records is particularly revealing. The document reads, "we the jurors find the indented servant Phebe . . . to be the *property* of Elihu Stout." The jurors confirmed Stout's claim and awarded him $775 in damages. Before the court Phebe was a piece of property with a specific dollar value.[40]

Servant holders in Indiana regularly bought and sold African Americans; although technically the term of service was sold, the documents did not always make the distinction. The buying and selling of indentures brought servitude even closer in line with chattel slavery. In Kentucky, Peter Smith held slaves, who became indentured servants when he moved to Indiana. Smith transferred his contract with Sylvia to his wife, Mary Smith, for two hundred dollars in 1808. Upon his wife's death, he once again found himself in possession of Sylvia, and he sold her again, this time to Alexander Craig. The legal heritability of the contracts mirrored the legal heritability of slaves in Kentucky. In another example, Toussaint Dubois sold his servant Sam to Jacob Kuykendall. In addition slaves and servants were bequeathed in wills as part of the estates. Henry Vanderburgh, for example, bequeathed two slaves and two indentured servants to his wife. Indeed William Henry Harrison saw little difference when he wrote to a correspondent in New Jersey that he "would freely take one or two negroes either male or female and get the favor of you to keep them till an opportunity of sending them occurred—it would make no difference whether they are slaves for life or only serve a term of years."[41]

Harrison and his allies crafted the system of chattel servitude to encourage slaveholders from Kentucky to settle in Indiana and therefore established the procedure for converting a chattel slave into a chattel servant. The 1805 act allowed slaveholders to sell their slaves after sixty days' residence in the new territory, which clearly indicated that crossing the river did not raise African Americans from the status of property into persons. Only through the actions of whites could African American slaves become indentured servants, which took away most of their bargaining power in the relationship. If they refused to sign an indenture contract, they faced certain sale. This allowed whites to exact ridiculous contracts from their former slaves. The most common terms were for twenty and forty years, but some contracts were for ninety-nine years, essentially making the African Americans slaves for life under the guise of servitude. The indenture laws strengthened the connection between Indiana and Kentucky, as slaveholders moved into the territory with their slaves and others already in Indiana bought slaves in Kentucky and indentured them in the territory. Of the eighty-six indentured African Americans recorded in all county court books between 1805 and 1810, sixty were from Kentucky. In Knox County, with Vincennes as the county seat, twenty-seven of the forty-six indentures were from Kentucky.[42]

While chattel servitude approached chattel slavery, it *was* different. If we call Kentucky's system chattel slavery and Ohio's indentured servitude, the appropriate name for the system in Indiana was chattel servitude. Servants were regularly bought, sold, and traded, which made it more like chattel slavery than indentured servitude, but unlike chattel slavery, the system was not interminable for all servants. The official contracts put time limits on servitude, and some of those time limits were reasonable enough that servants could hope to outlive their contracts. In addition, although servitude was heritable, sons had to work for the holder until age thirty and daughters until age twenty-eight. This, at least in name, put an end to service, which distinguished it from chattel slavery.

The distinctions between servitude and slavery seem minimal to modern eyes, but inhabitants of the Indiana Territory, both whites and blacks, and white slaveholders in Kentucky recognized the differences between chattel servitude in the territory and chattel slavery in Kentucky. Harrison complained:

I am totally at a loss what to do with Molly. Because I am yet uninformed whether she has been emancipated in KY and bound for 15 years or whether you have made a contract with her former master to have her set free in 15 years—if she has not been indentured it must be done in 30 days after her arrival in the vicinity or loose her service altogether—& if she refuses to indent herself I must remand her in 60 days or likewise loose her service. But in case of Refusal where am I to remand her? No person in Kenty. Will buy an Indented Servant. Indeed I would send her back & sell her at any rate but for your contract to free her at the end of 15 years for reasons not sent at all.

Inhabitants of the territory recognized the difference between the two most clearly when they crossed the border. While slaveholders could convert their Kentucky slaves into Indiana servants, they quickly discovered that they could not convert their servants into slaves by heading south across the river.[43]

Sometime before the spring of 1804, three enslaved African Americans named Peggy, Hanah, and George made their way from Virginia to Vincennes. Peggy, Hanah, and George had all been the slaves of John and Elizabeth Kuykendall in Virginia, who, upon their death, bequeathed them to their children. In one document, the deponent claimed that the slaves escaped "without the knowledge or consent" of the Kuykendalls. In another document, Peter and Henry Kuykendall claimed that Hanah, Peggy, and George "were brought from . . . Virginia" without their knowledge or consent. It is difficult to discern exactly what happened based on these contradictory statements. However, in one document Jacob Kuykendall, the brother of Peter and Henry, spoke on behalf of Hanah and stated that she was not a slave for life. In addition Henry and Jacob Kuykendall appear in the census records as residents of Indiana. Based on this evidence, possibly certain members of the Kuykendall family brought Hanah, Peggy, and George to Vincennes but did not register them with the courts.[44]

The murkiness of the court documents stems from the confusion surrounding border crossing. The deponent who claimed that the slaves had escaped from Virginia wanted to validate his own claim to them as slaves. Perhaps Peter Kuykendall claimed that they left Virginia without his knowledge because he wanted to reclaim what he believed to be rightfully his to inherit. Jacob Kuykendall may have spoken on Peggy's behalf in order to thwart his brother's efforts. Another possibility was that once they crossed the Ohio River, Hanah, Peggy, and George no longer considered themselves slaves for life. With this belief, they immediately began negotiating, any way they could, for an end to their servitude. However they got there, Peggy, Hanah, and George's paths toward freedom began once they arrived in Vincennes. However, it was a combination of family disagreements among the Kuykendalls, distaste among Indianans for making servants into slaves, *and* the active pursuit of freedom by Peggy, Hanah, and George that led to their eventual freedom.[45]

The conflict began in the spring of 1804. Simon Vannorsdall, claiming that he was acting on behalf of the heirs of John and Elizabeth Kuykendall, seized George and Peggy in Vincennes and attempted to carry them back to Virginia. Upon hearing this, William Henry Harrison issued a proclamation forbidding Vannorsdall from carrying out his "nefarious and inhuman design." He commanded all magistrates and civil officers to stop Vannorsdall. Vannorsdall was arrested, and habeas corpus proceedings were brought for the release of the two former slaves. Exactly what prompted Harrison to stop and arrest Vannorsdall cannot be known, but he left clues as to his motivation. In his proclamation he stated that "some evil disposed persons are about to transport from the territory, certain indented servants of colour without their consent first had and obtained, with a design as is supposed of selling them for slaves contrary to the law and dignity of the United States." Harrison understood Peggy and George to be indentured servants and did not want them reduced to chattel slaves. In September of the same year, the court ruled that there was insufficient evidence to prove that the two were fugitives from justice or slavery. It seems clear that the two were not fugitive slaves because neither Harrison nor Henry Vanderburgh, one of the acting judges, believed that they had run away.[46]

Vannorsdall did not give up so easily, however, and upon his release he seized Peggy and George once again. Habeas corpus proceedings were instituted once again, and all awaited the trial, which was set for June 1805. Before the June term, Harrison indentured George for a term of eleven years, and Vannorsdall dropped his claim to him. Either George or William Harrison could have initiated the contract. From George's perspective, although he was a servant, at the very least his indenture to the territorial governor protected him from a lifetime of bondage. Perhaps Harrison had some selfish motives for his interference or he just wanted to capitalize on the situation. He could have offered George the indenture contract in exchange for his protection. Newspapers seized on this, making the appropriate observation that if George was not a slave, then he should not have to serve Harrison, and if he was a slave, then Harrison interfered with justice. However, the fact remains that without Harrison's interference Vannorsdall could have carried George back to Virginia.[47]

Henry Vanderburgh sat as the lone judge in the June term, and so he postponed the hearing until at least one other judge was present. Vanderburgh explained that "when a cause comes before me in which the freedom or slavery of a human being is involved I feel such diffidence to determine the important question, that in the case of habeas corpus continued to this term I determined to postpone it until the next, when I hope to have the assistance of either or both of my brethren." The court finally heard Peggy's case in April 1806, with Vanderburgh and Judge Davis presiding. The judges released Peggy because she was not a fugitive from justice or slavery, but they added, "this order is not to impair the right that Vannorsdall or any other person shall have to the said negro girl Peggy, provided he, Vannorsdall, or any other person, can prove said negro Peggy to be a slave." In other words, they could not say how Peggy arrived in Vincennes, and for now that uncertainty protected her from a lifetime of bondage.[48]

In September 1805, while still awaiting the hearing for Peggy, Vannorsdall seized Hanah, another of the Kuykendalls' former slaves. Before this case went to court, however, Vannorsdall transferred ownership to Daniel Sullivan. Apparently Hanah agreed to work for Sullivan for twelve years in return for his purchase of her freedom. Rather than face losing everything, and perhaps another arrest, Vannorsdall readily agreed to rid himself of the trouble. Hanah gained a promise of future freedom.[49]

Peggy's and Hanah's troubles continued. Although released by the court, Vannorsdall apparently failed to release Peggy from his custody, since Peggy sued Vannorsdall for assault and false imprisonment in September 1808. Peggy claimed that Vannorsdall forcibly seized her in January 1806 and held her for two years and nine months. She asked for lost wages as damages. Vannorsdall once again claimed that Peggy was a slave for life, which authorized the detention. Because she was under twenty-one, Jacob Kuykendall spoke on Peggy's behalf and said that she was not a slave for life. Ostensibly Peggy initiated the suit to gain her freedom from Vannorsdall's custody. But why would she wait nearly three years to bring Vannorsdall to court when she had already been freed twice? The timing of this suit and Jacob Kuykendall's presence offer interesting possibilities as to Peggy's status. It is possible that Jacob Kuykendall initiated the suit against Vannorsdall because Vannorsdall failed to pay him for her services, which would suggest that Vannorsdall and Kuykendall were acquaintances. Jacob Kuykendall may have wanted to keep Peggy in the Indiana Territory without freeing her and so left her in Vannorsdall's custody. But when Vannorsdall failed to return Peggy, Kuykendall sued him. The court ruled in Vannorsdall's favor, which is highly suspect because two years earlier the territorial judges had released Peggy from Vannorsdall's custody. The ruling seems to reflect Peggy's confused status. She was not a slave, but neither was she free because Vannorsdall did not have to pay her for her labor. While Peggy may have been freed from slavery, she remained under the control of her former owner.[50]

Hanah faced her own problems in the Indiana Territory. After he purchased Hanah, Daniel Sullivan sold the indenture to Benjamin Beekes in 1808. Beekes petitioned the court to invalidate the indenture on the grounds that Hanah was legally an escaped slave from Virginia. Beekes hoped to eliminate the time limit on Hanah's servitude and keep her as a slave for life. Luckily for Hanah, the court did not rule in Beekes's favor, and she remained an indentured servant. However, Beekes may have maintained possession of Hanah beyond her contract, since the 1820 census schedule lists a free black female of Hanah's age in the Beekes household. Clearly Hanah existed somewhere between slavery and freedom, as did many chattel servants in the Indiana Territory.[51]

George, Peggy, and Hanah all gained freedom from chattel slavery by crossing the Ohio River. Considering all the obstacles they encountered, the three former slaves would not have gained their freedom if they had not actively pursued it. Much of the credit for their success assuredly is owed to their persistence. The fact remains, however, that they could not have been successful without the aid of white Indianans. Harrison's initial proclamation stopped Vannorsdall. This in itself was remarkable because Vannorsdall was a shady character. In December 1805, while awaiting Peggy's hearing, Vannorsdall stole and secreted William Bullitt's indentured servant Abraham from Indiana into Kentucky without Bullitt's consent or knowledge. Harrison's contract with George elevated him from fugitive slave to indentured servant, which protected him. Jacob Kuykendall's desire to maintain possession of Peggy kept her in the Indiana Territory and under his direction. As selfish as their motives may have been, these white Indianans had the power and resources to keep the servants from becoming slaves. George, Peggy, and Hanah all took advantage of white Indianans' selfish motives to obtain their own freedom. The process was a negotiation, with most of the power stacked against the former slaves. But George, Peggy, and Hanah forced Indianans to articulate the difference between servitude and slavery. Ironically their slaveholding liberators were the same men who were seeking to introduce chattel slavery into the Indiana Territory.[52]

In recognition and fear of the distinction between chattel servitude and chattel slavery, the servant holders of Vincennes spearheaded a movement to suspend article six of the Northwest Ordinance and legally establish chattel slavery in the Indiana Territory. Inhabitants began petitioning the federal government for the suspension in 1796 and continued until 1808. Congress repeatedly refused to act on the petitions, which led Harrison and the legislators to establish chattel servitude, but they continued to appeal to the government. They may have done this out of respect for federal authority, but their repeated petitioning also suggests that they feared the stability of their servitude system. One man stated of servant holders that, "having been accustomed to treat their slaves with severity, they generally spoil the tempers of their bound servants, whom they have not so much under their command."[53]

Supporters of the introduction of slavery were most concerned with how the transformation of slaves into servants concomitant with crossing the Ohio River deterred slaveholders from entering the territory. In their petitions to Congress, supporters of slavery contended that the "abstract question of liberty and slavery was not involved." The territory "must be settled by emigrants from those in which slavery is tolerated, or for many years remain in its present situation," they claimed. If all states allowed slavery, "a large proportion of them [emigrants] would naturally be drawn from the Southern states." While this argument was self-serving, the petitioners also revealed that at least some southern migrants were hesitant to migrate north of the river because of the slavery ban. While some crossed the river with their slaves, as historians have argued, article six at the very least made others hesitate about heading north.[54]

Supporters of slavery asked for a temporary suspension of article six for ten years in order to eliminate the Ohio River border and unite the Ohio Valley. Petitioners claimed that the diffusion of the slave population could then eventually lead to emancipation because "in less than a century the colour would be disseminated as to be scarcely discoverable." They used Kentucky as one of their examples: "from a reference to the states of Kentucky and Tennessee at the time of the last United States census, it is believed that the number of slaves would never become so great as to endanger either the internal peace or future prosperity of the territory." Petitioners suggested that slavery was a necessary evil in the settlement of the new territory but that it would ultimately outlive its usefulness and be replaced by free labor. Counterintuitively, the introduction of slavery would lead to emancipation. It is unclear whether petitioners actually believed this argument. However, their primary objective was to bring white southern settlers across the river. If emancipation followed, that would be a nice side bonus.[55]

William Henry Harrison's effort to capitalize on bound labor does not entirely explain why he was willing to lead the movement to bring slavery into the territory. Harrison was a Virginian and hoped to establish a plantation and live as a gentleman in the new territory. The same could be said of Thomas Worthington, and yet Worthington led the movement to keep slavery out of Ohio. Both Harrison and Worthington owned thousands of acres in their respective territories and wanted to see settlers fill the vacant land because that translated into personal profit. Settlers rushed into the Ohio Territory, and as a direct result Indiana populated slowly. Ohio had a mix of settlers, with some coming from New England, Pennsylvania, New Jersey, Kentucky, and Virginia. Harrison and the other petitioners, some of whom were speculators, knew that most settlers in Indiana came from the southern states, and they complained that the ban on slavery kept slaveholders out of the new territory. Allowing slavery, therefore, was part of Harrison's plan to populate the territory and dispose of his real estate investments. Both Harrison and Worthington sought the same ends, but while an antislavery position profited Worthington, Harrison hoped to profit from a proslavery stance. Harrison actually sought Worthington's support for his efforts to introduce slavery into the territory. Worthington refused, which upset Harrison, who told Worthington that he "did not consider this subject sufficiently or you would not have given such an opinion."[56]

Ironically, the ease with which white Americans crossed the border undermined the proslavery movement, because as Euro-Americans moved into the southeastern portion of Indiana, Harrison's power and influence began to decline. By 1810 Knox County, which contained Vincennes, was still the most populous county with 7,945 residents, but not by much. The county of Dearborn in southeastern Indiana boasted 7,310 residents, and Clark County in south-central Indiana numbered 5,670. These numbers included only those enumerated in the territorial census, but most likely there were more residents in southern and eastern Indiana, where squatters were especially prevalent. North Carolina Quakers began migrating to Indiana during the territorial period and established the community of Richmond in eastern Indiana in 1806. Despite their small numbers, Quakers were a legitimate antislavery force because they settled together and formed tightly knit communities. The commitment to antislavery partially motivated Quakers' migration to Indiana, and they did not want to see slavery introduced in their new home.[57]

Other settlers from Kentucky crossed the river to escape the influence of slaveholders. They had watched the institution of slavery choke out their hopes for a fresh start in Kentucky, and they saw in Harrison the same threat of aristocratic dominance. These new Indianans did not want their movement across the river to be meaningless. In 1807 residents from Clark County petitioned the federal government *not* to suspend article six. In their petition they plainly stated, "Slavery is either right or wrong." No amount of expediency or temporary benefit sanctioned the extension of slavery to the territory. The petition from Clark County was enough to convince the federal government that there was not universal support for the introduction of chattel slavery in the Indiana Territory. In reality, once antislavery Indianans made their presence known, there was little chance for Harrison's government to suspend article six.[58]

Ambitious politicians turned opposition to slavery into a political weapon. Whereas the antislavery movement in Kentucky was largely religiously motivated, and leaders in Ohio used antislavery as a means of maintaining their social power, the antislavery movement in Indiana was more overtly political. Harrison's opponents called themselves the "people's party." They lambasted Harrison as an aristocrat and targeted chattel servitude as the ultimate symbol of his aristocracy. Much as Republicans had done in Ohio, the new people's party used simple dichotomies to distinguish themselves from Harrison and his supporters. The similarity between chattel servitude and chattel slavery proved especially detrimental to the Harrison faction. Thus they successfully sidelined issues of expediency, ignored the dearth of available labor, and turned it into a question of principle; one was either for slavery and Harrison or in favor of freedom and the people's party. Antislavery leaders complained that the racial proscriptions and interminable contracts common to chattel servitude too strongly resembled chattel slavery. The problem was that the chattel principle put one person in complete control of another, which bred vice in the owner. Antislavery activists claimed that the fact that servant holders *possessed* their laborers led them to look down on all who labored for themselves. This in turn bred "a habit of servility and despondence in those who possess no

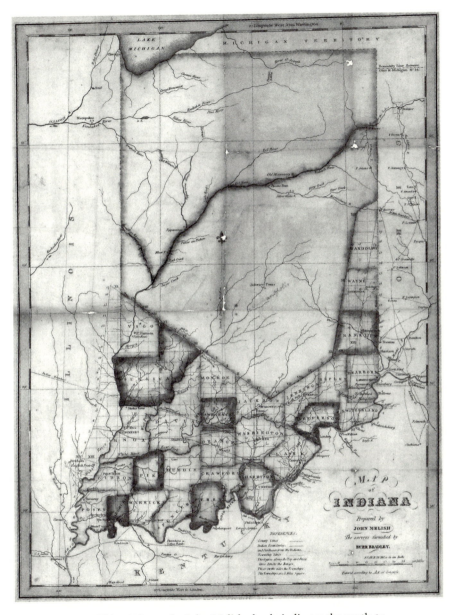

Figure 2. This 1819 map by John Melish clearly indicates the south-to-north pattern of settlement in Indiana. Courtesy of the Indiana Historical Society.

negroes." Thus Indianans had to stop the chattel principle at the river in order to preserve Indiana for virtuous free white laborers.[59]

It is difficult to determine if the battle over slavery in the Indiana Territory was primarily ideological or political. It was probably a combination of the two. In many cases little separated many of the most outspoken critics of slavery and the most vociferous proponents of slavery. In the new territory, ambition reigned supreme among all of the young men in politics. Once the debate reached politics and the press, each had to pick a side. However, for at least some, convictions about slavery came before politics and even proved detrimental to their political status. John Badolett was a leader of the antislavery movement and genuinely morally opposed slavery. Badolett came to America sometime around 1786, and he owned a farm in western Pennsylvania on the Monongahela River. In 1803 Albert Gallatin, Badolett's childhood companion in Switzerland, suggested to Thomas Jefferson that Badolett become the register of the land office in Vincennes. Badolett headed out in 1804, and initially he supported Harrison and the territorial government. He wrote of Harrison that he was "a man of true honour, of an unimpeachable honesty, and an excellent officer." However, even at this early stage Badolett wrote to Gallatin, "Negroe Slavery is also going to be introduced & that circumstance alone would prove sufficient to drive me from hence."[60]

In the end Badolett's antislavery convictions alienated the most powerful men in town, including Harrison, and stifled his political career. Harrison explained in a letter to Albert Gallatin that "an intimacy and confidence" existed between Badolett and himself "until I discovered that Mr. Badolett was the author of a petition to the territorial legislature . . . against the law for the introduction of Negroes." Harrison went on to explain that he had been aware for several years that Badolett did not support slavery but that Badolett, upon learning of Harrison's support of slavery, took politics too personally and alienated those around him. Badolett explained, "I have been more than two years his [Harrison] complete dupe, believing him a very good man," but that changed over time. As testament to Badolett's conviction, he apparently interrupted Harrison's Fourth of July toast in support of slavery, making him "swallow in the middle of his adherent." Badolett was also disgusted by self-serving politicians' decisions to further their political careers rather than pursue the public good. He wrote, "A man warm on our side is made sheriff of Harrison County [Spier Spencer] as is become since mute, another also enemy to slavery receives a commission of a justice of the peace, changes sides, becomes clamorous for it."[61]

While Badolett denigrated politicians' lack of principle, he still recognized that the antislavery movement combined principles and self-interest, as residents crossed the river in search of economic opportunity. He conceded that "it is not true that to *hold* slaves is to be a friend of slavery; in a country where no other labouring hands are to be found, imperious necessity compels the best of men to use negroes on their farms, or to abandon cultivation." However, Badolett insisted that the antislavery movement more accurately reflected the overall views of the population: "The emigration from the neighboring State of Kentucky is chiefly composed either of men who detest slavery from principles, or of such, as being in modest circumstances, & owing their bread to their own labour cannot well brook the haughty manners of their opulent neighbors the slave-holders." Thus, for Badolett, the slavery issue was a question of principle. Residents' backgrounds, whether or not they held slaves, simply did not matter. The more pertinent question was whether a person supported Harrison and his "darling object of slavery." Slavery was slavery, in Badolett's opinion, and it did not matter on which side of the river it existed; "the immigrating master will bring with him his passions and his habits . . . the negroe . . . will be sold like a beast, his family bartered away, and his back lacerated with as much composure on the Wabash, as in Georgia."[62]

Jonathan Jennings quickly became the face of the political antislavery movement, but his ardent agitation against slavery began as agitation against Harrison. Jennings did not own any slaves or hire any slaves and likely was legitimately opposed to slavery. Jennings settled in Vincennes in 1807 for a short time and tried to get in with Harrison. Records indicate that Jennings commonly played billiards at the same tavern as did Harrison and other leading men of the territory. He worked in the land office for a short time but was frustrated by the domination of the Harrisonians and moved in 1808 to Jeffersonville in Clark County, where he befriended other political leaders. In Clark County leaders shared Jennings's dislike of privilege, slavery, and most importantly William Henry Harrison.[63]

In 1809 Jennings campaigned for a position as territorial delegate to Congress as an anti-Harrison candidate. Jennings was skilled at face-to-face politicking and made the rounds among the farmers throughout southern Indiana. As the historian Daniel Walker Howe states, "people spent most of their waking hours working, with scant opportunity for the development of individual talents and interests unrelated to farming." Jennings likely introduced the political conflict to many Indiana farmers. He claimed that he was campaigning for white farmers, and he probably left his audience to determine exactly what that meant. The election results reveal just how uninterested in politics many were, as Jennings won with a total of 428 votes to his opponent's 402. Fewer than 1,000 people voted, and there were over 20,000 people in the territory. Despite Badolett's claims for principle and despite Jennings's success, some farmers may have shared this sentiment: "I would not have upon my conscience the moral guilt of extending slavery over countries now free from it . . . but, if it should take place, I do not see why I should not make use of it. If I do not have servants I cannot farm; and there are no free labourers here."[64]

However, as the political antislavery movement gained momentum, it picked up more supporters, some with far less ardent convictions than John Badolett's. Nathaniel Ewing was among the early advocates against slavery in Knox County in 1805. Ewing was not an obvious choice for the antislavery movement. In 1793 he, then a trader in Vincennes, was one of the men hired by Henry Vanderburgh to seize and export Peter and Queen McNelly. In addition Ewing owned a slave and continued to own a slave until 1820, long after slavery had been legally eliminated in Indiana. General Washington Johnston had been an ardent supporter of Harrison, but in 1808 he suddenly declared his antislavery stance. He claimed that he had always been antislavery and had supported slavery only at the behest of his constituents. However, the 1820 census lists Johnston as owning one male slave. Despite the fact that they held slaves, Ewing and Johnston successfully hitched their fortunes to the burgeoning antislavery and anti-Harrison movement.[65]

Slavery became the dividing line in the world of personal politics. Unlike in Ohio, where there was a political divide between Federalists and Republicans, in the Indiana Territory everyone claimed to be a Republican. Men such as Ewing and Johnston claimed that they owned slaves out of a need for labor but wanted to move away from that dependence on slavery. In the meantime, however, they would continue to possess their own slaves. The way antislavery politicians talked in circles to emphasize their difference from the proslavery party is dizzying, but where similarities outnumbered differences, the slightest differences took on the greatest meaning in the world of politics.

The 1809 election for the territorial legislature proved decisive as the antislavery party won the majority of the seats. In 1810 the territorial legislature repealed the indenture laws in Indiana, signaling the first victory for the antislavery party. With the ascent of the antislavery movement, members of the proslavery party quickly reversed their positions. Thomas Posey, formerly a supporter of Harrison and slavery, changed his position after replacing Harrison as territorial governor in 1813. In 1799 Posey had petitioned Congress to allow former Virginia soldiers to bring their slaves across the Ohio River. However, in 1814 he wrote, "I am as much opposed to slavery as any person whatever, I have disposed of what few I had some time since to my children and by emancipation. I am sure I shall never sanction a law for slavery or any modification of it." Waller Taylor, who had indented a former slave to serve him until 1850, renounced his support of slavery in 1812 and was eventually one of Indiana's first senators. Much as in Ohio, antislavery men warned Indianans to be on guard against the introduction of slavery right up until the constitutional convention. By the time of the convention, residents seemed to have gained more interest in politics. One traveler reported hearing debates about the future of slavery in Indiana, and voter turnout had increased dramatically by the latter half of the decade. In 1816 the Indiana Constitution officially proclaimed that slavery and indentured servitude were banned in the state of Indiana. The slaveholding liberators claimed this as a great political victory; Indianans had defeated the slave aristocracy.[66]

While, as one traveler noted, "the members of the late Convention . . . put the question at rest forever, by excluding the *principle* of slavery from the state constitution," the gap between excluding slavery in principle and slavery in practice was wide. The leaders of the political antislavery movement may have seen their victory as a step on the way toward emancipation in the state. Much like their neighbors in Ohio, Indianans had ensured that the Ohio River marked the limit of the spread of slavery. Because they ensured that slavery had no future, the present existence of slavery in the state did not matter. The men at the head of the antislavery movement did not have any motivation to clarify the antislavery clause in the state constitution because many owned slaves and had long-term indentures! As a result the political victory, much like the Northwest Ordinance, failed to free any slaves or indentured servants already in the state. Another traveler wrote, "The constitution or government in this new country is similar to that of the other neighbouring states, excellent in theory, but too often vile and corrupt in practice. It declares, in pompous language, that all men are free; but if their skins be black, they are not included in this declaration, slaves being necessary for the ease and comfort of the freemen of Indiana."[67]

In 1816, just prior to Indiana's constitutional convention, an Ohioan announced to Indianans, "The eyes of thousands are looking upon you, waiting to see the form of your constitution." In his pamphlet "An Address to the Inhabitants of the Indiana Territory on the Subject of Slavery," Alexander Mitchell tried to persuade Indianans to ban slavery in their state constitution and join Ohio among the ranks of free states. Mitchell wrote, "Slaves when free must either become citizens or be strangers and aliens among you. In either case your society would be better without them." Mitchell's pamphlet reveals that a sense of difference between free and slave states was emerging among residents of the Ohio Valley. Mitchell associated progress with freedom, attributing Ohio's superior progress to the state's freedom from slavery. Not only did Mitchell want Indiana to become a free state like Ohio, but he also stated that banning slavery would keep an unwanted African American population out of the state. As Mitchell's pamphlet suggests, white Ohioans' and now Indianans' concern was not for any enslaved African Americans personally but more for freeing their states from slavery. However, much as George, Peggy, and Hanah had done, other African American chattel servants capitalized on the work of their slaveholding liberators to gain immediate personal freedom from slavery.[68]

African Americans in the Indiana Territory added substance to the political antislavery movement through their efforts to gain personal freedom. African Americans used the courts to enforce the term limits of their indentures. In 1815 the Clark County court freed Silvia Parker from Alexander Craig. Parker's mother had been indentured to Peter Smith for fourteen years beginning in 1799, and Smith had then signed control over Silvia Parker to Craig. By 1815 the indenture had expired, and the court freed Silvia Parker. General John Gibson took his escaped servant, Jack Green, to court, but Green had escaped after his contract expired, and the court upheld Green's freedom. These success stories, however, were the exceptions. In Knox County fifteen African Americans initiated seven suits for their freedom in 1817 and 1818, and in each case the court ruled in favor of the servant holder. In fact the Knox County court continued to hold that chattel servants had to fulfill the terms of their contracts for the next three years. However, the repeated resistance of African Americans weakened the system because their persistence proved that they rejected the terms of their servitude.[69]

The 1820 census showed 190 slaves still in the state, and many of the free African Americans were likely chattel servants. It was not until 1820 and 1821 that the court officially banned slavery and indentured servitude respectively in the state. While white lawyers initiated the suit that banned slavery in the state, the case against indentured servitude began with an ambitious female servant. Mary Clark was a slave in Kentucky when Benjamin Harrison brought her to Indiana in 1815. He indentured her for thirty years, but a year and a half later Harrison manumitted her. On the same day she bound herself to General Washington Johnston for twenty years, but five years later she applied for her freedom. The Knox County court denied her claim, but the state supreme court reversed the decision in a broad ruling that covered indentures made prior to the state constitution. Johnston had led the political charge against slavery in the state, but his indentured servant forced him to put his rhetoric into practice. After Mary Clark's landmark case several more African Americans were discharged from service in Knox County. Of course, this case did not instantly free all indentured servants in Indiana, and many African Americans continued to labor as indentures for years to come. However, the case gave African Americans hope for gaining legal freedom.[70]

The efforts of African American chattel servants gave new meaning to border crossing. Whites could no longer force slaves in Kentucky to become servants in Indiana. In perfect historical irony, white Indianans' efforts to extend slavery across the river led to the creation of an antislavery state. Harrison and his supporters' egregious violation of the spirit of the Northwest Ordinance left them open to criticism and gave men such as Jonathan Jennings and John Badollet a cause to which they could rally support. What white politicians started, bound African American servants finished. Their efforts to enforce the limits of their contracts destabilized the labor system and demonstrated that their servitude was far from voluntary. This pushed the court toward interpreting the antislavery clause in the constitution broadly enough to put slavery and servitude on the path to extinction in the state. This process, in combination with Ohio's rejection of slavery, more clearly defined the Ohio River as a divide between free and slave territories. Exactly what the status of newly freed African Americans would be in free territory was another question altogether, but this process stopped the chattel principle at the Ohio River.

*   *   *

The development of the labor systems in the states along the Ohio River and the transition to statehood marked the Ohio Valley's transition from western territory to borderland of slavery and freedom. The creation of a geographical border between slavery and freedom forced Americans to confront the multiple legacies of an American Revolution devoted both to securing liberty and to maintaining slavery. Rather than working toward an autonomous public good, as elites had hoped, residents of the new American West almost uniformly acted out of self-interest when defining the meaning of American freedom. Whether it was land speculators trying to sell their land, young white men seeking political recognition, or African American servants binding themselves for finite periods of service, individuals tried to assign to the Ohio River border meanings (and with them freedom itself) that were most beneficial to them personally.[71]

Thomas Worthington was speaking truthfully when he said that he moved to Ohio because it was free from slavery. However, it is important to remember the multiple meanings and layers to that statement. Worthington, like many other Americans, likely truly disliked chattel slavery in principle, and his movement across the river allowed him to act on that belief. However, he also moved to escape from slaveholders as much as slavery because slaveholders dominated the political and social landscape of southern states. Free states offered the chance to climb the social ladder. Thus his devotion to freedom was tinged with a bit of selfishness.

Similarly, his devotion to liberty did not translate into color-blind equality. Looking back from the present, Worthington's decision to keep African Americans as lifetime servants appears contradictory to his self-espoused devotion to antislavery principles. It is entirely possible that Worthington did not see anything hypocritical in his Adena estate. Worthington feared the potential growth of the free black population, and he feared the social upheaval that might accompany immediate emancipation. Racism and selfish ambition in part undergirded those fears, but Worthington could also look on Haiti as an example of a revolution gone wrong. What began in 1793 as a slave rebellion in Saint Domingue turned into a bloody race war that showed no signs of abating ten years later, proving that revolutions left unchecked could bring social disorder and chaos. Thus Worthington used his fears of the Molotov cocktail that was the combination of slavery and revolution to define the meaning of freedom and the limits of America's Revolution. As personified in Thomas Worthington, the debates over the Ohio River border suggested that greed, ambition, and fear were equal partners with hope, liberty, and equality in America's future.[72]

The end result was a line on a map that divided slave states from free states in the area from the Atlantic Ocean to the Mississippi River. In many ways this line simply divided bound labor between slavery on the southern bank and servitude on the northern one. Ultimately what separated the states was the chattel principle. Whereas Kentuckians firmly embraced their human property, Ohioans and Indianans thoroughly rejected human ownership in their states. Once these differences were established as political realities, residents of the Ohio River Valley continuously negotiated the meaning of the border between slavery and freedom until the Civil War ultimately destroyed it. Some areas became flashpoints of conflict only to become models of accommodation ten years later. Thus in many ways the Ohio River borderland defied simple characterization or geographical limits. However, even if residents of Louisville, Kentucky, held widely divergent viewpoints on slavery from those of tobacco plantation owners in Harrison County, Kentucky, and laborers of Cincinnati had different ideas about fugitive reclamation than those of small farmers of Clark County, Indiana, two factors provided coherence to their experiences: first, the Ohio River was a *border*; second, the Ohio River was a *river*. The uniqueness of the river border distinguished the Ohio River border from the Mason-Dixon Line separating Pennsylvania and Maryland. The Mason-Dixon Line was drawn in the sand, while the Ohio River was an economic conduit tying the region together. Indeed over the next forty-five years the meaning of the Ohio River border shifted and meandered as residents living along its banks struggled to fix a static border on a river that would not sit still.[73]

CHAPTER FOUR

Steamboats and the Transformation
of the Borderland

After being arrested on the mere suspicion of being a fugitive, Elisha Green, an African American minister from Kentucky, explained, "I was more of a slave after I bought myself than before. Before . . . I could go many places without interruption, but when I became a freeman I could not cross the Ohio River." Green's statement illustrates the contradictions of black freedom in the Ohio Valley by the 1830s. His freedom of mobility declined when he became legally free because he could no longer travel through slaves states; as a slave, in contrast, he could "go many places." In this brief statement, Green revealed that residents used both social custom and the law to separate slavery and freedom. Thus legal freedom failed to free Green from the regulation of his movement because, when coupled with his movement across the river border, Green's dark skin color elicited suspicion from white residents. It was not just that he was black but that he was black *and* crossing the river that gave Green the appearance of a fugitive from labor. In short, this combination constituted a transgression of an unofficial barrier.[1]

This chapter and the next detail the political, economic, and social changes that forced residents to redefine the Ohio River border by the 1830s. The politics of border making are the subjects of the next chapter, while in this chapter the social and economic shifts underlying political debates are explained. In the 1820s, as politicians fiercely battled over defending the geographical border between free and slave states, locally residents adapted to the rise of a steamboat economy that was transforming the region. The burgeoning river economy spurred a population boom that increased the size, diversity, and mobility of the population along the river.

African Americans moving into the region capitalized on the new jobs offered by the steamboat economy, and they transformed the labor situation along the river. Both free and enslaved African Americans worked on the docks, in shipyards, and on the steamboats that plied western rivers; they settled in black neighborhoods of river cities, routinely crossed the river on errands, and socialized with other workers in taverns and other social spaces. While some of these men and women earned wages as free laborers, others paid their wages back to their owners, and still others earned no wages at all, toiling as enslaved workers. There were social and legal differences between slavery and freedom, but observers often failed to distinguish between free and enslaved blacks along the river. While white Americans found the expanding market exciting, they looked with trepidation on this mobile workforce. In particular, many worried about fugitives from labor who used the tools made available by the river economy to forge identities as free persons. Essentially participation in the market economy offered opportunities to forge new identities; white Americans began to fear that the self-made man could be black or white.

* * *

Prior to the growth of the steamboat economy, the bound-labor system along the Ohio River provided structural coherence to white Americans' assumptions of African American dependency. Bound-labor contracts, by their definition, fixed African Americans as economic dependents. As the historian Seth Rockman has suggested, in the early republic, white Americans used existing methods of controlling enslaved populations to control the emerging free laboring population. Along the Ohio River, bound labor contracts defined the status of African Americans somewhere between chattel slavery and complete individual freedom. From the perspective of whites, the contracts prevented the growth of an unemployed and rootless black population by subsuming African Americans within white households. In contrast to the intentions of the contracts, African Americans used bound labor as a means to protect their freedom and establish a reputation of respectability.[2]

In early America one method of gaining respectability was to become independent through the acquisition of wealth and property. However, the bound-labor system limited African Americans' opportunities for independence. In fact many African Americans in Ohio and Indiana still resided within white households in the 1810s and early 1820s. In Indiana in 1820 there were 270 white households with African Americans, and one-third of those households contained nominally free African Americans. These black Americans may have been former slaves or perhaps were indentured servants. In some cases the census records clearly indicated that owners freed their slaves and the slaves remained in the households despite the change in their legal status. For example, the Kuykendalls had two slaves in 1820 and four free blacks in the household in 1830. Nathaniel Ewing's household had one slave in 1820, a female under the age of ten, and in 1830 there was one black female between the ages of ten and twenty-four listed as free.[3]

In the eyes of white Americans, residence within a respectable white household gave all members respectability. When describing his family, the Indianapolis lawyer Calvin Fletcher referred to the orphans in his household as his own children. He wrote of one boy, "I have no need of him to assist in my domestic concerns neither can I make him a farmer, but I take him out of a respect to the child and his destitute situation but thro' the assistance of devine Providence I hope to be able to cloth and instruct him so he may be useful to his God his country and himself." Fletcher believed it was his, and every other citizen's, moral duty to care for those less fortunate and turn them into respectable citizens.[4]

Some census records suggested that white residents considered their former African American slaves part of their households. In 1820 Phillip Catt's household had four members, three white and one free black. In 1830 his household still had four members, but all were listed as free and white. Catt was older, listed as over forty-five in 1820 and between sixty and seventy in 1830. The free black male in 1820 was under fourteen, and the 1830 census indicated that the only other male was between fifteen and twenty. It seems likely that the black man remained in the Catt household but was listed as white in the later census. In another example, in 1820 Christian Groater showed five white members in his household, four males and one female, and four slaves, two male and two female. The 1830 census listed nine members in the Groater household, six males, three females, all free, and all white. It seemed that when African Americans became part of a white household, they also became white, as recognized by the census.[5]

African Americans also traded labor for protection from figures of authority. This may have been a common method of gaining freedom since according to Indiana's 1820 census, in 42 of 270 white households with at least one free or enslaved African American, the heads of the households

were figures of authority—justice of the peace, judge, or other public official. Another 21 were members of the military. Both of these numbers suggest a relationship between figures of authority and bound laborers. In
addition the courts bound African Americans who tried to break their labor
contracts, or were accused of being fugitives, to judges for protection.
Judges received young African Americans into their homes as they would
orphans, becoming responsible for their well-being and gaining farm labor
at the same time.[6]

It seems that African Americans took advantage of their limited occupational opportunities and gained respectability by working within white
households either as indentured servants or as unofficial laborers. Between
1824 and 1836 African Americans in Highland County in southern Ohio
registered thirty-seven indenture contracts with the state. All of these contracts involved minors. African American parents likely indentured their
children both to learn occupational skills and to receive protection from
the white household. Some of the children indentured were too young, at
three or four years old, to provide significant labor. In these cases parents
may have indentured their children out of financial necessity, but the contracts also guaranteed their children protection from kidnapping. Nearly
half of these contracts were for skilled jobs such as blacksmith and wagon
maker, which suggests that free blacks used indentured servitude as a
springboard for future occupations. The indenture system may have been
a small step from chattel slavery, but living within a white household gave
that step significance.[7]

In the 1820s existing customs for regulating the boundary between slavery and freedom eroded under residents' feet. White Americans had relied
on social and economic structures of dependency to regulate the border,
but they believed that the law gave those systems legitimacy. However, the
local political debates between 1818 and 1823 revealed the potential impotence of state law at settling local disputes over the border. Just as politics
unsettled interstate relations, economic development along the river destabilized the existing social and economic structures that gave the border
meaning.

In 1819 the country experienced its first major national depression. The
Panic of 1819, as historians have labeled it, shook Americans' faith in the
emerging market economy. In the West as the credit market collapsed,
banks closed, and the flow of capital contracted, residents looked for any
solution to the economic crisis. In Illinois the panic spurred a contentious

debate over legalizing slavery in the state. Farther east residents considered the slavery question settled, as Indianans resoundingly voted against a constitutional convention in 1823. However, the depression contributed to a shift in labor relations along the river by creating a demand for cheap labor. African Americans capitalized on the depression by finding work in the emerging steamboat industry. The resulting social and economic transformation of the borderland changed perceptions of the slave/free dichotomy, the lived experience of enslaved and free laborers, and methods for regulating the slave/free border.[8]

Perceptions of the slave/free dichotomy at both the state and personal levels, the lived experience of bound and free laborers, and the legal and social methods for the regulation of border crossing all contributed to black and white residents' understanding of the geographical division between slave and free states. African Americans recognized both unofficial and legal borders, and they challenged them. Ranging from the mundane to the bold, African Americans' actions pushed against white residents' social and legal distinctions between freedom and slavery and their political distinctions between free and slave states. White Americans pushed back, resulting in a closer linkage between race and status, and by the end of the decade both white and black Americans recognized that they could not separate slave and free from black and white. The existing customs did not disappear altogether, and the evidence suggests that they maintained their resonance throughout the antebellum period. However, increasingly white residents relied on race to do the work that the border simply could not accomplish. African Americans identified the link between race and freedom in their narratives, and for many, transitioning from enslaved to free persons involved crossing racial barriers. It was not that distinctions between free and slave mattered more or less than racial distinctions; they both mattered.[9]

*   *   *

The growth of the population and resulting changes in living conditions altered local residents' perceptions of the ostensibly natural and obvious differences between slavery and freedom. The populations of Ohio and Indiana roughly doubled between 1820 and 1830, and Kentucky's population rose by nearly 300,000. However, in Indiana the pace of growth of the white population along the river was slower than in the rest of the state.

The total white population of the state grew by over 130 percent, whereas the counties along the river experienced less than a 50 percent rate of growth. In fact, whereas over 30 percent of the population was concentrated in river counties in 1820, by 1830 less than 20 percent of Indianans lived along the Ohio River. These numbers reflect the availability of land. Settlers moved into the interior in large numbers because land was inexpensive, whereas much of the land along the Ohio had already been purchased. After moving their state capital from Corydon, a mere twenty-five miles from Louisville, to the centrally located Indianapolis in 1825, Indianans flocked to the state capital and the surrounding area. Instead of an overall expansion, growth along the river was concentrated within the emerging urban areas. Floyd County's population rose by 130 percent from roughly 2,800 in 1820 to over 6,300 in 1830. Many of these residents settled in New Albany, directly across the river from Louisville. Similarly Jefferson County's population, home of Madison, increased by over 3,500 residents.[10]

Indiana's free black population experienced concentrated growth along the river as well. The total black population in Indiana tripled from over 1,200 to over 3,600 residents in 1830 and more than doubled along the river from roughly 400 to nearly 1,000. In particular Floyd, Clark, and Jefferson Counties picked up 196, 105, and 128 new black residents respectively. The African American population of Floyd County rose nearly 300 percent, and by 1830 over 7 percent of the free black population of the entire state lived in Floyd County, many having settled in New Albany. When set in comparison, amazingly, the free black population grew at a faster rate than did the white population, especially along the river. The free black population along the river grew by nearly 130 percent, whereas the white population experienced only a 47 percent growth rate.

Kentucky's free black population nearly doubled between 1820 and 1830, and the slave population increased by over 40,000 in the same decade. Indeed slaves never made up a higher percentage of the population of Kentucky than they did in 1830 (roughly 24 percent). To truly understand the trajectory of growth along the Ohio River in Kentucky, we need to expand the inquiry beyond 1830. The enslaved population of Jefferson County, which contained Louisville, climbed to nearly 7,000, making it the second-highest concentration in the state, but that population increased by less than 100 between 1820 and 1830. According to census data, the total population of Jefferson County increased by only 15 percent. However, Kentucky was still in the process of fixing county lines, and Jefferson County decreased in total size between 1820 and 1830. Between 1830 and 1840 the enslaved population increased by 24 percent to roughly 8,600. The enslaved population increased by another 2,000 between 1840 and 1850. Clearly the enslaved population was on the rise in Louisville. Similarly, whereas the free black population in Jefferson County grew by fewer than 100 total residents between 1820 and 1830, the population doubled between 1830 and 1840 and again between 1840 and 1850. Louisville grew rapidly between 1820 and 1840 and passed Lexington as the largest city in Kentucky.[11]

In Ohio the free black population increased from roughly 4,700 residents in 1820 to over 9,500 by 1830. Many of the African American immigrants settled in the Queen City. Between 1826 and 1829 the African American population of Cincinnati increased by over 300 percent from roughly 700 to over 2,250. By 1829 blacks made up nearly 10 percent of the city's total population. As these numbers suggest, the trajectory of growth for the free black population in each state was one of concentrated growth in urban areas.[12]

River cities were centers of movement, with diverse and transient populations that frequented the taverns and brothels as they proceeded down the river. One traveler noted that his hotel was filled with "mercantile gentlemen of New Orleans, many of whom are waiting for the troubling or rising of the waters, and consequent movement of the steamboats." Another visitor described Louisville as a commercial hive bustling with activity. "The stores are filled with the commodities and manufactures of every clime, and every art, dazzle the eye—the ringing of the bells and roaring of the guns, belonging to numerous steamboats in the harbor the cracking of the coachman's whip, and the sound of the stage driver's horn, salute the ear," he wrote. Capturing the excitement of the city, he continued, "The motley crowd of citizens, all well dressed, hurrying to and fro—the numerous strangers from all parts of the world almost, visiting the place, to sell or to buy goods—the deeply loaded dray cart, and the numerous pleasure carriages rolling to and fro, arrest and rivet the attention of a mere traveler like myself."[13]

Although not mentioned specifically in this description, African Americans were part of the "motley" crowds of the city. Some migrated to burgeoning river cities, where city life offered unique opportunities; others were brought by white owners; still others temporarily stopped in as laborers or human chattel on steamboats. Free African Americans lived and

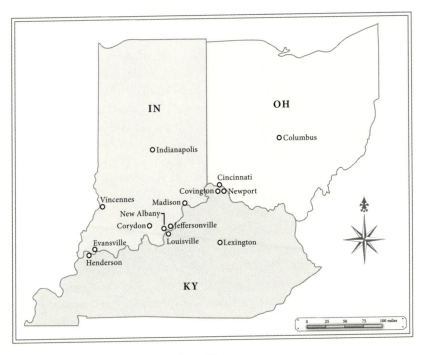

Figure 3. Ohio river towns in the 1830s.

worked with some enslaved blacks, and in the bustle of commercial activity boundaries between slavery and freedom blurred. This is not to suggest that slavery in Kentucky was somehow milder than in the Deep South or that slavery and freedom were interchangeable categories for African Americans. Instead any attempt to make a clear distinction between the conditions of slavery and those of freedom requires the oversimplification of a complex situation. The fact was that where freedom and slavery blurred, racial barriers limited the range of experiences for residents, which put African Americans in a precarious position. There could be very real differences between freedom and slavery for African Americans, but often skin color undermined the security that freedom supposedly guaranteed.[14]

In Kentucky state laws stripped free African Americans of their rights and made skin color prima facie evidence of status. The state appellate court specifically ruled that "color and long possession are such presumptive evidences of slavery as to throw the burden of proof on a negro claiming freedom." While Kentuckians had long held color presumptive of status, as the African American population increased, white Americans in Ohio and Indiana increasingly viewed African Americans as an alien population defined by their skin color. Whites north of the river targeted black immigration as a threat to their social fabric. In 1827 Henry Scribner, a founder of New Albany, Indiana, wrote, "Persons slip over the river . . . have regular papers of manumission recorded here and the negroes become citizens. . . . none have become a county charge, but they are a troublesome part of community . . . these are the very refuse . . . of their masters slaves, ought they not to give security for their good behavior . . . to save the county from their support." Scribner feared that African Americans who were able to "slip" over the river would bring vice into the community. Scribner suggested that manumission papers failed to eliminate what he considered "slavish" qualities. Instead, through this technically legal but clearly unwanted immigration, slavery extended into the free state of Indiana. In his address to the General Assembly in 1829, Governor James Brown Ray of Indiana complained that "the scourge of the oppressed is not confined, as it should be, exclusively to the land of the oppressor." Ray claimed that the black population in Indiana was on the rise because Kentucky slaveholders "dumped" their old slaves in across the river. Census data, of course, proved otherwise. However, perception was Ray's reality. The growth of the African American population along the river upset his and other whites' understandings of the difference between free and slave states.[15]

In addition to sheer growth, the apparent independence of African American immigrants upset white Americans' observed differences between slavery and freedom at the personal level. New African American immigrants settled with other African American residents, forming enclaves, which was particularly unsettling for white Americans. Whereas previously many African Americans in Indiana and Ohio settled in white households, these free African Americans seldom lived in white households. In particular, African Americans migrated to burgeoning river cities, where city life offered unique opportunities. Enslaved African Americans lived and worked in Cincinnati, earning wages to pay for their purchase from their Kentucky owners. Even in Kentucky city life broke down traditional signs of African American dependence. In Louisville a select few self-hired slaves chose their employers, rented houses, and maintained a certain measure of control over their lives. Some enslaved people who hired their own time resided in the same wards as free blacks.[16]

It is important to note that, despite the independence, urban living conditions could be quite squalid for African Americans. In Cincinnati the majority of African Americans lived in the neighborhoods of "little Africa" and "Bucktown," nicknamed for their racial homogeneity. African Americans earned low wages, which limited their housing opportunities, and many crowded into temporary shacks and shanties, abandoned buildings and shops, or houses that had been divided into apartments. Living independently granted African Americans more autonomy than if they lived in white households, but racism limited their opportunities in Cincinnati and Louisville to acquire satisfactory housing. When African Americans crowded into ramshackle housing that offered little above protection against the elements, white Americans viewed the squalid living conditions as evidence of blacks' inferiority. These conditions undermined African Americans' ability to attain "respectability" in the eyes of whites while reinforcing perceptions of racial difference.[17]

Linking the squalor of black neighborhoods with the apparent independence of the African American population, white residents and visitors looked with trepidation on any group of African Americans gathered in city streets. One visitor wrote, "The first thing that struck my attention after arriving in this city, was the crowds of negroes, parading the streets after night." These fears often translated into frequent complaints in the press identifying African Americans as the source of vice and basically all conflict and catastrophes that arose. In Cincinnati the editor of *Liberty Hall* warned "that the rapid increase of our black population, to say nothing of slavery, is of itself a great evil." Across the river in Louisville, papers warned of "night walkers, lewd persons, and those who lounge about without any visible means of support" and called for a town watch to prevent the "illegal assemblage of slaves," warning that "without them, the most fatal results may be apprehended." In the *Louisville Public Advertiser* one writer complained of "Local Evils":

We are overrun with free negroes. In certain parts of our town throngs of them may be seen at any time—and most of them have no ostensible means of obtaining a living. They lounge about through the day, and most subsist by stealing, or receiving stolen articles from slaves at night. Frequently, they are so bold as to occupy the side-walks in groups, and compel passengers to turn out

and walk round them. Their impudence naturally becomes conta-
gious. . . . We are not alarmists—but we do believe prompt measures
to drive the vagrant negroes from among us, to prevent servants
from hiring their own time, and to subject the entire slave population to rules sufficiently rigid to preserve order and insure perfect
subordination, are necessary to our security.[18]

The emergence of black neighborhoods in urban areas both offered African
Americans more freedoms than in the countryside and undercut those freedoms by increasing whites' suspicions. Whites attempted to regulate the
African American population through curfews and town watches. In Louisville the local paper praised the efforts of the volunteer town watch. In
1826 members of the Louisville City Council declared a three-man watch
insufficient, authorized additional members to join the watch, and gave
them these special instructions: "to be very particular as it regards the collection of colored people . . . about the Market House and groceries." In
Cincinnati the Overseers of the Poor was charged with the responsibility of
"regulating" the African American population. These efforts contributed to
African Americans' awareness of the limitations to their liberties. As Isaac
Throgmorton, who worked as a barber in Louisville, later explained, "I
lived with free people, and it was just as though I was free." Note, however,
that he said not that he *was* free but only that it was "as though" he was
free. Throgmorton made the important point that he lived like a free person
but was not, in fact, free. Thus he and others like him experienced characteristics of both freedom and slavery. The Ohio River border, the representation of the slave/free divide, ironically was a place where dichotomies
could not apply.[19]

*   *   *

Rather than representing a line dividing slavery and freedom, the Ohio
River became the place where enslaved and free labor met and became
enmeshed in one system. As borderland slavery and borderland free labor
blended, enslaved and free African Americans experienced characteristics
representative of both slavery and freedom. In theory the division between
freedom and slavery was a sharp dichotomy representing antithetical forms
of labor. Historians have argued that the decline of indentured servitude
and bound labor in general in America furthered the separation of freedom

and slavery in Americans' minds. They suggest that over the course of the antebellum period, sectional animosity and the rise of the free-labor ideology in the northern states erased the connections between slavery and freedom, so that by 1860 white Americans understood the commodification of labor power and the commodification of laborers as two entirely opposite things: freedom and slavery. However, the emerging market economy demanded the commodification of labor power *and* laborers, and economic self-interest often trumped political, legal, and even moral distinctions between slavery and freedom. In reality in antebellum America, African Americans could be capital, labor power, and laborers.[20]

The commodification of labor power meant that a worker was able to move from job to job because only his/her labor was commodified. Thus a free person could quit a job precisely because he/she was not owned. At the same time, a laborer earned wages for the labor performed, thus giving labor power, not the person, a cash value. The labor contract was the nexus of the power relations that defined the commodification of labor; the contract symbolized the negotiation between employed and employee. A worker had the freedom to sign a contract, while the employer had the power to assign value to a person's labor. In contrast, a bill of sale represented the uneven power negotiation between the slaveholder and the enslaved in the commodification of a laborer. The document gave a person a price, effectually flattening everything that person said or did into a single dollar amount. Thus ownership of labor power was intrinsic in the ownership of a laborer; in a sense chattel slavery involved the commodification of the laborer *and* his/her labor power.[21]

This Ohio River labor system, just emerging in the 1820s, combined the commodification of labor with the commodification of laborers. The hiring out of enslaved African Americans exemplified the combination of commodified labor and commodified people. Slave hiring followed the same principles as free labor, especially if the slave was self-hired and living on his/her own. Essentially, in the case of self-hiring, the slave was selling his/her labor, not his/her person, on the market. Even when slaveholders were responsible for negotiating a contract, they sold the labor on the market while maintaining their claim to ownership of the person. Slave hiring complicated the distinction between free and slave labor because the commodified labor was the product of a commodified laborer.[22]

While hiring out was present throughout the South, the presence of the Ohio River and its symbol as a border gave it unique features in this region.

Hired Kentucky slaves performed virtually every type of labor from field work to factory work to work on a steamboat to work in a hospital; they could be barbers, musicians, draymen, or most commonly domestic servants. Historians have estimated that as much as 20 percent of the enslaved population of Louisville was leased at any one time during the antebellum period. Across the river the 1842 Cincinnati directory revealed that the occupations of free blacks included barber, laborer, cook, river worker, domestic, and washerwoman—that is, the same types of jobs held by enslaved people in Kentucky.[23]

In fact, the mixture of slave and free labor allowed for the development of illicit fugitive labor. Working toward freedom became a viable means of escape for the enslaved, and white Americans north of the river either looked the other way or capitalized on the situation. Advertisements for fugitives are suggestive in their association of escaped slaves with their labor talents. "Mensor," for example, was a shoemaker, and his owner, William Huston, suggested that he would "again attempt to follow said business." Slaveholders commonly listed the skills of runaways in advertisements, suggesting that they might try to hire themselves as free persons. "Henry" was listed as a blacksmith, "Charles" as a carpenter, and "Billy" as a barber and a steamboat cook. During his escape Henry Bibb got a job as a cook in Ohio and was so successful that the landlady wanted to hire him permanently. He declined, but he "got a job of chopping wood during that winter which enabled me to purchase myself a suit, and after paying my board the next spring." Business owners in Cincinnati hired slaves from Kentucky. African American workers helped turn Cincinnati into the Queen City of the West. Certainly many African Americans in Cincinnati were free, but many were just as certainly fugitive slaves. When Josiah Henson stopped in Cincinnati while traveling from Virginia to Kentucky with his owner's slaves, African Americans in the city tried to convince him and the others to run away. Henson opted not to leave, but his story suggests that African Americans in Cincinnati were accustomed to taking in fugitive slaves.[24]

To be certain, the rise of the river economy gave some African Americans new opportunities. Joshua and Jessie Wilson arrived in Floyd County, Indiana, in 1812. Joshua was a pilot on the Ohio River and engaged in river transportation. Joshua Wilson owned and commanded his own fleet of steamers and by 1817 was regarded as the wealthiest man in Indiana. The Wilsons built the first homes made of brick in the area, and Joshua's mansion cost him upward of ten thousand dollars. Joshua Wilson was referred to as "Yellow Wilson" in Ohio river navigation directions that used his large brick home as a benchmark. The 1820 census counted him as a white man. He married a white woman in 1822. The 1830 census showed him again as white with two black females under ten and two black males between ten and twenty-four in his household. He was not mentioned as a "man of color" until the time of his death, when his will was probated. In Louisville, Washington Spradling purchased his freedom in 1814, worked as a barber in Louisville, and by 1850 had accumulated assets totaling thirty thousand dollars. For these men, the acquisition of considerable wealth offered respectability.[25]

Few African Americans could hope for the success of the Wilsons or Spradling. The blending of slave and free labor also locked African Americans in a meager economic web. John Malvin, a free black man, commented on the dire situation: "I thought upon coming to a free state like Ohio that I would find every door thrown open to receive me, but from the treatment I received by the people generally, I found it little better than in Virginia." Certain jobs, such as menial labor along the docks, work in the service industry, and barbering, were the domain of African Americans, which made it difficult for free blacks to break out of the system. The racialized labor system cut off one avenue toward respectability because white Americans viewed the work of black Americans as degrading. African American leaders recognized this perception as well; they called for blacks to find work in "respectable" positions.[26]

While advertisements suggested the interchangeability of free and slave labor, ads also made some subtle and some clear distinctions between free and enslaved people. Whites regularly submitted advertisements declaring their desire to hire an African American. These ads usually did not indicate whether they sought a slave or a free person. A common advertisement read, "Good Wages will be given for a negro woman capable of cooking and washing for a family." Often the ads did not even specify the work entailed in the job, for example, "Wanted a smart negro or mulatto boy from 16 to 18 years of age who can be recommended for honesty and sobriety." These advertisements revealed the desire for people, not just for the labor. Thus the people were on the market, and the labor was part of the package. Similarly the ads for runaways listing occupations suggested ownership of the persons. Even if runaways attempted to use their labor, they could not escape from the slaveholders' claims to ownership of them. Distinctions such as these mattered to African Americans in the region.[27]

Enslaved and free African Americans used principles outside the slave/ free dichotomy to define their place in the world, or perhaps they refused to let the slave/free dichotomy define them, even as they could not escape its influence. As John Malvin suggested, the conditions of freedom were not perfect. At the same time, being well fed or properly clothed did not convince enslaved African Americans that slavery was preferable to freedom. Henry Bibb wrote, "Freedom to act for oneself though poorly clad, and fed with a dry crust, is glorious when compared with American slavery." As these statements suggest, slavery and freedom were not the only categories structuring the lives of African Americans along the Ohio River. Instead they were only part of their worldview, not the defining features of it.[28]

The mobility generated by the Ohio River economy further complicated the lived experience of enslaved and free laborers. Steamboats made rivers fluid arteries of movement for people and capital. Prior to the improvement of the steamboat for travel in shallow waters in 1817, Americans loaded their goods on flatboats and traveled down the Ohio and Mississippi Rivers but had to return on foot. The steamboat cut this three-month trek down to a three-week excursion. In addition steamboats reduced the cost of travel from Pittsburgh to New Orleans from sixty dollars to just six dollars.

As they wound their way along the river's path, steamboats brought a diverse population into close contact. The casualty reports from steamboat crashes give us a window into the heterogeneity of life and work along the Ohio. One report from June 1829 listed among the dead "Collins, carpenter; Bradley, white fireman, Peter, a white French boy; Hunstman and Ferral, sailors; five Negroes, four of them firemen, and a sailor." The injured included "the mate of the boat, a black fireman, and a sailor." Another crash in May 1830 listed among the casualties "Philip Orne of Kentucky; John Sheridan of Indiana, Jonas Chamberlain of Indiana, four colored men, firemen; Hardy Carlisle of Indiana, Charles Moore (colored man), Parmenius Palmer of Kentucky, and Christmas Disney an Indian interpreter." In both cases the newspapers did not make it clear whether black firemen were slaves or freemen. The absence of an occupation next to his name seems to indicate that Charles Moore, the "colored man" from the second crash, was a passenger.[29]

As steamboats widened Americans' spheres of interaction, they forced some to evaluate and articulate their views on slavery and race. White travelers could not avoid contact with black workers and slaves on their trips.

Some made sense of their experiences by drawing racial barriers that encompassed both free and enslaved African Americans. During his trip down the Ohio River in 1824, the Scotsman Donald McDonald wrote of a group of African American slaves headed south for sale at slave market, "These poor beings did not at first appear in a very good humour, but afterwards they seemed to recover themselves." He continued, "I could not distinguish between them and some others who were employed on board as part of the crew." McDonald quickly grouped all African Americans together without any distinction between the workers on the boat, who may have been free, and the enslaved individuals.[30]

In other cases steamboat travel forced white Americans to confront the omnipresence of slavery and the slave trade. When Benjamin Lundy traveled down the Ohio in 1821, he encountered a Louisiana planter and his Virginian nephew traveling with their slaves. Lundy, already committed to antislavery, expressed his dislike of the men's manners and morals and linked their dissipation with slaveholding. When he traveled down the Ohio River in 1841, Abraham Lincoln witnessed the slave trade firsthand. He wrote of the enslaved heading to Deep South markets, "Amid all these distressing circumstances, as we would think them, they were the most cheerful and apparently happy creatures on board." Lincoln later cited this as a key moment in his developing antislavery attitudes. Writing of it fourteen years later to Joshua Speed in 1855, "The sight was a continual torment to me; and I see something like it every time I touch the Ohio."[31]

Indeed many associated the Ohio River with the slave trade. Cheaper travel and a greater capacity for people and goods on steamboats allowed white Americans in Kentucky to turn slave trading into a lucrative business. White Americans began settling the southwestern territory in earnest in the late 1810s and 1820s, and their demand for slaves was insatiable. Between 1820 and 1830 Alabama's slave population increased from roughly 47,000 to 117,000, and in Mississippi the slave population more than doubled from roughly 32,000 to 65,000 slaves. It is true that large companies dealing exclusively in slaves began to appear in Kentucky only in the mid-1840s; however, during the 1820s the Ohio River was still a slave-trading highway, and large-scale slave trading also existed even without the large companies. Even at this early stage, Kentuckians supplied more than 1,000 slaves annually to Deep South states. Historians usually downplay the extent of the slave trade in early Kentucky, because much of the trading took place at the local level. However, it was precisely the combination of local and interstate slave trading that made the impact of slave sales so profound along the river.[32]

Advertisements for the sale of and seeking the purchase of slaves regularly appeared in Kentucky newspapers in the 1820s. Some ads offered "CASH . . . for likely young NEGROES." Others requested groups of slaves to work on farms or in rope-making factories, while others wanted to acquire single domestic servants. White Kentuckians bought and sold slaves in plain public view at the front doors of public gathering places such as printing offices and taverns. The thriving local trade in enslaved blacks increased the visibility of slave sales, which enticed some Kentuckians to join in the trade. In the 1820s businessmen added trading in slaves to their other business endeavors. By the 1830s nearly fifty businesses dealt in slaves, and some of those advertised in Louisville newspapers. At the local level, through sale white Kentuckians attempted to transform enslaved African Americans into mobile capital. Interstate sales widened the influence of this process of commodification. On board steamboats enslaved and free blacks worked side by side as stewards, servants, barbers, or laborers, as slaveholders traveled with personal servants and slaves bound for Deep South markets. North of the river business owners accommodated white Americans traveling with slaves.[33]

The Ohio River facilitated the transfer of mobile capital from Kentucky down to Natchez and New Orleans, which contributed to the commodification of enslaved Kentuckians. The historian Walter Johnson explained the variety of ways that slaveholders assigned cash value to physical, emotional, and psychological traits of enslaved African Americans. This process sped the flow of human capital because in classifying African Americans by representational qualities, slaveholders crafted a common language. For example, slaveholders greased the skin of enslaved blacks in their effort to demonstrate youth and vitality. However, this process of sale also revealed who was for sale in the market and who was in charge of the market. While slaveholders found endless ways to differentiate their human capital, skin color was the ultimate representational quality that white Americans used to commodify African Americans. Overall, skin color overshadowed distinctions between free and enslaved African Americans, which meant that either free or enslaved African Americans could be sold "down the river" at any time. This is not an argument about the relative persistence of kidnapping. Instead commodification spread the threat of sale to legally free African Americans, and that threat undermined the security that freedom supposedly granted.[34]

Instead of separating the experience of the free from that of the enslaved, the slave trade flattened distinctions between free and enslaved blacks because mobile black laborers worked along the Ohio River amid the thriving slave trade. When former slave William Wells Brown worked on a steamboat, the freedom of the passengers on board sharpened his awareness of his own bondage. Brown worked for a slave trader and had the responsibility of maintaining his owner's human cargo and preparing them for sale. He wrote that "in passing from place to place, and seeing new faces every day, and knowing that *they could go where they pleased*, I soon became unhappy, and several times thought of leaving the boat at some landing-place, and trying to make my escape to Canada, which I had heard much about as a place where the slave might live, *be free, and be protected*." For Brown, other enslaved blacks, and free African Americans, steamboats carrying black bodies down the Ohio and Mississippi Rivers symbolized the material link between enslavement in the Ohio Valley and that in the Deep South. While steamboats allowed Brown to travel up and down western rivers, his movement was not free.[35]

Sale invaded the psyches of free and enslaved African Americans, making life in the borderland uncertain. The slave trade and resulting commodification of black Americans undermined the freedom of blacks living north of the river. Both enslaved and free African Americans were in a precarious position because the threat of the Deep South was omnipresent. As John Chapman explained, "I was originally from Kentucky, but removed into Indiana at fourteen. I did not feel safe in Indiana, and removed with my family into Canada at Gosfield."[36]

* * *

Kentuckians relied on both formal legal methods and informal social customs to regulate the movement of African Americans. In order to facilitate the transfer of mobile capital and capitalize on mobile black laborers, Kentucky slaveholders tried to control the movement granted by the Ohio River. In their efforts to capitalize on the new economic importance of the Ohio River, the Kentucky courts and legislature claimed jurisdiction over the river itself. The court ruled that because Virginia ceded only the territory north of the Ohio River, the river was still a part of Kentucky. In 1824, as an extension of this reasoning, the Kentucky legislature passed a law that made steamboat captains liable for slaves who used the steamboat to escape from their masters.[37]

Within Kentucky slaveholders used written passes to regulate the movement of the enslaved. Passes granted enslaved African Americans a proscribed mobility. Even domestic and personal servants moved between households on the authority of passes. The correspondence of the Miller family in Kentucky, especially between the mother and her daughters, reveals how these servants labored. Mrs. Miller had her slaves take pieces of furniture and other household items to her daughters. Slaves delivered messages and ran errands, and on one occasion Mrs. Miller sent three female domestic slaves to help her ill daughter tend to her children. Other domestic servants ran errands across the Ohio River into Cincinnati, Madison, and New Albany.[38]

However, two factors complicated the apparent simplicity of written passes. First, some passes were incredibly liberal in their provisions. For example, the slaveholder John Jarret penned the following pass: "Know all men by these presents, I, J. Jarrett, of Livingston, and State of Kentucky, do agree that this black man Allen, do bargain and trade for himself until the first day of May next; and also, for to pass and repass from Livingston county, KY, to the Mongalia county, state of Virginia, Morgantown and then to return home to the same Livingston county, Kentucky, near the mouth of Cumberland river, Smithland." Second, whites constantly worried that African Americans would forge their own passes or claim to have verbal permission to travel, and many likely did. In this way the presence of literate and mobile slaves undermined the certainty of the written word. In response, patrols led by whites surveyed dark roads, exploiting their authority by stopping and questioning all African Americans traveling alone.[39]

The Ohio River border further complicated the use of passes to control the movement of enslaved and free blacks. River cities such as Louisville had large and transient populations constantly in flux on the docks. With travelers arriving daily with baggage in tow and others running errands across the river on ferries, African Americans took advantage of the anonymity to free their movement. Upon arriving in Louisville, Donald McDonald wrote, "This town being in the slave state of Kentucky, we everywhere saw a great many black slaves." It is as if the mere fact that he was in a slave state confirmed that all blacks were enslaved. But the reader has to wonder if some of those "slaves" he observed were actually free black workers. Some African Americans operated ferries along the river, while others relied on their reputations to cross the river on the ferries. In some instances enslaved African Americans simply informed the ferry operators that they were running errands for their owners, and the ferry operators allowed them to cross the river. In order for this to happen, clearly the enslaved African Americans must have run errands so regularly as to make them commonplace. In another case the captain of a steamboat "made a contract with the slave, or permitted some one engaged on board the boat, to make the contract, by which the slave was received on board as a hand, and performed one trip out from Louisville," without the consent of the owner. Indeed it took two months before the steamboat captain "restored" the escaped slave to his owner. This suggests that not all movement was, or even could be, regulated with written passes.[40]

Adding to the confusion, slaveholders granted some enslaved African Americans the freedom to cross the Ohio River almost at will. Three enslaved musicians, for example, lived in Louisville and played at parties across the river in Madison and Cincinnati with the written permission of their owner. In another case William Thompson granted his slave Willis Lago permission "to go to any free state and there remain." In his narrative Josiah Henson recalled that he traveled well into Ohio preaching with the full permission of his owner. Henson wrote of a trip he took in fall 1828: "Somewhat to my surprise, Master Amos made no objection; but gave me a pass to go to Maryland and back. . . . Furnished with this, and with a letter of recommendation from my Methodist friend to a brother preacher in Cincinnati . . . I had an opportunity of preaching in two or three of the pulpits of Cincinnati, when I took the opportunity of stating my purpose, and was liberally aided in it by contributions made on the spot." Henson continued, "The annual Methodist Conference was about to be held at Chillicothe, to which my kind friend accompanied me, and by his influence and exertions I succeeded well there also. By his advice I then purchased a suit of respectable clothes, and an excellent horse, and travelled leisurely from town to town, preaching as I went, and, wherever circumstances were favorable, soliciting aid in my great object."[41]

To be certain, Henson and the traveling musicians did not represent the majority of the enslaved population. Indeed many enslaved Africans Americans spent their lives contained on the small farms of their owners. However, the significance is not in the frequency of these cases but in the implications of the presence of such liberality of movement. African

Americans were regularly jailed on the mere suspicion of being runaways. Whites published notices in the newspaper to alert claimants, but the language of the notices revealed the depth of whites' suspicions because it called virtually everything about the detainee into question. One notice read, "a negro man who *calls* himself William and *states* that he is the property of Andrew Barnett." This notice implicitly undermines William's credibility, suggesting that the reader cannot necessarily take William at his word. The courts supported such suspicion, as one judge ruled, "Experience teaches, that there is no danger to be apprehended from too great an alacrity, or passionate ardour, in apprehending slaves as runaways, without probable cause." Within the state Kentucky slaveholders had to rely on the suspicions of their neighbors to control the movement of the enslaved precisely because written passes were not always reliable.[42]

Kentucky slaveholders feared that their free-state neighbors either could not or would not employ the same methods to limit the movement of the enslaved. In their ads for runaways, slaveholders warned their neighbors that enslaved African Americans would turn white Americans' reliance on the written word into an avenue for gaining freedom. Some enslaved blacks may have learned of the need for written proof of freedom from free African Americans in the region. For example, an advertisement for "Jacob" read that "he may procure forged papers and attempt to pass as a free man." Jacob Herral's owner feared the possibility of a market for free papers in the black community. Clearly Herral had enough contact and interaction with the free black community along the river to know how to obtain some papers. Many enslaved African Americans undoubtedly understood the importance of the written word through observation. Some mobile black laborers used their autonomy to learn how to read and write. Literacy among slaves in Kentucky was low, but it was more common among runaways. "James," who had considerable "knowledge of the country on the other side of the Ohio River," also knew how to read. Slaveholders feared that literate slaves such as James would forge their own papers. In another example, Frank's owner wrote that he could "read and write, and it is likely that he has got a pass of his own writing."[43]

While the enslaved could manipulate existing language and texts, they could not control the dissemination of information, and sadly enslaved African Americans' ability to use the written word to their advantage at least partially undermined its power. Essentially slaveholders used advertisements to undermine the power of written authorizations of freedom by calling all papers into question on both sides of the river. Some advertisements suggested that the runaway slaves had legitimate claims to freedom, but the advertisers simply dismissed any written proof as false. For example, George was freed by his deceased owner's will but was forced to flee when his new owner tried to quash his freedom legally. George's new owner wrote that he had "a copy of Violett's will with him, and passes as free; but he is a slave." The new owner had the power to invalidate George's legitimate written claim to freedom. Through their advertisements slaveholders called any written proof of freedom into question. For example, Bobb's owner wrote that he "has passed himself for a freeman, and may or may not have a pass, or some forgery to that effect." An advertisement such as this essentially made any African American man in the Ohio Valley a suspected fugitive.[44]

Kentucky slaveholders knew they had to rely on the assistance of white Americans in Indiana and Ohio to control the movement of African Americans across the river. Just as the process of sale reified racial difference on both sides of the river through commodification, so too did reclamation strategies bring white Americans together in the practice of racial policing. In 1824 William Buckner of Paris, Kentucky, wrote a letter to a man in Covington, Kentucky, a city directly across the river from Cincinnati. He "had not the pleasure of a personal acquaintance" with this man but sought his help in recovering his runaway slave. Buckner asked his new acquaintance to make the escape "known to all your acquaintances in Covington, Newport and Cincinnati, and request that they will make use of some exertion to stop him." Buckner believed that his best hope for recovery was to utilize the ferry drivers. But if his slave escaped beyond Cincinnati, Buckner had little chance for recovery. While Buckner could count on the assistance of white Cincinnatians, he worried that his slave may have been hiding out among free blacks in Cincinnati. He suggested the possibility of bribing a free black person in Cincinnati to search for his slave but worried that "there are so few that can be relied on." Even without any facts to support his fear, Buckner immediately suspected the free black community as an obstacle to the reclamation of the escaped slave. Yet Buckner was willing to trust a man he had never met to help in the recovery of his escaped slave. In 1826 Edward Stone of Bourbon County floated down the Ohio River with seventy-seven slaves bound for the New Orleans market, before they mutinied. Indianans quickly formed a posse, rounded up all escapees, and transported them back to Kentucky. Kentuckians relied on racial solidarity with their free-state neighbors and a shared mutual suspicion of both free and enslaved African Americans.[45]

Slaveholders' suspicion crossed the banks of the Ohio River and made Kentucky's legal reclamation procedures social practice in free states, which undermined the security of freedom of African Americans in free states. Much as in Kentucky, Indianans published notices in local newspapers when they jailed suspected runaways. In the 1820s Indiana law did not yet require African Americans to register their freedom in the local courts, as did Ohio law, but African Americans still felt uneasy in their freedom. David Prosser, for example, asked his former owner, Charles Phillips, for papers proving his emancipation after a "mob of ruffians" arrested him. However, as the advertisements and Prosser's arrest suggest, even in the free state of Indiana, African Americans were enslaved until proven free. The omnipresence of white suspicion helps explain why Ohioans had laws requiring African Americans to register their freedom upon entering the state. While Ohio's law was seldom enforced, the existence of the law put the burden of proof for freedom on African Americans. In response to this uncertainty, Martin Baker attempted to use the press to secure his freedom. Baker had a notice published in Madison, Indiana, in Cincinnati, Ohio, and in Lexington, Kentucky, in which he gave a physical description of himself and stated that he had "clear and indisputable evidence" of his freedom. Baker explained, "This description is published that it may be known by all persons to be free wherever I may go." Baker's description is both an example of the innovative ways African Americans secured their freedom and evidence of the insecurity of black freedom. Baker would not have had to publish a claim to freedom if he had no reason to fear having it taken away.[46]

The work of Indiana and Ohio Quakers to free kidnapped African Americans highlights the tension between legal freedom and the increasingly racialized limitations to practiced freedom. In their yearly meetings, Indiana Quakers reported on their efforts to protect African Americans from kidnapping. In one example a boy was taken from Richmond, Indiana, and sold as a slave to work on a steamboat that plied the Ohio River between St. Louis, Missouri, and Louisville, Kentucky. Indiana attorneys found the boy, proved his claim to freedom, and returned him to his home "after much fatigue and expense." Evidently, with the pursuit of cases such as this, Indiana Quakers exhausted their funds, suggesting that there was no shortage of kidnapping cases. In fact, the expense of proving legal freedom likely prevented many African Americans from redeeming their freedom.[47]

In their writings white residents and politicians universally deplored kidnapping and argued that written proof of freedom protected African Americans under the antikidnapping laws in Ohio and Indiana. In addition Kentucky courts upheld African Americans' claims to freedom when they could demonstrate residence in a free state. However, these legal measures did not ensure the safety of African Americans along the river. They provided African Americans with the legal recourse to prove their freedom, but they still required African Americans to *prove* their freedom, something white Americans did not have to worry about. Thus the written word could prove status, but race often served as the shortcut.[48]

Using physical appearance as a shortcut for determining status had a long history in America. In particular, clothing had long been a marker of status in America because the absence of hereditary nobility necessitated new definitions of class. In colonial America, Virginia planters mimicked the clothing and lifestyle of the English gentry as means of establishing their power through social practice. During the American Revolution, homespun clothing became a symbol of patriotism in the New England colonies. Following the American Revolution, Americans experienced a shift in values that established the self-made man as the American ideal. However, the self-made man had a sinister cousin, the confidence man. The confidence man used the appearance of gentility and class to lure, seduce, and debauch innocent young men recently arrived to the cities from rural areas. The parallel stories of the confidence man and the self-made man revealed Americans' fascination with and fear of social mobility. In the early republic, many Americans believed that participation in the market granted any person the chance of becoming successful. But while America as a land of opportunity was a defining feature of American nationalism, it also offered corrupt individuals the chance to take advantage of the fluid society. Thus appearance was both essential in defining character but ultimately flawed because it was unreliable.[49]

Along the Ohio River, changing clothes allowed free blacks to create new identities in the marketplace and offered escaped slaves the chance to merge with the free black population. Advertisements for runaways from that time revealed that both whites and blacks recognized the importance of clothing in determining status. Most such ads included detailed descriptions of the fugitives' clothing, but those were more than straightforward descriptions of an objective reality. Milly, who escaped from Kentucky, wore a cotton dress that, according to her owner, "may easily be changed."

Milly was a "bright mulatto" woman with light eyes, "well-made" hair, and had a daughter who was "as fair as most white people." Everything about the description of Milly's physical appearance suggested that she could pass as a white woman, including her ability to change her dress. Therefore it was likely that Milly was *not* wearing her cotton dress. Descriptions such as this made any light-skinned woman with "well-made" hair into a potential fugitive.[50]

African Americans throughout the South clearly recognized the importance of clothing in transgressing the confines of bondage. In the Deep South, plantation owners commonly issued one or two sets of clothing annually for their enslaved laborers. African Americans wore out their clothing, not surprising considering their arduous work in the cotton fields, and had to patch up their clothes and shoes throughout the year. As a result clothing was an easily recognizable physical marker of servitude. The historian Stephanie Camp has argued that in Georgia, women used clothing to protest slavery by reclaiming their bodies. For secret gatherings, called frolics, enslaved women made their own clothing, weaving and dyeing color and patterns into it using roots and berries. In some cases they imitated the popular hoop skirts with grapevines and limbs from trees and made hats and accessories. Camp argues that through these actions enslaved women transformed their bodies from objects of labor and humiliation to ones of pleasure and self-expression.[51]

Along the Ohio River, sartorial strategies of resistance had an increased social impact because they flouted physical markers of status. In advertisements for runaways, slaveholders both identified the clothing of the fugitives and indicated that the fugitives could not be easily identified by sight because they had all the outward appearances of free persons. For example, the description of Frank read, "It is probable he will change his name and clothes," and for William or Billy, "His clothing cannot be well described, they were pretty good." When John escaped from his owner, he took a "variety of clothes," and it was also likely that he would "pass as a white man." Considering the fact that many white Americans had only a couple of changes of clothing, John's "variety of clothes" was remarkable for any man in nineteenth-century America, let alone someone who was enslaved. Nothing about John—not his clothes or his skin color—suggested that he was enslaved. Similarly this advertisement suggested that free African Americans also dressed differently than enslaved blacks did. John changed his clothes in order to cross the border between slavery and freedom, suggesting that, in river cities, both free and enslaved African Americans might look exactly the same.[52]

Ironically, in defeating one barrier to freedom, African Americans initiated a new, more stubborn racial barrier. By indicating that white Americans could not recognize slaves by their clothing, slaveholders redrew the boundaries of recognition to make African Americans on either side of the river potential slaves unless proven otherwise. More broadly, white Americans along the Ohio River reworked the boundary between slavery and freedom every time African Americans challenged it. When African Americans moved into the area and settled in river cities, white residents used the squalid conditions of black neighborhoods to define African Americans as unfit for freedom. When black workers sought to take advantage of the river economy, they found their occupational opportunities limited by race and lived with a daily fear of sale to the Deep South. In addition, when African Americans sought to rely on legal protection, white residents relied on racially motivated suspicion to regulate black freedom and overcome incompatible state laws.

*   *   *

In response to the changes developing in the 1820s, white Americans along the Ohio River increasingly understood the world in racialized terms. As Ohioans' passage of black laws as early as 1803 suggests, white settlers had long practiced racial politics. However, as the consequences of economic development upset the social landscape, the language of race changed. In earlier decades white settlers with antislavery convictions linked emancipation with the need for uplift. Reformers such as David Rice argued that slavery degraded the black population and so African Americans required some "preparation" for freedom. In part, Ohio's black laws reflected this understanding of limiting dependence through uplift. In short, slavery was the problem and emancipation was the solution. As the Ohio River labor system emerged and the conditions of slavery and freedom blurred, white Americans defined race as the key to controlling the problem of slavery. As a reflection of the growing importance of race, colonization gained popularity on both sides of the border throughout the 1820s. In 1825 the Ohio legislature passed a resolution that called for Congress to consider instituting a plan for gradual emancipation and the colonization of freed slaves. Indiana governor William Hendricks and Indiana legislators passed their own resolution in support of the plan for colonization. White residents formed state auxiliaries of the American Colonization Society in Ohio in 1826 and in Indiana and Kentucky in 1829.[53]

Colonization supporters defined all African Americans, regardless of status, as members of a degraded class. The Indiana judge and colonizationist Isaac Blackford argued that slavery degraded African Americans initially but prejudice kept them in a degraded state. The colonization advocate Henry Clay explained that "the free people of color are, by far as a class, the most corrupt, depraved and abandoned . . . they are not slaves, and yet they are not free." The issue, according to white colonizationists, was not just slavery but slavery and racial prejudice. Thus emancipation, in their view, simply unleashed a new problem because it created a "corrupt" and "depraved" population. As one writer stated, "A manumitted slave remains a negro still, and must ever continue in a state of political bondage," and "he is always degraded in the estimation of the community, and the deep sense of that degradation enters into his soul, and makes him degraded indeed." Colonizationists argued that because prejudice made uplift impossible, removal was the only solution. As one supporter argued, "The colonization society holds out to the free man of color the only possible method by which he can hope to attain the dignity or enjoy the blessing of a free man."[54]

While the words of Henry Clay and the colonizationists were not actually true, they were at least psychologically true. As the black population increased along the river, white Americans expressed deep misgivings about the place of African Americans in their vision for not only their state but also their region. Colonizationists repeatedly framed slavery and racial conflict as regional issues. Residents on both sides of the river expressed similar concerns about the emancipation of the enslaved population. In Kentucky slaveholders and nonslaveholders looked to colonization as a means of freeing the state from a potentially dangerous free black population. Fears of disrupting the social order stalled Kentucky's emancipation movement in the 1790s, and by the 1820s Kentuckians had framed colonization as the solution to a national problem. In Ohio and Indiana whites associated the black population with slavery, so colonization would limit the growth of the black population and sever their states' connections to southern slavery. David Smith, of the Ohio Colonization Society, argued that emancipation would inevitably lead to a race war and so colonization of the freed black population was the only way to avoid devastation. Thus, in Smith's estimation, racial conflict made slavery an Ohio Valley issue, not a southern problem. In an official publication of the Ohio Colonization Society, Smith wrote, "Though hundreds of us have fled to Ohio as the asylum of freedom; who will desire her pleasant plains and valleys as a residence? Who would not then prefer a residence in a slave-holding state?" No matter what the immediate goals, through colonization white Americans on both sides of the river forged a common language of race that defined both free and enslaved African Americans as unfit for freedom whether in a slave state or a free state.[55]

While the urban environment made racial conflict particularly volatile, the press helped spread this image of black depravity across the white countryside in Indiana and Ohio. Some white residents who lived in racially homogenous regions of southern Ohio and Indiana had little interaction with African Americans. Therefore their perceptions most likely came from newspapers that typically depicted African Americans as violent and depraved individuals. Editors also ran articles describing the alarming growth of the free black population in the state. The constant stream of articles claiming that African Americans brought vice into the community stimulated whites' fears about the growth of the black population. White residents' racism was not innate; they based their racism on the only experience they had, and for some that was discussion of the news in local taverns.[56]

*　*　*

By the end of the 1820s, white Americans had attempted to simplify their world into black and white. Residents along the Ohio River could not separate the practice of race from the emerging labor system. In fact, the growing importance of racial distinctions reflected the ways in which labor conditions blended the experiences of enslaved and free black laborers. Recently historians have argued that in Maryland, another border state, the economy combined both slave and free labor. However, rather than seeing this as a place where slavery and freedom blended, the historian Max Grivno has argued that where these labor systems collided was precisely where "the slavery–free labor boundary emerged." In teasing out the differences between the lives of the enslaved and those of free laborers in rural Maryland, Grivno argues that there were clear distinctions between slavery and freedom that could never be erased. This argument is convincing and cannot be disputed. However, arguing that racial restrictions closed the gap between the experiences of the enslaved and those of free African Americans is not the same thing as arguing that slavery and freedom were interchangeable. Slavery and freedom were not interchangeable categories for African Americans in Kentucky, Maryland, or anywhere else in the country. At the Ohio River border, racial distinctions had a special relationship with distinctions between slavery and freedom. White residents used race to control the mobility of black workers along the Ohio River because they refused, or failed, to distinguish between free and enslaved black workers. Racial control gave residents on both sides of the river a common ground on which to negotiate because it allowed them to sidestep the more volatile issue of defending and defining the slave/free border.[57]

However, in sidestepping the issue, whites left the issue of fugitiveness unresolved. Enslaved blacks continued to escape across the river and challenge the boundaries of freedom throughout the antebellum period. As a result, while racial distinctions limited conflict along the border, the reclamation of fugitives from labor continued to smolder as a potentially explosive issue. After a confrontation with an Ohio farmer in whose haystack he had surreptitiously hidden, Milton Clarke, a light-skinned fugitive from Kentucky, understood that though he had crossed the geographic divide between slavery and freedom, the racial boundary remained. The day after Clarke had hidden in his hay, the farmer confronted "Mr. Austin," a local white at whose home Clarke was staying, "to know if it was so." Clarke remembered the farmer angrily announcing that "if he had known that a nigger slept there, he would have burned the hay and him all up together." He then turned to Clarke, unaware that he was the runaway, and asked him if he had seen "that nigger." "I told him I had," replied Clarke. Austin then asked the farmer "what he would say if they [slave catchers] should come and attempt to take" Clarke "into slavery." "Why," replied the farmer, "I would shoot them." For Clarke, the lesson was clear: The farmer's "philanthropy was graduated, like many others, upon nothing more substantial than color." He knew that his light skin carried the assumption of freedom, but his story also highlighted the tenuousness of assumed freedom. Clarke, like many other free blacks north of the Ohio River, realized that he could only "pass" as a free person.[58]

CHAPTER FIVE

Politics of Unity and Difference

After Indianans banned slavery from their state in 1816 (and Illinoisans did in 1819), the Ohio River, which had been a border in principle under the Northwest Ordinance, became the legislated border between slave and free territory in the Ohio River Valley for the rest of the antebellum period. The politics of statehood created this border, but politicians on both sides of the river struggled to come to terms with the differences between internal debates over slavery and maintaining harmony between "sister states." Leaders from Indiana and Ohio, who had concerned themselves with ridding their states of slavery, sought to translate those concerns into protecting the border between slavery and freedom. Across the border Kentucky leaders sought concessions from their free-state neighbors in order to establish a community dedicated to protecting the property rights of their slaveholding citizens. When these debates exploded into conflicts between executives and echoed in the halls of Congress, local leaders realized that protecting state sovereignty while engaging in interstate diplomacy over slavery was a difficult and potentially dangerous balance to strike.

The rapid emergence of political conflicts over slavery around 1820, and the absence of any definitive resolution to those conflicts, revealed much about the influence of power on the dynamics of this borderland. Power struggles are central to the emergence of borderlands. As Richard White has argued about the colonial Great Lakes region, when two powers meet, the absence of a dominant party necessitates accommodation. White's description of the "middle ground" is often misinterpreted as meaning a place only of accommodation and creativity. However, as White suggests, conflict makes that accommodation and creativity both possible and necessary as a means of either resolving or avoiding future conflicts.[1]

In the Ohio River Valley when Indianans and Ohioans clashed with Kentuckians over the reclamation of fugitive slaves, they met as theoretical equals. James Madison had imagined the equal sovereignty between independent states as central to the stability of the young republic. Therefore only a federal authority had the power to resolve disputes between states. Indeed residents and politicians on both sides of the Ohio River appealed to the higher authority of the federal government as a mediator in their debates. However, the rancor of the debates during the Missouri Crisis weakened federal legislators' willingness to interfere in interstate conflicts over slavery. Instead local politicians and residents had to develop their own solutions to interstate disputes. As a result politicians on both sides of the river promoted commerce as a necessary point of compromise and legislated racial barriers to both quiet conflict and give meaning to the Ohio River border.

This chapter demonstrates that the social context and the political imagining of the Ohio River border cannot be separated from each other; they reinforced each other even when they were at odds. That effort, of enacting a political border against a social context having little to do with that border, made this borderland a unique place where confrontation coexisted with accommodation and disunity highlighted similarities. For borderlanders, the Ohio was a river of freedom and a river of slavery; it encouraged unity as it imposed division; and it was a border that separated states even as it drew people together.[2]

*   *   *

After Kentuckians defeated emancipationists with their conventions in 1792 and 1799, Ohioans confirmed the state's commitment to free soil with their antislavery state constitution in 1802, and Indianans banned slavery in their state in 1816, it became less likely that Illinois, or any other state under the Northwest Ordinance, would become a slaveholding state. Just as it solidified the Ohio River border, ironically the ratification of Indiana's antislavery constitution also threatened the region's unity. In earlier visions of the West, Americans imagined the Ohio River as the great highway traveling through a united "Western Country." However, as the state constitutions demonstrated, the very river that was to unite the region was also a symbol of division. The common regional identity of the "Western Country" threatened to dissipate just as it began to take shape.[3]

The unique dynamics of Indiana politics exacerbated the latent conflict between the newly forming free states and slave states. While the future of slavery in their states was an important issue for politicians and voters in Kentucky and Ohio, Indiana politicians built their power on the conflict between slavery and freedom. Once they settled the contest within the state, Indiana politicians quickly took the battle to the border to further their political aspirations. In his first message to the General Assembly in 1816, Governor Jonathan Jennings recommended legislation to regulate the retrieval of fugitive slaves and to protect free blacks from kidnapping. Jennings asked for a law "to prevent more effectually any unlawful attempts to seize and carry into bondage persons of colour, legally entitled to their freedom, and at the same time . . . to prevent those who rightfully owe service to citizens of any other state, from seeking within the limits of this state a refuge from the possession of their lawful owners." At the governor's request, the Indiana legislature passed an "Act to Prevent Manstealing," which put local Indiana officials in charge of reclaiming fugitives from labor. The Indiana law required the claimant to secure a warrant for the arrest of the fugitive from either a justice of the peace or a judge of the circuit courts. Most important, the law required a local sheriff or constable, rather than the claimant, to make the arrest. Not only did the law standardize the retrieval of fugitives, but it also punished with a fine of five hundred to one thousand dollars any person who did not follow the proper procedure.[4]

In the fall of 1817, in response to Indiana's law on man stealing, members of the Kentucky legislature passed a resolution requesting their governor, Gabriel Slaughter, to correspond with Jonathan Jennings about "the difficulty said to be experienced by our [Kentucky] citizens in reclaiming their slaves who escape into Indiana." In his correspondence with Jennings, Slaughter emphasized the commercial importance of the Ohio River and the unavoidable constant intermingling among residents along the Ohio. Slaughter blamed Indianans for the difficulties in reclamation: "Whether it is a defect in your laws, or the want of promptitude and energy in those who administer them, or the prejudice of your citizens against slavery, or to all those causes," the people of Kentucky wanted to remove the obstacles "real or supposed by your citizens." It took a community to properly shackle a slave, and Kentuckians sought to extend that community across the river. In response the Indiana House of Representatives formed a committee to discuss the matter and reported that the Kentucky legislature was incorrect to accuse Indianans of any "want of promptitude and energy" in helping them reclaim their fugitive slaves. The committee reported further that the complaints were coming from "individuals who have been disappointed in their attempts to carry away those, whom they claimed as slaves, without complying with the preliminary steps required by law." Members of the committee argued that Kentuckians' efforts to force Indianans to follow their customs for fugitive reclamation were an affront to the "dignity of our laws and the sovereignty of our state." By this definition, keeping slavery south of the Ohio River protected the free soil and free labor of Indiana.[5]

Jennings and Indiana legislators probably did not want to generate a disruptive conflict with their slaveholding neighbors, but they were acutely sensitive to the importance of defending the state against the influence of slavery on residents. However, in this case, defending the state against slavery put them in direct conflict with the policies and will of their southern neighbors. As this early correspondence revealed, the problem was that in some cases only the federal government could regulate interstate relations. However, the 1793 Federal Fugitive Slave Law failed to give responsibility for enforcement to any one person or official; nor was the requirement of proof precise. When Kentuckians questioned the constitutionality and legality of Indiana's Act to Prevent Manstealing, they appealed to the federal law and the Constitution; Indianans believed that federal regulations were ineffectual. The ambiguity of the federal law created a troubling situation for Indiana legislators, because they feared it left their constituents subject to the will of Kentucky slaveholders.[6]

Almost immediately Kentuckians and Indianans clashed over the proper procedure for reclaiming fugitives from labor. In November 1818 two agents of Squire Brooks and James Nabb, of Jefferson County, Kentucky, attempted to carry away Isaac Crosby, a black man living in Indiana. The agents found Isaac at the house of General Bartholomew in Charlestown in Clark County, Indiana. Isaac Crosby had escaped from his owner in Kentucky and taken up residence with the general, and he apparently worked on Bartholomew's farm. Brooks's agents found Crosby outside Bartholomew's house, but Bartholomew and Crosby resisted the arrest and forced the Kentuckians into the house, preventing their departure.

Squire Brooks arrived at the general's house and produced a legal claim to Crosby from the Knox County Circuit Court, but Bartholomew refused to allow the Kentuckians to take Crosby. Before this incident Brooks had spoken to the local sheriff, asking the consequences if he were to capture

Isaac himself. He claimed that "He did not wish to do anything in violation of the law of the country." In referencing the "law of the country," Brooks appealed to the federal law in order to circumvent Indiana's state law. Brooks's claim for the higher authority of the federal law was not unfounded, since earlier in 1818 Judge Benjamin Parke of the Indiana Federal District Court had ruled that the Federal Fugitive Slave Law of 1793 superseded state law. Squire Brooks was clearly familiar with this ruling since he asked General Bartholomew if he had seen Judge Parke's opinion on the subject of fugitive slaves. In fact Brooks wanted to take Crosby to Jeffersonville because he believed the justice of the peace would be sympathetic to his circumstance. Bartholomew, however, demanded that Brooks take Isaac before the local circuit court in Charlestown, where Davis Floyd, the "great emancipator," was president.[7]

Everyone involved knew that the meaning of the law depended on who enforced it, and they tried to manipulate the legal system to further their own ends. It is no wonder that Brooks ran into trouble; not only did he receive contradictory advice from local Indianans, but in addition state and federal judges could not clear up the situation. During the territorial period, circuit court judge Davis Floyd attached himself to the antislavery party, whereas federal judge Benjamin Parke had been an ally of Harrison and the proslavery party. Davis Floyd, still carrying a personal antislavery image, now vigorously fought to defend Indiana's free soil from any encroachment by Kentucky slaveholders. Parke, a slaveholder himself, ruled that Indiana's free soil could not hinder the national institution of slavery. Divisions over slavery carried over from the territorial period into the new state's government, undermining the stability of the legal system and ultimately confusing the situation for Brooks.[8]

Because the law was subject to interpretation, Brooks, Bartholomew, and Crosby knew that the Ohio River border was an unofficial point of no return. Bartholomew's only chance to maintain custody of Crosby was to confront Brooks and keep Crosby in Indiana. In contrast, Brooks knew that once he carried Crosby across the border into Kentucky his claim was safe. Isaac Crosby was more than a mere pawn in this game. He tried to use the system to defend his freedom. Isaac Crosby could not rely on the law to secure his freedom, so he worked for Bartholomew with the hope that the general would aid in his fight for freedom. Despite the efforts of Crosby and General Bartholomew, Crosby may have been removed to Kentucky since the justice of the peace of Jeffersonville was indicted for carrying

Crosby "forcibly out of the state." In addition Crosby did not appear in the 1820 census as an individual or as part of Bartholomew's household. Crosby's fate demonstrated that the odds were stacked against African Americans; working within a respectable household offered hope for freedom north of the border, but south of the border Crosby's fate was sealed.[9]

While this conflict received little public attention, in 1819 a local conflict over the arrest and extradition of an escaped slave from Kentucky ignited a two-year political conflict between the executives of Indiana and those of Kentucky. Susan escaped from her owner Richard Stephens in Kentucky into Indiana in 1816 and filed for her freedom in an Indiana circuit court. The jury ruled that Susan did indeed belong to Stephens and should be returned to him. Susan's attorney motioned for and received a new trial, and the case continued for several terms of court. In 1818 Richard Stephens, tired of the delay, sent his son, Robert, to Indiana to bring Susan back to Kentucky by force. Davis Floyd, the local judge, immediately issued a warrant for Robert Stephens's arrest and brought the case to the attention of Governor Jonathan Jennings. Nearly one year after Robert's indictment, Jennings demanded his extradition to Indiana to stand trial for "mansteal- ing." Richard Stephens was a member of the Kentucky legislature and rallied his fellow legislators, and they refused to extradite his son to Indiana. Over the course of the next two years, Jennings and Gabriel Slaughter, the governor of Kentucky, engaged in a heated correspondence about Robert Stephens and the legality of his actions. The Indiana legislature forwarded the correspondence between the governors to President James Monroe, but when Monroe failed to respond, the case was dropped in 1823.[10]

The anticlimactic resolution to the Stephens controversy belies the importance of the event in shaping not only political interstate relations but also residents' understandings of their state and regional identities. Before it became an interstate political imbroglio, the Stephens controversy ultimately began as a local conflict between Indianans. While Robert Stephens tried to circumvent Indiana's legal system to reclaim Susan, he did not want to provoke conflict. He sent a letter to the sheriff of Harrison County, Indiana, John Tipton, asking him to help with the removal of Susan. He asked if they could reclaim Susan "without alarming the family" and also if Tipton would talk to Daniel Lane, the owner of the home at which Susan was staying. Robert Stephens's friends told him that Lane was a "Gentle- man" who would potentially help with the reclamation. In a later letter Richard Stephens told Tipton, "I was advised when I was there also in

Charlestown to take my negro by forse but I thought I would advise with some others of the barr I went to a Mr. Nelsen who . . . told me the better way was to let her alone but tomason advised . . . to take her away by fors . . . I want al ill blood settled between our side of the river and yourn." As Stephens's letters suggest, he received contradictory advice from Indianans on how best to reclaim Susan. Some suggested that he leave Susan alone, while others suggested that he take her "by fors." Those Indianans who suggested taking Susan by force likely did not view Stephens's actions as an affront to Indiana's state sovereignty because he had a legitimate legal claim. It is also possible that Mr. Nelsen suggested that Stephens leave Susan alone because he knew that the slavery issue was controversial and had the potential to erupt into a major conflict. Clearly, Indianans did not agree on their responsibilities to their slave-holding neighbors, which frustrated the expectations of slaveholders such as Richard Stephens.[11]

If we look deeper, the personal animosity between the two primary Indiana officials involved in the affair, John Tipton and Davis Floyd, may have been what turned the local conflict into an interstate controversy. In contrast to Davis Floyd, who had earned the reputation of "emancipator," Tipton, while acting as sheriff of Harrison County, repeatedly aided in the recovery of fugitive slaves. In fact Floyd and Tipton had a history of animosity. Prior to the Stephens affair, Tipton aided in the recovery of Perry, who claimed that he had been set free but whose former master, William Stith, was trying to bring him back into slavery. The Indiana General Court issued a certificate for Perry's removal, but Perry had escaped into Harrison County. Davis Floyd wrote Tipton asking him to let the alleged slave go free and told him that the government would compensate him for his efforts. Tipton, angered at the questioning of his actions, shot back, "I have no objection to you or any other Jentleman taking an active part in administering Justice even to the African (if he was oppressed) You think the court has Erred I think Different if the members of the Legislature has requested you to Interfere with the affairs of our County as an Individual this time and you have Done so, I hope they will now Desist and hereafter mind their own business and not meddle with the Sivil officers of our County." It hardly seems a coincidence that Floyd issued the warrant for the arrest of Robert Stephens immediately after Tipton aided Stephens's removal of Susan. Davis Floyd clearly held strong enough antislavery convictions to repeatedly clash with fellow Indianans over the issue of slavery.

In fact it is quite possible that Floyd was a contentious individual who rubbed many people the wrong way, Tipton among them. Floyd may have issued the warrant even if Tipton had not been involved, but Tipton's involvement may have sweetened the deal.[12]

From Tipton's perspective, he was acting as a friend in his efforts to aid Stephens in Susan's removal. In the summer of 1820, as the affair dragged on, Richard Stephens wrote to Tipton, "I address you I return you my harty thanks for your honest and upright Conduct towards my boys during there being over in your Country after my property." Tipton's actions were a personal favor to Richard Stephens, but Stephens had a legitimate legal claim to Susan, which Tipton simply honored. Tipton's actions do not necessarily demonstrate support for slavery but seem instead to be a different approach to maintaining interstate harmony. Even as the conflict raged between the governments of Indiana and Kentucky, Tipton and Stephens remained friends. In fact Robert Stephens asked Tipton, "Please to use your utmost influence to put an end to the affair." Despite Tipton's involvement in the incident and his sympathy for Stephens, the available sources do not indicate that Indiana officials ever questioned Tipton's actions as sheriff. In fact Jennings put Tipton in charge of arresting Robert Stephens and bringing him back into Indiana![13]

The Stephens controversy moved from a local concern to the governor's office, which made it peculiar. Floyd issued the warrant for Robert Stephens's arrest in July 1818, but Jennings waited until November 1819 before he demanded the extradition of Stephens from Kentucky. Why was there a year-and-a-half lag? In that time the debate at the federal level over the admission of Missouri into the Union had dramatically changed the political climate. While Jennings had always advocated antislavery, the Missouri Crisis had ignited the antislavery feelings of northerners, making it especially politically advantageous to oppose the extension of slavery in the fall of 1819. Jennings could make an example of Stephens to demonstrate Indiana's total freedom from slavery and, in the process, make a name for himself as a defender of freedom. However, the conflict over Missouri undermined the possibility of compromise and hardened the positions of both Indianans and Kentuckians, and Jennings's motives were not lost on Kentucky legislators. Thus the interstate debate over the extradition of Robert Stephens became intertwined with the national debate over Missouri, and the conflict spilled out of the halls of Congress across the pages of newspapers and into local taverns.[14]

In February 1819 New York senator James Tallmadge proposed an amendment to Missouri's statehood bill. Tallmadge called for a ban on the "further introduction of slavery" once Missouri became a state. The Tallmadge amendment set off a fierce debate in both halls of Congress and across the nation over the place of slavery in the country's future. Thomas Jefferson famously called the Missouri Crisis a "firebell in the night" because it revealed the devastating divisiveness of the slavery issue. As congressmen found out when they went home for their summer recess, the debate ignited the public. Some congressmen watched as crowds publicly burned them in effigy. Historians have made much of the Missouri debate as a political turning point responsible for the rise of Andrew Jackson and the two-party system. Recently the historian Matthew Mason characterized the Missouri debates as both the culmination of previous debates over slavery and a moment of redefinition. This duality best captures its effect on the Ohio River borderland.[15]

Prior to the Missouri statehood bill, border-state congressmen were ambivalent about their responsibilities to their constituents with regard to slavery. In January 1817 representatives considered passing a new, more stringent fugitive slave bill, and they continued the fruitless discussion up until the Missouri debates in February 1819. In the U.S. House of Representatives, Indiana's representative voted against the bill and all Kentucky representatives voted in its favor. The votes, however, were not strictly sectional, as one representative from Ohio voted for the bill and another abstained from voting. In the Senate both Ohio senators voted down the bill, while both Kentuckians voted for the bill's passage. In this vote, however, Indiana's senators split. The debates and votes for a bill that never actually became law may seem trivial, but they reveal much about the pre-Missouri politics of the borderland. First, Henry Clay said that the bill was of "peculiar interest" to Kentuckians, suggesting that the local conflicts over fugitive reclamation reached the ears of national representatives. Thus border-state controversies over the reclamation of alleged fugitive slaves inspired the proposal of the new bill, and indeed the committee responsible for drafting the bill was made up of representatives from Virginia, Ohio, and Kentucky. However, the voting also reveals representatives' ambivalence over the relationship between "sister states." The Missouri debates made that ambivalence a political liability.[16]

The difference between the votes on the Missouri bill in spring of 1819 and those in spring of 1820 signaled the temporary evaporation of ambivalence from the border politics of slavery. During the initial votes on the amendments, Indiana's representative and all Ohio representatives with the exception of William Henry Harrison voted for the slavery restriction. Every Kentucky representative voted against the restriction. Ohio representatives split, three in favor and three against, on the enactment of a gradual emancipation clause in Missouri's constitution. In the Senate, Waller Taylor from Indiana abstained from the vote on the gradual emancipation clause but voted against striking out the prohibition of slavery in the state. However, when voting on whether to send the bill back to committee to reintroduce the prohibition of slavery, Taylor broke with his fellow Indiana representative, James Noble, and voted in the negative.[17]

While there was only a slight deviance from a strictly sectional vote, that deviance is telling. Waller Taylor was a slaveholder and William Henry Harrison's former aide-de-camp. Just as they had during Indiana's territorial debate, Harrison and Taylor once again joined together to allow the spread of slavery into a new territory. Harrison, the lone Ohio representative to side with the South on the restriction clause, lost the governor's election in 1820 and lost his bid for the House of Representatives in 1822. The Indiana legislature censored Waller Taylor for his vote on the Tallmadge amendments.

When Congress returned later in the year, the debate continued, but the sentiment had changed. By the spring of 1820 Jesse Thomas from Illinois had introduced an amendment that allowed slavery in Missouri but banned slavery in all future territories north of the 36/30 latitude line. When he voted on Thomas's amendment, Waller Taylor voted with Noble against the new compromise. In the House all representatives from Ohio and Indiana voted against striking out the prohibition clause, while all representatives from Kentucky voted in favor of it. As these results suggest, the fallout from the Missouri Crisis led representatives to take a strong stance on slavery. But while these votes highlight the hardening of positions on slavery, they do not entirely explain why that hardening happened. As former speaker of the house Tip O'Neill once suggested, all politics are local, and in this case the shift from ambivalence to certainty can be found not in the *Annals of Congress* but instead in records of local debates.[18]

When Jonathan Jennings demanded the extradition of Robert Stephens from Kentucky in November 1819, he linked issues of state sovereignty with slavery, and his timing tied local and national politics together. Kentucky's governor, Gabriel Slaughter, denied Jennings's request because he claimed that in cases of differences in the "policies" between states, he did not have the legal right to interfere. Jennings responded that in taking Susan himself Stephens was "insulting the sovereignty of our state." Slaughter stuck to his legal argument but expanded on it by arguing that the U.S. Constitution superseded the authority of Indiana's state law, and that there was no evidence that Stephens had violated federal law. Jennings responded by again suggesting that Indiana's sovereignty was at stake in the matter. Jennings insisted that it was not Slaughter's place to determine the legitimacy of the crime; he should simply respect the equal sovereignty of Indiana's laws. According to Jennings, when Indiana courts convicted Stephens, that should have been sufficient for Slaughter to honor the extradition request. Jennings forwarded all of his correspondence with Slaughter to Indiana's state legislature and issued a special message to the state senate in January 1820. Jennings again linked Indiana's "manstealing" law with the defense of state sovereignty: "Such violations of our penal laws, with impunity, while they are qualified to detract from the dignity, are equally calculated to impair the rights of the sovereignty of the state; and so long as a portion of our citizens shall countenance or encourage such infractions upon claims to protection under the constitutional laws of the state, so long may we expect the deleterious effects of their influence."[19]

In the correspondence between executives, only Jennings invoked arguments of state sovereignty, whereas Slaughter remained committed to his legal argument. However, when this controversy reached the newspapers, the tenor of the debate changed. The first article on the controversy to appear in Kentucky newspapers labeled Jennings's extradition request an affront to Kentucky's state sovereignty. The *Kentucky Reporter* read, "What does Governor Jennings mean? Does he intend to insult the state of Ky by dragging her reps from the legislative floor to be tried as criminals for reclaiming their own property?" When Jennings renewed his demand for Stephens in late January, Kentucky newspapers printed a barrage of articles denouncing Jennings and all Indianans *and* Ohioans who stood in the way of fugitive reclamation.[20]

Kentuckians continued their printed defense of Stephens throughout February, March, and April and into May. In the editorials, Kentuckians employed a variety of arguments rooted in the defense of their rights as slaveholders, while sidestepping the morality of slavery itself. First, they isolated the problem by claiming that most Indianans and Ohioans respected the dignity of Kentucky's laws and did not harbor fugitives.

Instead they suggested that a few harbored fugitives just for their labor. With this argument they sought to undermine the ostensibly philanthropic motives of Indianans and Ohioans by claiming that they just wanted slavery by another name. Second, Kentuckians suggested that Indianans and Ohioans adopt Kentucky's stance of making skin color presumptive evidence of status. In other words, while Indianans and Ohioans should protect free blacks from kidnapping, they should consider all African Americans enslaved until proven free. Thus Kentuckians warned that rather than worrying about slaveholders reclaiming their property, Indianans and Ohioans should be more concerned with the dangers of slaves escaping across state lines.[21]

In making the protection of slaveholders' rights an interstate issue, Kentuckians began the articulation of a new regional identity rooted in shared interests across distinct state borders. Kentuckians argued, "The time is rapidly coming on, when the united power, weight and influence of the whole of the western states will be required to prevent Indiana, Illinois, and Missouri, from being sacrificed on the altar of Eastern interest, avarice, ambition and pride." As this statement suggests, Kentuckians tied the Missouri debates together with the fugitive debate in their effort to craft a western identity. This argument followed a long tradition of westerners defining themselves in opposition to easterners, but it also admitted the difference between free and slave states. In this new vision, the Ohio Valley was no longer a singular "Western Country" but rather was a delicate balance of sovereign states based on compromise on differences and the promotion of shared interests. This was a critical moment in the development of the borderland because it signaled a shift in sensibilities toward the celebration of compromise across lines of difference.[22]

However, in the heat of the debate not all agreed on compromise. In fact Kentucky newspapers repeatedly issued threats to Indianans and Ohioans. Kentuckians seemed particularly offended that Indiana's law on man stealing punished violators with public flagellation. One Kentuckian wrote that "it would be unwise in the state of Indiana to impose 100 lashes on the bareback of a Kentuckian . . . let her do so, and take the consequences." In another example, a writer claimed, "Unless a radical and honest change shall take place in the feelings and practices of some of the people of Ohio and Indiana, and in the conduct of the government in those states, it is feared that we shall see *civil war* between them and Kentucky." In order to avoid violent conflict, Kentuckians suggested appealing to the federal government.[23]

Indianans were only too happy to turn to the federal government to resolve the conflict. In fact Indiana newspapers printed the correspondence between the governors and the reports of the legislatures but refrained from editorializing on the issue. The state legislature also forwarded all of the correspondence to Secretary of State John Quincy Adams in the winter of 1820. However, this heated debate came at the precise moment that national representatives were voting on the admission of Missouri to the Union, which heightened the sense of crisis. The newspaper articles took the debate from the halls of government to the streets. Newspaper editors routinely printed stories as means of stirring up debate, which furthered the popularity and notoriety of their papers. Americans commonly read stories aloud in crowded public arenas such as taverns. When the editorials in newspapers presented the Stephens affair as a crisis of great magnitude alongside columns about the crisis in Congress, local residents felt called to join in the debate. The newspapers reflected genuine political rancor, and the publication of the political rancor increased the conflict among residents. One student mentioned a conversation he had in a Louisville tavern about "dissensions that had taken place between Indiana and Kentucky on account of slaves who had escaped."[24]

The controversy stirred up more than debates in taverns; in some cases it inspired local residents to take the law into their own hands. Seth Woodruff was a judge in New Albany, Indiana, who owned and purchased at least two slaves in his life, but in 1821 he stood against the reclamation of a known fugitive slave. In February 1821 Abraham Fields of Kentucky sent an agent across the Ohio River to reclaim Moses, who had run away over ten years prior. Woodruff stopped Fields's agents at the ferry and demanded they accompany him to the courthouse (which just happened to be his own home). Seth Woodruff and Moses were probably acquainted because Woodruff was one of the most prominent men in New Albany and Moses had lived in the city for ten years. Woodruff saw himself as the leader of New Albany, and he wanted to protect the city's residents, including Moses, from intrusive outsiders.[25]

The next day when forty-three Kentuckians came across the river to reclaim Moses, white Indianans rallied to defend the suspected fugitive. A crowd of armed Indianans and Kentuckians gathered at Woodruff's home and turned the situation into a battle of wills where brute force determined righteousness. Woodruff invoked the militia in hopes that a military presence could keep the tense situation from erupting into violence. The local justice of the peace declared Moses a free man, but as he approached the door, the crowd of Kentuckians seized Moses and took him into the street with the intention of carrying him back to Kentucky. The militia and local residents confronted the Kentuckians, and a scene of confusion ensued. Around one hundred combatants shoved and shouted in the streets in front of nearly two hundred spectators. Eventually the Kentuckians acquiesced to the strength of the militia and settled for some parting verbal insults. Amid the tumult Moses was safely "conducted out of the crowd."[26]

The story of Woodruff and Moses reveals an interesting dynamic in the interstate conflict. Newspapers on both sides of the river printed the story, helping to fuel the conflict while making claims that these incidents had to stop to prevent further violence. Woodruff's defense of Moses was printed in newspapers in New Albany, Vincennes, Louisville, and even Cincinnati, and the publicity helped spread word of the event up and down the Ohio River. Indeed Kentucky newspapers printed the story with the following warning: "We are well convinced that the strong arm of the national legislature must be interposed or such degrading scenes will continue to occur." However, the crisis also masked some existing accommodations between the states. While the publicity contributed to Indiana's free-soil image and Woodruff's reputation as a defender of Indianans' freedom, Woodruff owned his own slave at the time. He purchased another slave from Kentucky years later and brought her to his home in Indiana. This suggests that state sovereignty and pride were at issue more than the rights and protection of African Americans.[27]

The crisis over fugitive reclamation revealed the limits of white philanthropy north of the river. African Americans could not always count on the local judge coming to their defense as happened with Moses. However, white residents were more willing to interfere in fugitive reclamation if they identified with the alleged fugitive as a citizen of Indiana or Ohio. African Americans established respectable reputations as one means of overcoming racial policing. Once white residents recognized African Americans as "respectable" citizens, they were willing to protect them, whether legally free or not, from enslavement. Peter McNelly, the man who escaped from Kentucky in 1793, continued to reside in Knox County, Indiana, in 1820 despite the fact that he was a known fugitive slave and was listed as a slave in the federal census. Reputation was a powerful principle because it allowed white residents to identify with African Americans.[28]

Unfortunately in these rhetorical, and sometimes physical, battles, whites treated the African Americans involved as pawns in a larger game.

After John Quincy Adams forwarded the correspondence between Jennings and Slaughter to James Monroe, Monroe let it sit on his desk. The historical record is virtually silent on the fate of Susan, the escaped slave. After Stephens forcibly removed her to Kentucky, an editorial in one Indiana paper suggested that she escaped from a steamboat. After that she disappeared. The lives of the Stephenses and Tipton changed very little. Robert Stephens remained a member of the Kentucky legislature, and he and his father carried on amicable relations with John Tipton throughout the entire affair. Tipton's actions were never questioned, and he continued to climb the political ladder in Indiana.[29]

The crisis over the Ohio River border was short-lived in part because local residents had to find ways to avoid conflict on a daily basis. Because the Ohio River was a shared space, a highway that united residents and connected them to the rest of the country, Americans had to interact constantly on the banks of the river. So while Jennings and other politicians preached vigilance, residents who shared familial, business, religious, and cultural connections with their southern neighbors along the river followed a path of less resistance. Residents believed in the differences symbolized by the Ohio River border, but the growth of large cities such as Louisville and Cincinnati along with smaller cities in Indiana such as Madison and New Albany highlighted the centrality of the river economy. Residents sought to situate their sense of difference within their reliance on interaction across borders, resulting in long stretches of peaceful accommodation punctuated by moments of intense conflict. The ostensibly contradictory simultaneous sense of unity and division came to define life along the river. Borderlanders understood that the river necessitated this accommodation, and so they developed a unique cultural outlook that would eventually separate the borderland region from the remainder of the state.[30]

*   *   *

Just as the resolution of the Missouri Crisis temporarily removed slavery from national politics, in the absence of a definitive resolution to the Stephens affair local politicians let the issue of fugitive reclamation drop. The national debate over Missouri and the local debate over the border revealed the dangers of conflicts over slavery and affirmed the necessity of compromise in the minds of borderland politicians. Therefore, in the aftermath, politicians devised ad hoc solutions to maintain the détente. The lack of a definitive policy gave politicians the appearance of inconsistency on the issue of slavery. In addition the steamboat industry rapidly changed the local economy and forced residents to redefine the codes of social behavior. As a result there was not a straight line of development in border politics. Gradually the development of commerce and the changes to the social landscape increased the saliency of race in state politics along the river. Race did not suddenly become the defining feature of state politics, nor did every state follow the same trajectory.

Apparent contradictions existed, indeed abounded, as politicians in each state offered seemingly contradictory solutions to the border problem. In Ohio white residents of Cincinnati engaged in a race riot to drive out the African American population, but two years later politicians passed a more stringent antikidnapping law to protect free African Americans in the state. Indianans softened their antikidnapping law and passed an immigration law requiring African Americans to register their freedom upon entering the state. Across the river in Kentucky, politicians passed a nonimportation act to limit the growth of the enslaved population, which some Kentuckians interpreted as a proslavery measure while others viewed it as an antislavery law.

White residents could not agree on the best means of controlling the border, but they all could agree that conflicts over the border were potentially dangerous. Therefore white residents and politicians committed themselves to maintaining amicable border relations. But solutions were far from simple, because politicians had to balance harmony against sovereignty. Maintaining interstate harmony with "sister states" while protecting state sovereignty caused political conflict, but that conflict coexisted with accommodation. Politicians on both sides of the river broadly agreed that regulating the African American population was the key to maintaining interstate harmony. Thus, while politicians disagreed over means, they shared a common bond in their attempt to control the black population. In this way race played a key role in political debates over the division between freedom and slavery. In sharing a border, white politicians shared concerns over the African American population. Emancipation in Kentucky affected Indianans and Ohioans just as much as fugitive reclamation did. While politicians north of the river sought to defend their state from slavery and politicians south of the river tried to protect slavery in their state, they shared a race "problem."

As the historian Stephen Middleton has suggested, by 1830 white Ohioans had made Ohio a "white man's republic." While they had passed laws requiring blacks to prove their free status on arrival and on demand over twenty years prior, the development of the river economy in the 1820s increased white Ohioans' desire to enforce them. The laws provided the framework for racial inequality, but by the end of the decade Ohioans practiced their racial politics in the streets. This issue was particularly explosive in urban areas where the free black population was on the rise. As white Americans increasingly viewed African Americans as an alien population defined by their skin color, they targeted black immigration as a threat to their social fabric. In Cincinnati by 1829 the old system of border regulation had been so badly damaged by the river economy that white residents felt it necessary to physically force alleged fugitives out of the city. Local residents began demanding enforcement of the 1807 law requiring registration for black immigrants. Politicians heeded the call of their constituents but tried to reassure black residents that "it is only the runaway slaves and idle vagrants that have occasion for alarm." While elite leaders tried to reassure black residents with this statement, they also indicated that African Americans would be suspected unless they could prove their freedom.[31]

Unable and unwilling to recognize the difference between free and enslaved African Americans, white residents stepped up their efforts to warn off all black Americans from the city. In June 1829 the Overseers of the Poor submitted a notice to the *Cincinnati Daily Gazette* warning African Americans in the city that "the act to regulate black and mulatto persons . . . will hereafter be rigidly enforced." The notice also gave black residents thirty days to pay their bond and register with the courts. African American leaders tried to organize a mass migration to Canada and asked the public to hold off enforcing the law. By August 1829 time had run out, and working class whites initiated, and wealthy gentlemen supported, a week of mob violence that left black-owned buildings, homes, and shops in ruins. Participants in the mob violence targeted black homes and businesses without regard to status. By the end of the violence, fifteen hundred blacks had left the city, some by choice and others as refugees.[32]

The Cincinnati riot was a violent indication of the new place of race in border regulation, and it effectually heightened all residents' awareness of racial barriers. White residents had tried to drive African Americans out of the city in order to prevent further immigration of formerly enslaved blacks. They exhibited their racism violently in order to solidify the border and keep slavery, and with it African Americans, on the southern bank. After the riot, many legitimately free blacks left the city, abandoning their earlier attempt to extend the space of black movement across the river. These free blacks viewed the border as a barrier to the enjoyment of their freedom, because when the racial limitations of slavery crossed the border, these undermined the security that freedom supposedly guaranteed. Indeed many of the black residents who remained in Cincinnati were poor people bound to the city. Contrary to the efforts of white Cincinnatians, however, these men and women rebuilt Cincinnati's black community and continued to welcome formerly enslaved blacks into the city. In the eyes of white Ohioans, the rebirth of the free black community in Cincinnati was a visual reminder of how African Americans undermined Ohio's freedom from slavery.[33]

However, white Ohioans cannot be categorized so easily. Ohio legislators were devoted to the commercial development of the state and therefore sought to minimize conflict while maintaining state sovereignty. By 1830 Ohio was second only to New York in the number of miles of canals in the state, greatly increasing the state's connections with the national market. However, the increase in connections also divided the export of goods, forging sectional economic links. The canal system allowed Ohioans to ship wheat north, while along the Ohio River, Cincinnatians shipped pork and whiskey south. The emergence of this divided economy in the 1820s and 1830s laid the groundwork for later social and political divisions as well. The historian Kim Gruenwald has suggested that the emergence of northern and eastern economic connections diminished the economic importance of the Ohio River, which in turn weakened Ohioans' ties to the South. At this early point, however, white Ohioans clearly struggled with the tension between commercial development and their economic and political ties with their southern neighbors.[34]

Instead of a gradual transition to a more northern and antislavery identity, Ohioans had a schizophrenic response to social and economic changes. Ohioans participated in a violent riot to drive African Americans out of Cincinnati, but two years later, seemingly in direct contradiction with the intentions of the Cincinnati riot, the legislature passed a law protecting African Americans from kidnapping. The 1831 law prohibited the illegal abduction and transportation of free blacks or mulattoes out of the state. With this law Ohioans tried to establish a limit to their willingness to placate their southern neighbors. However, Kentuckians regularly complained about Ohioans' unwillingness to help in the retrieval of fugitive slaves, which put Ohio leaders in a delicate political situation. In 1832 Democratic governor Robert Lucas worried that conflicts over fugitive slaves threatened Ohio's trade with the South. In an address to the Ohio Assembly, Lucas said about Kentucky, "Commerce" must "pass through her territory or touch her borders." Two years later the Ohio legislature tried to walk the line with a new statute. The legislature said that all African Americans who conformed to state law were legal residents of the state, but nothing would "bar the lawful claim" of any alleged runaway slaves. It was as if, to white Ohioans, the existence of a free African American population in the state was their "necessary evil." Ohioans did not want their state to be a pawn of southern interests, but neither would the state be a haven for fugitives. Therefore the question facing Ohioans was how best to manage the African American population. At this early stage, white Ohioans began making a key distinction between lawful and illicit border crossing, effectively dividing the African American population. White Ohioans began the process of marginalizing fugitive slaves as a means of defending and defining state sovereignty.[35]

In Indiana the local and national crises between 1818 and 1822 both highlighted the tension between state sovereignty and interstate commerce and suggested that Indianans had to find a better way to strike a balance between the two. Locally Indianans maintained their commitment to protecting their state against the encroachment of slavery. In 1823 Indianans considered the possibility of forming a convention to revise the state constitution, and the issue of the convention became intertwined with the issue of slavery. Kentuckians felt compelled to comment on Indiana's convention debate and the issue of slavery. In the *Louisville Public Advertiser*, one writer argued,

Whether the introduction of slaves to aid in clearing and cultivating their soil and in the performance of most other kinds of labor, would tend to increase their wealth and prosperity, and their relative weight in the confederacy, they are doubtless more capable to determine than we are. There is one important fact, however, which the opponents of the convention, seem to have entirely overlooked, viz., that the introduction of slaves into the new states, or the dissemination of them over a large tract of country, while it would enhance their value by opening new markets for them, and consequently ameliorate their condition, would not add one to the list of those in bondage.

The writer tried to remove morality from the issue, arguing that "the question therefore, may be fairly construed as a question of policy, and not as one of freedom or bondage." However, to a population already sensitive about the presence of slavery in the state, this read as a plot to make Indiana a slaveholding state. In response to this piece, the *Indiana Gazette* printed a piece saying, "A call of a convention, we have no doubt, is quite a popular theme throughout Kentucky. . . . It would afford such a fine market for their negroes." Indianans overwhelmingly voted down the convention, which the *Gazette* praised as a successful stand against the "plot to introduce slavery."[36]

But while Indianans overwhelmingly ratified the state's freedom from slavery, Indiana politicians also moved toward compromise with their southern neighbors. After failing to enforce the Act to Prevent Manstealing, Indiana legislators passed a new law more sympathetic to their southern neighbors in 1824. Judge Benjamin Parke, a former ally of Harrison, a slaveholder, and a well-known apologist for slavery, supervised the revision of the law. The new law allowed the claimant to secure a warrant from any county clerk and to make the arrest himself. After the arrest, the justice of the peace determined the case "in a summary way," and if decided in favor of the claimant, he/she received a certificate authorizing removal. The new law also limited the appeal process, requiring the appellant to pay the cost of the first trial and give security for the cost of the appeal. Essentially the new 1824 law changed the two factors that had caused the controversy over the removal of Susan, by allowing Kentuckians to make the arrest and limiting the financial accessibility of a legal appeal. Parke and others argued that the revisions simply brought Indiana's law closer in line with the Federal Fugitive Slave Law of 1793, which allowed slaveholders to apprehend alleged runaways anywhere in the country and offer only oral testimony as proof of their claims. Parke's revision suggests a move toward defusing the potentially volatile issue of fugitive reclamation. In addition in 1825 Indianans moved the state capital from Corydon, which was located just twenty-five miles from Louisville, to Indianapolis, which was about one hundred miles away. While Indianans chose Indianapolis because it was centrally located within the state, as an unintended consequence the move also took Indiana's seat of government out of the shadow of the Ohio River.[37]

After 1824 the issue of kidnapping virtually disappeared from Indiana newspapers, suggesting that the contest between freedom and slavery was losing its political saliency. However, Indiana politicians struggled to develop strategies that limited conflict, promoted commerce, and protected state sovereignty, a challenge complicated by the development of a labor system along the river that blended the characteristics of slavery and freedom. In 1825 James Brown Ray became the state's first governor not tied to the antislavery Jennings political alliance, which signaled the emergence of a new political era. Ray's decisions and statements about slavery reveal white Indianans' unsure responses to the social and economic changes of the 1820s.

On at least two occasions Governor Ray went out of his way to aid a Kentucky slaveholder in the retrieval of a runaway slave. In January 1826 Benjamin Ferguson petitioned Governor Ray to pardon Charles, an African American convicted of larceny. The petitioners claimed that Charles had committed his crime to protect himself from the claim of his master. The petitioners wrote, "As both the laws of congress and the laws of this state are silent upon the subject . . . we believe some remedy should be provided . . . both in regard to the private interest of the slaveholder and as it respects relations between non-slaveholding and slaveholding states bordering upon each other." Ray granted the petition and returned Charles to his alleged owner. In March 1826 Ephraim Dillingham petitioned Ray to pardon an African American man named Perry as "the most expeditious way of recovering his property." In this case the petitioner once again made the case for interstate harmony, arguing that "extending your prerogative in the present case would have a good effect [MS torn by seal] would have a tendency to remove the prejudices which slave holders entertain against us and also reconcile the feelings of our sister state." Again in this case Ray granted the pardon.[38]

However, in a controversial case in 1829, Governor Ray demonstrated that he was not an apologist for slavery. William Sewell, a Virginian emigrating from Virginia with four female slaves, a woman and three children, was detained for a few days because of high water in Indianapolis. Someone told the woman that in Indiana, a free state, they were free, and so they left Sewell. He retook them, and they were then brought to court on a writ of habeas corpus. The ensuing case apparently caused a considerable stir in Indiana's political community. Calvin Fletcher wrote of the event in his diary, "The house was full. Most of the members of the legislature were present. Great excitement among the people of the county. Their sympathies alive for the woman and children while the members of the legislature and some few who in our own place yet countenance the horrid traffic were almost clamorous for the pretended owner." Fletcher's entry suggests that legislators may have leaned more toward placating southerners' claims, while residents sympathized with the woman and her children. Fletcher testified on behalf of the woman and her children, but other politicians testified on behalf of the owner. The judge ruled against Sewall, arguing that his time in Indianapolis constituted residency, which negated any claims to ownership of the four females. Of the decision Fletcher wrote, "This decision will produce excitement. Most at least a majority of the members of the legislature were of opinion from some exciting cause just at this time not from sober reasoning from the principles contained in the constitution and laws of the country."[39]

Ray testified on behalf of the woman, which alienated him from political leaders in Indiana. James Noble, a longtime political leader in the state, publicly denounced Ray's testimony: "This governor Ray, had not long ago, through an erroneous judicial opinion, when a man was compelled to pass through the borders of the state, in consequence of freshets produced high rains, declared that the slaves he carried with him were free and entitled to all the rights of freemen; in consequence of which unjustifiable procedure, the individual was deprived of his property, which he held under the laws and constitutions as they now stand." Ray defended his actions by explaining that if a slaveholder entered a free state "not as an emigrant, but with an intention of making his slaves serve him, as such, in a free state, they could rightfully claim their freedom."[40]

Ray's actions, and his willingness to risk political alienation, suggest that he truly believed slavery was wrong. In speeches Ray denounced slavery as an "unnatural and unchristian" practice and called it a "mortifying spectacle . . . in the temple of human freedom." Indeed there is no reason to doubt the sincerity of Ray's statements, but they require further contextualization. Ray both disliked slavery and believed that slavery made African Americans unfit for freedom. He therefore sought to chart a course that freed Indiana from slavery, and all of its evils, as much as possible. He promoted the state's economic independence in a speech to the Indiana Assembly: "It is an error to presume that the people of Indiana can be induced or forced to abandon their favorite internal improvement and domestic manufacturing systems to secure to themselves the comfort and honor of wearing Georgia or Carolina cotton, whilst their own climate and soil, are capable of producing their variety of superior raw materials." But at the same time he asked the legislature to pass a law to "regulate for the future, by prompt correctives, the emigration into the State" by the "scourge of the oppressed." Ray clearly sought to free Indiana from slavery *and* from African Americans.[41]

In 1831 Indiana legislators passed a law that required every African American to post a five-hundred-dollar bond upon entry into the state and to register with the local courts. Legislators reasoned that if they could keep African Americans south of the border, they could keep the evil of slavery out of the state as well. This open exhibition of racism was legislators' declaration of Indiana's freedom from slavery, but one that would not upset their slaveholding neighbors. The law also made Indianans who employed unregistered African Americans subject to fines. Indiana Quakers protested the law as unjust and oppressive and took particular offense at the labor provisions of the law, suggesting that they may have hired black workers, perhaps even fugitive slaves. In linking freedom, free labor, and whiteness politicians crafted a vision for Indiana's lily-white future.[42]

Indiana Quakers were in the minority in their protests because the majority of white Indianans were on their way to dissociating the state from slavery. In 1831 Indianans elected the Virginia transplant Noah Noble as governor. During the election, a story appeared in the *Indiana Journal* claiming that Noble had sold a black girl back into slavery after she had gained her right to freedom by residence in a free state. Noble answered back, explaining that he and his bride had brought the woman west with the understanding that his father-in-law expected to reclaim her. The Nobles had stopped in Brookville, Indiana for two days before they arrived in Kentucky. They left the enslaved girl in Kentucky with Noble's mother. Noble's father-in-law then decided to stay in Virginia and instructed Noble to sell the girl, which he did in 1820. The publication of this story and Noble's response suggest that antislavery credentials were still important in the 1831 election. Noble carefully explained that he did not intend to keep a slave in Indiana. Therefore his decision to sell the woman, while an odious reminder of the evils of southern slavery, did not undermine Indiana's free soil; slavery remained south of the river. This story did little to damage Noble's reputation, as he still won the election and carried counties with large Quaker populations. When he settled in Indianapolis in 1833, Noble built a home in the Virginia style, complete with servants' quarters, and employed some emancipated slaves from Virginia as domestic servants.[43]

The apparent hypocrisy of Noble's actions likely did not violate Indianans' antislavery principles. By the end of the 1830s, white Indianans defined

African Americans as unfit for freedom politically, legally, and socially. If anything, Noble likely believed that in freeing his slaves and employing them as domestic servants he exhibited benevolence. He freed them from the chains of bondage and gave them gainful employment in positions that suited emancipated African Americans. His household symbolized "freedom" in Indiana.[44]

Similarly, John Tipton's ascension to the United States Senate in 1831 marked Indiana's racially defined freedom from slavery. Tipton kept black servants while living in Indiana, referring to "my black buoy" in his letters and his diary. However, on the Senate floor, Tipton fiercely defended free labor in Indiana. When he voted in favor of a protective tariff, he admitted to a friend, "my southern friends are all offended with me." Tipton distinguished his defense of free labor from agitation over slavery: "The tariff policy makes such a division of labour that the free states thrive, thrive indeed faster than the south who stick to nearly one occupation this is giving them a preponderance in the councils of the nation which the southron does not like to perceive, because he fears they may have sort of unholy enthusiasm and disturb the slavery relations which exist among them." Tipton made a clear statement that, in promoting free labor, he was not agitating against slavery. Instead he defined slavery as a uniquely southern institution and problem. There was no contradiction in Tipton's mind between aiding southerners in retrieving their human property, defending Indiana's freedom from the influence of southern slavery, and keeping black indentured servants at his residence in Indiana because he viewed freedom as a white man's privilege. He employed black servants because he believed that that occupation suited African Americans; he aided in the recovery of fugitive slaves because he believed that it was his duty to protect property rights and that it was not his place to attack southerners' social system; and he promoted free labor in Indiana because it offered the most promise for white Indianans.[45]

Racism among white Indianans was not a new phenomenon in the late 1820s. However, by the late 1820s white Americans' racism had begun to take on a new tone. The social changes wrought by the economic development along the river spurred a political response that defined Indiana's freedom along racial lines. White legislators and wealthy citizens in Ohio and Indiana increasingly viewed the presence of African Americans as a threat to their own freedom. Legislators used race to make fugitive slaves marginal citizens and permanently exclude them from society. In so doing they created a racial barrier to respectability by limiting employment opportunities. The law effectually made all African Americans in the state suspected fugitives, in that it forced all black Indianans to prove their freedom. Even in the free state of Indiana, dark skin color carried the assumption of slavery. Ironically this effort to free the state from slavery actually extended the domain of slaveholders across the river.

By the early 1830s Kentuckians had had to come to terms with the social realities of the state's need for slave labor. After the Panic of 1819 shook the economy, recovery in the 1820s had only increased the size of the black population. In 1830 African Americans made up nearly 25 percent of the total population, the highest proportion the state reached in the antebellum period. In addition to the size, the enslaved population in urban areas and along the river was increasingly mobile. Kentuckians' political response reflected fears over the growing black population but was a tacit recognition that slavery was a critical component of the Kentucky economy. Therefore in their efforts to control, and limit, the black population, they hung their hopes on gradual and "natural" emancipation.[46]

Kentuckians continued to make demands on the governments of Indiana and Ohio. In 1822 Kentucky's legislature asked legislators from Indiana, Illinois, and Ohio to sponsor a conference to discuss the problem of runaway slaves. Ohio agreed to appoint two commissioners, but nothing came of it in that state. Indianans revised their law on "manstealing" shortly after this request. Kentucky made similar requests in 1829 and again in 1837. Newspapers made public these requests and the results of the commissions. Typically legislators claimed that they were responding to the complaints of their constituents in their pronouncements. The publicity of these requests is significant because with it Kentucky legislators kept the issue present by renewing the requests. The public announcements were declarations of state sovereignty that forged a connection between elected leaders and citizens based on the protection of slavery. In this way Kentucky leaders publicly affirmed their commitment to slavery.[47]

However, Kentucky politicians had always prided themselves on the "mildness" of slavery in Kentucky, and they struggled with residents' increasing commitment to slavery. Legislators passed a nonimportation act in 1833 that satisfied both Kentuckians' commitment to slavery and their discomfort with that commitment. The act prohibited the importation of slaves for sale within the state, and all immigrants had to swear that they intended to become citizens of the state and did not intend to sell slaves.

Much like their northern neighbors, Kentucky legislators attempted to regain control of the Ohio River border by reducing the number of African Americans in the state. The goal was to control the growth of the African American population by limiting the importation of out-of-state slaves. However, residents were free to sell enslaved blacks within or outside the state.[48]

Legislators' had mixed motivations for passing this law. Some saw it as a means of lessening the states' dependence on slave labor and as a step toward gradual emancipation. Coupled with colonization, the nonimportation act gave these conservative antislavery Kentuckians the quixotic hope that slavery would naturally die away. Nonimportation promised to limit the growth of the population, and colonization would free the state from an emancipated black population. As this reasoning suggests, even into the 1830s Kentuckians had made little progress from the emancipation movement of the 1790s. Kentuckians still viewed slavery as a necessary evil, and they sought to limit the evils of slavery.

Some legislators voted for nonimportation because they believed it strengthened slavery in the state by reducing the threat of slave rebellion that accompanied a large enslaved population. In addition, by keeping interstate slave traders out of the state, the law promised to raise the price of slaves in the state by controlling market competition. Some of the proslavery supporters of the nonimportation act also supported colonization because they believed it strengthened slavery by eliminating the free black population. While these men were clearly committed to slavery, they had to be careful about their public pronouncements. When Robert Wickliffe, president of the Kentucky Colonization Society, made a speech explaining that the society had no intention of interfering with slavery or ridding slavery from the state, he found himself so alienated that he resigned from his position. While some Kentuckians may have been satisfied with the belief that slavery was necessary, they remained committed to viewing it as an evil.[49]

Kentuckians' support of nonimportation and colonization revealed the shared perception between legislators on both sides of the border that the safety of white freedom depended on maintaining racial barriers. This position distinguished Kentuckians from slaveholders in the Deep South who believed that white freedom depended on black slavery. Historians cite 1829–1833 as a turning point in the southern defense of slavery. In the Deep South, in response to the abolitionists' attacks on slavery, slaveholders began to see slavery as a central feature of southern life. In South Carolina apologists began defending slavery as a positive good. In the southwestern states, slaveholders defined slavery as vital to their economic opportunity. Kentuckians, however, continued to espouse slavery as a necessary evil, which was a perceived break with both strains of thought in the Deep South. The necessary-evil approach proved to be the perfect position for Kentuckians to balance their northern and southern interests.

In Kentucky and Deep South states, racial dominance was critical to white leaders' understandings of social power and stability. However, there were subtle distinctions. In Deep South states, leaders feared a disproportionate growth of the black population, but they remained committed to slavery as a social and economic system. Kentuckians, on the other hand, admitted to the "necessity" of slavery but expressed a reluctant commitment to the institution. The slave/free and black/white dichotomies were deeply intertwined in both regions, but the emphases differed. It might be fair to suggest that Deep South southerners would argue that enslavement required racial dominance, whereas Kentuckians might argue that racial dominance required enslavement. Definitions of freedom, in part, depended on comparison. White Indianans and Ohioans defined their freedom by comparing their states' whiteness to Kentucky, and Kentuckians defined their freedom by comparing their state's blackness to the blacker Deep South.[50]

*   *   *

No longer as a response to a specific incident or arising out of a general fear of dependents, white Americans by the 1830s specifically targeted the African American population itself as a problem. By 1833 the laws of the states on both sides of the Ohio River ensured that fugitives never stopped "passing" as free persons because African Americans needed proof of their freedom. Of course the irony of the reduced meaning of the border for black Americans was that it made the border gain meaning in the eyes of white Americans. In the 1830s white residents in both Ohio and Indiana celebrated their victory over slavery and heralded the Northwest Ordinance as a great bulwark against slavery. White Americans in Ohio and Indiana dissociated themselves from slavery by excluding black Americans from the body politic and making fugitives marginal citizens. In contrast to what was happening in eastern cities such as Boston and Philadelphia, where black

Americans' promotion of racial uplift sparked reactionary violence, along the Ohio River white Americans hardened their understanding of racial difference precisely because they believed that uplift was impossible. If slavery made African Americans unfit for freedom, racial prejudice prevented them from ever earning their freedom. The presence of the border made this circular logic of colonization both convenient and convincing because it made emancipation a concern for whites on both sides of the river. Slavery may have been a southern problem, but northerners and southerners shared the "problem" of a growing black population. Thus for many white Americans in the borderland, freedom from slavery meant, even depended on, freedom from African Americans.[51]

CHAPTER SIX

Fugitive Slaves and the Borderland

In the 1850s Richard Daly enjoyed considerable freedom for a man in bondage. Daly lived in Trimble County, Kentucky, on a plantation along the Ohio River owned by two brothers, Samuel and George Ferrin. He worked on the farm and regularly attended the market in Madison, across the river in the nominally free state of Indiana. He married Kitty, a house servant from a neighboring plantation, and they had four children before Kitty died in childbirth at the age of twenty. Daly protected his family the best he could and visited his children nightly. According to Daly's later description, in the 1850s he yearned to be free, but he also recognized that despite his enslaved status he still enjoyed some opportunities and autonomy. Daly understood that he could obtain freedom whenever he wanted, but he later claimed that he never thought about running away. He did not accept the legitimacy of slavery, nor was he satisfied with his enslaved status; by his own estimate he helped thirty slaves escape from bondage. However, Daly did not believe that the uncertain status he would hold in the "free" states was necessarily better. More important, his affection for his family overshadowed the advantages of freedom. Bondage conditioned his life, but love motivated him. He loved his family more than he wanted freedom. Only when "Mrs. Hoaglin," the woman who owned Daly's children, decided to give his daughter Mary to her own daughter in Louisville did he decide to escape slavery. For Daly, who had not considered escape before, running away or "stealing" his freedom and the freedom of his children became the only way he could keep his family intact. In 1857 the devoted father escaped to Canada with his four children.[1]

Daly's story provides a window into how personal considerations and the geographic border between slavery and freedom complicated the decisions of African Americans in the Ohio River Valley. The boundary between slavery and freedom carried special significance for African Americans because in crossing it they enjoyed the possibility of escaping their enslaved status. However, rather than defining a boundary that slavery could not penetrate, the Ohio River represented a periphery of both slavery and freedom, and the resulting racial and labor ambiguities both provoked violence and muddied distinctions between slave and free status. Consequently enslaved blacks faced substantial barriers to freedom that did not end at the Ohio River. The Fugitive Slave Laws of 1793 and 1850 enabled slaveholders to retrieve their escaped property throughout the country, meaning that fugitives' legal status did not change when they escaped to a free state. Fear of pursuit, punishment, and death strongly discouraged slaves from escaping north. As the former Kentucky slave Andrew Jackson noted, "If anyone wishes to know what were my feelings during this time, let them imagine themselves a slave, with the strong arm of the law extended over their heads—doomed, if retaken, to a severe punishment, and almost unendurable torture."[2]

In the Ohio River Valley, fugitives never stopped "passing" as free persons because African Americans needed proof of their freedom. Whites questioned and even jailed black Americans traveling without papers in Ohio, Indiana, and Kentucky on the suspicion that they were runaways. Madison Jefferson, a slave living along the Ohio River, was jailed in Ohio on three separate occasions while trying to escape. In Kentucky an appellate court ruled that "color and long possession are such presumptive evidences of slavery as to throw the burden of proof on a negro claiming freedom." The laws of the states on both sides of the Ohio River required free blacks to carry written proof of their freedom. In Ohio and Indiana free blacks had to post bonds and register with the local county court upon entering the state. Due largely to the efforts of the antislavery lawyer Salmon P. Chase, by 1841 the Ohio Supreme Court had determined that slaves brought voluntarily by their owners into Ohio were free. Fugitives, however, remained technically enslaved and, equally important, confronted a largely hostile white population in the state. The sheer number of kidnapping and violent reclamation incidents that appeared in Ohio newspapers attest to the dangers that black Americans faced in the region. Slavery was only an unvigilant moment away because the law put the burden of proof on African Americans, and dark skin color undermined the security that freedom supposedly guaranteed.[3]

Racism, in short, made free blacks "slaves without masters" throughout the country, a situation that was no different in the Ohio River Valley.

Indeed black Americans on both sides of the river found their occupational opportunity and physical mobility limited by race regardless of their legal status. For a small number of African Americans, freedom offered the opportunity to work for oneself. Moreover free blacks kept all of their wages and could better provide for themselves and their families. A few free blacks even amassed considerable fortunes. Washington Spradling, freed in 1814, worked as a barber in Louisville and by 1850 had amassed over thirty thousand dollars, much of which he used to purchase the freedom of thirty-three slaves. However, Spradling was in the minority, and many found little opportunity for advancement. After gaining his freedom, former slave J. C. Brown hoped to join the ranks of financially successful free blacks in the Ohio Valley. Brown tried to conduct his mason business on both sides of the Ohio River, but whites threatened him with violence and conspired to kidnap and sell him south, which ultimately convinced him to head to Canada. Brown's experience suggests that the racial limitations followed African Americans throughout the Ohio River Valley.[4]

After 1830 Kentucky's economy grew increasingly diverse, which in turn prompted many slaveholders to hire out their slaves. The freedoms associated with hiring out revealed the similarity of slave and free labor in the Ohio Valley. Hired bondspeople generally performed the same kinds of labor that free workers did. They worked in fields and factories, on steamboats and in hospitals, and as barbers, musicians, draymen, and most commonly as domestic servants. A select few self-hired slaves chose their employers, rented houses, and maintained a certain measure of control over their lives. Such work facilitated movement across the river and created unique opportunities for enslaved river workers. Some enslaved people who hired their own time resided in the same wards as free blacks. These hired slaves were well aware of what freedom along the border did and did not offer. As the Kentucky slave John Davis noted, "I can't say that I suffered anything particular down South; but they always kept my nose down to the grindstone, and never gave me anything for my labor." When Davis set out in pursuit of freedom, he did not settle in the free states immediately to the north. Instead he traveled to Canada because he believed that only there could he enjoy economic freedom; after sixteen years he had amassed thirty-five hundred dollars worth of property.[5]

The border juxtaposed the lived experiences of slavery and freedom in a way that gave enslaved Americans "a clear view of life outside of slavery." From this vantage point, border slaves could see the opportunities that freedom offered as well as those it limited. Consequently in their published narratives and recollections former slaves tended to portray the Ohio River as a borderland in which a slavelike experience characterized life on both banks. Some fugitives even concluded that because of the constraints imposed by race north of the Ohio River, freedom as a fugitive was not a desired state in and of itself. All things being equal, of course, African Americans chose freedom over slavery; however, all things were *not* equal, and slaves understood better than anyone the nature of slavery and freedom in the borderland. Former border slave Frederick Douglass said it best: "We knew of no spot this side of the ocean we could be safe. We had heard of Canada, then the only real Canaan for the American bondman, simply as a country to which the wild goose and swan repaired at the end of winter . . . but not as the home of man."[6]

In their narratives Kentucky slaves often described a point when an opportunity to escape presented itself but they decided not to run. These moments of decision—or indecision—reveal that enslaved African Americans along the border constantly evaluated the costs and benefits of an escape attempt. Historians can easily explain why field hands toiling on cotton plantations in antebellum Mississippi did not run away in large numbers. The sheer power of the white community combined with the forbidding distance to free territory ensured a minimal likelihood of success, while failure guaranteed severe physical punishment and perhaps sale. Proximity to the border, in contrast, offered enslaved people more opportunities to flee, but the barriers to successful escape remained high, as did the price of failure. African Americans understood that the stigma of slavery followed them across the border. So while they may have had the opportunity to flee across the river, they could not escape from slavery that easily. Thus many slaves along the border escaped only after a triggering event threatened to tear them away from their community or forced them to reevaluate their enslaved condition. The complicated motivations of slaves in the borderland suggest that while the desire for freedom always gave them a reason to escape, some enslaved people needed an additional rationale.[7]

In short, African Americans' experiences in the Ohio River Valley led them to view the region as a borderland in which slavery and freedom did not always represent antithetical conditions. While black Americans recognized the marked differences between the status of enslaved people south of the river and that of free people to the north, many concluded that freedom did not offer all the privileges that slavery denied, nor did slavery deny all the privileges of freedom. As a result, the decision to escape from bondage was rarely simple because the choice between slavery and freedom was far from intuitive. Recognizing the complicated motives of fugitives also enhances our understanding of them as rebels. As the historians John Hope Franklin and Loren Schweninger note, "To examine the motives of those who challenged the system does injustice to the complexities of the human experience," but at the same time exploring "the conditions and factors that caused slaves to go 'on the run' is one of the best ways to comprehend the attitudes of slaves." The present study, then, examines these human "complexities," particularly how personal and geographic conditions became reasons to flee. But such factors were only part of the story, because often the same reasons that induced some slaves to escape convinced others to endure bondage. To understand this apparent contradiction requires considering borderland slaves' understandings of slavery, their initial decisions not to escape, and the factors that sparked their ultimate decisions to run.[8]

*   *   *

Following his escape, former Kentucky slave Henry Blue explained that "some poor, ignorant fellows may be satisfied with their condition as slaves, but, as a general thing, they are not satisfied with being slaves." With this pithy comment, Blue made a careful distinction between the idea and the practice of slavery. He articulated how slaves both rejected the legitimacy of bondage and tolerated their conditions as slaves. Certainly, being well fed or properly clothed did not convince enslaved African Americans that slavery was preferable to freedom. Thus to African Americans freedom and bondage were about more than living conditions. Nonetheless there was a relationship between living conditions and slave/free status. Henry Bibb, when offering an account of his motivations for escape, wrote to his former owner, "You had it in your power to have kept me there much longer than you did. I think it is very probable that I would have been a toiling slave on your plantation today, if you had treated me differently." Bibb rejected the legitimacy of bondage; yet he admitted that his living conditions, and most importantly changes in those conditions, affected his personal motivations for rebellion. Historians have devoted thousands of pages to explicating the methods African Americans employed both to reject and to endure their bondage. In the borderland, where geography intermingled with slaves' personal motivations, the reasons for and methods of tolerating slavery were both unique and profoundly ordinary.[9]

As a slave in Madison County, Kentucky, south of Lexington, Lewis Clarke hired his own time, provided for his own room and board, and enjoyed considerable geographic mobility. In order to retain his liberties as a hired slave, Clarke denied his desire for freedom. As he later explained, "Now if some Yankee had come along and said 'Do you want to be free?' What do you suppose I'd have told him? . . . Why, I'd tell him to be sure that I didn't want to be free; that I was very well off as I was. If I didn't, it's precious few contracts I should be allowed to make." Clarke certainly wished for freedom, but he also wanted to remain in Kentucky because his close proximity to the border made gaining freedom a tangible possibility. So he put on the mask of a happy slave in order to protect his current situation. Only the threat of sale to the Deep South prompted Clarke to make his escape in 1841.[10]

During his flight, Clarke encountered a Baptist minister who suspected that he was a runaway and, according to Clarke, attempted to "read [his] thoughts." In order to allay the minister's suspicions, Clarke emphasized his favorable situation as a slave, noting, "I wondered what in the world *slaves could* run away for, especially if they had such a chance as I had had for the last few years." This apparently satisfied the minister, who believed that a slave who enjoyed so many privileges would not run away. Clarke closed this tensely comic conversation by adding, "I do very well, very well, sir. If you should ever hear that I had run away, be certain it must be because there is some great change in my treatment." With these words Clarke actually explained to his credulous white interlocutor why he was fleeing. Clarke had long entertained the idea of escape, but sale was the "great change" that convinced him to run away. On a Deep South cotton plantation Clarke would have few or no opportunities to hire out his time and live independently. More important, sale away from the border extinguished his hope for eventual freedom. Nearness to the North did not ameliorate the conditions of bondage; indeed slaves such as Clarke regularly detailed the injustices of slavery in the borderlands. However, they tolerated harsh treatment because they believed that the relative proximity of the free states held out the possibility of eventual freedom.[11]

While the border provided hope for freedom, escape was still a risky endeavor precisely because the insatiable demand for bondspeople in the "cotton kingdom" of the Deep South transformed the border South into a slave-exporting region. Indeed selling slaves south became a profitable business during the antebellum period, and planters commonly punished unsuccessful runaways with sale south. The internal slave trade moved close to one million slaves from the Eastern Seaboard and the upper South to the cotton plantations of the Southwest. Kentucky exported about 22 percent of its male slaves between the ages of ten and nineteen in the 1850s, whereas Mississippi imported 27 percent of its male slaves of the same age. Between 1830 and 1860 the percentage of African Americans in Kentucky's population dropped from about 25 to 21 percent. Most slaves either experienced sale personally or witnessed the sale of family members, friends, and fellow slaves, often at public auctions. Sale was the fullest expression of the brutal individuating force of slavery because it broke all ties of kinship, leaving slaves totally isolated.[12]

The slave trade along western rivers represented a material link between the Ohio River borderlands and the Deep South, one that placed Kentucky slaves in a precarious position. Sale generated the greatest fear among slaves in the upper South and became the most common trigger for escape. Sale left borderland slaves with two options: take a chance at freedom by heading north or endure a lifetime of servitude and die a slave in the Deep South. As Kentucky slave Harry Smith recalled, "going to New Orleans was called the Nigger Hell, few ever returning who went there." When local enslaved people became "aware of the presence of . . . slave buyers," he noted, "a number of them would run away to the hills and remain often a year before they returned. Some would reach Canada for fear of being sold." Likewise, when Louisville slave Henry Morehead learned of his family's potential sale to the Deep South, he decided it was time to act. "I knew," he remembered, "it was death or victory." The slave trade brought the oppression of bondage in the Deep South to the borderland, a fact that the antislavery novelist Harriet Beecher Stowe dramatized in her account of Eliza Harris's escape attempt across the Ohio River in the opening pages of *Uncle Tom's Cabin*. Robert Nelson, another Kentucky slave, ran north after his master mortgaged him. "The sheriff got after me," Nelson recalled, "and I ran to Canada" without money or an apparent plan because "I was to have been taken to a cotton farm in Louisiana."[13]

Of course, slaves ran away for a variety of reasons. The historians Franklin and Schweninger provide a detailed survey of the many factors that prompted escape throughout the antebellum South, ranging from fear of punishment, to change in ownership, to simple opportunity or emotion. Many slaves required no specific trigger at all, finding enough motivation in their hatred of slavery and desire for freedom. In their published narratives, in contrast, most former Kentucky slaves described their flight as a rational response to specific events. In particular, many carefully evaluated how escape would impact their hopes for self-purchase, family unity, and self-improvement. Each of these triggers, however, functioned both as prompts to escape and as deterrents against flight. In short, the very factors that enabled former slaves to endure their bondage eventually prompted them to escape. This duality lies at the heart of understanding why and when Kentucky slaves decided to escape their bondage.[14]

*　　*　　*

Though slave hiring enabled a small number of Kentucky slaves to earn enough to pay their owners and save money to purchase their freedom, most hired slaves could only pay their owners and feed and clothe themselves. Lavinia Bell, for example, hired herself as a washerwoman for eleven years and made just enough money to cover food, shelter, doctors' bills, and clothing for her young children. Her husband earned three hundred dollars a year working in a hotel but was able to keep only five dollars a year for himself. Their owner hired their children out when they turned eleven. For the Bell family, hiring out was hardly a step toward freedom, and as Lavinia lamented, it separated her from her children for long periods of time. As census data reveal, moreover, the Bells' experience was common. Between 1790 and 1860 the percentage of African American freemen in Kentucky remained low, rising from roughly 1 to 4.5 percent of the state's black population. In the border slave state of Maryland, in contrast, the free black population grew from around 7 to nearly 50 percent of the state's African American population in the same years. While some slaves who purchased their freedom moved to free states and Canada, the slow growth of Kentucky's free black population indicates the limited opportunities for self-purchase in the state. Even in Louisville, where owners commonly hired out their slaves as domestics and in the tourism and manufacturing sectors, free blacks made up only 3 percent of the city's African American population in 1850. Indeed former slaves who escaped from the state commonly cited a broken promise of self-purchase as their reason for fleeing. The frequency of this trigger reveals the bias of published narratives, which tended to be written by privileged bondsmen rather than by field hands, but it also suggests that those slaves who had the opportunity to purchase their freedom were more likely to escape.[15]

The causal relationship between self-purchase and escape was complicated, however, because the promise of future freedom operated as a contract between slaveholder and slave. Self-purchase functioned like a free labor contract, putting a time limit on servitude and creating a mutual obligation between enslaved and slaveholder. African Americans' need for proof of freedom allowed owners to extract labor from extremely mobile slaves while reducing the threat of escape. Once they had entered into an agreement, slaves strove to earn and expressed great pride in their ability to purchase their freedom. "If a slaveholder offers his servant freedom, on condition that he will earn and pay a certain sum, and the slave accepts freedom on that condition," explained ex-slave Henry Blue, "he is bound in honor to pay the sum promised." Other slaves worked in Cincinnati to purchase their freedom from Kentucky owners. Richard Keys paid $20 per month for twelve years and then paid an additional $850 for his freedom, while another individual worked in the city and sent his master $100 every year for seven years before receiving his free papers.[16]

Not all slaves accepted this logic, but some former slaves stated quite plainly that the prospect of self-purchase kept them from running away. Josiah Henson led fellow slaves from Virginia to his owner's brother in Kentucky via the Ohio River. Despite prodding from free blacks in Cincinnati, Henson encouraged his fellow slaves not to run. "The idea of running away," Henson later explained, "was not one that I had ever indulged. I had a sentiment of honor on the subject, or what I thought such, which I would not have violated even for freedom." Henson's "sentiment of honor" seems to have embarrassed him later in life when he dictated his narrative, and he likely used the phrase pejoratively. Nonetheless while enslaved he apparently accepted the appropriateness of purchasing his freedom. Owners used the future prospect of freedom to secure short-term loyalty and labor from their slaves. And because it functioned as a deterrent to escape, owners allowed their most trusted and privileged bondsmen considerable mobility and freedom to labor. Mobility was, however, a double-edged sword, convincing some slaves to make their escape.[17]

Slaveholders' willingness to break these contracts by refusing freedom, raising the price of purchase, or selling the slave down the river also frequently triggered escape. The Kentucky slave Alfred Jones explained that he made an arrangement to purchase his freedom for $350, but "before the business was completed, I learned that my master was negotiating with another party to sell me for $400." Upon learning of this betrayal, Jones wrote himself a pass and left for Canada. Likewise the enslaved millwright Jonathan Thomas contracted with his owner to buy himself for $1,000 and by the age of thirty-three had paid his master $400. But the untimely death of the master left the estate to a son, who promptly sold Thomas to a slave trader. An angry Thomas approached the son and informed him of the agreement "with old master for my freedom" and that he "had paid . . . four hundred dollars towards it." The son, however, denied knowledge of the agreement and "cared nothing about it." In response, Thomas made arrangements for his free wife and children to travel to Canada and then made his escape.[18]

The contract of self-purchase functioned as a pathway to freedom for Blue, a reason not to run for Henson, and, once broken, a motivation for escape for Jones and Thomas. In all these cases their participation in the market economy informed their understanding of freedom and slavery. These former slaves recognized self-purchase as a morally just method of "earning freedom," and its prospect made temporarily enduring bondage more honorable than escape, which broke the contract. Historians' discussions of self-hiring and self-purchase as steps toward freedom or as other forms of exploitation are incomplete when they focus on the end result because self-purchase began with slaves' understanding of freedom as a product of the market. For them, self-ownership was freedom, and this market conception of liberty enabled them to tolerate market slavery in the borderland. As the Kentucky slave Israel Campbell explained after having to delay his self-purchase: "Now that my hopes were deferred, I settled down to the conviction that things were not so bad, after all,—that I was well treated, had plenty to eat, allowed a fine riding horse, kept cattle, hogs, chickens, bees, had shoemakers' and carpenters' tools; and I settled down to the conviction that it would be better for me to remain as I was awhile longer." Campbell's grudging acceptance of his enslaved situation suggests that he believed freedom in the borderlands would effect only limited change in his work and physical conditions. Still, Campbell wanted to buy his liberty, and the fact that he conceived of freedom as something he could purchase reveals his understanding of how the market shaped both slavery and freedom. Freedom had a price.[19]

In the 1850s the price of freedom increased dramatically for Kentucky slaves, fueled by the growth of the interstate slave trade. Prime field hands valued at $400 in the 1830s sold for more than $1,500 twenty years later. In 1849 Kentucky repealed a nonimportation law enabling whites to bring slaves into Kentucky for the purpose of sale. The repeal increased the volume of slave sales within the state, spurring the growth and increasing the sophistication and profitability of the domestic slave trade. By the 1850s several large slave-trading firms based their operations in Kentucky, and the state's white residents shipped thirty-four hundred slaves annually to the Deep South. In order to regulate the rising trade, the city of Louisville passed an 1851 ordinance requiring slave vendors to purchase a $300 license each. The sharp spike in slave prices put the prospect of self-purchase out of reach for many enslaved people, as the price of freedom rose from under $1,000 in the 1830s and 1840s into the thousands in the decade before the Civil War. The washerwoman Mrs. Lewis Bibb, for example, paid $323 for her freedom in 1833, while in 1859 Lydia Reed and her husband used their lottery ticket winnings to purchase their freedom for $2,125. In short, the increasing difficulty of purchasing freedom made escape the only option for many Kentucky slaves.[20]

Family ties influenced the lives of even more enslaved African Americans in Kentucky than did the prospect of self-purchase. Historians have demonstrated that family provided the first line of defense against the isolation of bondage throughout the antebellum South. Familial affection both eased the suffering under bondage and created ties that made slaves think twice about escape. Group flight presented multiple challenges, making it more difficult for runaways to blend into the surroundings, find shelter, and gather food, but individual escape required fugitives to abandon their families to the yoke of bondage. William Wells Brown's affection for his mother and sister tied him to slavery more than the force of his master did. Brown worked on steamboats that plied the Mississippi River and admitted that he had many opportunities to escape. When he thought of escaping to Canada, however, his "resolution would soon be shaken by the remembrance that my dear mother was a slave in St. Louis, and I could not bear leaving her in that condition." Brown felt a tension between his desire for freedom and his affection for his kin, but he endured slavery to remain with his family.[21]

Throughout the South family ties complicated slaves' decisions to run, but for borderland slaves the nearness of the free states emphasized the matter of choice in escape. The proximity of the border both increased the chance of successful escape and highlighted the tension between family ties and the desire for freedom. Some slaves sacrificed freedom to save their families. Mrs. L. Strawthor, a free black woman from Kentucky, recalled that her husband had earned enough to purchase his family before he was sold to the Deep South. Strawthor never saw her husband again and was unsure if he remained alive. In other cases the loss of family members convinced those remaining to make their breaks. The wife and children of enslaved Kentucky blacksmith George Ramsey belonged to another owner who sold them to the Arkansas Territory. "I went after her once, and got her," Ramsey recalled, "but they took her away from me. Canada was not in my head till I lost her completely, and then I thought I would go." Similarly, J. D. Green explained, "From 18 to 27 I was considered one of the most devout christians among the whole Black population, and under this impression I firmly believed to run away from my master would be to sin against the Holy Ghost—for such we are taught to believe—but from the time of my wife's being sent away, I firmly made up my mind to take the first opportunity to run away." In each of these examples distance interacted with family ties. Former slaves lamented that sale to the Deep South shattered the connection between husband and wife, but they also realized that those family members transported far from the border had little chance to gain freedom. While families remained together slaves endured their bondage because they hoped eventually to gain freedom as a group. When sale extinguished this hope—when a spouse or child was lost to slavery—those who remained in the upper South saw no reason to suffer bondage further. Without family, only freedom mattered.[22]

However, escape north also threatened family ties. Mary Younger fled to Canada without her children and sadly recalled, "The barbarity of slavery I never want to see again. I have children now who have got the yoke on them. It almost kills me to think that they are there, and that I can do them no good. There they are—I know how it is—it brings distress on my mind." William Brown, another former slave who escaped to Canada, expressed similar grief: "It is three years ago that I left my family, and I don't know whether they are dead or alive. I want to hear from them." In contrast, at least one slave used escape to Indiana to keep his family together. John Moore ran away from his owner in Kentucky in 1850, hiring his time in Indiana. Two months later he returned to Kentucky, gave his wages to his master, and announced that "he was sick of freedom, and the abolitionists."

He also pretended that he wanted nothing to do with his wife and children, who lived on a neighboring farm. Moore hoped that his subterfuge would enable him to gain the confidence of local slaveholders and make it easier for him to free his family. His plan worked. Convinced that the family had no plans to escape, the neighboring owner gave Moore's wife permission to visit her husband on Saturday night and return on Sunday. Once together, the couple fled to Canada. In short, Moore's temporary foray into Indiana was a stepping stone in his effort to free his family. When the Moores sought permanent freedom, they escaped to Canada beyond the reach of the Fugitive Slave Law.[23]

Former Kentucky slave Henry Bibb's escapes from slavery highlight how distance from the Ohio River borderland sharpened the distinction between freedom and slavery. Bibb demonstrated incredible devotion to his family in his repeated attempts to rescue his wife and child from bondage. He lived as a slave in Shelby County, Kentucky, near Louisville, and escaped north on three separate occasions, finally securing his freedom in 1841. Each time Bibb escaped, however, the duplicity of white and black Americans in southern Ohio made him vulnerable to recapture. He could escape the grasp of his master in Kentucky, but he could never become truly free in Ohio because of the constant risk of recapture. Nonetheless Bibb placed himself in danger and returned to Kentucky because he wanted to save the wife and child he had left behind. "I felt," he wrote, "as if love, duty, humanity, and justice, required that I should go back." For Bibb, freedom was not as sweet without his wife. Bibb made his final escape after his owner sold him and his wife and they were taken to the Deep South. With permanent slavery looming, Bibb's commitment to freedom became equally permanent. When sale separated him from his wife in Louisiana, Bibb decided to make his final escape and did not stop until he reached Detroit, far enough north to secure his freedom once and for all.[24]

Even after Bibb reached Detroit, he did not give up hope of saving his wife. He returned to Madison, Indiana, four years later in 1845 to inquire after her and learned that she was "living in a state of adultery" with her owner. Feeling betrayed, Bibb announced, "she has ever since been regarded as theoretically and practically dead to me as a wife." Before this discovery, however, Bibb remained committed to his family. In an 1844 letter to his former owner, Bibb explained that the master's constant whipping of his wife and child "drove me from home and family, to seek a better home for them." Slavery left Bibb helpless to safeguard his family, and he originally escaped in order to find a way to protect them. The fate of his wife demonstrated, however, that Bibb's vulnerability followed him into freedom. Bibb had wanted liberty to protect his family, but the tenuousness of that freedom prevented him from saving his family from slavery. The loss of his wife destroyed Bibb's hopes of having both family and liberty, leaving individual freedom as his only choice.[25]

Bibb demonstrated that family devotion could be a powerful motivation for escape. As mothers charged with the care of their children, enslaved women shared motivations for escape similar to those of male slaves. Indeed more female than male slaves resided in Kentucky, especially in Louisville, and women were as likely to be sold and hired out as men were, though they usually served as domestic workers and washerwomen. Nonetheless men made 80 percent of the escape attempts from Kentucky before 1850 and 73 percent thereafter. Though the percentage of women runaways in Kentucky was higher than elsewhere in the South, they still fled in far fewer numbers than did enslaved men. The historians Franklin and Schweninger argue that fewer women escaped because they had to care for children and most could not withstand the physical demands necessary to escape. More broadly, limited opportunity and a sense of responsibility for the welfare of their families stifled female escape attempts.[26]

Slave women in the borderland often lived apart from husbands, many of whom resided on other farms or were hired out to work elsewhere. As a result the responsibilities of child care fell largely to women. Hired female slaves had to earn enough to pay their owners and support themselves and their children. The Kentucky slave Charlotte, for example, worked as a washerwoman to support her family. She took pride in her ability to fend for her family, even covering the difference when her employed children failed to make their contractual earnings. "I get along very well," she stated; "you couldn't pay me to live at home, if I could help myself. My master doesn't supply me with anything . . . no more than if I didn't belong to him." Charlotte tolerated her bondage because she lived on her own and could provide for her children. If given the option, slave women such as Charlotte undoubtedly would have purchased their freedom, but few had that choice. A number of factors worked against them. Multiple children placed the purchase price out of reach for many. Equally important, gender limited the occupational opportunities of female slaves. Most worked as domestic servants, washerwomen, and in other service professions, jobs that offered low wages and limited their mobility in comparison to the work performed by some enslaved men. For example, Cox worked as a steamboat steward and earned "$250 a year for myself when I hired my time." Cox made enough money to pay his owner and purchase his freedom for $2,100, an amount beyond the reach of a washerwoman such as Charlotte. In short, enslaved women's circumscribed opportunities limited the possibility that self-purchase could become a motivation for escape.[27]

Charlotte was relatively fortunate compared to other slave women because she did not witness the sale of her children. In the upper South approximately one of three slave children suffered separation from their families through sale. Most cruelly, slaveholders made slave women care for their children until they reached an age when they could work and then tore them away by sale. Advertisements for runaways indicate that the threat of such sales inspired some enslaved women to attempt escape with their children. However, female slaves' limited mobility and the difficulty of traveling with children reduced the number of women who ran away. Instead women protected their children at home. Households depended on women for their survival, and many enslaved women viewed escape as the abandonment of their responsibilities to their families. Enslaved women's resistance to slavery was more likely to take the form of temporary truancy than permanent escape. In addition slaveholders punished enslaved women more frequently than they did men for verbal and physical resistance. The separation of husbands and wives coupled with the constant threat of sale likely heightened enslaved women's protectiveness of their children. They best protected themselves and their families by staying put.[28]

Enslaved women also sought to defend their bodies. They understood the difficulties of escape, the possibility that failure could result in sale, and that transfer to a new owners could increase their risk of sexual exploitation. Historians do not know how widespread rape was among slave women, but the rapid growth of the mulatto population and its prevalence in slave narratives suggests that interracial sex was widespread. Women who were not sexually exploited likely understood that they could protect their bodies by remaining in their current situations. Stasis, then, could be a means for enslaved women to resist bondage and control their bodies within the unequal power dynamics of slavery. Although Kentucky bondswomen faced difficult circumstances in slavery, many may have concluded that freedom was not worth running the risk of sale.[29]

The actions of Margaret Garner, a slave woman who lived eighteen miles from Cincinnati in Boone County, Kentucky, highlight how the threat of rape and attempts to protect family shaped the perspective of slave women. Garner served as a nurse for her owner's child and even accompanied the family to Cincinnati in 1840. In 1849 her owner sold his slaves, including the pregnant Garner, to his brother. She soon gave birth to two daughters, Mary and Cilla, who contemporaries described as "nearly white" and "bright mulatto," respectively. Though no conclusive evidence exists, Garner's new owner may have fathered these children. What is certain is that after the birth of her two girls, Garner determined that escape was the only means to protect her family and herself. The opportunity to flee came during the harsh winter of 1856. When the Ohio River froze, the Garner family crossed the river on foot and hid in the Cincinnati home of Elijah Kite. Alerted to the presence of the fugitives, federal marshals descended on the Garners. When they burst into Kite's cabin, they saw Garner holding a knife dripping with blood, screaming that she had killed one child and would murder the rest rather than see them reduced to slavery. Garner's actions represented an extreme manifestation of enslaved women's protective instinct. But the same protectiveness motivated female slaves who lived with their children and did not suffer sexual exploitation to forgo freedom and endure their bondage. In short, the experiences of women highlight how and why their families influenced slaves' decisions to flee.[30]

For slaves who lacked nuclear families or whose families had been torn apart by sale, the African American community provided emotional, psychic, and sometimes physical support. In response to the isolation, prejudice, and instability that were part of life in the Ohio River Valley, mobile slaves mingled with free African Americans and built communities that emphasized racial solidarity and muted the distinctions between slavery and freedom. This process took place most often in urban places that afforded greater opportunities for interaction between free and enslaved African Americans, but it embraced the entire black community. Slaves who worked on small farms and plantations often ran errands in urban centers and interacted with African American residents. The church formed the center of the black community on both sides of the river, and within it African Americans, enslaved and free, developed racial solidarity. Black ministers traveled throughout the Ohio Valley and preached sermons of deliverance and liberation in the black churches. For rural slaves who had limited interaction beyond the plantations, the division between black and white mirrored the division between enslaved and free. However, the correlation between race and status muted the distinction between slavery and freedom because in the experience of plantation-bound slaves the division between black and white superseded the division between enslaved and free. Thus even among less mobile rural slaves race reinforced status.[31]

Whether blacks were enslaved on isolated hemp plantations in the Kentucky interior, hired out in Louisville, or lived as free people in Cincinnati, the African American community provided better protection against the hazards of white racism than the law did. When whites kidnapped Frank Cranshaw, a Louisville slave active in the black religious community, and held him on a docked steamboat, crowds of local African Americans, mostly fellow members of his church, marched to the river. The protest prompted the sheriff to check the boat, where he discovered Cranshaw. Learning that Cranshaw had been illegally seized, the sheriff released him. In Cincinnati the African Methodist Episcopal Church served as a safe house for fugitives, and church members often harbored and aided fugitives. Despite repeated attacks by white mobs, Cincinnati's African American community grew and matured through the antebellum years.[32]

In contrast, blacks found that isolation increased their vulnerability. As Mrs. Colman Freeman, a free black woman, explained, "I lived in Ohio ten years, as I was married there,—but I would about as lief live in the slave States as in Ohio. In the slave States I had protection sometimes, from people that knew me—none in Ohio." Freeman believed that she was vulnerable to white racism regardless of which side of the river she lived on. Personal contacts had a greater impact on her safety than did geographic location. For African Americans such as Freeman who found solace in the protection and solidarity afforded by the black community, the river did not constitute a clear border. Indeed for many slaves escape meant leaving behind friends and the protection of the black community for an uncertain and potentially dangerous future.[33]

Still, many borderland slaves found the known future of slavery more distressing than the uncertainties of freedom. As Henry Bibb noted, the "idea of utter helplessness, in perpetual bondage," was "distressing" because there was "no period even with the remotest generation when it shall terminate." Slaves such as Bibb and Margaret Garner strained against the bonds of slavery in part because their helplessness undermined notions of personal improvement. Nothing highlighted how slavery destroyed the possibility of future improvement more than raising enslaved children. African Americans in the Ohio Valley believed that education was the key to their children's future, and once out of bondage they set to work educating their children. After purchasing his wife and children, former slave Andrew Fredhew sent two of his daughters to Oberlin College. Likewise Cox, the steamboat steward, sent his children and his nephews to school after he purchased his freedom. In contrast, enslaved parents had few opportunities to improve their children's situations. Both Bibb and Garner fled from bondage in hopes of salvaging their children's future. But crossing the river did not ensure greater access to schools. In fact, Ohio blacks complained bitterly about the unequal educational opportunities in the state. As Henry Johnson explained: "I left the States for Canada, for rights, freedom, liberty. I came to Buxton [Ontario] to educate my children. I lived twenty-three years in Massillon, Ohio, and was doing well at draying and carting— wanted for nothing—had money when I wanted it, and provisions plenty. But my children were thrust out of the schools, as were all the colored children—one must know how I would feel about it."[34]

When enslaved people viewed bondage as the ultimate impediment to personal improvement, freedom became the only viable alternative. Notions of improvement depended on individual identity and varied from slave to slave. For some, it rested in their children's future. In contrast, after his religious conversion Kentucky slave Francis Fedric equated freedom with spiritual development. "Work, work, work, one day like another," he wrote, "only I had now been to several prayer-meetings, and had got a knowledge of religion, which comforted me. I thought about the future, when I should be free from my master." Fedric decided to run away after his master flogged him for attending a prayer meeting, which Fedric viewed as an impediment to spiritual growth. For Fedric, religion marked the distinction between slavery and freedom; only as a free man could he overcome the barriers to spiritual progress created by slavery. Fugitive slaves who shared Fedric's belief in individual progress distinguished between the physical conditions and the personal limitations of slavery. Lewis Clarke, for example, admitted that he did not suffer much as a slave in Kentucky and that he had as much autonomy as most free African Americans. He lamented, however, that "a slave can't be a man! Slavery makes a brute of a man." "It was not my enslavement, at the then present time, that most affected me," explained Frederick Douglass; "the being a slave *for life*, was the saddest thought." Many fugitive slaves suffered the physical cruelties of slavery, but their concern for individual improvement convinced them of the unbearable personal limitations of bondage.[35]

Historians link Americans' fascination with self-improvement to the nineteenth-century rise and maturation of the market economy. The new middle class embraced personal growth, they argue, in response to the market economy's disruption of the traditional social order. Slaves at the border who lived and worked among white and black free persons may have imbibed this desire for improvement from their free neighbors. But the narratives and recollections of former slaves suggest that something else was at work—namely, that bondage itself contributed to their interest in self-improvement. For upper South slaves, proximity to the border offered hope for liberty, hope for the future, and hope that their aspirations for self-improvement might be achieved.[36]

*   *   *

In their narratives, borderland fugitives recognized how the limitations imposed by race on both sides of the river often overshadowed the differences between the border slave states and free states. For African Americans in the Ohio Valley, slavery was national. As former Kentucky slave Lewis Clarke wrote after he escaped his bondage: "I am yet accounted a slave, and no spot in the United States affords an asylum for the wanderer. True, I feel protected in the hearts of the many warm friends of the slave by whom I am surrounded; but this protection does not come from the LAWS of any one of the United States." Despite his successful flight across the Ohio River, Clarke could not legally escape from slavery entirely. In fact, Clarke suggested that the law offered him no protection. Instead the antislavery community kept him out of bondage.[37]

Without a clear sanctuary, enslaved and free African Americans made efforts to "establish relations and values suitable to a world without enslavement." Ironically, their ability to do so allowed slavery to function at the border. Historians have long understood the attempt to turn a human being into chattel, or the chattel principle, as the central contradiction inherent to human slavery. As the historian James Oakes has argued, "slaves affected the political system by intruding themselves into it as runaways, criminals, victims and witnesses. Because every time the law recognized the slave as a person it reputed the very essence of slavery." However, on the borderland whites viewed enslaved African Americans as *human* property. In fact, they relied on the humanity of the enslaved to limit the threat of escape, and in so doing limit the potential for conflict with their free-state neighbors.[38]

In the borderland the perspective of the enslaved, a point of view made possible by the liminality of the lived experience of slavery and freedom, revealed a disconnect between more formal political antislavery actions and personal resistance. Antislavery activists could not make the Ohio River a firm barrier because they had to recognize the legitimacy of fugitive reclamation. Instead they made distinctions between illegal kidnapping and legal reclamation. However, as Lewis Clarke's statement suggested, from the perspective of the enslaved, there was no difference between the two, and the legality of reclamation meant that the region would always be a borderland. On this borderland the fugitive could never be entirely free.

CHAPTER SEVEN

The Nature of Antislavery in the Borderland

In 1851 Harriet Beecher Stowe used the borderland, a region that white Americans built through compromise, to inflame the conflict between the North and the South, with her book *Uncle Tom's Cabin*. Stowe's story began in Kentucky and was set in motion by the movement of one enslaved African American toward freedom and another toward slavery. The threat of sale compelled Eliza to take her child and escape across the Ohio River toward freedom and a new life. In contrast, sale took Uncle Tom to New Orleans, where he found increasingly difficult bondage and eventually died. Slavery pulled Tom farther south against his will, whereas Eliza had to actively pursue her freedom. Stowe used this characteristic pattern of movement in the borderland to excite the sympathies of white northerners. Outside the borderland, Stowe's book electrified northern resistance to the Fugitive Slave Law and propelled the country toward civil war. As a resident of Cincinnati, Stowe had firsthand experience with white Americans' resistance to radical action, and her book was a call to action for borderland residents who preferred a more "natural" solution to the issue. While the antislavery movement grew in strength as a result of Stowe's book, in the borderland the antislavery movement could not escape the influence of the very border that Stowe tried so hard to politicize.[1]

In the 1830s and 1840s borderlanders developed formal and organized antislavery movements based on the informal antislavery activities of residents along the border. In many ways the black convention movement, the white abolition movement, and the legal distinctions between kidnapping and reclamation were distillations of the unorganized, and sometimes contradictory, day-to-day antislavery conflicts along the river. The informal antislavery actions of white and black Americans were tied to the social conditions of the borderland. In particular the slave trade created a racial divide in residents' economic relationship to the Ohio River. In response to increasing sales to the Deep South, free and enslaved African Americans tried to protect themselves from commodification. In contrast, white Americans moved along and across the river in order to take advantage of both legitimate and illicit river commerce. Their freedom of movement encouraged a diversity of opinion on the border, because, unlike black Americans, they did not have an imminent common threat. White northerners attempted to defend their states from intrusions by outsiders but recognized Kentuckians' legal right of reclamation. Kentuckians defended their rights to reclamation but imagined a gradual and peaceful process of emancipation freeing them from the necessary evil of slavery. Residents clashed, often violently, but social and economic connections limited political differences even over slavery. Borderland residents refused to let the border between slavery and freedom define their interactions, even though they could not escape its influence.[2]

*   *   *

Beginning with the growth of the slave trade and ending with the convention movement in the late 1840s, there was a chain of action that connected the social conditions of the borderland with black Americans' formal protests against slavery. The growth of the slave trade in Kentucky expedited the unwilling movement of black Americans down the river to the Deep South. This constant threat of coerced movement forced black Americans along the river to defend themselves. Self-defense, in its variety of forms, was the most common informal act of resistance. As this informal antislavery activity transitioned into the more formal protests of the convention movement in the late 1840s, free black leaders advocated legal protection against kidnapping through the repeal of the black laws. Therefore, in order to understand the rise and the goals of the black antislavery movement in the Ohio River Valley, we must first understand how the river border influenced the movement of black Americans.

The growth of the slave trade throughout the 1830s and 1840s made Kentucky a point of departure for enslaved blacks. Steamboats and coffles regularly transported enslaved blacks down to the bustling markets in Natchez and New Orleans. As demonstrated, sale also induced the movement of blacks across the Ohio River to Ohio and Indiana. Some enslaved blacks who escaped settled in cities such as Louisville, Cincinnati, New Albany, and Madison. These patterns of movement, in combination with the racial limitations to freedom and the commodification of laborers, destabilized life for African Americans.

Commodification complicated the lives of free African Americans who lived and worked along the river. Aaron Siddles lived in Indiana, but he recalled that "it was not safe, for any loafing white might destroy or steal, and unless a white man were by to see it, I could get no redress." He remembered an incident when seven white residents broke the windows of his home "without provocation." Siddles "put some small shot in the backs of two of them" as they ran away. Siddles stated that he was "much esteemed and respected" in Indiana but that he still had to defend himself. The lack of protection eventually convinced men such as Siddles to move to Canada. Whereas white Americans lived and worked along the Ohio in order to take advantage of the river's connections with the South, black Americans did so in spite of those connections. As a result, in the borderland African Americans rooted their antislavery actions in the necessity of self-defense.[3]

For many enslaved blacks, controlling and protecting their bodies were necessary steps on the path to freedom. Enslaved African Americans understood that the Ohio River controlled their movement in two ways. First, the flowing water of the Ohio posed a formidable barrier. Henry Bibb explained, "I have fled to the highest hills of the forest, pressing my way to the North for refuge; but the river Ohio was my limit. To me it was an impassable gulf." The ferries and steamboats that plied the river joined the natural barrier of the flowing water. Bibb said, "I have stood upon the lofty banks of the river Ohio, gazing upon the splendid steamboats, wafted with all their magnificence up and down the river, and I thought of the fishes of the water, the fowls of the air, the wild beasts of the forest, all appeared to be free, *to go just where they pleased*, and I was an unhappy slave!" In this statement Bibb juxtaposed the natural movement of wildlife with the human technology of steamboats. Much as he did of the fish swimming freely, Bibb could look on the movement of the steamboat only with envy. Although the steamboat moved freely, Bibb knew that he could not take advantage of the technology. Later, as a steamboat carried him back to slavery in Kentucky, he contemplated jumping from the deck and swimming to freedom. The steamboat confirmed Bibb's slavery because it was as much a barrier to his freedom as was the river itself.[4]

Second, linking river transportation with unfreedom, enslaved African Americans viewed the flow of commerce along the Ohio River as a barrier to their freedom. Steamboats symbolized how the free flow of commerce along the river relied on the coerced movement of black bodies. Black laborers and enslaved blacks en route to markets in Natchez and New Orleans occupied the same space as white travelers, but they traveled as salable commodities. Self-defense, therefore, involved overcoming white attempts to commodify black labor. Enslaved blacks who used steamboats to escape from slavery either passed as free persons or hid among other African Americans. In passing as free persons, they escaped coercion and used the steamboat to facilitate their own mobility. By passing as laborers or hiding among the cargo, fugitives capitalized on the free flow of river commerce to create an illicit movement all their own. They used the racial preconceptions of whites to hide as commodified laborers and make their movement invisible. In both cases enslaved blacks had to manipulate the apparently free movement of steamboats because white Americans regulated those spaces.[5]

The fact that African Americans had to manipulate space and movement in order to escape from slavery suggests that sale and coerced movement were fundamental aspects of borderland slavery. In addition, in the borderland, physical violence and the threat of sale blended into one mutually destructive threat against enslaved bodies. Former slaves commonly lamented how slavery stripped away their ability to defend themselves. Lewis Clarke recalled that vulnerability, and the inability to defend himself, was not only a cruel aspect of slavery but the foundation of human bondage: "It wouldn't do to let the slave think he is a man. That would spoil slavery, clean entirely. No; this is the cruelty of the thing—a slave can't be a man." African Americans knew that if they confronted a white person in Kentucky, they faced retribution at the hands of the entire white community, which could ultimately result in sale as punishment. The threat of sale therefore made the threat of violence particularly acute in the borderland. Kentucky slave Peter Bruner wrote that "if you attempted to fight them back they would take you to the whipping post and give you 39 lashes, or sell you down the river."[6]

Once they had escaped, fugitive slaves existed in a space somewhere between slavery and freedom, which complicated the notion of self-defense. Fugitives remained subject to recapture and sale, but their acts of escape also meant that bondage had to be forced back on them. Therefore enslaved

African Americans looked to capitalize on the unique conditions of the borderland to resist recapture. Former Kentucky slave, Andrew Jackson wrote, "The penalty is very severe upon slaves who strike a white man, but I was after a prize, for which I was willing to risk my life. . . . And if it was right for the revolutionary patriots to fight for liberty, it was right for me." Lewis Clarke put his situation even more succinctly: "I set my face in good earnest toward the Ohio River, determined to see and tread the north bank of it, or *die* in the attempt. I said to myself, One of two things,—FREEDOM OR DEATH!" At this point Clarke was between freedom and slavery, and he had to commit himself to the pursuit of freedom. Both Jackson and Clarke recalled their determination to fight for their liberty, which was remarkable. White Americans made every effort to ensure that bondage crushed enslaved blacks' ability to defend themselves, and yet both of these men were willing to defend themselves physically from reenslavement or die trying. That willingness to fight indicated their rejection of bondage and their move toward a new self-understanding.[7]

Despite this willingness to fight, the unpredictability of violence and a universal distrust of humanity made fugitive slaves just as likely to avoid confrontation along the river. Fugitive slaves did not know whom they could trust and looked at everyone as potential traitors. As William Wells Brown explained, "I had long since made up my mind that I would not trust myself in the hands of any man, white or colored. The slave is brought up to look upon every white man as an enemy to him and his race." In the South slaves faced certain retribution if they confronted a white person. North of the river the situation was less certain but certainly still volatile. When Henry Bibb escaped from his captors in Cincinnati, he explained, "I . . . reached the fence and attempted to jump over it before I was overtaken . . . . I kicked and struggled with all my might to get away . . . but they never let me . . . they succeeded in dragging me from the fence and overpowered me by numbers." He continued, "The office being crowded with spectators, many of whom were colored persons, Mr. G. was afraid to keep me in Cincinnati, two or three hours even . . . so they took me across the river, and locked me up in Covington jail, for safe keeping." Despite the fact that Cincinnatians aided the capture of Bibb, his owner still worried that a group of black Ohioans would free Bibb.[8]

In crossing the river, enslaved blacks could more readily resort to physical resistance, but the close proximity of the river made this risky. The connections forged by the river meant that white slaveholders had friends

and associates on both sides of the Ohio. In addition they issued advertisements for runaways and had unfettered access to ferries and steamboats.
This all increased the likelihood that a fugitive slave would be recognized
and confronted at some point. Fugitive slaves knew that creating a scene
could make observers come to the aid of the slave catchers, especially if it
was apparent that those African Americans were runaways. Henry Bibb
wrote, "When I saw a crowd of blood-thirsty, unprincipled slave hunters
rushing upon me armed with weapons of death, it was no use for me to
undertake to fight my way through against such fearful odds." He knew
that resistance at that point was futile.[9]

Fugitives' use of violence depended on the situation but not necessarily
on which side of the river they were located. When David Barret escaped
from his master in Kentucky, he "was accosted by three men. I fought them
like a Turk for some time." But later when he was in Ohio, three white
men confronted him and asked for his papers; rather than fight, he fled
into the woods. During his escape, J. D. Green stowed away on a steamboat
headed toward Cincinnati. Once the boat docked, he waited for the other
passengers and the crew to leave the boat before disembarking. On his way
up the hill from the river, Green met his master's nephew, who seized him.
According to Green, "A sharp struggle ensued. He called for help but I
threw him and caught a stone and struck him on the head, which caused
him to let go, when I ran away as fast [as] my legs could carry me, pursued
by a numerous crowed, crying "stop thief." The ability of the owner's family to cross the Ohio River so easily led them to expect Green's enslavement
to follow him across the river. But to Green, the river represented a barrier
against his enslavement. He wanted to make crossing it akin to crossing a
point of no return. Both Green and Barret understood that violent resistance was a practical necessity of escape on either side of the river. But
both men tried to avoid confrontation and turned to violence only when
absolutely necessary.[10]

Sources offer different interpretations of fugitive reclamation, but they
corroborate the individual nature of fugitive resistance. Abolitionist editors
depicted the resistance of individual fugitive slaves as examples of defenseless
slaves in need of white Americans' help. They sensationalized the stories of
white Americans coming to the rescue of fugitive slaves but printed those
stories alongside examples of slaveholders carrying African Americans back
into bondage. In one story, "a fugitive was given over to an irresponsible
magistrate, surrounded by slave-hunters, and his consignment to chains was

hailed with shouts of joy by the bystanders." In another example, five "ruffi-anly negro-hunters" seized Henry Colwell and carried him to Kentucky. Thereafter "some fifteen or twenty men" convinced the "ruffians" to let Col-well free. Here white Ohioans confronted Colwell's captors, but initially Col-well was on his own to defend himself. Abolitionist editors published these stories to excite the sympathies of white northerners who might have other-wise watched or simply ignored the reclamation of fugitive slaves.[11]

Similarly, Kentucky legislators complained about the inaction of white Ohioans and Indianans in the reclamation process. In 1838 the Kentucky government sent commissioners to speak to Ohio's governor about improving the process of reclamation. In their communication the com-missioners claimed that "experience has shown, that without the concur-rent legislation of our sister states, bordering on the north side of the river Ohio, the laws of Kentucky . . . cannot be effectually enforced." The Ken-tucky commissioners who went to Indiana admitted, "The citizens of those states are comparatively few, by whose artifice, crude, ill digested and fanatic notions of civil rights, the injuries referred to are inflicted." They suggested that, for the most part, Indianans failed to interfere in the recla-mation of fugitives.[12]

The situation was highly volatile because in crossing the border, enslaved blacks challenged the power of slaveholders. Furthermore their willingness to defend themselves physically made reclamation that much more difficult. Recapture and retribution, while possible north of the river, were not certain. Enslaved blacks exploited that uncertainty. The reclama-tion of fugitive slaves was not an easy task for slaveholders, and thus any interference caused problems, and the actions of a few caused troubles beyond their numbers. Because enslaved blacks were willing to defend themselves, interference, or even noninterference, by white northerners fur-ther challenged the power of slaveholders because it limited the influence of the slaveholding community.

The growth of the African American population along the river further challenged the slaveholding community, since an engaged free black com-munity could turn an individual's act into collective resistance. The bur-geoning river economy encouraged free blacks to settle in the region. This was particularly true in major urban centers. Between 1840 and 1850 the free black population of Jefferson County, Kentucky, more than doubled from 765 to 1,631. In Hamilton County, Ohio, the free black population increased by more than 1,000, rising to 3,600 by 1850. The smaller towns

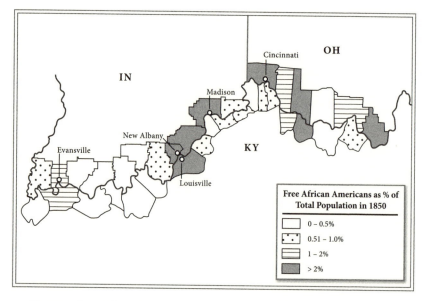

Figure 4. Free African Americans as a percentage of the total population in 1850.

across the river from these cities also experienced growth. In Floyd County, Indiana, across from Jefferson County, the free black population increased from 402 to 574. Kenton County and Campbell County, across from Cincinnati, also experienced dramatic growth. The free black population increased in almost every county on both sides of the Ohio River but was most dramatic in more urban counties. For example, rural Spencer County, Indiana, had a free black population of only 27, and across the river Hancock County had a free black population of 15. The numbers suggest that African Americans moved to the northern bank for two reasons: the availability of jobs; and the existence of a free black community.[13]

The rising free black population in Kentucky suggests that some enslaved workers had been emancipated. Also it is certainly possible that free blacks moved to Kentucky's river cities in search of employment. For example, Mason County's enslaved population decreased by 25 between 1840 and 1850, but the free black population rose by over 100. Some of the enslaved blacks may have been freed and then remained in Mason County. Henderson County's enslaved population increased by over 1,000, but the free black population rose from 48 to 123 by 1850. Employment in the town of Henderson may have attracted free black workers, while white slave owners used slave labor to power rural tobacco plantations. In either case some free blacks chose to live in Kentucky.

Many black Americans who lived in river cities were former slaves, and possibly even fugitives themselves, which made them aware of the devastation of sale and willing to defend escapees. Free black communities in Evansville, Madison, Louisville, and Cincinnati were "stations" on the Underground Railroad, but they were more than stations that fugitives passed through. In fact free black Americans' participation in the river economy allowed them to defend fugitive slaves against recapture, making these cities destinations. These Americans worked along the docks, as ferrymen, and on steamboats, which gave them the unique ability to ferry enslaved blacks across the river. When five Kentuckians seized Thomas Fox in Brown County, Ohio, several African American residents came to his aid and "loosed the captive." The Kentuckians returned the next day with constables to arrest the men responsible for stopping the reclamation, but local residents again interfered, and the Kentuckians dispersed.[14]

The black community along the river provided physical protection against the threat of sale for both free and enslaved African Americans. At the hands of white mobs, African Americans in Ohio and Indiana could not rely on neighbors or the law. The black laws of Ohio and Indiana forced African Americans to register their freedom with courts and stripped African Americans of their right to testify in cases against white residents. Protection against sale or kidnapping therefore often required the aid of the larger black community. African American residents knew that the difference between fugitive slave reclamation and kidnapping was a slippery legal distinction that slaveholders crossed nearly at will, and so they used collective resistance to combat both kidnapping and reclamation. Personal safety was the primary issue, and African Americans had to physically defend their freedom from unscrupulous whites trying to make a profit on the trade in black bodies. When a mob attacked Frederick Douglass in Pendleton, Indiana, in 1843, he was forced to flee in a "fearfully true picture of the flight of the fugitive slave."[15]

While African Americans were willing to resort to physical violence, they also knew that collective violence struck fear in the hearts of white residents along the river. When black residents showed collective force to meet a threat, their actions precipitated more violence. In August 1841

black resistance to white mob violence escalated into a race war in Cincinnati. When black residents refused to turn over an alleged fugitive, white
residents attacked the building housing the fugitive, but they failed in their
reclamation efforts. News of blacks' resistance spread through the city and
across the river, and tensions increased. Black residents organized and
armed themselves and awaited the impending mob attack. White residents
of both Kentucky and Cincinnati formed a mob and approached the black
neighborhood. When the mob arrived, the armed black men fired into the
crowd. The crowd dispersed only to return with a cannon and proceeded
to fire into black homes and businesses. When the militia finally arrived,
they declared martial law, arrested black residents, and detained them until
they paid bond. Kentuckians were able to examine the prisoners and determine if they were fugitive slaves.[16]

Explosions of racial violence, such as in Cincinnati, linked the experiences of free and fugitive African Americans north of the river. After the
riot, white Cincinnatians demanded that the militia enforce the black law
of 1807 and the Fugitive Slave Law of 1793. But while they placed the blame
for the riot on the presence of "undesirable" fugitive slaves, they attacked
African Americans indiscriminately. First, this pattern of racial violence stabilized the borderland by reducing the meaning of border crossing for black
migrants. Collective black resistance encouraged white Kentuckians to join
together with white Ohioans. Whites on both sides of the river shared a
fear of disruption to the racial order and used that fear to regulate the
movement of black Americans. This revealed that, despite their disagreements over slavery, the threat of a race war convinced white Americans to
overlook their differences. After this riot, many free African Americans settled in northern Ohio and even Canada in fear for their safety. Second, the
threat of collective white violence made African Americans in the borderland hesitant to respond with violence. For African Americans, the Cincinnati riot of 1841 revealed both the danger of collective resistance and its
ineffectuality without a legal baseline.[17]

As this informal antislavery activity transitioned into formal protest, free
black leaders struggled to reconcile the need for self-defense with whites' fears
of collective resistance. During the 1830s and 1840s few free black leaders
openly advocated violent resistance, which has led historians to conclude that
nonviolence remained the watchword among black leaders until the turbu-
lent 1850s. However, African Americans' concern for personal safety under-
pinned the legal focus of the 1840s, especially in states such as Indiana and

Ohio, which bordered the South. African Americans knew that violence was not an adequate form of self-defense, and they sought to overturn the black laws as a nonviolent corollary to the necessity of personal self-defense.[18]

Free black leaders in Ohio tried to strike a balance between civil rights and physical resistance. During the 1840s free African Americans held conventions in many states throughout the North, including Ohio and Indiana, at which they discussed the best course of action. At the Ohio convention in 1849, free black leaders declared their right to "sternly resist, by all the means which the God of Nations has placed in our power, every form of oppression or proscription attempted to be imposed upon us." Then, in their proclamation to the citizens of Ohio, they denounced the black laws and said that their right to defend their liberty was "beyond the reach of legislation," appealing to a "higher judicature." Thus they called on Ohio politicians to bring state laws into conformity with their natural rights, including the right of self-defense. Black Americans collapsed the difference between kidnapping and reclamation and advocated universal protection against the pull of slavery. Ultimately, free black leaders sought the best means to protect and enable African Americans' freedom of movement by defending themselves against coerced movement.[19]

Through the 1830s and 1840s racial violence yielded a measure of stability to the borderland by limiting the outlets for black-led antislavery action. African Americans did not have the right to vote, so they had to try to convince white residents and politicians to support their cause. America's two-party system was a significant check against their cause. The Whig and Democrat Parties were cross-sectional alliances that avoided controversial issues. The strength of these parties undermined the democratic process by preventing outsiders from gaining access to politics. The political system's checks against radicalism therefore reduced the chance for revolutionary action. Up until 1850 free black leaders seldom directly linked their cause of fighting racial prejudice with a call for enslaved African Americans to collectively fight against enslavement. Free African American leaders decided that legal protection was the best means of combating both vulnerability and actual threats from groups of whites.[20]

*   *   *

While the Ohio River border heavily influenced the movement of free and enslaved African Americans throughout the 1830s and 1840s, the border remained just one of many factors that influenced whites' movement. The centrality of the Ohio River to the economy destabilized the lives of African Americans because it made them susceptible to sale and bondage in the Deep South. In contrast, white Americans took advantage of river commerce, utilizing the centrality of the river to increase their economic and personal opportunities. This freedom allowed white Americans to define the meaning of their movement. Whether that meant emphasizing accommodation across the border to facilitate commerce, imposing restrictions on black immigration to keep slavery south of the river, or following the call of abolitionism, white Americans gave meaning to their actions based on their experience with the river border. Therefore, whereas the river border gave black Americans a common cause in their antislavery movement, white Americans were divided in their antislavery opinions precisely because they had the freedom to be so.

By the 1830s and 1840s the cheap and easy-to-purchase land that had lured white Americans to the Northwest Territory at the turn of the century was no longer available along the river. As a result, the movement of white Americans across the Ohio River slowed. Counties along the Ohio continued to experience population growth, but census data reveal that by 1850 the majority of residents were born in their states of residence. The population of Posey County in southern Indiana increased by nearly 30 percent, but Kentuckians made up only 2 percent of the total population. In Daviess County, Kentucky, Indianans comprised merely 1 percent of the population and native Kentuckians 84 percent. Lawrence County, Ohio, located on the border with Kentucky, contained mostly native Ohioans and more Virginians than native Kentuckians. Newport, Kentucky, directly across from Cincinnati, had fewer than ten proprietors from Ohio listed in the city directory. These data suggest that by the later antebellum period, fewer residents crossed the river to settle. Likely the river flattened distinctions between the banks, creating economic zones. In other words, counties directly across the river from each other may have been more economically similar to each other than to counties farther downriver. Therefore residents could capitalize on the economic opportunities of the region from either side. If they truly sought something new, they would have to head farther down the river or out of the region entirely.[21]

Land was still available in northern Ohio and Indiana, but Kentuckians did not head to either location. During the first years of settlement, many Kentuckians crossed the Ohio in pursuit of economic opportunity and settled in southern Indiana and southwestern Ohio. However, most of the immigrants to northern Ohio and Indiana came from the Northeast. In northern Ohio the Erie Canal had opened a new path of migration with the East, and also a new path for trade. As available land disappeared in Ohio, these eastern settlers continued west to northern Indiana. They shipped their goods, grain in particular, along this new canal system to eastern markets. As a result the settlers of the Western Reserve in northern Ohio and northern Indiana held no personal or economic ties to their southern neighbors. The settlement of northern Indiana and Ohio created a separation within these states, which reinforced the southern region's unique connection to the Ohio River.[22]

Clark County, Indiana, was an exception to the slowing of movement along the river. However, this area was a distinct economic zone with clear economic connections to the river. Those Kentuckians who moved across the river to Indiana, perhaps to escape slavery, maintained their close connections to the river. In Clark County, Indiana, directly across from Louisville, only 58 percent of the residents were born in Indiana and Kentuckians made up nearly 15 percent of the population in 1850. Meanwhile more residents of Louisville were from Ohio than from Indiana. Due to the sheer size of Louisville, it made sense that the smaller cities were within its sphere of influence. Residents could live across the river in Indiana and still take advantage of the commercial and manufacturing opportunities in Louisville. Similarly, upriver Cincinnati gave Kentuckians greater opportunities. Ohioans rarely moved across the river to Newport or Covington. However, Kentuckians in those cities could take advantage of their situation, perhaps owning slaves, but still remain close enough to Cincinnati to benefit from its economic production. Thus there was a duality to white Americans' view of the river border.

Even if they chose to live in Ohio and Indiana to be free from slavery, they perched themselves on a river that connected the region with the rest of the South. The Ohio River was the lifeblood of the region, and local residents knew it. Kentuckian John Corlis wrote to his wife, "I am still of the opinion that the vicinity of the river is the best place for farming, as there will be always a growing and unceasing market. The communication will become so easy and cheap that much of the produce of Kentucky and Ohio will reach the Atlantic market." Corlis was right, as his business associate Lloyd Halsey later wrote to him, "Yankees will be plenty enough in your part of the country" to purchase Corlis's pork. White Americans' control over their movement allowed them to take advantage of the unique economic opportunities of the river economy.[23]

White Americans capitalized on the economic connections between the Ohio Valley and the South by moving along the river rather than across it. The promise of the cotton kingdom likely attracted Kentuckians to Mississippi, since many Kentuckians who moved to the interior of Mississippi became planters. These migrants rarely traveled as families. Male migrants often married Mississippi women and then started families, and many of the female migrants married Mississippi planters. Not every migrant to Mississippi became a cotton planter, but the health of the slave economy attracted whites in search of economic opportunity. The migration of Ohio Valley residents to Warren County, Mississippi, revealed the connections of the river economy. Vicksburg, located in Warren County, was a thriving commercial center located on the Mississippi River, and it attracted migrants from both sides of the Ohio River. Most of the Kentuckians living in Vicksburg worked as river workers or as laborers in the manufacturing sector. While Ohioans seldom moved to Kentucky, many were attracted to Warren County, Mississippi, in the Deep South. Ohio migrants typically worked as river workers, skilled laborers, or as professionals. The presence of Ohioans in Vicksburg symbolized the economic connections created by the river trade.[24]

White residents' decisions about which side of the border to live on were personal, and numerous factors contributed to their choice. But white skin color gave them the freedom to make that choice. White residents could cross the Ohio River with impunity, and thus the simple fact of having white skin gave them the power to define the meaning of their movement, or lack of movement. Many white residents developed an understanding of the Ohio River border that allowed them to take full advantage of the river economy but also to imagine a meaningful difference between free and slave states. On the north side of the river, white residents resented intrusion by outsiders, especially groups of Kentucky slave catchers. But to suggest that they refused to accommodate their southern neighbors at all would be an overstatement. Many recognized that in order to maintain amicable relations, they had to allow Kentuckians to reclaim fugitives from labor. This combination of resistance and accommodation yielded multiple responses from northerners to the border issue—from limiting black immigration, to assisting in reclamation, to defending escaping fugitives, to forcing open discussion of the issue of slavery, to making legal distinctions between reclamation and kidnapping.

*   *   *

Some white residents' experience with southern slavery convinced them to pursue more radical antislavery views north of the river. The conservatism and gradualism of the colonization movement made it a popular antislavery stance both locally and nationally. However, the tenor of the national antislavery movement had changed by the 1830s. In the late 1820s free black leaders in eastern cities such as Boston and Philadelphia rejected gradualism and began advocating for an immediate end to slavery. Free African Americans in Boston strongly influenced the reformer William Lloyd Garrison's views on slavery. Funded by the free black community, Garrison began printing the *Liberator* in January 1831 and called for an immediate end to slavery. Garrison and free black leaders tried to convince Americans of the hypocrisy of the colonization movement in order to convert them to abolitionism. Others came to abolitionism through the evangelical fervor unleashed by the Second Great Awakening in the 1820s. These abolitionists refused to compromise on the issue of slavery, and they cast the issue as a simple decision to reject it as a sin. Southerners and northerners alike denounced the radicalism of the abolitionists. Along the Ohio River, abolitionists threatened to upset the balance of the border, and many accused them of trying to incite a slave rebellion. However, radical abolitionists along the Ohio River based their understanding of the river border on personal experiences, and their strategies of resistance reflected that experience.[25]

Three abolitionist leaders who lived and traveled in southern states moved to Ohio in the 1830s. All three began advocating immediate emancipation after witnessing southern slavery and the impotence of conservative antislavery. Theodore Weld toured several southern states in the 1820s in support of manual-labor schools. Weld never resided south of the Ohio River, but he chose to begin his abolitionist career in Cincinnati. John Rankin developed his antislavery views in Tennessee and Kentucky but felt compelled to move across the Ohio in order to continue his antislavery work. Between 1826 and 1836 James Birney moved from Alabama to Kentucky and then to Ohio, and as he did, he transitioned from slaveholder to colonizationist and then to abolitionist.[26]

James Birney's increasingly radical antislavery views pushed him from the Deep South to Kentucky and then eventually across the river to Ohio.

Birney was an Alabama slaveholder with little concern about human bondage until 1826, when he converted to Christianity. Birney became convinced of the evil of slaveholding and began his antislavery work in Alabama as an advocate for colonization. Rather than forcing him out, colonizationist leaders in Alabama recruited him as a leader and spokesperson. He soon decided to leave Alabama because he worried about the effect that slavery had on his children. Although he wanted to move to Illinois, he relocated to Kentucky in 1833 to be near his ill father. Birney believed that Kentucky offered "a better field for operations than that in which I have been laboring," because slavery was weaker there than in Alabama. As he saw it, the influence of slavery existed on a continuum with the Upper and Lower South as anchors. After organizing a disastrous expedition to Liberia and making little headway on emancipation in Kentucky, Birney became convinced that colonization was impractical. By the winter of 1833–34 he had become an advocate for immediate emancipation in Kentucky.[27]

After he distributed a circular declaring his intention to print an antislavery newspaper in Danville in the summer of 1835, Birney received condemnation from slaveholders and nonslaveholders alike. The nonslaveholder Lewis Bond wrote, "If you say it is for the purpose of convincing us that slavery is wrong, you would only be beating the air, for we all know it is wrong," but Bond worried that the paper would "stir up the negroes in rebellion against the whites." Bond and other nonslaveholding whites accepted the mechanisms for controlling slavery. Slaveholders feared that if slaves thought they had support from whites they would be more likely to resist their owners or, even worse, rebel collectively against the institution. So slaveholders silenced all opposition to slavery with brute force. The historian David Grimsted uncovered hundreds of instances from the later antebellum period where white mobs viciously attacked outspoken critics of slavery, sometimes even killing the victims. Even if they did not accept slavery itself, these men and women joined the white collective that upheld slavery.[28]

The presence of the border offered antislavery activists in Kentucky two choices in response to the threat of violence: join or move. S. S. Dismukes, Birney's potential publisher, confessed to Birney that he "had been anxious for a long time to get out of the business—that if his establishment should be attacked and destroyed it would ruin him—that he was anxious to go to

Missouri where his father resided." The publisher moved laterally to another slaveholding state to join his family.[29]

Rather than compromise his antislavery principles, Birney moved across the river. Unlike the antislavery leaders of the early statehood period who were politicians first, Birney and these new activists were career reformers. Their commitment to their cause convinced them to move across the river. One man who moved from Kentucky to Ohio said, "the people of Ky. would shun me as they would a rattlesnake." Birney wrote to Theodore Weld that he could not "remain in Ky" and asked if he could take a position as an agent for the American Antislavery Society in Ohio. He moved to Cincinnati late in 1835 and began his efforts in a free state. Along the border the potential for violence both quelled moderate antislavery whites and expelled radical antislavery activists from the state, which helped to stabilize slavery in Kentucky.[30]

Even their pursuit of radical antislavery failed to sever white Americans' social ties with their southern neighbors. When fugitive slaves or even freed slaves crossed the river, they had to divorce themselves from their past in order to protect themselves from reenslavement. In contrast, while Birney could not continue his antislavery work in Kentucky, he moved directly across the river, where he could, and did, remain in contact with friends in Kentucky. In one letter Birney wrote, "Mrs. B. and part of our family are still in Kentucky." In his grandfather's biography, William Birney indicated that his father and mother remained friends with many people in Kentucky throughout their lives. Cincinnati's vibrant print industry and location along the Ohio River connected Birney with the national flow of information. Birney's move across the river increased his connections and gave him unique opportunities found only in the large river city.[31]

Cincinnati and northern Kentucky residents repeatedly attacked Birney in Cincinnati, and each time they threw his printing press into the Ohio River. This was more than an act of destruction. It was a symbolic effort to use the river to flush Birney and abolitionists away. In throwing the press into the river, the mob made the statement that the Ohio River could swallow the incendiary words of Birney and the abolitionists. Yet every time they threw it in, Birney pulled the press out of the river and continued publication of his newspaper. Birney made his own statement that the border was more powerful than nature, and his movement across it had meaning.[32]

While abolitionists' move across the river did not protect them from mob violence, even radically antislavery whites did not have to fear kidnapping or enslavement as did black Americans. In Cincinnati white Americans from both sides of the river commonly mobbed abolitionist meetings and drove away abolitionist speakers. In a letter to Lewis Tappan, Birney wrote, "we were dreadfully mobbed by a drunken rabble . . . yet the Lord held them back from interfering with our meetings." But while abolitionists often claimed that they narrowly escaped bloodthirsty mobs bent on destruction, antiabolitionist mobs in Ohio and Indiana did not intend to kill them. Birney, Weld, and Rankin survived every one of their attacks and proceeded to tell the world about them. Weld wrote in a letter to Birney, "The mobs at New York have greatly helped our cause all over the East. Of this I am advertised by almost daily letters. Truth has always been the gainer when men resort to bludgeons, and think to overmaster her by pains and penalties." Few abolitionists died during these riots. Abolitionists had an ambivalent relationship with violence because they both feared it and believed that it was beneficial to their cause. Yet their ability to both survive and publicize the violence suggests a real difference between mob violence in slaveholding Kentucky and such violence in the free state of Ohio. The border allowed white abolitionists to advocate their cause because it provided protection against the deadly mob violence of slave states.[33]

Abolitionists throughout the North attempted to exploit the violence of the Ohio River borderland to further their cause. The abolitionist firebrand William Lloyd Garrison wrote of James Birney's attempt to establish his paper in Kentucky, "Mr. Birney . . . attempts to talk anti-slavery in the den of the lion." By August 1835 Garrison had been publishing his abolitionist newspaper, the *Liberator*, in Boston for over four years and had yet to garner a single subscription from a resident of a slaveholding state. His own failure in slaveholding states likely contributed to Garrison's view of the Ohio River as a barrier. Birney's paper, therefore, was an opportunity to take the fight between "liberty and despotism" into enemy territory. When residents of Danville threatened to destroy Birney's printing press, Garrison called it a "murderous and violent opposition." In Garrison's words, Birney "had to flee . . . from Kentucky to save his life . . . and durst not go back to get his family. All this because he thinks that slavery is not right!" When Birney established the *Philanthropist* in Cincinnati, Garrison's vision of the border was confirmed. Whereas the forces of slavery would not tolerate an abolitionist newspaper, once Birney crossed the border he could speak out against slavery.[34]

James Birney and Ohio abolitionists developed their own method of protest in relation to their understanding of the border. Birney experienced violent censor in Kentucky and again in Ohio. Therefore he advocated and promoted the open discussion of the issue of slavery. In order to craft a distinction between free and slave states, and give meaning to his own movement across the border, Birney refused to be censored. Instead James Birney and Ohio abolitionists depicted the borderland as a war zone between the violently opposed systems of slavery and freedom in order to excite white Americans to action. Abolitionists claimed each mob attack as proof that the influence of slavery did not stop at the river. After the 1836 Cincinnati riot, the Ripley antislavery society reported, "We view the origin of this disgraceful affair to have had its rise in the nature and system of slavery. As slavery was first established by violence and continued by force, mobocracy is only one of the ways in which it exhibits its legitimate results and develops its true character." Members of the Ripley antislavery society linked slavery with threats to white freedom: "It no longer remains a solitary question whether slaves shall be free but whether we shall be free ourselves." Through this rhetoric of battle and invasion, the abolitionists of Cincinnati tried to convince white Ohioans that the Ohio River was a border in need of defense. Gamaliel Bailey, Birney's successor as editor of the *Philanthropist*, explained, "Our situation peculiarly exposes us to the insidious and incessant inroads of the spirit and practices of slavery . . . slavery itself, as she passes through our midst, is suffered to rattle her chains, unrebuked." In other words, it was up to Ohioans to speak out against and resist the intrusion of slavery.[35]

The fiery rhetoric excited the public in Ohio but created a division in antislavery opinion in the state. Settlers of the Western Reserve in northern Ohio held no personal or economic ties with their southern neighbors. As a result, they more readily supported the antislavery movement. Along the border white residents may have supported, and even shared, abolitionists' desire to end slavery, but many rejected their means. One Ohioan wrote, "For my own part I am not a very strong abolitionist, for I cannot see how they can affect their object by their present course, and it appears to me that their efforts only tend to rivet the fetters of the slave tighter because they only exasperate the slaveholders." An Ohio newspaper read, "The controversies of those States have produced much bad blood, and alienated feeling, and done infinite ill to trade." Ira Bean, a resident of Cincinnati, wrote to a friend, "Although I deprecate slavery as much as any can I am astonished that thinking, sensible men cannot see that immediate emancipation unless obtained by mutual compromise would be unconstitutional unjust and dangerous in its consequences." In fact, Ira Bean's father (who lived outside the borderland) was an abolitionist, and they exchanged letters about their antislavery positions, but Ira Bean never converted. Even Joshua Giddings admitted, "Indeed in here lies the only thing about which our people contend. It is the term abolition. On all constitutional principles and on all questions of policy we agree but we contend about a mere name."[36]

Abolitionists had minimal influence in Indiana, especially in the southern part of the state. Unlike in Ohio, settlers did not begin settling northern Indiana in great numbers until the 1840s and 1850s, which severely retarded the growth of the abolitionist movement there. The only antislavery society in Indiana was formed in 1839, but it quickly died out. White residents in the hills of southern Indiana drew their community lines narrowly and wanted to regulate within that community, but outsiders were free to do what they wished. Thus they wanted to free themselves from the sin of slavery and let southerners deal with the problem. To many white residents in this region, violence proved that abolitionists' course was misguided because it prompted such anger from their slaveholding neighbors.[37]

While radical abolitionists threatened to upset the balance along the border by refusing to compromise, other white Ohioans and Indianans, inspired by their decision to live in free states, both justified conflict and accepted the necessity of accommodation. When white residents made the decision to cross the river, some wrestled with how best to leave slavery behind. When Esther Hollowell wrote to her brother about moving to Indiana, she expressed her concern about the future of the enslaved blacks in her household, saying, "I cannot bare the thoughts of leaving them here." In fact, she explained that she wanted to "get them away to a land of freedom . . . if it was not too great an undertaking." Hollowell wanted to migrate to a free state, but she needed help to do it because she wanted to bring her freed slaves with her. Others sought to leave slavery entirely behind. When an Indiana man wrote to his cousin in Kentucky, he explained that "the price of . . . [Jane] would purchase you a comfortable home in this country. If it is right to keep her it is right to sell her but my advise [sic] would be to hire her out till she is 25 and then give her her liberty you will feel a great deal better when you come to die." In both cases their freedom depended on their ability to determine the future of enslaved African Americans. In fact, white Americans' belief that they could, and should, control the movement of black Americans was constant whether they remained in Kentucky or left for free states. White borderlanders targeted the movement of blacks in order to control the boundaries of their own communities. In borderlands, debates over border crossing target both the actions and the people involved. Acceptable people make acceptable transgressions, but residents restrict the movement of those whom they view as a threat. Their movement becomes unacceptable as a means of keeping them out of the community.[38]

Residents of southern Indiana and Ohio had a long history of trying to limit the immigration of African Americans both legally and by force. In the 1810s and 1820s Indianans petitioned the government to prevent southerners from bringing their freed slaves with them when they moved to the state. Both states had laws requiring blacks to register with the local courts and agree to five-hundred-dollar security bonds based on good behavior. In the summer of 1846 residents of Mercer County, Ohio, tried to drive black settlers away by force. An observer noted that the local authorities contributed to the mob violence, writing that the state attorney was a "lawyer for the mobocrats and has a high fee for driving the negroes from the county." Ohio's governor issued an executive order demanding that order be restored: "If the coloured people against whom the excitement has been raised, have violated any law, disturbed the peace of the state or trespassed upon the rights of others, the legal remedy should be applied, but not unlawful violence should be applied." Ultimately whites' efforts to limit immigration had mixed results, as the free black populations of both states increased between 1830 and 1840, but the growth was slow.[39]

White borderland residents developed definitions of acceptable and unacceptable border crossings that applied to the movement that the river induced. Whites imagined the movement of mobs of Kentucky slave catchers across the river as invasions of their territory and threats to their sovereignty. Their efforts to resist "invasions" allowed them to give meaning to their choice to live north of the river by defending free soil from the intrusion of slavery. At the same time, reclamation did not always equal invasion.

Indianans and Ohioans recognized Kentuckians' rights for *lawful* reclamation, but on their terms. In 1838 Kentucky sent commissioners to Ohio and Indiana to discuss the issue of reclamation. Noah Noble, Indiana's governor, in a speech to the General Assembly said, "Upon all questions connected with the institution of slavery, the citizens of this state have been exempt from excitement. Ever mindful of the duties which devolve on her as a member of the great family of American States . . . the State of Indiana has religiously abstained in her principles and her policy from every act that could be construed into a disposition to tamper with, or disregard the domestic institutions of her sister states." The Kentucky legislature reported that Indiana, "regardful of the rights of her sister states of [the] South," had taken an action that called forth "the most decided and unqualified approbation of this legislature" and that was "such as might have been expected from our enlightened, liberal, and patriotic, sister state." After the commission, Ohio legislators passed a more conciliatory fugitive slave law in 1839, but popular protest led to its repeal just four years later.[40]

The movement of fugitive slaves was more disruptive than lawful migration because it threatened the stability of the border by invoking the questions of when a slave became free and conversely what enslaved a person. White Americans sought to control the movement of fugitives by making a distinction between reclamation and kidnapping. White residents clashed, sometimes violently, over the distinction between reclamation and kidnapping, but those conflicts revealed whites' shared perception that unrestricted black movement would destroy the border. From the perspective of slaveholders south of the river, the protection of slavery depended on the unrestricted movement of white posses controlling the movement of African Americans. Kentuckians regularly crossed the river, usually in small groups, to reclaim escaped slaves and did so quite lawfully. The United States Constitution and the Fugitive Slave Act protected slaveholders' rights to their slaves everywhere in the country.[41]

White residents north of the river recognized the need for peaceful reclamation as well. Editors of northern papers regularly printed advertisements for runaways. In addition enslaved blacks' fears of recapture did not disappear as soon as they crossed the river. Many recalled that white Americans north of the river questioned them. They would not have viewed the region as a borderland if white northerners had protected them from recapture. As one Ohio editor wrote: "whatever might be the difference of opinion between the two states as to holding negroes in slavery . . . it would necessarily lead to disruption between the states, for either now to attempt to enforce its peculiar practices on the other. Ohio would not for a moment submit to any attempts on the part of Kentucky to force slaves upon us—neither could it be supposed that Kentucky would quietly look upon our citizens stealing away slaves from them."[42]

Yet white Americans in Ohio and Indiana also supported escaping fugitive slaves. Some were even proud of their ability to resist slaves' reclamation. One Ohio woman wrote to her sister, "No news except there is several runaway slaves here and their masters have come here after them but they will not get them." Abolitionist editors printed stories of whites coming to the aid of enslaved blacks, and Kentuckians constantly complained that their slaves were "enticed" away by a small minority of "evil disposed persons." When slaveholders seized Milton Clarke in Ohio, the local sheriff rounded up farmers to protect him. He wrote, "The people were gathered, all this time, around the windows, and in the road, discussing the matter, and getting up the steam, to meet the Kentucky bowie knives and pistols." The public writings of James Birney and other abolitionists shed light on this apparent contradiction. In the descriptions of kidnappings in the *Philanthropist*, the editor often described the victims as "respected," "quiet," and "hard-working" and gave the length of their residence in Ohio or Indiana. The key was that at some point reclamation became kidnapping, and white Ohioans and Indianans interfered on behalf of the alleged fugitives when they suspected the latter.[43]

White Americans in Ohio and Indiana valorized the act of escape precisely because fugitive slaves were perennial outsiders. Once they escaped, fugitive slaves existed in a liminal space somewhere between slavery and freedom. Liminal characters are useful in the definition of identity because they embody values that a society treasures and those they reject. They are perennial outsiders, which makes it safe to valorize certain characteristics because their very outsidership prevents them from ever being part of the community. Ohioans and Indianans established laws ensuring that fugitives could never become residents. Yet white residents reasoned that the free soil must have been attractive enough for slaves to risk life and limb in its pursuit. So when they fought off Kentucky slave catchers, whites were defending freedom within the state.[44]

Abolitionists, the most ardent advocates of protecting fugitives from reclamation, wanted white northerners to protect individual fugitive slaves against the superior numbers of slave catchers. But their rhetoric primarily supported white collective violence to meet the show of force by slaveholders in order to defend white freedom. In depicting fugitives as helpless individuals, white abolitionists distanced themselves from supporting black collective action. On numerous occasions James Birney stressed that his desire for abolition did not imply racial equality. When free black residents came to the aid of an alleged fugitive in Cincinnati, whites from both sides of the river rallied to quell the potential rebellion. Ohio's most abolitionist politician, Joshua Giddings, argued that once they crossed the Ohio River fugitive slaves had the right to self-defense. He wrote, "While in a slave State he may not resist the violence of his master, by any act of self-defense; if he do so, he may be instantly slain." However, once he/she crossed into Ohio "he may defend himself, with just so much force as becomes necessary to protect his person and his personal liberty." While this was a radical support of black resistance, Giddings also isolated it to individual resistance, stating that it was "a matter entirely between themselves."[45]

The only form of kidnapping that elicited united resistance from white Ohioans and Indianans was the arrest of suspected *white* fugitive abettors. In 1838 Kentuckians accused the Ohio minister John B. Mahan of enticing slaves away while in the state of Kentucky. The governor of Kentucky requested the extradition of Mahan, and Governor Vance of Ohio complied. The *Philanthropist* described this case as an example of the slave power's violent assault on freedom. Political papers in Ohio also denounced the governor's actions, calling him a hypocrite who bowed to the "dark spirit of slavery." Editors exploited the incident as an example of how slavery threatened to pull even whites into slavery. One editor wrote that if "such proceedings are tolerated, no man is safe in Ohio. He may be torn from his family at any moment; no writ of habeas corpus or other judicial procedure will save him." Seven years later another case sparked the outrage of the Ohio public. In July 1845 six slaves escaped across the river, and some white Ohioans met them on the northern bank. Slaveholders followed the runaways and captured the escaped slaves as well as three white Ohioans. They took them across the Ohio and put them in jail. White Ohioans were outraged by this "invasion of Ohio." Cases such as these excited white Ohioans' fears that slavery threatened white freedom.[46]

Arising from this fear of invasion and radicalism, Ohio antislavery activists developed a formal legal protest against slavery. In a series of state supreme court cases agued by the antislavery lawyer Salmon P. Chase, the Ohio courts had determined by 1841 that slaves brought voluntarily by their owners into Ohio were free. Whereas previously the legal system had granted slaveholders the right to retain possession of their enslaved laborers as long as they had no intention of settling in free states, these decisions legally prevented slave owners from traveling through free states with their slaves. The decisions redefined the division between slave and free states. Chase presented the argument that freedom was the natural state of being and that slavery was a state law forced onto individuals. This was a powerful argument, because along the border many slaveholders traveled into Ohio with their slaves or sent them on errands across the river. Clearly Chase recognized the power of his argument in the context of the borderland. On the surface these decisions lent no support to the act of escape, but now any fugitive who had once traveled across the border had legal grounds for freedom. At the same time Chase recognized Kentuckians' rights of reclamation. His argument, and the court's decision, repudiated the radical "battle" of abolitionists. It demonstrated the extent and limits of formal antislavery protest north of the river.[47]

*   *   *

As was the case across the river, Kentuckians' antislavery strategies reflected the social and economic conditions of the state. Historians use the drop in the proportion of African Americans in the total population from 24 percent to 19 percent between 1830 and 1850 as evidence of the decline of slavery in the state. However, while slavery was declining in some areas, it was rapidly expanding in others. Between 1840 and 1850 the total slave population increased by nearly twenty-nine thousand, which was a 16 percent increase in a decade when slavery was supposedly on the decline. Slavery remained stable in the central bluegrass section but spread and began to thrive in new areas of the state. The growth of slavery along the Ohio River in western and southwestern Kentucky outpaced the state total. In addition the slave population of Jefferson County (containing Louisville) became the largest in the state by 1850.[48]

The Ohio River gave life to slavery in the state of Kentucky and brought bound labor right to the border. Slavery thrived in river towns, such as Louisville, because of its flexibility and resemblance to free labor. In Louisville, James Rudd turned slave-hiring into his business. In the 1820s Rudd worked as a mechanic in Louisville, and his success allowed him to purchase a few slaves. He proceeded to rent these slaves out, and by the end of the 1830s hiring out provided an enormous supplementary income. He hired out anywhere from five to ten slaves annually, bringing in one hundred dollars for female hires and as much as two hundred dollars for male hires. Some of the most powerful men in slaveholding regions were slaveholders, and men such as Rudd believed that slavery was vital to the economy. While the majority of white Kentuckians did not own slaves and the state did not have the large-scale cotton and sugar plantations of the Deep South, slavery was vital to certain industries. Kentucky's hemp industry thrived on the expansion of the cotton kingdom in the Deep South. Southerners packed their cotton in bags made from Kentucky hemp. In addition the labor involved in the production of hemp was arduous and dirty, and white laborers refused to do it. The border protected Kentucky's hemp industry from competition in southern Ohio or Indiana.[49]

Kentuckians also wanted to take advantage of the slave trade, local and interstate, to further their economic opportunities. For example, when Hector Green left his parents in Henderson, Kentucky, to establish himself, he headed for Louisville. Hector took three of his parents' slaves with him, with the intention of selling at least two in town. Hector's parents hoped that the money made from the sale would help Hector establish a business for himself. Louisville was a point of departure for the slave trade and likely offered higher prices than in western Kentucky. Hector's decision to move to Louisville and his intention to sell slaves in order to establish himself suggest that he hoped to take advantage of the thriving commerce along the river.[50]

White Kentuckians had never openly supported abolitionists, but in the 1830s and 1840s the state's pattern of growth and economic ties to the river facilitated a conservative antislavery movement there. They shared their free-state neighbors' belief in the uniqueness of the borderland. Cassius Clay began a newspaper dedicated to promoting antislavery in the state. Clay lived in the central bluegrass area and was therefore witness to both the dominance of slavery in the region and its stagnation in the later antebellum period. Lexington, once the dominant commercial city of the state, was outpaced by Louisville and its mixture of enslaved and free workers. Residents of Lexington quickly shut down Clay's paper, but he reassembled the press in Cincinnati and continued printing the paper. He grew bored with the job and ceased his editing of the paper before he rode off to the Mexican War, but John Vaughn moved the press to Louisville and continued the emancipationist paper. Residents' tolerance of an antislavery paper in Louisville was not surprising. While Jefferson County had the highest number of enslaved workers in the state, Louisville was in the midst of a massive migration of Germans. Whereas slaves made up roughly 18 percent of the population in 1850, thanks to the migration of German forty-eighters, by 1860 that number was closer to 11 percent. This immigrant population was receptive to the antislavery message because it meant eliminating competition from enslaved laborers.

Cassius Clay appealed to the economic self-interest of white nonslave-holders, making the argument that slavery retarded the economic development of the state. Articles compared the economic growth of Kentucky with that of Ohio and determined that Kentucky "could and would keep pace with its sister States, and even outstrip many of them" if slavery were removed. Antislavery men such as Cassius Clay and John Vaughn argued that Kentucky's connection with her northern neighbors could make emancipation a peaceful process. They distanced themselves from both proslavery South Carolinians and abolitionists, claiming a middle ground. As they explained, radicals "do not understand the position and feelings of the people of Missouri, Kentucky, Virginia, and large portions of them in North Carolina and Tennessee." Conservative Kentuckians blamed violence along the border on radicals and claimed that Kentucky, Ohio, and Indiana shared many economic interests.[51]

By 1850 white borderlanders had developed a variety of opinions about the Ohio River border. Kentuckians demanded the right to reclamation just as some expressed their hope that slavery was on the road to extinction. Radical abolitionists imagined the border as a war zone dividing the violently opposed systems of freedom and slavery. Less radical Ohioans and Indianans sought to defend the state, and themselves, against invasions by slave-catching "ruffians." Still others aided Kentuckians in the retrieval of fugitives from labor. On the streets and during tense political meetings whites regularly clashed over their understanding of the border. The Ohio River border was a place of near constant conflict.

*   *   *

By 1850 slavery and freedom had become potent but increasingly mutable political categories. The border was a political creation, and it set up a false dichotomy. The reality was that the slave/free dichotomy could not possibly capture the range of human experiences in the region. That did not, however, mean that the border lacked political salience. In fact, quite the contrary occurred. This puzzle of the politics of this borderland becomes

Figure 5. This painting demonstrates that Louisville ca. 1850 shared similarities with Cincinnati. When set in juxtaposition, the cities appear more similar than different. Courtesy of the Filson Historical Society, Louisville, Kentucky.

Figure 6. This 1851 painting by Wallace Middleton highlights the cross-river connections between Cincinnati, Newport, and Covington. Courtesy of the Cincinnati Museum Center.

slightly clearer in a social context that closely linked race and status. Even then it is only slightly clearer. In fact, multiple loyalties and divisions that appeared and disappeared defined the borderland as a place of ambiguity. As tempting as it is to rationalize and apply analyses that clarify the picture in hindsight, it is more accurate to describe the ambiguity. Between 1830 and 1850 the border between slave and free states gained political meaning, but not always as a symbol of division. Even as the importance of the border increased, contradictions abounded as residents developed different perspectives on the border depending on their personal circumstances. Even more troubling, the emerging political categories of slavery and freedom relied on inventions that, while inspired by it, did not always accurately describe reality.

The combination of socioeconomic developments, informal and formal antislavery protests, and political maneuvering helped residents define the Ohio River Valley, narrowly conceived, as a borderland. Neither free nor enslaved black residents could escape the pull of the slave trade toward the Deep South. As a result, self-defense was the top priority of the black antislavery movement. In contrast, white Americans capitalized on the river economy without fearing the devastating consequences of commodification. They therefore had the freedom to give meaning to their movement and consequently the Ohio River border. White borderlanders, in large part, understood their own freedom by defining and controlling the movement of African Americans. This social context suggests that casting the border as a straightforward division between free and slave states is inadequate. White borderlanders used the border as a means of controlling the movement of African Americans, which made the border politically important. But at the same time the centrality of the border limited the appeal of radical antislavery sentiment. Escalating sectional conflict in the 1850s would test the stability and coherence of this emerging definition of the borderland.

CHAPTER EIGHT

The Borderland and the Civil War

At midcentury borderlanders debated the meaning and the future of the Ohio River border. These local debates reflected the growing national crisis over slavery. The years 1848–1852 were a period of intense political debate in Congress as representatives faced the deepening sectional rift. The debates over what to do with the territory acquired from the Mexican War led to the Compromise of 1850 and also revealed the possibility of southern secession. In Indiana, Ohio, and Kentucky midcentury debates led to a political configuration that held the region together against the pull of sectionalism that split the country into warring nations. Deep divisions characterized this configuration, but those divisions limited the appeal of disunion.

In contrast to the national narrative of America's descent into civil war, the story of the Ohio River borderland in the 1850s is a narrative of noncausation. Historians have spilled much ink debating the multiple causes of the bloody conflict that resulted in the deaths of over 660,000 Americans. While they differ in emphasis, historians agree that both political and social factors contributed to the sectional rift. But the Civil War failed to split the Ohio River borderland at the seam. Explaining the absence of war requires a slightly different approach than arguing for causation. In an effort to explain the area's resilience, this chapter explores what factors mitigated the appeal of disunion in the borderland.[1]

As the country careened toward civil war in the 1850s, residents along the border developed a regional counternarrative that emphasized a tradition of compromise and accommodation. Residents denounced radical sectionalism and understood their region as a borderland set apart from the uncompromising North or South. Theirs was not a third in-between, as is often the case in international borderlands. Instead they believed that their borderland was a true expression of the nation because they put the union ahead of personal or sectional interests. This emphasis on unionism limited the appeal of increasing radicalism. Ironically, unionism triumphed in the borderland precisely because residents divided over the best course for the region's future. The absence of consensus prevented any one group from dominating, and therefore conflict required resolution and, ultimately, accommodation.[2]

This study of the triumph of the borderland is broken down into analyses of political and social factors. First, for each state individually, the discussion traces the limits of radical sectionalism, the nature of conflicts over slavery, and the importance of controlling the movement of African Americans in the forging of political accommodations. Second, an analysis of 1860 census records reveals the emergence of distinct economic zones that crossed the Ohio River. These zones reveal the continued importance of cross-river social and economic interactions despite the ferocity of sectional conflict. This political and social definition of the borderland helps explain the power of borderland unionism during the fateful election of 1860, the winter of secession, and the rapid formation of the Confederacy.

*   *   *

Sectional debate over slavery threatened to tear the United States in two at midcentury. In 1846 Congressmen David Wilmot, in a move that the historian Michael Holt has likened to opening "Pandora's Box," proposed an amendment that would ban any slavery or involuntary servitude in any territory acquired from Mexico. The Wilmot Proviso never actually passed on any bill, but it set off a firestorm of controversy and debate in Congress that lasted until 1850. Southerners called for a convention to devise a common response should the Wilmot Proviso pass. While this Nashville convention was sparsely attended (no Kentuckians attended) and resulted only in southerners agreeing to hold another convention in five months, it revealed the growing dangers of sectionalism.[3]

As debate over the future of slavery threatened to tear the nation apart, Henry Clay stepped forward to forge one final compromise. Eventually, based on Clay's ideas, Congress agreed on five provisions to the bill that would become known as the Compromise of 1850: 1) the admission of California as a free state; 2) New Mexico and Utah as popular sovereignty territories; 3) Texas's boundary set at the Rio Grande River and the assumption of Texas's debt by the United States; 4) the Fugitive Slave Law; 5) no public slave trade in Washington, D.C. After an exasperated Clay left Congress following the failure of his omnibus bill, Stephen Douglas stepped up to take the lead on the compromise. Douglas split the bill up and used the sectional split to pass provisions using southern majorities for proslavery measures and northern majorities for free-soil measures. Because of this sectional vote, the historian David Potter has called the Compromise of 1850 an armistice rather than an actual compromise. At the time Representative Salmon P. Chase of Ohio declared, "The question of slavery in the territories has been avoided. It has not been settled."[4]

The armistice of 1850 revealed the increasing radicalism of both northerners and southerners at midcentury. For the first time southerners outside of South Carolina accepted secession as a possible, even legitimate, response to threats against slavery. Similarly, northern leaders revealed their willingness to stand against the "slave power." Following this armistice, one controversy after another enflamed sectional tensions. Each controversy also seemed to grow more violent. Passage of the Kansas-Nebraska Act in 1854 ignited armed conflict between pro- and antislavery forces in the Kansas Territory. After the sack of Lawrence, John Brown and seven others took it upon themselves to act as divine retribution. They killed five proslavery men, dragging them from their homes in the middle of the night and splitting their skulls with broadswords. This Pottawatomie Creek massacre ignited more violence in Kansas and was not the last the country would hear from John Brown.

In Congress, Charles Sumner from Massachusetts railed against proslavery violence in a two-day speech he called the "Crime against Kansas." "Murderous robbers from Missouri, hirelings picked from the drunken spew and vomit of an uneasy civilization," he said, committed "a rape of virgin territory, compelling it to the hateful embrace of slavery." Sumner also attacked Andrew P. Butler of South Carolina, saying that Butler was "Don Quixote who had chosen a mistress to whom he has made his vows. Though polluted in the sight of the world, is chaste in his sight—I mean the harlot, Slavery." Two days after the speech, on 22 May, Preston Brooks, Butler's cousin, walked into the nearly empty Senate chamber, approached Sumner's desk, and began to rain blows down on Sumner with his cane. He pummeled him over thirty times. Sumner's legs were trapped under the bolted-down desk, and he eventually pried it from the floor and collapsed in a bloody mess. Sumner did not come back to his Senate seat for two and a half years! The northern press called this incident an outrage, whereas the southern press lionized Brooks. A South Carolina newspaper declared that Brooks "stood forth so nobly in defense of the honor of South Carolinians." In addition Brooks received dozens of new canes, some with inscriptions reading "Hit him again!"[5]

The political turmoil in Congress and escalating violence threatened to turn the Ohio River borderland into a war zone. The Fugitive Slave Law of 1850 had particular relevance to residents along the border. The new law reaffirmed white slaveholders' claims to their human property in free states and forced residents north of the river to aid in the retrieval of fugitive slaves. In addition the law stripped accused African Americans of the right to a jury trial or even to testify in their own defense. The special commissioner in charge of determining an alleged fugitive's fate received ten dollars if he returned the fugitive to slavery and five dollars if he freed him/her. In response to this law, some in the region followed the path to radicalism. Newspapers detailed dramatic escapes by enslaved African Americans and whites' defiance of the Fugitive Slave Law. In politics after 1850 Salmon P. Chase, the senator from Ohio, became increasingly outspoken in his antislavery views. Conflict abounded along the border in the 1850s.[6]

The Federal Fugitive Slave Law of 1850 radicalized the black antislavery movement in Indiana and Ohio. Free black Americans believed that the law took them closer to slavery. As a result, free African Americans explicitly linked the individual fugitive's right to resist with their own condition. The link between fugitive self-defense and kidnapping propelled African Americans toward the support of collective violent resistance. African Americans formed vigilance committees to protect fugitives against recapture. Members of the Ohio convention resolved that the Fugitive Slave Bill taught them "that liberty is dearer than life, and eternal vigilance its only guarantee." African Americans had suggested the need for violent self-defense for many years, but they had coupled it with the legal fight.[7]

The political turn in the 1850s symbolized the failure of their legal efforts and increased their resolve to resist physically. African Americans moved toward a more radical position, linking northern racial prejudice with the plight of southern slaves. At the 1851 convention, C. H. Langston declared, "I would call on every slave . . . to arise and assert their liberties, and cut their masters' throats if they attempt again to reduce them to slavery." As an example of this shift, Frederick Douglass, once a proponent of nonviolence, considered violence the only solution by the 1850s. African American leaders recognized that the existence of slavery prevented them from ever gaining the political and civil rights they desired. Therefore they fought against the connections between freedom and slavery by defending fugitive slaves from recapture. Blacks' freedom depended on the abolition of slavery and the destruction of the border.[8]

The Federal Fugitive Slave Law also radicalized some of the pioneers of the white abolitionist movement. James Birney and other original abolitionist leaders lost faith in the antislavery movement. Theodore Weld abandoned the abolition movement altogether after becoming frustrated with the lack of progress and the violent backlash. James Birney began advocating disunion by midcentury because he believed that the Union protected slaveholders. Birney and Weld saw the connections between slave and free states as the reason for the failure of the abolition movement. From their perspective, rather than a division, the border symbolized the interconnectedness of slavery and freedom in America. Birney decided that the only way to break away from the influence of slavery was to break the Union in half.[9]

However, while whites militantly defended their states from invasion by outsiders, in contrast to abolitionists and southern fire-eaters, most of them failed to see the logic of disunion. North of the river, residents believed that the border protected them from a flood of immigration by blacks. South of the river, residents believed that a border between sovereign states with a shared federal government better protected slavery than a border between sovereign enemy nations. Therefore the increased radicalism of black and white abolitionist leaders in Ohio and Indiana pushed them to the margins. In advocating for collective resistance, black abolitionists ignited the fears of white residents along the border, and abolitionists' call for disunion threatened to turn the borderland into a war zone. In the political mainstream, borderland whites remained wedded to their commitment to maintaining the Union through compromise. One Ohio paper read, "One half our commerce floats on the waters of the Mississippi . . . the other half finds its way East by the Lakes. Will you split Ohio, Indiana and Illinois in half, and let the Northern sections go with your Eastern confederacy, and the Southern sections, with the South Western?" As this editorialist suggested, southern Ohio and Indiana were becoming distinct from the northern sections of the states. Indeed division within northern states limited the power of the antislavery movement along the river.[10]

* * *

In 1849 Ohioans repealed many of the state's black laws, suggesting that the state was becoming more open to African Americans. However, the politics behind the repeal revealed the depth of the divisions in the state. Joshua Giddings, from the Western Reserve in northern Ohio, was a classic conscience Whig and was outspokenly antislavery. Giddings and his fellow conscience Whigs wanted to repeal the black laws and remain dedicatedly antislavery. However, Giddings's stance and his refusal to compromise with southern Democrats alienated him from southern Ohioans. Southern Ohio Democrats both supported the Wilmot Proviso and opposed the repeal of the black laws. Support for the black laws remained strong in the southern part of the state, where residents despised the radicalism of abolitionism and slavery equally. Salmon P. Chase stepped in to strike a deal to secure the repeal of the black laws and satisfy the southern Democrats. Chase, like Giddings, was strongly antislavery, but he was also better attuned to the sentiment of southern Ohioans. He worked as a lawyer and served on the city council in the 1840s in Cincinnati. Chase bargained for his own election as U.S. senator and the repeal of the black laws in return for the election of two Democrats as representatives. In the end, the success of the grassroots movement against the black laws came down to a political deal between Democrats and Whigs. The deal ended the Whigs' hopes for redistricting and helped the Democratic Party break the power of the Whigs. Salmon P. Chase became a free-soil Democrat.[11]

As the black laws political deal suggests, Ohioans remained divided in 1850. While some Ohioans stepped up their efforts to defend the state against intrusions by the "slave power," others worried about the consequences of the radicalization of the country. In contrast to those in the rest of the state, who more closely identified with the Northeast, southwestern Ohioans continued to look in both directions. These Ohioans identified with the free-soil North, but their close proximity to the border forced them to look south as well. Historians have long recognized the region's close economic connections with the South. But in addition to these economic concerns, residents along the river looked at the Ohio River border as protection against migration by both free and enslaved blacks from Kentucky. This divided outlook encouraged conflict but also made some seek accommodations to maintain social stability. Thus in the case of Ohio, division actually weakened radicalism.[12]

Southwestern Ohio never followed the rest of the state's drift toward the stronger antislavery position of the Republican Party in the 1850s. But it would be inaccurate to argue that residents of southwestern Ohio completely sympathized with their Kentucky neighbors. Instead residents of southwest Ohio remained divided and ambivalent in their antislavery opinions. In 1857 three U.S. deputies and five Kentuckians tried to arrest Addison White, an escaped Kentucky slave, in Mechanicsburg in central Ohio. White exchanged gunfire with the deputies, and thirty Ohioans came out and helped him escape. A federal posse returned less than a week later and arrested four of the men who had helped White escape. As they traveled south in a carriage, a crowd followed firing pistols. A sheriff stopped the carriage, but the deputies pistol-whipped him. Eventually a force of about two hundred Ohioans overpowered and arrested the deputies. The deputies were charged with assault for injuring the sheriff, and the case was presented in Cincinnati at the U.S. District Court. The judge ruled in favor of the deputy marshals and their use of force. In response, indictments were issued against all Ohio officials who had tried to stop the marshals. At this point the governor, who just happened to be Salmon P. Chase, negotiated a compromise. All charges were dropped, and one thousand dollars was paid to Addison White's Kentucky owner.[13]

On the surface this case demonstrated Ohioans' growing resistance to the Fugitive Slave Law and southern intrusions. However, the case also highlighted the divisions in the southwestern section of the state. The first men to resist the deputies were from central Ohio. However, the conflict became especially heated when the marshals tried to arrest white Ohioans. Ohioans resented any threat to their sovereignty and defended themselves from any perceived invasion by their slaveholding neighbors. As they had for years, they united when slavery threatened white freedom. However, divisions emerged as the case reached the courts. Southern Ohio Democrats, in particular Clement Vallandigham, represented the deputy marshals. In addition the U.S. district judge upheld federal authority and ruled in favor of the marshals. It is clear that some Ohio politicians and authorities believed in accommodating southern slaveholders. In offering financial compensation to White's owner, Chase's compromise recognized the rights of Kentucky slaveholders.

Ohioans' understanding of the border still turned on their distinction between illegal kidnapping and lawful reclamation. Even though Ohioans still recognized the Kentuckians' rights of reclamation into the 1850s, the free black population increased in every county in Ohio along the river between 1850 and 1860. The repeal of the black laws likely contributed to this growth, but the numbers also suggest that Ohio's free soil was attractive to free African Americans. In 1856 the Ohio court ruled that any slave except a fugitive became free when entering Ohio. This was a major step in strengthening the power of Ohio's free soil, but it still upheld the long-held distinction between reclamation and kidnapping. Ohioans understood that the more clearly they defined the river border, the more it could compel African Americans to cross it in pursuit of freedom. This put them in a difficult position. Ohioans would defend the border against invasion, but only the border could protect them from Kentucky's African American population. While they could not stop it, Ohio borderlanders understood that negotiation and accommodation across the border limited the immigration of African Americans, an appealing position in a region that never fully supported the repeal of the black laws.[14]

In Indiana politicians firmly rejected the sectionalism both locally and nationally. In 1850 Indiana's governor stated, "Indiana takes her stand in the ranks, not of Southern destiny, nor yet of Northern destiny. She plants herself on the basis of the Constitution; and takes her stand in the ranks of American Destiny." In Congress, Indiana politicians turned doughface compromising into a political platform. Jesse Bright was the best example of this compromising position. In his personal life, Bright married a woman from Kentucky, Mary Turpin, and maintained a slave plantation in Kentucky. In Congress, Bright represented Indiana Democrats. Bright repeatedly voted with the South on the Compromise of 1850, but he denounced both southern fire-eaters and northern Free-Soilers as radicals. As Bright explained, "with me, the voters of Indiana unite in opposing and repudiating Disunionists South and Abolitionists North." Another Indiana congressman, Richard Thompson, wrote to one of his constituents, "The ultra feelings of neither of these parties have yet to carry very great extent—reached the West. Here we occupy a conservative position denouncing slavery as an evil on the one hand and admitting all the constitutional rights of the slave states on the other. This is a high position." As these examples suggest, Indiana politicians celebrated compromise as the ultimate expression of patriotism. Whereas "Disunionists" and "Abolitionists" threatened the future of the country with their "ultra feelings," Indianans celebrated their ability to put interest aside in pursuit of the public good.[15]

Indiana politicians' conservatism reflected the feelings of their constituents along the Ohio River. Whereas white Kentuckians feared that abolitionists could inspire slave rebellions in the state, white Indianans feared

Table 1. Comparison of Voting Percentages in Favor of the Exclusion Clause in Indiana

Ohio River Counties	Percentage in Favor of the Exclusion Clause	Northern Counties	Percentage in Favor of the Exclusion Clause
Clark	97	De Kalb	53
Crawford	90	Elkhart	38
Floyd	94	LaGrange	39
Harrison	96	Lake	61
Jefferson	86	LaPorte	68
Perry	92	Marshall	68
Posey	94	Noble	61
Spencer	96	Porter	71
Switzerland	92	St. Joseph	53
Vanderburgh	86	Steuben	30
Warrick	98		
STATE AVERAGE	84		

that news of whites' fighting for black freedom could incite a flood of unwanted black migration. This fear of unrestricted black freedom led whites to facilitate peaceful coexistence by regulating the border crossing of African Americans. White residents in Indiana sought to control the move-ment of African Americans by stopping the migration of free blacks across the river. Around Louisville, enslaved African Americans crossed the Ohio River on errands, traveled with their owners on steamboats, and worked along the docks with free workers. These behaviors served as constant reminders of how slavery crossed the border. Clearly, the 1831 law requir-ing African Americans to post bonds upon immigration failed to meet white Indianans' goal of limiting black migration. Despite petitions and protests from free blacks and white Quakers in the state, Indiana politicians in 1851 passed a new constitution that banned all African American immi-gration. As shown in Table 1, in each county along the Ohio River, Indian-ans voted for the restriction clause at a higher percentage than the state average. In contrast, sixteen counties north of Indianapolis voted below the state average, including three counties where Indianans voted against the restriction. Of these sixteen counties, twelve had fewer than forty black residents compared to at least four thousand white residents in each county.[16]

Despite their nearly unanimous support of the immigration restriction, there were examples of Indianans aiding in the dramatic escape of enslaved blacks from Kentucky. Newspapers in New Albany regularly printed stories of conflicts between Kentuckians and Indianans over reclamation. In one event in 1857, Charles Bell; his father, David; and Oswald Wright, a black man, helped a slave escape. In response Kentuckians arrested Charles while he was in Kentucky; they then went to Indiana to arrest the elder Bell and Wright and took them to Brandenburg. In response to threats of violence from Indianans, Kentucky's governor called out the militia to defend Brandenburg. Charles Bell's brothers raided the Brandenburg jail and freed him and their father but not Wright. The Kentuckians retaliated by capturing one of Charles's brothers, and they took him back to Brandenburg. In response 120 Indianans from New Albany crossed the river fully armed and ready to take Bell back. Town leaders negotiated a deal, the Indianans returned north, and Horace Bell was freed on bond. However, Oswald Wright remained in jail![17]

While events such as this demonstrated the potential for armed conflict between Indianans and Kentuckians, the details of this particular event reveal the limits of Indianans' antislavery militancy. Most important, the residents of New Albany protested and threatened violence each time Kentuckians captured and jailed a *white* man. In addition they agreed to go back to Indiana once Kentuckians promised to release the jailed white man but not the black man involved. Oswald Wright's involvement was equal to that of the Bells, but his loss was not worth violence in the minds of the New Albany residents. There was not an army of free blacks marching into Kentucky to free Wright, likely because whites on both sides of the river feared blacks' collective action. Along the border, whites' fear of radical collective action by African Americans became the shadow behind every antislavery action. Therefore they would rally to defend white Indianans from kidnapping but stopped short of fighting for, or with, black Americans.

African Americans in Indiana recognized the limits of their protection. The combination of the Fugitive Slave Law, Indiana's anti-immigration law, and white residents' general intolerance for black radicalism convinced many African Americans to leave the region. Whereas the free black population increased in the state overall between 1850 and 1860, it decreased along the river. In fact the free black population decreased in eight of eleven counties along the river. The free black population significantly increased in Floyd County, but that growth was likely a product of neighboring

Louisville's continued growth and development. As a demonstration of their views on African Americans, 94 percent of white residents of Floyd County voted for the immigration restriction. They used the border to limit both legal and illegal migration by African Americans, but they also defended it against intrusions by slaveholding Kentuckians. In southern Indiana white Americans' commitment to racial supremacy remained constant, but through a combination of accommodation and conflict they, like their neighbors across the river, hoped to see a future "whitening" of the population along the Ohio River. In short, white Indianans used the border to define their freedom.[18]

Across the river Kentuckians debated the future of slavery in their state at midcentury. In February 1849 the Kentucky legislature repealed the Non-Importation Act. Kentuckians' vote to repeal that act reflected the reality that slavery was part of the state's economy but did not necessarily indicate their commitment to perpetualism. The repeal increased the volume of slave sales within the state, spurring the growth and increasing the sophistication and profitability of the domestic slave trade. The price of slaves spiked sharply in the 1850s, which also increased the profitability of the trade and highlighted the economic importance of the commodification of black bodies. By the 1850s several large slave-trading firms had based their operations in Kentucky and the state's white residents were shipping thirty-four hundred slaves annually to the Deep South. In order to regulate the rising trade, the city of Louisville passed an ordinance in 1851 requiring slave vendors to purchase three-hundred-dollar licenses. The repeal of the Non-Importation Act revealed a commitment to the form of slavery already present in Kentucky. The Ohio River connected the state with the markets of the Deep South, and in the 1850s slaves were valuable commodities. The growth of the slave trade after the repeal strengthened Kentucky's economic link with the Deep South.[19]

In August 1848 Kentuckians had approved the calling of a constitutional convention, sparking debates over convention candidates for the next year. The repeal of the Non-Importation Act in February 1849 led some Kentuckians to look for antislavery candidates to bring the law back. The political antislavery movement lacked unity, but candidates still campaigned fiercely and stirred up conflict in the process. After a debate Cyrus Turner, the son of a proslavery candidate, confronted the emancipationist Cassius Clay. Clay responded by drawing his bowie knife but was surrounded, hit in the head with a club, and stabbed in the lung. Clay fought back, regained control of his knife, stabbed Cyrus Turner in the stomach, and promptly lost consciousness. Cyrus's brother aimed a gun at Clay's head, but the gun misfired. Cyrus Turner died from his wounds, but Clay, amazingly, survived. In addition to this bloody scene, there was a mass escape and threat of a rebellion in the central bluegrass region amid the constitutional convention debates. From the perspective of proslavery Kentuckians, violence and upheaval seemed to follow the emancipationists.[20]

Ultimately emancipationists gained little support among white Kentuckians, which reflected the realities of Kentucky's position at the edge of the South. Some Kentuckians hoped that the state was on a natural course toward gradual emancipation. These men worried that the emancipationists would cause more harm than good. As one politician wrote, "I fear, however, that the imprudent goal of the emancipationists may lead to the adoption of ultra views and throw open the state to the importation of slaves." This man, like others, hoped that Kentuckians would be free from slavery one day in the future based on the gradual reduction of the slave population in their state at the top of the South. When Kentuckians voted on candidates, the emancipationists filled just two seats and gained less than 10 percent of the vote throughout the state. At the constitutional convention, Kentuckians once again guaranteed the future of slavery in the state.[21]

The defeat of the emancipation candidates sapped the strength of the political antislavery movement in the state. After the state convention, Kentucky politicians abandoned talk of emancipation and instead traded votes over who could best protect and maintain slavery. However, most Kentuckians failed to follow their Deep South brethren toward sectional nationalism or the defense of slavery as a positive good. Instead the debate taught Kentuckians the dangers of radicalism. Radical proslavery ideas emerging in the 1850s found little traction in Kentucky. White Kentuckians had long prided themselves on the mildness of slavery in their state. Politicians made regular demographic comparisons between Kentucky and states of the Deep South to highlight the weakness of slavery in the state. Of course, these numbers only masked the iron grip that slavery actually had on the state, but the perception of mildness mattered deeply to Kentuckians. Similarly, Henry Clay's legacy of compromise mitigated extremism among politicians. Instead politicians understood themselves as great compromisers because they had lived so peaceably with their free-soil neighbors. Kentuckians explicitly distinguished themselves from the more radical fire-eaters of the

Deep South, instead taking pride in the fact that the region was a borderland.[22]

By the 1850s Kentuckians had accepted slavery as economically profitable and socially useful. Kentuckians', as they had for many years, wedded their commitment to slavery to their desire to maintain the racial order. They therefore looked with increasing ire on threats to slavery. Some antislavery reformers began to work outside the political mainstream and, as they did, became increasingly radical in their tactics. John G. Fee, for example, established the community of Berea, where he passed out Bibles to slaves and supported the admission of blacks to the college. Kentuckians violently opposed Fee's actions. They burned several schools sponsored by his followers, threatened to drown him in the Kentucky River, and eventually ousted him from the state in 1859. In another example, William Bailey printed an antislavery newspaper in Newport, across the river from Cincinnati. Proslavery businesses boycotted his paper, the building where he printed his paper was burned, and he was attacked and sued. In 1859 Kentuckians threw his press into the Ohio River and warned him to leave the state. Fee and Bailey represented the increasing radicalism of antislavery advocates in Kentucky. However, Kentuckians' violent responses to their work revealed the population's intolerance for radical antislavery. In reality, though, Fee's and Bailey's actions could not have taken place farther south, so the fact that they could and did work in Kentucky suggests that Kentucky was more open to antislavery protest than the Deep South.[23]

The increased radicalism of the pro- and antislavery movements only marginalized radical sectionalism and cemented the conservative center in Kentucky. In 1859 Reverend James Craik denounced radicalism in a speech in front of the Kentucky House. Craik called abolitionism a "stupid crime"; he felt that in their call for the national government to end slavery, abolitionists violated state sovereignty and threatened the very integrity of the Union. At the same time Craik called disunion a "more flagrant stupidity" because only the Constitution could protect state sovereignty against a despotic federal government. Rather than radicalism, Craik called for "reason, argument, and justice and right" from his fellow Americans.[24]

Kentuckians coupled their rejection of pro- and antislavery radicalism with an argument that "whitening" the state would naturally free Kentucky from slavery. The steamboats traveling along the Ohio River continuously moved enslaved blacks to the Deep South. In Jefferson County the enslaved population dropped by 5.6 percent between 1850 and 1860. In Louisville,

Kentucky's most developed industrial center, the enslaved population dropped by 10 percent and made up only 7.5 percent of the city's population in 1860. In addition, as part of the constitutional convention, Kentuckians had banned the migration of free blacks to the state. Across the river Indiana had already been proved inhospitable to free blacks. Therefore, through sale, Kentuckians would eventually be free from both slavery and African Americans. Conservative politicians stressed moderation and compromise for the best of both worlds: Kentucky could maintain its ties to the South through the slave trade but also trade with its northern neighbors. If emancipation came to the state, it would have to be gradual and "natural."[25]

Local and national political turmoil at midcentury marked both the culmination of the previous two decades of antislavery conflict and the separation of the borderland from the states and the nation. Politicians from the Ohio River borderland repudiated the polarization of the nation. They portrayed both northern abolitionists and southern fire-eaters as dangerous to the integrity of the Union. Their emphasis on compromise and accommodation set them apart even from other sections of their respective states. Northern Indiana and Ohio became Republican strongholds, whereas politicians such as Jesse Bright of Indiana and Clement Vallandigham of Ohio remained loyal to the Democratic Party. The persistence of northern doughface politicians in southern Indiana and Ohio reflected the region's rejection of radicalism.

In rejecting sectionalism as dangerous, residents along the river in turn made their commitment to compromise and the Union into an expression of patriotism. From farther away, people imagined the border as separating two entities in conflict. But while it separated two entities, along the border conflicts oddly allowed for coexistence. While they fought over fugitive reclamation, residents on both sides of the river feared radicalism's potential for social disruption. Instead white Americans' commitment to racial supremacy shielded the region from the divisions of the 1850s; while they may have disagreed over how the border could best limit racial conflict, white Indianans and Kentuckians could agree that the border was the best means of limiting racial interaction and conflict. In using the accommodation across the border to define the region, politicians and residents set the borderland up as the rhetorical opposite of sectional conflict. Borderlanders imagined the Ohio River Valley as a unique region rooted in compromise across a potentially divisive border.

*   *   *

The European Alexis de Tocqueville toured the United States to learn about American democracy. Based on his observations, Tocqueville wrote his famous work *Democracy in America*, in which he described the origins, nature, and limits of democracy. As part of his tour, Tocqueville traveled down the Ohio River. He wrote that from the Ohio, one had only to "cast glances around himself to judge in an instant" the differences between slave and free territories. Tocqueville wrote that in Kentucky "society is asleep" and in Ohio there is "a confused noise that proclaims from afar the presence of industry." In Tocqueville's understanding, slavery was an aberration in America's otherwise free and classless society. Therefore he depicted the Ohio River as a clear border dividing two distinct worlds.[26]

While Tocqueville based his description on brief and select observations, Mark Twain used his years of life experience along the Mississippi and Missouri Rivers to craft his account. In *The Adventures of Huckleberry Finn*, Twain depicted the border between slavery and freedom as elusive. Setting their sights on Cairo, Illinois, Huckleberry Finn and Jim floated the river in hopes of finding freedom for Jim. They realized that the current could push them past the city of freedom, but Jim assured Huck that he would "be mighty sure to see it, because he'd be a free man the minute he seen it, but if he missed it he'd be in a slave country again and no more show for freedom." Fog obscured the shore, and they drifted right past Cairo. On their raft Huck and Jim were subject to the river's current, which propelled them toward slavery. Jim and Huck failed to distinguish free-soil from slave territory because for the runaway slave and his friend, the river obscured the differences between the two. When they tried to paddle upstream, a steamboat, the very representation of commerce, appeared and smashed their raft, and with it Jim's hope for freedom.[27]

Whereas Tocqueville's observations may have suited a regional comparison on a national scale, Twain's fictional account better captured the liminality of the Ohio River borderland. Historians and observers have long drawn attention to the different economic trajectories of the North and the South in the antebellum era. By 1860 the North was more heavily industrialized, and small farms dotted the rural landscape. The South, in contrast, lagged behind the North in industrialization and had an economy built on the growth and cultivation of slave-powered cotton plantations. Regional generalizations, however, paper over the diversity of both the northern and southern landscapes. The closer the analysis, the less distinct the sections seem, especially at the border. Analysis beginning at the state level and moving to the county level reveals the similarities and differences across the Ohio River. In the end, the cross-river similarities in agricultural and manufacturing production in the Ohio River Valley reveal that rather than a line dividing two distinct economic worlds, residents used the river to foster strong economic connections in a borderland.[28]

*   *   *

Both agricultural production and manufacturing production in Ohio, Indiana, and Kentucky followed the traditional regional patterns associated with the North and the South respectively, as shown in Table 2. Ohio's large population, dense agricultural production, and high manufacturing production made it similar to other industrial centers in the North. While not on the same scale as Ohio, neighboring Indiana had a large population, dense agricultural production, and solid manufacturing base. Indiana's low ranking in cash value per farm but moderate cash value per acre demonstrates the dominance of small farmers in Indiana and the dense cultivation of the land, making it more similar to other northern states. Indiana also had a higher annual value of manufacturing products than all southern states with the exception of Virginia.[29]

Despite being settled before Ohio or Indiana, Kentucky had a lower total population, fewer total farms, and a lower cash value of those farms than either of its northern neighbors. Indicative of the difference between farming in free states and farming in slave states was the value of farmland per acre. Kentucky was well below its free-state neighbors at only fifteen dollars per acre. Kentucky ranked fifteenth in manufacturing production, which was lower than its free-state neighbors, but fourth among other slaveholding states behind Virginia, Missouri, and Maryland. Thus at the state level Ohio and Indiana more closely fit the northern model, whereas Kentucky was more southern in its agricultural and manufacturing production.

While the state comparison revealed clear regional associations, the counties along the Ohio River did not follow the patterns of the rest of the states. As shown in Table 3, in Ohio the value per farm and the value per acre were significantly higher along the river than the state averages. In particular, Hamilton County's farmland was worth three times the state

Table 2. State and Regional Comparison of Economic Development Based on 1860 Census Data

	Total Population	Number of Farms	Total Cash Value of Farms	Cash Value per Farm	Cash Value per Acre	Ratio of Improved/ Unimproved Land	Total Manufacturing Production
Ohio	2,339,511 (3)	173,383 (2)	$678,132,991 (2)	$3,911 (10)	$33.12	62/38	$121,691,148 (4)
Indiana	1,350,428 (6)	126,898 (5)	$356,712,175 (6)	$2,811 (22)	$21.77	50/50	$41,840,434 (10)
Kentucky	1,155,685 (9)	83,689 (8)	$291,496,955 (7)	$3,483 (15)	$15.21	40/60	$37,931,240 (15)
Non-Slaveholding States		1,233,175	$4,068,824,199	$3,299	$25.86	56/44	
Slaveholding States		698,958	$2,550,237,608	$3,649	$10.39	30/70	
All Counties in Indiana and Ohio				$3,446	$28.07	57/43	
Northern River Counties				$3,245	$28.35	51/49	
Southern River Counties				$4,365	$24.14	48/52	

Note: The numbers in parentheses indicate the state's rank for all states in the country.

average per acre, and the value per farm was twenty-seven hundred dollars higher than the state average. Table 5 shows that, similar to Ohio, in Kentucky farmland along the Ohio River was more valuable than that in the rest of the state. Farmland had the highest value in Jefferson County, where the value per farm exceeded ten thousand dollars, nearly tripling the state average. The high land values were likely related to the presence of a large urban center, Louisville. Much like Hamilton County, Ohio, which was the location of Cincinnati, Jefferson County, Kentucky, had extremely high farmland values compared to those in the rest of the region. The fact that land values were high in both counties with major urban centers reveals the influence of development on land values. In contrast to Ohio and Kentucky, in Indiana farmland along the Ohio River was less valuable than that in the rest of the state. While the river counties made up 11 percent of the total number of farms, they made up only 9 percent of the total cash value for the state. Notice in Table 4 that only two of eleven counties had farm values higher than the state average. In fact, Crawford County averaged one thousand dollars per farm, nearly two thousand dollars below the state average. Overall, both the value per acre and the value per farm in Indiana were significantly lower along the Ohio River than in the rest of the state.

In addition to land values, the rate of land development differed along the Ohio River. The 1860 census records divided farmland into the categories of improved and unimproved to signify the difference between cultivated and uncultivated land. Along the Ohio River in both Ohio and Indiana, the land was less densely cultivated than that in the rest of the state. This shift toward more unimproved land is especially significant when compared to Kentucky. As a state, Kentucky had a cultivation rate typical of southern states. However, along the Ohio River the land was more densely cultivated. These shifts made cross-river averages closer than state averages.

Manufacturing production was proportionally high along the river in all three states. Cincinnati dominated manufacturing in Ohio and the region. Hamilton County accounted for 39 percent of the state's total manufacturing products, 19 percent of total manufacturing establishments, 33 percent of capital invested in manufacturing, and 40 percent of the labor force. In Indiana three of the five top counties in manufacturing production in the state were along the Ohio River. In all three counties, river cities were production centers. In Kentucky five of the top six counties in manufacturing production were along the Ohio River. While the numbers were different for each state, the relative increase in manufacturing production along the

Table 3. Characteristics of Counties in Ohio That Border the Ohio River and Kentucky Based on 1860 Census Data

Ohio River Counties	Cash Value per Farm	Cash Value per Acre	Ratio of Imp./Unimp. Land (Percent)	Total Free Black Population	Free Blacks as Percentage of Population	Value of Manufacturing Products (Thousands)	Percentage of State Manufacturing Production	Percentage of Manufacturing in River Counties	Voting Results in 1860
Hamilton	$6,628	$99.31	69/31	4,608	2.13	$46,995	38.62	87.98	Lincoln
Clermont	$4,685	$45.33	62/38	833	2.5	2$1,292	1.06	2.42	Douglas
Brown	$3,740	$31.52	60/40	1,116	3.73	$1,273	1.05	2.38	Douglas
Adams	$2,796	$19.31	54/46	105	0.52	$695	0.57	1.30	Douglas
Scioto	$2,844	$21.18	51/49	323	1.33	$1,999	1.64	3.74	Lincoln
Lawrence	$1,949	$15.40	46/54	685	2.95	$1,160	0.95	2.17	Lincoln
River Totals	**$4,359**	**$40.71**	**58/42**	**7,670**	**2.21**	**$53,414**	**43.89**		
State Totals	**$3,911**	**$33.12**	**62/38**	**36,673**	**1.57**	**$121,691**			**Lincoln**

Table 4. Characteristics of Counties in Indiana That Border the Ohio River and Kentucky Based on 1860 Census Data

Indiana River Counties	Cash Value per Farm	Cash Value per Acre	Ratio of Imp./Unimp. Land (Percent)	Total Free Black Population	Free Blacks as Percentage of Population	Value of Manufacturing Products (Thousands)	Percentage of State Manufacturing Production	Percentage of Manufacturing in River Counties	Voting in 1860 Election
Posey	$2,699	$23.78	50/50	136	0.84	$544	1.30	5.84	Douglas
Vanderburgh	$1,922	$17.90	56/44	127	0.62	$1,645	3.93	17.67	Lincoln
Warrick	$2,004	$16.37	42/58	19	0.14	$517	1.24	5.55	Breckenridge
Spencer	$1,874	$15.14	39/61	2	0.01	$309	0.74	3.32	Lincoln
Perry	$1,091	$8.38	28/72	3	0.03	$470	1.12	5.05	Lincoln
Crawford	$1,002	$6.77	30/70	0	0	$52	0.12	0.56	Douglas
Harrison	$1,680	$13.01	47/53	114	0.62	$437	1.04	4.69	Douglas
Floyd	$2,829	$24.98	50/50	757	3.75	$1,833	4.38	19.68	Douglas
Clark	$3,178	$24.48	51/49	520	2.54	$653	1.56	7.01	Douglas
Jefferson	$2,567	$23.32	52/48	512	2.05	$2,474	5.91	26.56	Lincoln
Switzerland	$3,744	$35.02	60/40	42	0.33	$379	0.91	4.07	Lincoln
River Totals	**$2,254**	**$18.62**	**46/54**	**2,232**	**1.23**	**$9,314**	**22.26**		**Lincoln**
State Totals	**$2,811**	**$21.77**	**50/50**	**11,428**	**0.85**	**$41,840**			**Lincoln**

Table 5. Characteristics of Counties in Kentucky That Border the Ohio River, Ohio, and Indiana Based on 1860 Census Data

Kentucky River Counties	Cash Value per Farm	Cash Value per Acre	Ratio of Imp./Unimp. Land (Percent)	Total Free Black Pop.	Free Blacks as Percentage of Pop.	Value of Manufacturing Products (Thousands)	Percentage of State Manufacturing Production	Percentage of Manufacturing in River Counties	Enslaved Pop.	Enslaved as Percentage of Total Pop.	Voting in 1860 Election
Union	$5,620	$21.38	37/63	20	0.16	$1,219	3.21	5.32	3,105	24.27	Bell
Henderson	$5,858	$21.16	37/63	77	0.54	$1,089	2.87	4.75	5,767	40.44	Bell
Daviess	$3,426	$19.14	39/61	76	0.49	$419	1.10	1.83	3,515	22.61	Bell
Hancock	$2,122	$13.81	39/61	13	0.21	$119	0.31	0.52	818	13.17	Breckenridge
Breckenridge	$1,901	$8.00	36/64	17	0.13	$179	0.47	0.78	2,340	17.68	Bell
Meade	$2,804	$11.70	40/60	22	0.25	$126	0.33	0.55	1,932	21.71	Bell
Jefferson	$10,165	$64.76	67/33	2,007	2.24	$14,156	37.32	61.71	10,304	11.53	Bell
Oldham	$6,251	$28.05	68/32	37	0.51	$20	0.05	0.09	2,431	33.38	Breckenridge
Trimble	$2,718	$16.97	56/44	5	0.09	$287	0.76	1.25	831	14.13	Breckenridge
Carroll	$4,576	$25.79	57/43	42	0.64	$435	1.15	1.90	1,045	15.89	Breckenridge
Gallatin	$3,919	$21.91	59/41	14	0.23	$118	0.31	0.52	708	11.69	Breckenridge
Boone	$7,290	$42.89	63/37	48	0.43	$439	1.16	1.91	1,745	15.59	Bell
Kenton	$3,707	$30.15	59/41	85	0.33	$1,809	4.77	7.89	567	2.23	Bell
Campbell	$2,437	$41.45	63/37	88	0.42	$229	0.60	1.00	116	0.55	Douglas
Bracken	$2,153	$19.43	55/45	83	0.75	$72	0.19	0.32	750	6.81	Bell
Mason	$6,880	$38.85	83/17	385	2.11	$1,652	4.35	7.20	3,772	20.70	Bell
Lewis	$1,877	$8.93	31/69	17	0.20	$114	0.30	0.50	230	2.75	Bell
Greenup	$3,093	$9.73	27/73	47	0.54	$452	1.19	1.97	363	4.14	Bell
Counties Bordering Ohio	$3,678	$25.02	54/46								
Counties Bordering Indiana	$4,728	$22.93	45/55								
River County Totals	$4,365	$24.14	48/52	3,083	1.06	$22,937	60.47		40,339	17.89	
State Totals	$3,483	$15.21	40/60	10,684	0.92	$37,931			225,483	19.51	Bell

Ohio River suggests a link between the river and production. Thus the river gave counties on both sides of the divide a common ground.

Manufacturing is difficult to compare because of the dominance of Cincinnati. Hamilton County accounted for 75 percent of manufacturing production for all northern river counties. In comparison Jefferson County accounted for 62 percent of manufacturing production in Kentucky river counties. Removing Hamilton County from the calculations, Kentucky river counties far outproduced northern river counties. But removing both Jefferson County and Hamilton County from the equation, the remaining northern counties outproduced the remaining Kentucky counties. Thus major manufacturing centers dominated the landscape on both sides of the Ohio River. However, manufacturing was more heavily concentrated on the northern bank than in Kentucky. The absence of a major manufacturing center in Indiana suggests that southern Indiana's major cities were Louisville, Kentucky, and Cincinnati, Ohio.[30]

Along the river, Ohio, Indiana, and Kentucky retained the characteristics of their defining regions, but the distinctions became less defined. In order to examine the impact of slavery on the economic development of the region more thoroughly, the comparison is narrowed by state and by county. A closer analysis of the data reveals strong cross-river relationships in both agricultural and manufacturing production. As shown in Table 5, in the Kentucky river counties across from Ohio, the average value per acre was higher than Kentucky's full river county average and the value per farm was lower. These numbers reveal a higher number of small farms in this region than farther west. These numbers are closer to Ohio's averages, but there is still a clear difference. However, Hamilton County skews the average up considerably. Removing Hamilton County from the calculation brings Ohio's numbers closer to Kentucky's. Without Hamilton County, Ohio's value per farm was $3,484 and the value per acre was $28.38, which suggests that land values were quite similar across the river. The ratio of improved to unimproved acreage was also similar at 56 percent improved. In fact, the land values of Kentucky's river counties compare more closely with those in Ohio than with those in the rest of Kentucky.

On closer examination, the similarity in agricultural production between Ohio river counties and Kentucky river counties is most noticeable in bordering counties. In eastern Kentucky, it appears that the size of the enslaved population had less of an impact on development than did the quality of the land. Land quality was likely a feature shared across the river,

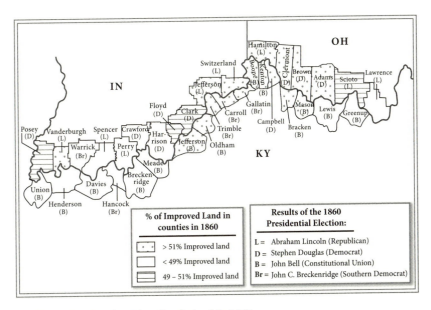

Figure 7. The Ohio River borderland in 1860.

so where land quality was low in Kentucky, it was also low in Ohio. Land values were directly influenced by land quality because improved land had a higher value than unimproved land. Thus land values were higher where the ratio of improved land was higher, because it yielded a higher value per acre.[31]

Ohio's easternmost county bordering Kentucky, Lawrence, had the lowest value per acre and the lowest ratio of improved land of Ohio's river counties. Similarly, Kentucky's eastern counties, Lewis and Greenup, had the lowest value per acre and were the least improved among Kentucky river counties. It is interesting that these counties also had small enslaved populations at only 3 and 4 percent of the population respectively. Mason County, directly west of Lewis County, in contrast, had a large enslaved population, high value per acre, and high rate of development. Directly across the river, Brown County had high values per acre and a high rate of development. Moving west, the Kentucky counties of Boone, Kenton, and Campbell all had small enslaved populations, high values per acre, and ratios of improved land at 59 percent and above. These counties bordered Hamilton County and Clermont County, both of which had high land values per acre and ratios of improved land above 60 percent.

The value of manufacturing products also reveals a cross-river relation-ship between Ohio and Kentucky. Clearly, Cincinnati was the dominant manufacturing center in the region. But, interestingly, Kenton County, directly across the river, was also a manufacturing center. The manufactur-ing production in this region had ties to the free black population. Kenton County and Campbell County, both situated across from Cincinnati, had the third and fourth largest free black populations of Kentucky river coun-ties. Hamilton County had a sizable free black population as well. Mason County, Kentucky, was a manufacturing center and had the second highest free black population of Kentucky river counties. In this case neighboring Brown and Adams Counties were not major manufacturing centers in Ohio, but that is because of the dominance of Hamilton County. In reality, Brown and Mason Counties had similar manufacturing outputs. Brown County also had a sizable free black population. Brown County was a known abolitionist hotbed, which also likely contributed to the growth of the free black population. However, the presence of a large free black popu-lation across the river in Mason County suggests that some free blacks may have chosen to remain in slaveholding Kentucky.

Moving west, the similarities between Kentucky river counties and Indi-ana river counties were striking. The remarkable similarity in rates of improved land once again highlights the importance of land quality in development. Figure 7 reveals that all counties in Kentucky from the border of Ohio to Jefferson County had more improved land than unimproved land. Similarly, as seen in Table 4, more than 50 percent of the land in all corresponding Indiana counties was improved. Beginning west of Jefferson County, all Kentucky counties had less than 50 percent improved land. Across the river all counties in Indiana with the exception of Vanderburgh County had less than 50 percent improved land as well. Evansville was in Vanderburgh County, and the area attracted more settlers than the more rural river counties did. Nonetheless the transition from more than 50 per-cent improved land to less is remarkable because it occurred at the same geographical point on both sides of the river. Looking closer, the far eastern county of Indiana had an average of 60 percent improved land and 40 percent unimproved land; Kentucky's border county had an average of 59 percent improved and 41 percent unimproved land. Farther west, Ken-tucky's least developed county was situated directly across from Indiana's least improved counties.

Kentucky's western counties, Henderson and Union, had large enslaved populations. This was Kentucky's tobacco growing region, and it typified the agricultural model of the South: large farms and less dense cultivation. However, looking at Kentucky's rate of development in comparison with Indiana's, it would appear that land quality also played a role in the density of cultivation. Other Kentucky counties, most notably Jefferson County and Mason County, had both large enslaved populations and dense cultivation. Thus this form of development had much to do with both land quality and the cultivation of tobacco.

The data on manufacturing production also reveal the cross-river relationship between Kentucky and Indiana and the role of manufacturing in the growth of the African American population. Jefferson County was the manufacturing center of the region, but across the river Floyd County, Indiana, also had a high manufacturing output. Jefferson County had a large free black population, and Floyd County had a relatively large free black population. Attracted by labor opportunities and the presence of a free black community, African Americans traveled to the area, settled on both sides of the river, and developed a cross-river community.

Farther west Henderson County, Kentucky, an area with a large enslaved population, also had significant manufacturing output. Henderson County had a small free black population, suggesting that enslaved workers contributed to the manufacturing development. This is significant because it highlights the flexibility of enslaved labor and demonstrates the power of enslaved labor to contribute to industrial development. Rather than retarding economic development, enslaved labor facilitated it. Also, likely because manufacturing was powered by enslaved labor, the free black population did not rise significantly in neighboring Indiana. Instead German immigrants powered the development of Evansville in Vanderburgh County.

Instead of dividing the region, the Ohio River allowed residents to forge distinct cross-river economic zones. These economic zones may have been influenced by the presence or absence of slavery, but they were not determined by it. First, there was a clear cross-river relationship in the ratio of improved to unimproved land. Thus where poor land quality limited agricultural production in Kentucky, it also limited production across the river in Ohio and Indiana. This is not to suggest that slavery had no impact on the rate of cultivation in Kentucky, but slavery did not absolutely slow the rate of agricultural production. Several factors, including land quality and what planters grew, affected agricultural production. The complexity of the situation belies any simple generalizations about free and slave states.

Second, land values along the river did not reveal a clear distinction between free and slave states. Despite this apparent inconsistency, there was a discernible pattern in land values. The fluctuations in land values between counties on one side of the river were matched by relative fluctuations on the other side. The cross-river relationship suggests that land quality played a significant role in land values. In addition slavery could not have been the deciding factor, first because Indiana averaged lower land values along the river than Kentucky did, and second because some Kentucky counties with large enslaved populations had high land values and others had low land values.

Third, if land values undermined the clarity of the border between freedom and slavery, Kentucky consistently had higher farm values than its free state neighbors did. Hamilton County, Ohio, was the clear exception to this generalization, but after removing Hamilton County from the calculations, Kentucky had higher farm values than those in Ohio counties, despite the fact that Ohio had higher land values per acre. In western Kentucky farm values were more than double Indiana farm values across the river. However, rather than symbolizing a dissipated work ethic among Kentuckians, as Tocqueville suggested, slavery actually facilitated agricultural production. Because land values and rates of development were tied to land quality, the higher farm values in Kentucky demonstrated that enslaved labor allowed white Kentuckians to have larger and more profitable farms. Thus, far from inhibiting productivity, slave labor aided white Kentuckians' agricultural development along the river.

Fourth, manufacturing did not demonstrate the clear superiority of free to enslaved labor in terms of production values. Not surprisingly, large cities were manufacturing centers, but overall the river facilitated the development of manufacturing throughout the region. The data on manufacturing revealed two cross-river links. First, major manufacturing centers on one side of the river typically faced smaller manufacturing centers on the other bank. Second, this cross-river relationship in manufacturing production was related to the free black population. Areas in Kentucky with large free black populations and significant manufacturing production typically were situated across the river from northern counties with corresponding large free black populations.

This relationship, however, was more complicated than it appeared. First, in western Kentucky counties with significant manufacturing production had large enslaved populations and small free black populations. It is interesting that across the river the free black population, while larger than those in some other Indiana river counties, made up less than 1 percent of the total population of the county. This suggests that manufacturing centers in Kentucky powered by enslaved labor did not necessarily give rise to a free black population across the river. Second, large free black populations in manufacturing centers in Indiana did not necessarily facilitate the rise of a corresponding free black community in Kentucky. This suggests that while free blacks in Kentucky may have been motivated to migrate across the river, in the absence of a major city the reverse was not true. At the same time, large manufacturing centers on both sides of the river seemed to have facilitated cross-river movement, perhaps in both directions.

In sum, the data on agricultural and manufacturing production suggest that economically residents had more in common with their neighbors across the river than they did with their fellow residents in other parts of their state. Despite the escalation of sectional conflict, cross-river economic connections remained strong in 1860. The Ohio River, long the economic center of the region, continued to draw residents together despite their differing views on slavery. Quite simply, characterizations of free and slave states as two separate worlds do not hold for areas along the Ohio River.

*   *   *

The election of 1860 was a pivotal moment on the nation's path to civil war. Abraham Lincoln's election set off a chain of secessions that led to the creation of the Confederacy and split the nation in two. In the Ohio River Valley, the presidential election of 1860 demonstrated how the Ohio River symbolized both division and coherence. The election was, in theory, a four-way race between Republican Abraham Lincoln, Democrat Stephen Douglas, southern Democrat John C. Breckenridge, and Constitutional Union candidate John Bell. In general, Lincoln carried northern states, Breckenridge carried the Deep South, and Bell carried the upper South states of Kentucky, Virginia, and Tennessee. Stephen Douglas was second in the popular vote at 29 percent, but he carried only twelve electoral votes. Lincoln received less than 40 percent of the popular vote in the country and won the election without carrying a single southern state. In fact, the Republican Party did not even offer a ticket in most southern states.[32]

Along the Ohio River, all four candidates gained at least one county each. But with two exceptions, the river marked the division of the northern election between Lincoln and Douglas and the southern contest between Bell and Breckenridge. In Kentucky, Lincoln received less than 1 percent of the popular vote, but he carried both Ohio and Indiana, a key factor in his electoral victory. Lincoln and Douglas split Ohio's six river counties, but Lincoln carried populous Hamilton County, which helped him carry the state. Lincoln carried five of eleven Indiana river counties, but in all but one of the counties he received less than 50 percent of the popular vote. Douglas carried five Indiana river counties, and southern Democrat John Breckenridge carried Warrick County, Indiana, albeit by receiving less than 40 percent of the popular vote. In Kentucky, John Bell carried thirteen of the eighteen river counties, Breckenridge carried four, and Douglas carried only one county. These results in part represented the division between the lower North and the upper South, since Lincoln and Douglas carried all but one northern county, while Bell and Breckenridge carried all but one of Kentucky's river counties.[33]

While the Ohio River represented the division between north and south in the election, there was still a cross-river relationship at various points. Before looking at the cross-river relationship, however, we should explore the variables that may have influenced voting patterns. Slavery impacted voting in Kentucky, but the diversity of results suggests that slavery was not the only factor voters considered. The county with the lowest percentage of the population enslaved went for Douglas. But all counties that went for the southern candidate, Breckenridge, had enslaved populations of 17 percent or less. In contrast, some of the most heavily enslaved counties went for Bell, including Henderson County, in which over 40 percent of the population was enslaved. These numbers suggest that some Kentuckians believed their best chance to preserve slavery was to preserve the Union. This in part could have contributed to the results. However, not all counties that went for Bell had large enslaved populations. In fact, in four of the Bell counties slaves made up less than 10 percent of the population. Seven of the Bell counties had declining enslaved populations, but six had rising enslaved populations, including two with greater than 30 percent growth rates between 1850 and 1860. All counties that went for Breckenridge had low levels of manufacturing output, whereas Bell carried all counties with significant manufacturing development. However, Bell also carried counties with the lowest levels of manufacturing development.[34]

The results in northern counties were similarly vexing. In Ohio, Lincoln carried the county with the highest manufacturing output, but for the remaining four counties there is not a clear connection between industry and voting habits. Similarly, Lincoln carried the county with the largest free black population, but Douglas carried the county with the second highest free black population. In Indiana, Douglas carried the two counties with the largest free black populations, but Lincoln carried the county with the third largest. Lincoln also carried counties with extremely small free black populations, the lowest rate of agricultural development, and the second lowest rate of manufacturing development. But lest this shows any developing pattern, Lincoln also carried the counties with the highest rates of agricultural and manufacturing development.

The influx of immigrants into river cities may partially explain the success of Lincoln in Cincinnati and Evansville and of Bell in Louisville. Historians have suggested that supporters of the Know-Nothing Party migrated to support the Republican Party in the North and the Constitutional Union Party in the upper South. In the 1850s large numbers of German immigrants settled in Cincinnati, Evansville, and Louisville. Nativism could have contributed to the popularity of the Republican Party in Hamilton County (Cincinnati) and Vanderburgh County (Evansville). Similarly there was strong antiimmigrant sentiment in Louisville, as demonstrated by the violent 1855 antiimmigrant riot that resulted in twenty-two deaths. As the Know-Nothing Party rapidly disintegrated, many voters in Jefferson County turned to the Constitutional Union Party.[35]

Outside of these urban areas, the absence of discernible patterns suggests that a variety of factors influenced Americans' voting habits. It seems clear that no one variable strictly determined residents' choice of a candidate. However, comparing election results along the river reveals some suggestive possible connections. While Kentuckians voted for Breckenridge, Indianans across the river voted for Lincoln. This suggests that in these particular areas, residents had potentially confrontational political views. It is interesting, though, that Ohio voters selected Lincoln but neighboring Kentuckians did not choose Breckenridge.

While the popularity of Lincoln and Bell in major urban centers was not surprising or necessarily unique to the borderland, the effect on the areas across the river revealed cross-river connections. In many regions the more centrist candidates, Douglas and Bell, seemed to do well across the river from major urban centers. In western Kentucky, Bell carried heavily slave-populated Henderson County across the river from Evansville in Vanderburgh County, Indiana. Farther east Douglas easily carried Harrison, Floyd, and Clark Counties, which all bordered Jefferson County, Kentucky. Farther east Bell carried two and Douglas carried one of the counties across the river from Hamilton County, Ohio. In addition Mason County, Kentucky, with the city of Maysville, went for Bell, and across the river Brown County went for Douglas. This was a remarkable result because Brown County was an abolitionist hotbed, and yet Douglas easily carried the county. It appears likely that unionism appealed to voters who lived in the shadow of major urban centers across the river.

A comparison of voting in the Ohio River borderland with voting along the Mason-Dixon Line and along the Mississippi River reveals the centrality of the river economy in forging social and political ties. In Pennsylvania, Lincoln carried eight of eleven counties along the border with Maryland and Virginia. Bell carried all bordering Maryland counties, Breckinridge carried two Virginia counties, and Douglas carried the other Virginia county. While Bell's success in Maryland suggests a strong unionist sentiment along the border in Maryland, Pennsylvanians failed to match that unionist sentiment. In contrast, the Mississippi River encouraged unionist sentiment from its confluence with the Ohio River until it emptied into the gulf. Even though he did not win in either Missouri or Arkansas, Bell carried nearly all river counties in both states. Farther south Breckinridge won in Mississippi with more than 59 percent of the popular vote. However, John Bell won eight of the eleven counties along the Mississippi River. In addition the path of the Mississippi River through Louisiana was lined with counties that went for either John Bell or Stephen Douglas. These results suggest that through their reliance on the western river economy, residents forged economic and social connections that were strong enough to withstand the fires of sectional conflict engulfing the nation. Therefore it was not just the border that encouraged compromise along the Ohio River; the Ohio River economy also forged connections that were strong enough to make borderlanders willing to compromise, even across a potentially divisive border.

The results of the 1860 election represented the limits of divisions along the Ohio River. The absence of Lincoln voters south of the river clearly showed that the Ohio River was a border. But the meaning of that border is more difficult to classify. Residents were divided over the best candidate for America's future. The success of Douglas and Bell along the river marked borderlanders' desire to preserve the Union, even if they divided over the best means to accomplish that end. In actuality the population was too divided to identify clearly with either sectional candidate. Lincoln carried more northerly counties of Indiana, and Breckenridge carried the mountain regions of Kentucky. It is interesting that the northern counties of Indiana had small free black populations and the mountain counties had small enslaved populations. These areas, further removed from the border and the reality of slavery and emancipation, more clearly identified with the more sectional candidates. At the border, in contrast, where residents interacted daily and had strong ties to the economic power of the Ohio River, residents hesitated to choose sides.

The centrality of the Ohio River to the regional economy and the results of the 1860 election reveal the uniqueness of the borderland in 1860. The Ohio River did not divide two different worlds rooted in dichotomous labor systems; nor would local residents be carried away by what the historian Michael Holt has called the "politicians' war." Instead the story of the Ohio River borderland in the 1850s is a narrative of noncausation. In 1860 many borderlanders remained committed to the Union. They may have disagreed over what the Union stood for, but they refused to accept the logic of sectional nationalism. It is likely that local residents' daily interactions across the river contributed to their commitment to the Union. They may have rooted their unionism in the selfish concern that war and disruption were bad for business. Or interaction may have taught them that accommodation was, in fact, possible. Politically, Henry Clay's legacy gave Kentuckians a model of compromise, of putting the Union ahead of sectional interests. Across the river Indianans and Ohioans had long accommodated the demands of their slaveholding neighbors. At times they stood up and defended their states against slaveholders' intrusions. At other times men such as Indiana's John Tipton and Ohio's Governor Robert Lucas made every effort to placate their sister states. Thus on both sides of the river there was a tradition of both conflict and accommodation. This political and social history taught borderlanders to look in two directions when defining their region. Looking across the border, they saw distinctly different neighbors. But looking in the other direction, they saw a region that was also different; southern Indiana and Ohio were not New England, and Kentucky was not the Deep South. As a result residents used the border

they shared to define the region. To borderlanders, the Ohio River represented a clear division between slaveholding and nonslaveholding states,
but their ability to coexist across this border set them apart from the rest
of the country. In this way they understood the region as a borderland, a
model of coexistence that gave hope to a country rapidly descending into
civil war.

*   *   *

Following the election, the seven states of the Deep South seceded from the
Union before Lincoln even took office. The initial resilience of the borderland in the face of violent and intense sectional conflict was remarkable.
Most residents and politicians refused to be carried away by either northern
or southern nationalism, and many clung to the belief that the borderland
could represent peace and reconciliation in the midst of conflict. Borderlanders understood the Ohio River Valley as a unique region rooted in
compromise across a potentially divisive border. Despite a long history of
conflict over fugitive reclamation, borderlanders were proud of the fact that
those conflicts had never led to open armed battles between Kentucky and
Ohio and Indiana. Their ability to coexist led many simply to reject the
dissolution of the Union as unnecessary.

In the heat of the secession crisis, Ohio and Indiana politicians
remained committed to their borderland identities. In January 1860 Indiana governor Ashbel P. Willard spoke at a banquet in Louisville, saying,
"Kentucky has no right to say to Indiana, you shall be a slave state; Indiana
has no right to turn upon the other side and say Kentucky shall be a free
State." Later in the winter, the governors of Indiana, Ohio, and Kentucky
agreed to create a border state council. Nothing came of this particular
meeting, and Indiana's new Republican governor, Oliver Morton, was too
removed from the border to recognize residents' desire for peace. In April
1861 representatives from New Albany, Jeffersonville, and Louisville met to
secure "the continuance of the amicable relations which have always sub-
sisted between them." Similar meetings took place in other border communities. Residents seemed particularly concerned that war would disrupt the
local economy, and newspapers printed numerous pledges to maintain
amicable relations no matter what happened. During the first month of the
Civil War members of the Indiana legislature made a pledge to Kentuckians
to "aid them as brothers, relatives, and friends in defense of their homes

and firesides." Kentuckians hoped that their shared perceptions and interests with their lower northerner neighbors made neutrality a possibility.[36]

Kentuckians declared their official neutrality, but from the outset, Kentuckians were divided over the best course of action for the state. Kentuckians clearly rejected radicalism and resented the implication that slavery was anything other than a state matter. Kentucky unionists declared their loyalty to their "sister Southern states," and much like the fire-eaters of the Deep South, they blamed the sectional conflict on Abraham Lincoln. Some Kentuckians believed that staying within the Union better protected slavery in the state than did secession. One politician wrote, "The profitable continuance of negro slavery . . . depends absolutely upon the existence of a common national government embracing both the Free States and the Slave States." In fact, Senator John Crittenden's call for compromise included a resolution declaring the government's intention not to interfere with slavery. Others hoped that slavery would naturally fade away from Kentucky. These men relied on demographics to explain slavery's limited influence in the state. From their perspective, it made little sense to go to war to protect a dying institution. In addition some Kentuckians identified with the newly formed Confederacy and even wrote a declaration of secession. In Louisville five companies of Confederate volunteers headed south immediately following the firing on Fort Sumter. However, supporters of the Union set up a recruiting station across the river in Indiana in hopes of attracting volunteers from Kentucky. The Louisville City Council set aside fifty thousand dollars to defend the city from attacks by Confederate or Union forces. In a state plagued by division, neutrality had little chance for success.[37]

Despite their rejection of radicalism and their call for compromise, borderlanders remained deeply divided over the best course of action. For many, their desire for peace, in part, was rooted in self-interest. They recognized the economic importance of the river and sought to preserve it as war broke out. But even those seeking compromise could not agree on the best way to maintain the Union. In addition not all borderlanders sought peace and reconciliation. Some northerners saw the war as a chance to sever the region's ties with slavery by destroying the border, and some southerners identified with the cause of the Confederacy. These divisions helped hold the region together because no one group could dominate. The absence of a dominant power, even in 1860, created conflict and necessitated compromise. Ultimately this region remained a borderland to the very end.[38]

In the end, only war could destroy the illusion of borderland neutrality, but the war failed to split the region at the seam of the Ohio River. Formally, Governor Beriah Magoffin rejected both Lincoln's and Jefferson Davis's calls for troops in 1861, as Kentuckians attempted to balance their northern and southern ties. Thousands of Kentuckians joined Confederate units in Tennessee and took horses, mules, food, leather, salt, and munitions with them to war. Soon people and goods began flowing north as well. Union agents ferried muskets across the river from Cincinnati into Kentucky, and Kentuckian Robert Anderson established Union recruiting camps for Kentucky volunteers on the Ohio side of the river. Confederate and Union forces jockeyed for position both on the landscape of Kentucky and in the hearts and minds of Kentuckians. Confederate forces moved into and occupied the southwestern city of Columbus. In response, Union forces occupied Paducah, and Union general Robert Anderson moved his headquarters from Cincinnati to Louisville. In September, Kentucky's legislature ordered all Confederate forces out of the state, effectively ending Kentucky's neutrality. But Confederate forces occupied Bowling Green, and representatives from sixty-five counties in southwestern Kentucky approved an ordinance of secession. The Confederate congress admitted Kentucky into the Confederacy. The remainder of the state remained loyal to the Union.[39]

*   *   *

During the Civil War, borderlanders continued to reject polarization. It is true that many Ohioans and Indianans readily answered Lincoln's call for troops to join the Union army to put down the southern rebellion. Indeed Ohio supplied more troops to the effort than any other state, and William T. Sherman and Ulysses S. Grant, the two generals most responsible for the Union's victory, hailed from Ohio. Indiana supplied over two hundred thousand troops to the war effort as well. However, southwestern Ohio was a hotbed of Copperhead opposition to Lincoln. Copperheads disrupted Republican events and developed a political movement that almost put Clement Vallandigham into the governorship in 1863. Vallandigham stressed the need to end the war and bring the South back into the Union peaceably, and without emancipation. This message of unionism and accommodation found fertile ground in the Ohio River borderland because it echoed the antebellum sentiments of many residents. In Indiana,

Senator Jesse Bright was expelled from Congress in 1862 for communicating with Jefferson Davis and attempting to facilitate the sale of arms to the Confederacy. In New Albany city authorities set up a guard at the ferry docks on either side of the river to stop African Americans who had no passes. In July 1862 there was a race riot in New Albany. Two white men were reported to have been shot by blacks. One of the two was killed, the other badly wounded. Indiscriminate acts of violence against blacks broke out. The rioters were never arrested. As a result of these riots some blacks moved to Kentucky for safety and others went to Canada.[40]

Kentuckians did not choose sides until hostilities broke out within the state, but even then Kentucky split in its loyalties. A former advocate of compromise, John Crittenden joined the Confederate army and encouraged others to do the same. Governor Magoffin abandoned his position of neutrality and resigned. Kentucky remained deeply divided throughout the war. Guerrilla warfare plagued the countryside. Perhaps no numbers better sum up Kentucky's stance than these: around seventy thousand white men fought for the Union; between thirty thousand and forty thousand fought for the Confederacy; and 71 percent of eligible young men chose not to fight at all![41]

In general many Kentuckians resented the shift in the Union war effort toward emancipation. Many Kentuckians who remained loyal to the Union also clung to the institution of slavery. In fact, some wrote to Lincoln claiming to support emancipation in principle but disapproving of his efforts to force emancipation on the state. Lincoln's Emancipation Proclamation failed to free any enslaved blacks in Kentucky, and Kentuckians voted against Lincoln in 1864. However, enslaved African Americans pushed the issue of emancipation by fleeing from their owners and finding work in Louisville or across the river. By 1865 tobacco production had dropped 57 percent, wheat 63 percent, hemp 80 percent, and the assessed value of slaves dropped 68 percent from the prewar numbers. By the end of 1865 ten thousand fugitives had left Kentucky. Nonetheless white Kentuckians refused to let go of the slave system and refused to ratify the Thirteenth Amendment.[42]

After abolition sank the border of slavery and freedom, local residents reinvented the borderland. Indianans and Ohioans constructed a historical memory based on antislavery action and loyalty to the Union. Ohioans and Indianans cling to the memory of the Underground Railroad. Despite historical evidence to the contrary, the myth of a sophisticated network of benevolent whites assisting helpless fugitive slaves remains. The historian David Blight has suggested that the myth of the Underground Railroad arose to assuage the guilt white Americans felt about their lack of antislavery activity before the war. This need to invent a new past was especially powerful along the border, where white Americans were a stone's throw away from slavery. Postwar conflict and internal strife precipitated Kentuckians' creation of an imagined Confederate past in which they stressed peaceful reconciliation and racial inequality. It is not that white Kentuckians immediately and explicitly linked their fate with the Confederacy but rather that they fought against African Americans' and the Republican-led Union government's attempts to "force" change on the state. This resistance to the Union government and the emancipationist narrative made Kentuckians more southern than ever. In some ways Kentuckians joined the Confederacy after the war ended. In short, postwar borderlanders reinvented the Ohio River border without slavery. Ironically, the Ohio River border became more distinct in the minds of borderlanders *after* its demise. In postbellum America the Ohio River was just the border between the North and the South.[43]

NOTES

Abbreviations

CHS   Cincinnati Historical Society, Ohio
FHS   Filson Historical Society, Louisville, Kentucky
HIS   Indiana Historical Society, Indianapolis
ISL   Indiana State Library, Indianapolis
OHS   Ohio Historical Society, Columbus

Introduction

1. Harriet Beecher Stowe, *Uncle Tom's Cabin or Life among the Lowly* (1853; New York: Signet Classic, 1998), 67–68.

2. The historian Andrew Cayton wrote that the Ohio River border was a "puzzle we have only begun to contemplate"; see Cayton, "Artery and Border: The Ambiguous Development of the Ohio Valley in the Early Republic," *Ohio Valley History* 1, no. 1 (2001): 19–26 (quote on 25). On the southern influence on the development of the old Northwest, see Richard F. Nation, *At Home in the Hoosier Hills: Agriculture, Politics and Religion in Southern Indiana, 1810–1870* (Bloomington: Indiana University Press, 2005); Andrew Cayton, *Frontier Indiana* (Indianapolis: Indiana University Press, 1996); Nicole Etcheson, *The Emerging Midwest: Upland Southerners and the Political Culture of the Old Northwest, 1787–1861* (Bloomington: Indiana University Press, 1996); James H. Madison, *The Indiana Way: A State History* (Bloomington: Indiana University Press, 1986); John D. Barnhart and Dorothy Riker, *Indiana to 1816: The Colonial Period* (Indianapolis: Indiana Historical Bureau, 1971); Andrew R. L. Cayton, *The Frontier Republic: Ideology and Politics in the Ohio Country, 1780–1825* (Kent, OH: Kent State University Press, 1990); John D. Barnhart, *Valley of Democracy: The Frontier versus the Plantation in the Ohio Valley, 1775–1818* (Bloomington: Indiana University Press, 1953); R. Carley Buley, *The Old Northwest: Pioneer Period, 1815–1840* (Bloomington: Indiana University Press, 1950); Andrew R. L. Cayton, *Ohio: The History of a People* (Columbus: Ohio State University Press, 2002); Darrel E. Bigham, ed., *The Indiana Territory, 1800–2000: A Bicentennial Perspective* (Indianapolis: Indiana Historical Society, 2001). On the uniqueness of Kentucky, see Craig Thompson Friend, *Along the Maysville Road: The Early American Republic in the Trans-Appalachian West* (Knoxville: University of Tennessee Press, 2005); Craig Thompson Friend, ed., *The*

Buzzel about Kentuck: Settling the Promised Land (Lexington: University Press of Kentucky, 1999); Stephen Aron, *How the West Was Lost: The Transformation of Kentucky from Daniel Boone to Henry Clary* (Baltimore: Johns Hopkins University Press, 1996); Joan Wells Coward, *Kentucky in the New Republic: The Process of Constitution Making* (Lexington: University Press of Kentucky, 1979); William Freehling, *The Reintegration of American History: Slavery and the Civil War* (New York: Oxford University Press, 1994); William Freehling, *The Road to Disunion: Secessionists at Bay, 1776–1854* (New York: Oxford University Press, 1991); Harold D. Tallant, *Evil Necessity: Slavery and Political Culture in Antebellum Kentucky* (Lexington: University Press of Kentucky, 2003).

3. The recent renaming of the *Filson Club History Quarterly* to *Ohio Valley History* is suggestive of a recent trend to interpret the area as a region. Recent work on the Midwest as a region has attempted to challenge regional boundaries. See Kim M. Gruenwald, *River of Enterprise: The Commercial Origins of Regional Identity in the Ohio Valley, 1790–1850* (Bloomington: Indiana University Press, 2002); John Craig Hammond, *Slavery, Freedom, and Expansion in the Early American West* (Charlottesville: University of Virginia Press, 2007); Andrew R. L. Cayton and Peter S. Onuf, *The Midwest and the Nation: Rethinking the History of an American Region* (Bloomington: Indiana University Press, 1996); Andrew Cayton and Susan Gray, eds., *The American Midwest: Essays on Regional History* (Bloomington: Indiana University Press, 2001). I have looked outside of historiography to craft an interdisciplinary understanding of borderlands; see Thomas M. Wilson and Hastings Donnan, "Nation, State and Identity at International Borders," in Wilson and Donnan, eds., *Border Identities: Nation and State at International Frontiers* (New York: Cambridge University Press, 1998), 1–30; Russ Castronovo, "Compromised Narratives along the Border: The Mason-Dixon Line, Resistance, and Hegemony," in Scott Michaelsen and David E. Johnson, eds., *Border Theory: The Limits of Cultural Politics* (Minneapolis: University of Minnesota Press, 1997), 195–220; Patricia Seed, "Afterword: Further Perspectives on Culture, Limits, and Borders," in Michaelsen and Johnson, *Border Theory*, 253–256; Gloria Anzaldua, *Borderlands/La Frontera: The New Mestiza* (San Francisco: Aunt Lute Books, 1987). For an excellent critique of Anzaldua's work, see David E. Johnson and Scott Michaelsen, "Border Secrets: An Introduction," in Michaelsen and Johnson *Border Theory*, 1–39. On the importance of mobility in border creation and identity formation, see Joel S. Migdal, "Mental Maps and Virtual Checkpoints: Struggles to Construct and Maintain State and Social Boundaries," in Migdal, ed., *Boundaries and Belonging: State and Societies in the Struggle to Shape Identities and Local Practices* (New York: Cambridge University Press, 2004), 3–26; Mark Simpson, *Trafficking Subjects: The Politics of Mobility in Nineteenth-Century America* (Minneapolis: University of Minnesota Press, 2005), 56–91; Peter Sahlins, *Boundaries: The Making of France and Spain in the Pyrenees* (Berkeley: University of California Press, 1989).

4. Stephen Aron and Jeremy Adelman attempted to give historical specificity to the terms "frontier" and "borderlands"; see Adelman and Aron, "From Borderlands

to Borders: Empires, Nation-States, and the Peoples in between in North American History," *American Historical Review* 104, no. 3 (June 1999): 814–841 (quote on 816); Stephen Aron, *American Confluence: The Missouri Frontier from Borderland to Border State* (Bloomington: Indiana University Press, 2006). For responses to Aron and Adelman, see *American Historical Review* 104 (October 1999): 1221–1239. My interpretation of the Ohio River borderland owes much to Aron and Adelman's model, but their definition overstates the ability of borders to divide. Whereas the creation of a border destroyed the borderland in their model, I argue that in the Ohio River Valley the border between slavery and freedom led to a redefinition of the borderland.

Herbert Bolton introduced the concept in the early twentieth century as the meeting place of rival European empires in the North American Southwest. Although Bolton used the term to describe a specific place, historians have used the concept to describe European–Native American relations throughout North America; see Herbert Eugene Bolton, *The Spanish Borderlands: A Chronicle of Old Florida and the Southwest* (New Haven, CT: Yale University Press, 1921). For three prime examples of the American nation closing a borderland, see Daniel H. Usner, *Indians, Settlers and Slaves in a Frontier Exchange Economy: The Lower Mississippi Valley before 1783* (Chapel Hill: University of North Carolina Press, 1992); Richard White, *The Middle Ground: Indians, Empires, and Republics in the Great Lakes Region, 1650–1815* (Cambridge: Cambridge University Press, 1991); James Brooks, *Captives and Cousins: Slavery, Kinship, and Community in the Southwest Borderlands* (Chapel Hill: University of North Carolina Press, 2002). These are excellent histories, and while I do not disagree with their interpretations, I think their focus on endings neglects the possibility that a new form of the borderland replaced the old. Examples from the Ohio River Valley include Cayton, *Frontier Indiana*; and Aron, *How the West Was Lost*. As these works argue, the shift from territory to state changed the power dynamic between Ohio Indians and Euro-American settlers, but it also heightened the importance of the border between slavery and freedom. Therefore as one borderland closed, a new one opened in its place.

5. Most historians who have evaluated the Ohio Valley as a region have focused on the social and economic importance of the Ohio River economy. This work has shed important light on trade, transportation, and community development on the Ohio River. The historian Darrell Bigham has produced two groundbreaking studies that examined African American community development along the Ohio River from the antebellum period through the early twentieth century. Bigham's work has highlighted the influence of the Ohio River on the experience of African Americans in both slavery and freedom. See Darrel E. Bigham, *On Jordan's Banks: Emancipation and Its Aftermath in the Ohio River Valley* (Lexington: University Press of Kentucky, 2006); Darrel E. Bigham, *Towns and Villages of the Lower Ohio* (Lexington: University Press of Kentucky, 1998); John A. Jackle, *Images of the Ohio Valley: A Historical Geography of Travel, 1740–1860* (New York: Oxford University Press, 1977); Keith P. Griffler, *Front Line of Freedom: African Americans and the Forging of the Underground Railroad*

in the Ohio Valley (Lexington: University Press of Kentucky, 2004); Robert L. Reid, ed., *Always a River: The Ohio River and the American Experience* (Bloomington: Indiana University Press, 1991); Joe William Trotter, *River Jordan: African American Urban Life in the Ohio Valley* (Lexington: University Press of Kentucky, 1998); Thomas C. Buchanan, *Black Life on the Mississippi: Slaves, Free Blacks and the Western Steamboat World* (Chapel Hill: University of North Carolina Press, 2004); George H. Yater, *Two Hundred Years at the Falls of the Ohio: A History of Louisville and Jefferson County* (Louisville: Heritage Corp., 1979); Richard C. Wade, *The Urban Frontier: The Rise of Western Cities, 1790–1830* (Urbana: University of Illinois Press, 1996); Richard Banta, *The Ohio* (New York: Rinehart, 1949); Paton Yoder, *Taverns and Travelers: Inns of the Early Midwest* (Bloomington: Indiana University Press, 1969); L. A. Williams and Co., *History of the Ohio Falls Cities and Their Counties with Illustrations and Bibliographical Sketches*, 2 vols. (Cleveland: L. A. Williams and Co., 1882).

6. Stanley Harrold has boldly taken the challenge to evaluate the entire border between slavery and freedom in America; see Harrold, *Border War: Fighting over Slavery before the Civil War* (Chapel Hill: University of North Carolina Press, 2010). For information on the Mason-Dixon Line, see Max Grivno, *Gleanings of Freedom: Free and Slave Labor along the Mason-Dixon Line, 1790–1860* (Urbana: University of Illinois Press, 2011). Edward Ayers and William Thomas have numerous articles and resources at their Web site dedicated to an examination of the border between Pennsylvania and Virginia; see "Valley of the Shadow," http://valley.lib.virginia.edu/ (accessed October 2012). On Illinois, see James Simeone, *Democracy and Slavery in Frontier Illinois: The Bottomland Republic* (De Kalb: Northern Illinois University Press, 2000).

7. An extended temporal focus sheds light on how imperial roots, especially the conflict with Native Americans and the trade in war-time captives, influenced the American settlement of the Ohio Valley and the early development of the borderland after the passage of the Northwest Ordinance. Historians who have focused on the issue of slavery have downplayed, if not ignored, the region's imperial past and the role of Native Americans. See Paul Finkelman, *Slavery and the Founders: Race and Liberty in the Age of Jefferson* (Armonk, NY: M. E. Sharpe, 1996); Peter S. Onuf, *Statehood and Union: A History of the Northwest Ordinance*, Midwestern History and Culture (Bloomington: Indiana University Press, 1987); David Brion Davis, "The Significance of Excluding Slavery from the Old Northwest in 1787," *Indiana Magazine of History* 84, no. 1 (1988): 75–89; Staughton Lynd, *Class Conflict, Slavery, and the United States Constitution: Ten Essays* (Indianapolis: Bobbs-Merrill, 1968). Meanwhile, Native American historians dismiss the issue of slavery as secondary; see, for example, White, *Middle Ground*, 413–433; Elizabeth A. Perkins, *Border Life: Experience and Memory in the Revolutionary Ohio Valley* (Chapel Hill: University of North Carolina Press, 1998). This trend stands out in the essay collections on the ordinance; see Lloyd A. Hunter, ed., *Pathways to the Old Northwest: An Observance of the Bicentennial of the Northwest Ordinance* (Indianapolis: Indiana Historical Society, 1988); Robert M. Taylor, ed., *The Northwest Ordinance, 1787: A Bicentennial Handbook* (Indianapolis: Indiana Historical Society, 1987); Frederick D. Williams, ed., *The Northwest Ordinance:*

Essays on Its Formulation, Provisions and Legacy (East Lansing: Michigan State University Press, 1989).

8. The historiography of the Northwest Ordinance has been primarily focused on the issue of effectiveness, but less attention has been paid to the nature and definition of the border. Perhaps framed by the arguments of Paul Finkelman and David Brion Davis, John Craig Hammond's most recent study of the expansion of slavery in the early West follows the historiographical debate on the effectiveness of the Northwest Ordinance; see Hammond, *Slavery, Freedom, and Expansion*. Older examples include Eugene H. Berwanger, *The Frontier against Slavery: Western Anti-Negro Prejudice and the Slavery Extension Controversy* (Urbana: University of Illinois Press, 1967); J. P. Dunn Jr., *Indiana: A Redemption from Slavery* (New York: Houghton Mifflin, 1905).

9. Marion B. Lucas, *A History of Blacks in Kentucky*, vol. 1: *From Slavery to Segregation, 1760–1861* (Frankfort: Kentucky Historical Society, 1992), 50. J. Winston Coleman Jr. proclaimed antebellum Kentucky a "romantic and picturesque" place and described slavery as "benevolent though despotic"; see Coleman, *Slavery Times in Kentucky* (Chapel Hill: University of North Carolina Press, 1940), 325. While Lucas's is the only book-length study on Kentucky slavery, numerous articles on the subject include, among others, Ellen Eslinger, "The Shape of Slavery on the Kentucky Frontier, 1775–1800," *Register of the Kentucky Historical Society* 92, no. 1 (1994): 1–23; Keith C. Barton, "Good Cooks and Washers: Slave-Hiring, Domestic Labor, and the Market in Bourbon County, Kentucky," *Journal of American History* 84 (September 1997): 436–460; J. Blaine Hudson, "Slavery in Early Louisville and Jefferson County, Kentucky, 1780–1812," *Filson Club History Quarterly* 73, no. 3 (July 1999): 249–283; J. Blaine Hudson, "Crossing the 'Dark Line': Fugitive Slaves and the Underground Railroad in Louisville and North-Central Kentucky," *Filson Club History Quarterly* 75 (Winter 2001): 33–83; Hanford Dozier Stafford, "Slavery in a Border City: Louisville, 1790–1860" (Ph.D. diss., University of Kentucky, 1982); Craig Thompson Friend, "Work and Be Rich: Economy and Culture on the Bluegrass Farm," in Friend, *Buzzel about Kentuck*, 130–151; Stephen Aron, "The Poor Men to Starve: The Lives and Times of Workingmen in Early Lexington," in Friend, *Buzzel about Kentuck*, 175–193, esp. 184–186. Some examples of this early focus on plantation slavery are John W. Blassingame, *The Slave Community: Plantation Life in the Antebellum South* (1972; New York: Oxford University Press, 1979); Eugene D. Genovese, *Roll, Jordan, Roll: The World the Slaves Made* (New York: Pantheon Books, 1974); Herbert Gutman, *The Black Family in Slavery and Freedom, 1750–1925* (New York: Vintage Books, 1976); James Oakes, *Slavery and Freedom: An Interpretation of the Old South* (New York: Knopf, 1990); Stanley Elkins, *Slavery: A Problem in American Institutional and Intellectual Life* (New York: Universal Library, 1963); Kenneth Stampp, *The Peculiar Institution: Slavery in the Antebellum South* (New York: Knopf, 1956).

10. The historian most responsible for turning our attention to the variations of American slavery is Ira Berlin; see his *Generations of Captivity: A History of African American Slaves* (Cambridge, MA: Harvard University Press, 2003); *Many Thousands*

Gone: The First Two Centuries of Slavery in North America (Cambridge, MA: Harvard University Press, 1998). Recent works that connected the experience of free and enslaved labor include the following: Grivno, *Gleanings of Freedom*; Seth Rockman, *Scraping By: Wage Labor, Slavery and Survival in Early Baltimore* (Baltimore: Johns Hopkins University Press, 2009); T. Stephen Whitman, *The Price of Freedom: Slavery and Manumission in Baltimore and Early National Maryland* (Lexington: University Press of Kentucky, 1997); Barbara Jeanne Fields, *Slavery and Freedom on the Middle Ground: Maryland during the Nineteenth Century* (New Haven, CT: Yale University Press, 1984); Christopher Phillips, *Freedom's Port: The African American Community of Baltimore, 1790–1860* (Urbana: University of Illinois Press, 1997); John Bezís-Selfa, *Forging America: Ironworkers, Adventurers and the Industrial Revolution* (Ithaca, NY: Cornell University Press, 2004). Historians have also explained how slavery functioned at the fringes of empire; see Brooks, *Captives and Cousins*; Usner, *Indians, Settlers and Slaves*.

11. Seth Rockman, "The Unfree Origins of American Capitalism," in Cathy Matson, ed., *The Economy of Early America: Historical Perspectives and New Directions* (University Park: Pennsylvania State University Press, 2006), 335–362; Stephanie Smallwood, "Commodified Freedom: Interrogating the Limits of Anti-Slavery Ideology in the Early Republic," *Journal of the Early Republic* 24 (Summer 2004): 289–298.

12. Historians have long pointed out the virulent racism of whites in the Ohio Valley but have treated it as a timeless variable. The timelessness of midwestern racism is most forcefully expressed in Berwanger, *Frontier against Slavery*; Stephen Middleton, *The Black Laws: Race and the Legal Process in Early Ohio* (Athens: Ohio University Press, 2005); Emma Lou Thornbrough, *The Negro in Indiana: A Study of a Minority* (Indianapolis: Indiana Historical Bureau, 1957); Leonard P. Curry, *The Free Black in Urban America 1800–1850: The Shadow of the Dream* (Chicago: University of Chicago Press, 1981); Leon F. Litwack, *North of Slavery: The Negro in the Free States, 1790–1860* (Chicago: University of Chicago Press, 1961); Juliet E. K. Walker, "The Legal Status of Free Blacks in Early Kentucky, 1792–1825," *Filson Club History Quarterly* 57 (October 1983): 382–395.

Historians have pointed to the crucial link between labor situations and racial views in antebellum America, but this theme has not been explored for the Ohio Valley. See especially Walter Johnson, "The Pedestal and the Veil: Rethinking the Capitalism/Slavery Question," *Journal of the Early Republic* 24 (Summer 2004): 299–308; David R. Roediger, *The Wages of Whiteness: Race and the Making of the American Working Class*, rev. ed. (New York: Verso, 1999); Jacqueline Jones, *American Work: Four Centuries of Black and White Labor* (New York: W. W. Norton, 1998); Sean Wilentz, *The Rise of American Democracy: Jefferson to Lincoln* (New York: W. W. Norton, 2005); Michael A. Morrison and James Brewer Stewart, eds., *Race and the Early Republic: Racial Consciousness and Nation Building in the Early Republic* (Lanham, MD: Rowman and Littlefield, 2002); Eric Foner, "The Idea of Free Labor in Nineteenth-Century America," the new introductory essay in Foner, *Free Soil, Free*

Labor, Free Men: The Ideology of the Republican Party before the Civil War (New York: Oxford University Press, 1995).

13. In his study of fugitive slaves in Kentucky, the historian J. Blaine Hudson estimated that forty-four thousand enslaved blacks escaped between 1810 and 1860, or a rate of loss of 0.5 percent annually; see Hudson, *Fugitive Slaves and Underground Railroad in the Kentucky Borderland* (Jefferson, NC: McFarland & Company, 2002), 161–162. Hudson and other historians have suggested that the escape of fugitives was a "slow bleed" that continuously weakened the institution in the state; see also Freehling, *Reintegration of American History*, 253–274; William W. Freehling, "Why the U.S. Fugitive Slave Phenomenon was Crucial," paper presented at "Unshackled Spaces: Fugitives from Slavery and Maroon Communities in the Americas," Fifth Annual Gilder Lehrman Center International Conference at Yale University, December 2002, http://www.yale.edu/glc/maroon/index.htm (accessed October 2012). This argument looks at the fugitive issue from the perspective of slaveholders but fails to explain adequately why the fugitive slaves did not stream across the Ohio River.

14. The proportion of African Americans in the population decreased in Kentucky between 1830 and 1860, but the number of slaves increased. In addition the diversity of the institution gave it strength beyond the numbers. Specifically, the question of why Kentuckians and their neighbors to the north convinced themselves that slavery was on the decline remains unanswered. Historians have made the argument that the diversity of labor in colonial America gave the institution enough strength to survive the Revolution; see Robin Blackburn, *The Making of New World Slavery: From the Baroque to the Modern, 1492–1800* (New York: Verso, 1997), 457–508; David Waldstreicher, *Runaway America: Benjamin Franklin, Slavery and the American Revolution* (New York: Hill and Wang, 2004), 175–224; Andrew O'Shaughnessy, *An Empire Divided: The American Revolution and the British Caribbean* (Philadelphia: University of Pennsylvania Press, 2000). Several historians have recognized how whites in Indiana and Ohio wanted to defend their border against the intrusion of slavery; see Harrold, *Border War*; Gruenwald, *River of Enterprise*, 155–158; Matthew Mason, *Slavery and Politics in the Early American Republic* (Chapel Hill: University of North Carolina Press, 2006), 130–157, 216, 233; Foner, *Free Soil, Free Labor, Free Men*, 301–318.

15. On the link between unionism and the protection of slavery in Kentucky, see Harrold, *Border War*, 183–213; William W. Freehling, *The South vs. the South: How Anti-Confederate Southerners Shaped the Course of the Civil War* (New York: Oxford University Press, 2001), 33–64.

16. This interpretation is directly at odds with Harrold's interpretation of the border as a place plagued and divided by an intractable border war. Instead my focus on compromise is informed by Peter B. Knupfer, *The Union as It Is: Constitutional Unionism and Sectional Compromise, 1787–1861* (Chapel Hill: University of North Carolina Press, 1991).

17. Political historians have based their explanations for the coming of the Civil War on national political debates. I do not believe that these explanations capture the

dynamic of the borderland because unionist sentiment prevailed along the border. On the breakdown of the political parties, see Michael Holt, *Political Crisis of the 1850s* (New York: Wiley, 1978); Michael Holt, *The Fate of Their Country: Politicians, Slavery Extension and the Coming of the Civil War* (New York: Hill and Wang, 2004). Works by historians who stress the irresolvable conflict between slavery and freedom are Foner, *Free Soil, Free Labor, Free Men*; Bruce Levine, *Half Slave and Half Free: The Roots of the Civil War* (New York: Hill and Wang, 1992); Eugene Genovese, *The Political Economy of Slavery* (New York: Random House, 1965).

18. Kenneth S. Greenberg, *Honor and Slavery: Lies, Duels, Noses, Masks, Dressing as a Woman, Gifts, Strangers, Humanitarianism, Death, Slave Rebellions, the Proslavery Argument, Baseball, Hunting, and Gambling in the Old South* (Princeton, NJ: Princeton University Press, 1996); Kenneth S. Greenberg, *Masters and Statesmen: The Political Culture of American Slavery* (Baltimore: Johns Hopkins University Press, 1985); John Ashworth, *Slavery, Capitalism, and Politics in the Antebellum Republic*, vol. 1: *Commerce and Compromise, 1820–1850* (New York: Cambridge University Press, 1995); William Freehling, *Road to Disunion*, vol. 2: *Secessionists Triumphant, 1854–1861* (New York: Oxford University Press, 2007). On the Toledo War, see James Z. Schwartz, *Conflict on the Michigan Frontier: Yankee and Borderland Cultures, 1815–1840* (De Kalb: Northern Illinois University Press, 2009). On the violence in Kansas, see Nicole Etcheson, *Bleeding Kansas: Contested Liberty in the Civil War Era* (Lawrence: University Press of Kansas, 2004).

19. Harrold, *Border War*, 183–207; David Grimstead, *American Mobbing, 1828–1861: Toward Civil War* (New York: Oxford University Press, 1998). Freehling, *Road to Disunion: Secessionists at Bay*, has demonstrated the benefits to integrating social and political history of the borderland. Taking a broad view, Freehling linked the emancipation of the old Northwest in the 1790s and 1800s with the emancipation movement in Kentucky in the 1850s. This broad perspective revealed both the importance of the border and its transient nature. Freehling argued that the upper South's lukewarm commitment to slavery divided the South, which both fueled secession and doomed the Confederacy to failure. The current study builds on Freehling's work by looking at the social processes that created the Ohio River border. See Freehling, *Road to Disunion: Secessionists at Bay*, 138–143. See also Tallant, *Evil Necessity*. For all of its broadness, Freehling's study fails to recognize that slavery thrived in Kentucky.

20. My approach to advertisements for fugitive slaves is informed by David Waldstreicher, "Reading the Runaways: Self-Fashioning, Print Culture, and Confidence in Slavery in the Eighteenth-Century Mid-Atlantic," *William and Mary Quarterly* 56, no. 3 (1999): 243–272. Several historians have recently made the effort to link the social and political history of slavery together; see James Oakes, "Political Significance of Slave Resistance," *History Workshop* 22, no. 1 (1986): 89–107; Ashworth, *Slavery, Capitalism and Politics*, vol. 1; Mason, *Slavery and Politics*; Freehling, *Reintegration of American History*; Steven Hahn, *A Nation under Our Feet: Black Political Struggles in the Rural South, from Slavery to the Great Migration* (Cambridge, MA: Belknap Press of Harvard University Press, 2003).

The importance of transgressions in the study of social boundaries inspired two sources that ostensibly had nothing to do with the history of the Ohio River Valley. In the introduction to *Almost Chosen People*, the historian Michael Zuckerman discusses how he had to use transgressions to study the rules for voting in colonial Massachusetts precisely because there was not a written code. Thus the only way to see the rules was to look for moments when someone broke them. In the 1950s the journalist John Howard Griffin traveled to the South disguised as a black man to highlight the psychological barrier posed by race. Griffin stated that as a black man he was always aware of racial boundaries even when they were not explicitly stated. The looks he received from whites constantly reinforced the racial boundary between them. Both of these books challenged me to look beyond the written law when examining the borderland. Because fugitive slaves had to cross from slavery to freedom in multiple ways, their strategies and rationales for escape revealed much about the border between slavery and freedom that may have otherwise remained hidden. See Michael Zuckerman, *Almost Chosen People: Oblique Biographies in the American Grain* (Berkeley: University of California Press, 1993); John Howard Griffin, *Black Like Me* (Boston: Houghton Mifflin, 1961).

21. Sterling Lecater Bland Jr., *Voices of the Fugitives: Runaway Slave Stories and Their Fictions of Self-Creation* (Westport, CT: Greenwood Press, 2000); Frances Smith Foster, *Witnessing Slavery: The Development of Antebellum Slave Narratives*, 2nd ed. (Madison: University of Wisconsin Press, 1994); James Olney, "'I was Born': Slave Narratives, Their Status as Autobiography and as Literature," in Charles T. Davis and Henry Louis Gates, Jr., eds., *The Slave's Narrative* (New York: Oxford University Press, 1985), 148–174; John W. Blassingame, "Using the Testimony of Ex-Slaves: Approaches and Problems," *Journal of Southern History* 41, no. 4 (November 1975): 473–492.

22. Historians have argued that the attempt to turn a human being into a thing was the central contradiction of slavery, and the ultimate source of conflict; see Walter Johnson, *Soul by Soul: Life inside the Antebellum Slave Market* (Cambridge, MA: Harvard University Press, 1999), 29, 128. My research suggests that in order for slavery to function at the border, slaveholders had to rely on the rationality of their slaves. Thus the concept of freedom as self-ownership became a language of negotiation in what Christopher Morris has called "articulation" in the master-slave relationship; see Morris, "The Articulation of Two Worlds: The Master-Slave Relationship Reconsidered," *Journal of American History* 85, no. 3 (December 1998): 982–1007. See also Walter Johnson, "On Agency," *Journal of Social History* 37, no. 1 (Fall 2003): 113–124.

23. Anzaldua, *Borderlands/La Frontera*.

24. Borderland residents' definitions of acceptable and unacceptable forms of border crossing target both the actions and the persons involved. Those in power, either politically or socially, act in self-interest to protect their position. Acceptable people therefore make acceptable transgressions, but residents restrict the movement of those whom they view as a threat. Their movement becomes unacceptable as a means of keeping them out of the community. This effort to regulate the border defines the

line between "us" and "them." While the action involved in "crossing" predates the borderland, the creation of the border transforms that act into a transgression. Border crossing therefore is an act of resistance only because those in power have defined it that way. See Migdal, "Mental Maps and Virtual Checkpoints," 3–26; Simpson, *Trafficking Subjects*, 56–91; Castronovo, "Compromised Narratives along the Border," 195–220.

25. Historians of the Jacksonian period have long made a case for the transformative power of the transportation revolution; see Daniel Walker Howe, *What Hath God Wrought: The Transformation of America, 1815–1848* (New York: Oxford University Press, 2007); Daniel Feller, *The Jacksonian Promise: America, 1815–1840* (Baltimore: Johns Hopkins University Press, 1995); Charles Sellers, *The Market Revolution: Jacksonian America 1815–1846* (New York: Oxford University Press, 1991). We are all indebted to George Rogers Taylor, *The Transportation Revolution, 1815–1860* (New York: Rinehart, 1951). Eric Foner recently made the argument that Americans' definition of freedom shifted during the antebellum period from the ownership of property to ownership of the self; see Foner, *The Story of American Freedom* (New York: W. W. Norton, 1998).

26. Norman Maclean, *A River Runs through It and Other Stories*, foreword by Annie Proulx, 25th anniversary ed. (Chicago: University of Chicago Press, 2001), 102.

Chapter 1

1. Richard White, *The Organic Machine: The Remaking of the Columbia River* (New York: Hill and Wang, 1995), 8–10; Scott Russel Sanders, "The Force of Moving Water," in Robert L. Reid, ed., *Always a River: The Ohio River and the American Experience* (Bloomington: Indiana University Press, 1991), 1–31.

2. Reid, *Always a River*, 2; World Resources Institute, Earthtrends: Environmental Information, "Watersheds of the World: North and Central America—Mississippi Watershed: Ohio Subbasin," multimedia.wri.org/watersheds_2003/na15.html (accessed October 2012).

3. "The Teays River," *GeoFacts No. 10*, Ohio Department of Natural Resources, Division of Geological Survey, http://www.dnr.state.oh.us/geosurvey/tabid/7882/default.aspx (accessed October 2012); Richard E. Banta, *The Ohio* (New York: Rinehart, 1949), 18–25.

4. Richard F. Nation, *At Home in the Hoosier Hills: Agriculture, Politics, and Religion in Southern Indiana, 1810–1870*, Midwestern History and Culture (Bloomington: Indiana University Press, 2005), 8–10; Darrel E. Bigham, *Towns and Villages of the Lower Ohio*, Ohio River Valley Series (Lexington: University Press of Kentucky, 1998), 11–13; Timothy R. Mahoney, *River Towns in the Great West: The Structure of Provincial Urbanization in the American Midwest, 1820–1870* (New York: Cambridge University Press, 1990), 3–15; John D. Barnhart and Donald F. Carmony, *Indiana, from Frontier to Industrial Commonwealth* (New York: Lewis Historical Publishing Company, 1954),

1–12; James H. Madison, *The Indiana Way: A State History* (Bloomington: Indiana University Press, 1986), 7–10.

5. On plant zones, see http://www.usna.usda.gov/Hardzone (accessed October 2012); Barnhart and Carmony, *Indiana*, 1–12.

6. Madison, *Indiana Way*, 3–7; Jared Diamond, *Guns, Germs, and Steel: The Fates of Human Societies* (New York: W. W. Norton, 1997), 35–66, 108–109, 151–152.

7. Daniel K. Richter, *Facing East from Indian Country: A Native History of Early America* (Cambridge, MA: Harvard University Press, 2001), 2–7; Alan Taylor, *American Colonies*, Penguin History of the United States (New York: Viking, 2001), 14–17. For an extensive treatment of prehistoric Indians, see Brian M. Fagan, *The Great Journey: The People of Ancient America* (New York: Thames and Hudson, 1987).

8. Richter, *Facing East*, 6; Stephen Aron, *How the West Was Lost: The Transformation of Kentucky from Daniel Boone to Henry Clay* (Baltimore: Johns Hopkins University Press, 1996), 6–7; Taylor, *American Colonies*, 261–262.

9. Richard White, *The Middle Ground: Indians, Empires, and Republics in the Great Lakes, 1650–1815* (New York: Cambridge University Press, 1991), 187–189; Aron, *How the West Was Lost*, 7–8; Richter, *Facing East*, 168–169.

10. Eric Hinderaker and Peter C. Mancall, *At the Edge of Empire: The Backcountry in British North America* (Baltimore: Johns Hopkins University Press, 2003), 92–95; Nation, *At Home in the Hoosier Hills*, 11–13; White, *Middle Ground*, 211–215; Aron, *How the West Was Lost*, 8–13; John Mack Faragher, *Daniel Boone: The Life and Legend of an American Pioneer* (New York: Holt, 1992), 98–140. My narrative closely follows the interpretations of White, Aron, Richter, and Hinderaker but differs in the emphasis on the river.

11. D. W. Meinig, *The Shaping of America: A Geographical Perspective on 500 Years of History*, vol. 1: *Atlantic America, 1492–1800* (New Haven, CT: Yale University Press, 1986), 209, 231–235.

12. Ibid., 200–202.

13. White, *Middle Ground*, 187–189.

14. Hinderaker and Mancall, *At the Edge of Empire*, 95–99; Richter, *Facing East*, 184–185; Aron, *How the West Was Lost*, 8–13; Reid, *Always a River*, 8–11. On agriculture as the only means of owning the land, see John Locke, *Two Treatises of Government*, ed. with introduction by Peter Laslett (New York: Cambridge University Press, 1988), 285–302; Joyce E. Chaplin, *Subject Matter: Technology, the Body, and Science on the Anglo-American Frontier, 1500–1676*, (Cambridge, MA: Harvard University Press, 2001), 322.

15. William Darlington, *Christopher Gist's Journals with Historical, Geographical and Ethnological Notes and Biographies of His Contemporaries* (Pittsburgh: J. R. Weldin & Co., 1893), 220, 226–231; Hinderaker and Mancall, *At the Edge of Empire*, 92–102.

16. Hinderaker and Mancall, *At the Edge of Empire*, 94–95, 100–102; Gayle Thornbrough and Dorothy Lois Riker, *Readings in Indiana History* (Indianapolis: Indiana Historical Bureau, 1956), 4–9; Eric Hinderaker, *Elusive Empires: Constructing*

Colonialism in the Ohio Valley, 1673–1800 (New York: Cambridge University Press, 1997); Taylor, *American Colonies*, 394–395; White, *Middle Ground*, 94–141.

17. Taylor, *American Colonies*, 428–430. For an in-depth description of the tangled world of village politics during the run-up to the Seven Years' War, see White, *Middle Ground*, 223–240.

18. Hinderaker and Mancall, *At the Edge of Empire*, 102–103.

19. White, *Middle Ground*, 240–259; Richter, *Facing East*, 188–189; Hinderaker and Mancall, *At the Edge of Empire*, 105–120. One of the better book-length treatments of the Seven Years' War is Fred Anderson, *Crucible of War: The Seven Years' War and the Fate of Empire in British North America, 1754–1766* (New York: Knopf, 2000).

20. Taylor, *American Colonies*, 433–437.

21. Meinig, *Shaping of America*, 284–286; Taylor, *American Colonies*, xiii. The classic depiction of the *courier du bois* is Richard White's *Middle Ground*, but see also Sylvia Van Kirk, *Many Tender Ties: Women in Fur-Trade Society, 1670–1870* (Norman: University of Oklahoma Press, 1983), for the importance of intermarriage in forging links between the French and Native Americans.

22. The modern spelling of Kentucky is used for consistency, but prior to becoming a state the spelling used was Kentucke. Aron, *How the West Was Lost*, 14–18; Richter, *Facing East*, 199–213; Hinderaker and Mancall, *At the Edge of Empire*, 117–124; White, *Middle Ground*, 269–340; Craig Thompson Friend, *Kentucke's Frontiers* (Bloomington: Indiana University Press, 2010), 39–41.

23. Aron, *How the West Was Lost*, 27–28; Richter, *Facing East*, 213–216; Hinderaker and Mancall, *At the Edge of Empire*, 157–160; Meinig, *Shaping of America*, 287.

24. White, *Middle Ground*, 366–396; Aron, *How the West Was Lost*, 35–47; Friend, *Kentucke's Frontiers*, 65–94; George H. Yater, *Two Hundred Years at the Falls of the Ohio: A History of Louisville and Jefferson County* (Louisville, KY: Heritage Corp., 1979), 2–14.

25. Friend, *Kentucke's Frontiers*.

26. Yater, *Two Hundred Years*, 15–25; Richter, *Facing East*, 224; Aron, *How the West Was Lost*, 49–53.

27. Banta, *The Ohio*, 175–176; Bigham, *Towns and Villages of the Lower Ohio*, 14–15. Meinig, *Shaping of America*, 352, offers a map of military bounty lands. Historians emphasize the division of authority at the river as one of the origins of the cultural separation between residents at the Ohio River. However, this assertion seems to be based on travel accounts, which often emphasized the difference between the orderly settlements north of the river and the scattered settlements on the south bank. First, travel accounts were usually written for a purpose and often attributed all differences between the north and south banks to the absence and presence of slavery. Second, most travel accounts date from the early decades of the nineteenth century, nearly twenty years after the initial division of authority. Third, travel accounts were based on quick observations and often failed to recognize the deep cultural and economic connections that crossed the river. Works that fairly evaluate the culture of the Ohio

River Valley are Hubert G. H. Wilhelm, "Settlement and Selected Landscape Imprints in the Ohio Valley," in Reid, ed., *Always a River*, 67–104; Andrew R. L. Cayton, "The Northwest Ordinance from the Perspective of the Frontier," in Robert M. Taylor Jr., ed., *The Northwest Ordinance 1787: A Bicentennial Handbook* (Indianapolis: Indiana Historical Society, 1987), 1–23.

28. I based this breakdown of the French and English Empires on Hinderaker, *Elusive Empires*. I have adapted his model of France's empire of commerce and England's empire of land, arguing that both forms of empire coexisted at the time of the creation of the American Confederation.

29. *Pittsburgh Gazette*, 2 June 1787, cited in Ellen Eslinger, ed., *Running Mad for Kentucky: Frontier Travel Accounts* (Lexington: University Press of Kentucky, 2004), 57; W. P. Strickland, *The Autobiography of James B. Finley, or Pioneer Life in the West* (Cincinnati: Methodist Book Concern, for the author, 1855), 24, cited in Eslinger, *Running Mad for Kentucky*, 43.

30. John D. Shane, interview with Mrs. Webb [1842], cited in Elizabeth A. Perkins, *Border Life: Experience and Memory in the Revolutionary Ohio Valley* (Chapel Hill: University of North Carolina Press, 1998), 47; Eslinger, *Running Mad for Kentucky*, 1–66; Kim M. Gruenwald, *River of Enterprise: The Commercial Origins of Regional Identity in the Ohio Valley, 1790–1850* (Bloomington: Indiana University Press, 2002), 7–24.

31. Ellen Eslinger, "The Shape of Slavery on the Kentucky Frontier, 1775–1800," *Register of the Kentucky Historical Society* 92, no. 1 (1994): 1–23.

32. Peter S. Onuf, *Statehood and Union: A History of the Northwest Ordinance*, Midwestern History and Culture (Bloomington: Indiana University Press, 1987).

33. On the mess that was Kentucky's land title system, see Aron, *How the West Was Lost*, 58–81.

34. Gruenwald, *River of Enterprise*, 10; White, *Middle Ground*, 418–419. On the expulsion of squatters, see Ensign John Armstrong to Lt. Col. Josiah Harmar, Ft. McIntosh, 12 April 1785, *Western Reserve and Northern Ohio Historical Society*, tracts 1–36 (1870–1877), no. 6: 3–4, as cited in Emily Foster, ed., *The Ohio Frontier: An Anthology of Early Writings* (Lexington: University Press of Kentucky 1996), 74; Cayton, "The Northwest Ordinance," 1–23.

35. On the use of bound labor in the settlement process, see Eslinger, "Shape of Slavery," 1–23. Although Eslinger does not specifically mention the presence of slaves north of the river, it seems unlikely that settlers would not bring or at least use slave labor north of the river. Slaves were a part of the settlement of Kentucky from the very beginning and were present even at Boonesborough and on Daniel Boone's long hunting trips; see Faragher, *Daniel Boone*, 68–140.

36. Shirley S. McCord, *Travel Accounts of Indiana, 1679–1961: A Collection of Observations by Wayfaring Foreigners, Itinerants, and Peripatetic Hoosiers*, Indiana Historical Collections, 47 (Indianapolis: Indiana Historical Bureau, 1970), 32, 35; White, *Middle Ground*, 422–433; Andrew R. L. Cayton, *Frontier Indiana* (Bloomington: Indiana University Press, 1996), 89–97; Cayton, "Northwest Ordinance," 1–23.

37. Christopher Hodson and Brett Rushforth, "Bridging the Continental Divide: Colonial America's French Quarter," *OAH Magazine of History* 25, no. 1 (January 2011): 19–24, quote on 22; Carl J. Ekberg, *French Roots in the Illinois Country: The Mississippi Frontier in Colonial Times* (Urbana: University of Illinois Press, 1998), 111–170.

38. On slavery, see bill of sale, 19 September 1766, 3 April 1771, letter, 11 October 1777, Lasselle Collection, ISL; James A. James, ed., *George Rogers Clark Papers, 1781–1784*, Illinois Historical Collections, 19 (Springfield, IL, 1926), 85. On the French slave trade, see Brett Rushforth, "Slavery, the Fox Wars, and the Limits of Alliance," *William and Mary Quarterly* 63, no. 1 (January 2006): 53–80; Brett Rushforth, "A Little Flesh We Offer You: Origins of Indian Slavery in New France," *William and Mary Quarterly* 60, no. 4 (October 2003): 777–809.

39. Memorial of Bartholomew Tarvideau, 8 July 1788, in Clarence W. Alvord, ed., *Kaskaskia Records, 1778–1790* (Springfield: Illinois State Library, 1909), 485–488; Meinig, *Shaping of America*, 242–243. Americans arriving in Vincennes commonly described the French settlers' lack of industry, using their minimal agricultural pursuits as evidence; see Emma Lou Thornbrough, *The Negro in Indiana: A Study of a Minority* (Indianapolis: Indiana Historical Bureau, 1957), 1–7. The settlements in the Illinois country were likely the upper reaches of what Daniel Usner has called the "frontier exchange economy"; see Usner, "The Frontier Exchange Economy of the Lower Mississippi Valley," in Peter C. Mancall and James H. Merrell, eds., *American Encounters: Natives and Newcomers from European Contact to Indian Removal, 1500–1850* (New York: Routledge, 2000), 215–239.

40. Barnhart and Carmony, *Indiana*, 78–83; White, *Middle Ground*, 421–433.

41. Merrily Pierce, "Luke Decker and Slavery: His Cases with Bob and Anthony, 1817–1822," *Indiana Magazine of History* 85 (March 1989): 31–49.

42. Eslinger, *Running Mad for Kentucky*, 1–66; Gruenwald, *River of Enterprise*, 7–24.

43. David Waldstreicher, *Slavery's Constitution: From Revolution to Ratification* (New York: Hill and Wang, 2009), 87–89.

44. William Grayson to James Monroe, 8 August 1787, cited in William W. Freehling, *The Road to Disunion* (New York: Oxford University Press, 1990), 138. The most famous proponent of the link between the constitutional debates and the Northwest Ordinance is Staughton Lynd, "Compromise of 1787," in *Class Conflict, Slavery, and the United States Constitution* (Indianapolis: Bobbs-Merrill, 1968), 185–213. In repudiation of Lynd, see James H. Huston, "Riddles of the Constitutional Convention," *William and Mary Quarterly*, 3rd ser., 44, no. 3 (July 1987): 415–418. Others who have taken up the discussion include Paul Finkelman, *Slavery and the Founders: Race and Liberty in the Age of Jefferson* (Armonk, NY: M. E. Sharpe, 1996), 37–57; Gary B. Nash, *Race and Revolution*, Merrill Jensen Lectures in Constitutional Studies (Madison, WI: Madison House, 1990); Edward L. Ayers, *All over the Map: Rethinking American Regions* (Baltimore: Johns Hopkins University Press, 1996), 11–37.

45. Onuf, *Statehood and Union*.

46. Finkelman, *Slavery and the Founders*, 37–57.

47. Ibid., 52. On the combination of ambivalence and idealism in the founding of the country, see David Brion Davis's classic study, *The Problem of Slavery in the Age of Revolution, 1770–1823* (New York: Oxford University Press, 1999), 255–284.

48. Hinderaker, *Elusive Empires*, 46–85, 176–186; Cayton, *Frontier Indiana*, 99–138; Andrew R. L. Cayton, "Separate Interests and the Nation-State: The Washington Administration and the Origins of Regionalism in the Trans-Appalachian West," *Journal of American History* 79, no. 1 (1992): 39–67.

49. Major John Hamtramck to General Josiah Harmar, 14 August 1789, as cited in Finkelman, *Slavery and the Founders*, 51; Arthur St. Clair to George Washington, 1 May 1790, in Clarence E. Carter, ed., *Territorial Papers of the United States*, 28 vols. (Washington, DC: Government Printing Office, 1934–1975), 2: 244–248; Bartholomew Tarvideau to Arthur St. Clair, 30 June 1789, Arthur St. Clair Papers, OHS.

50. Cayton, "Northwest Ordinance," 1–23.

51. Pierce, "Luke Decker and Slavery"; Waldstreicher, *Slavery's Constitution*, 89, 135.

52. Arthur St. Clair to Luke Decker, 1793, as cited in Thornbrough and Riker, *Readings in Indiana History*, 144. Finkelman, *Slavery and the Founders*, 51–58, demonstrates the evolution of St. Clair's interpretations of article six in a series of letters to George Washington and Thomas Jefferson. On St. Clair, see Andrew R. L. Cayton, *The Frontier Republic: Ideology and Politics in the Ohio Country, 1780–1825* (Kent, OH: Kent State University Press, 1986), 33–50.

53. Some historians, Paul Finkelman most prominently, cite the persistence of slavery and de facto slavery in Indiana and Illinois well into the nineteenth century as evidence of the weakness of the ordinance. On the other side of the debate, historians such as David Brion Davis and William Freehling argue that article six worked as a deterrent for the migration of slaveholders, which ultimately allowed for the success of the antislavery movement in the formation of states carved out of the Northwest Territory. The third position recently established by John Craig Hammond and Kim Gruenwald is that economic and personal opportunity outweighed slavery as a concern among Americans in the Northwest Territory. See Finkelman, *Slavery and the Founders*, 37–57, 58–80; Don E. Fehrenbacher, *The Slaveholding Republic: An Account of the United States Government's Relations to Slavery* (New York: Oxford University Press, 2001), 256–258; Onuf, *Statehood and Union*, 109–116.; David Brion Davis, "The Significance of Excluding Slavery from the Old Northwest in 1787," *Indiana Magazine of History* 84 (March 1988): 75–89; Phillip J. Schwartz, *Migrants against Slavery: Virginians and the Nation* (Charlottesville: University of Virginia Press, 2001), 1–15; Freehling, *Road to Disunion*, 138–141; Stephen Middleton, *The Black Laws: Race and the Legal Process in Early Ohio* (Athens: Ohio University Press, 2005), 7–17. These interpretations deemphasize the ordinance as the original impetus for migration; see John Craig Hammond, *Slavery, Freedom, and Expansion in the Early American West*

(Charlottesville: University of Virginia Press, 2007); Gruenwald, *River of Enterprise*, 3–38; Andrew R. L. Cayton, "Artery and Border: The Ambiguous Development of the Ohio Valley in the Early Republic," *Ohio Valley History* 1, no. 1 (2001): 19–26; Kim M. Gruenwald, "Space and Place on the Early American Frontier: The Ohio Valley as Region, 1790–1850," *Ohio Valley History* 4, no. 3 (2004): 31–48; Bigham, *Towns and Villages of the Lower Ohio*, 11–46.

Chapter 2

1. J. Blaine Hudson, "Slavery in Early Louisville and Jefferson County, Kentucky, 1780–1812," *Filson Club Historical Quarterly* 73, no. 3 (July 1999): 249–283; Joan Wells Coward, *Kentucky in the New Republic: The Process of Constitution Making* (Lexington: University Press of Kentucky, 1979), 63–65; Ellen Eslinger, "The Shape of Slavery on the Kentucky Frontier, 1775–1800," *Register of the Kentucky Historical Society* 92, no. 1 (1994): 1–23; Craig Thompson Friend, "Work and Be Rich: Economy and Culture on the Bluegrass Farm," in Friend, *The Buzzel about Kentuck: Settling the Promised Land* (Lexington: University Press of Kentucky, 1999), 130–151; Stephen Aron, "The Poor Men to Starve: The Lives and Times of Workingmen in Early Lexington," in Friend, *Buzzel about Kentuck*, 175–193, in particular 184–186; J. Blaine Hudson, *Fugitive Slaves and the Underground Railroad in the Kentucky Borderland* (Jefferson, NC: McFarland & Co., 2002), 14; J. Winston Coleman, *Slavery Times in Kentucky* (Chapel Hill: University of North Carolina Press, 1940), 1–17; Marion B. Lucas, *A History of Blacks in Kentucky: From Slavery to Segregation, 1760–1861* (Frankfort: Kentucky Historical Society, 1992), xi–xx.

2. Jeffrey Brooke Allen, "The Debate over Slavery and Race in Ante-Bellum Kentucky: 1792–1850" (Ph.D. diss., Northwestern University, 1973), 9; Eva Sheppard Wolf, *Race and Liberty in the New Nation: Emancipation in Virginia from the Revolution to Nat Turner's Rebellion* (Baton Rouge: Louisiana State University Press, 2006), 39–84; Ellen Eslinger, "The Beginnings of Afro-American Christianity among Kentucky Baptists," in Friend, *Buzzel about Kentuck*, 197–216.

3. David Rice left his slave Dick to his son, left the "use of Edith" to a daughter, and freed Edith's children, males at age twenty-five and females at twenty-three. Twenty-two years after his death the grandchildren of Edith filed for their freedom. The court ruled that because they were born while their mothers were still slaves they were "doomed" to slavery since the will said nothing about grandchildren; see Esther v. Akins, September 1842, in Helen Catterall, *Judicial Cases Concerning American Slavery and the Negro*, vol. 1 (Washington, DC: Carnegie Institution of Washington, 1926), 361.

4. Coward, *Kentucky*, 43; Lowell Hayes Harrison, *The Antislavery Movement in Kentucky* (Lexington: University Press of Kentucky, 1978), 18–37; Stephen Aron, *How the West Was Lost: The Transformation of Kentucky from Daniel Boone to Henry Clay* (Baltimore: Johns Hopkins University Press, 1996), 124–149.

5. David Brion Davis, *The Problem of Slavery in the Age of Revolution, 1770–1823* (New York: Oxford University Press, 1999), 285–342.

6. David Rice [Philanthropos], *Slavery Inconsistent with Justice and Good Policy* (Lexington, KY: J. Bradford, 1792), 34; Franklin, *To the People of Kentucky* (Lexington, 1795); George Nicholas, *To the Freemen of Kentucky*, 30 March 1799; all of the works cited above were found in *Early American Imprints, Series 1: Evans, 1679–1800*, Charles Evans, Roger P. Bristol, contributors (Worcester, MA: American Antiquarian Society, 2002), http://infoweb.newsbank.com.proxy.library.nd.edu (accessed 2006).

7. John Breckenridge to Isaac Shelby, 11 March 1798, Reuben T. Durrett Collection on Kentucky and the Ohio River Valley, Special Collections Research Center, University of Chicago Library, found in "The First American West: Ohio Valley 1750–1820," Library of Congress (online), http://memory.loc.gov/ammem/award99/icuhtml/fawhome.html (accessed October 2012). An example of Breckenridge's public stance against emancipation is A Friend to Order [John Breckenridge], *For the Kentucky Herald: To the Voter*, 20 April 1798, *Early American Imprints, Series 1: Evans, 1639–1800*.

8. On color-blind republican paternalism, see William W. Freehling, *The Reintegration of American History: Slavery and the Civil War* (New York: Oxford University Press, 1994), 82–104. On the Lynne estate, see "Kentucky Court of Appeals Ruling in Favor of Harry Innes, Executor for the Estate of Edmund Lyne," 9 December 1803; "Order Rescinding a Court Decision Setting aside Edmund Lyne's Will," December 1803; "Accounts for Maintenance of Milley, James, and Lucy, Emancipated African American Children," 1793–1803; "Bill and Receipt from Hannah Harris for the Maintenance of Milley, an Emancipated African American Child," 18 February 1799; "Bill and Receipt from Henry Thompson for the Maintenance of Lucy, an Emancipated African American Child," 25 April 1798; "Bill and Receipt from Robert Perry for the Maintenance of James, an Emancipated African American Child," 27 August 1797—all of the above documents can be found in the Edmund Lyne Papers, Reuben T. Durrett Collection on Kentucky and the Ohio River Valley, "The First American West: Ohio Valley 1750–1820."

9. On how the debate turned toward compensated emancipation, see Allen, "Debate over Slavery," 46–58.

10. Rice, *Slavery*, 16; Scaevola [Henry Clay], "To the Electors of Fayette County," 16 April 1798, as cited in Allen, "Debate over Slavery," 38.

11. Friend, *Along the Maysville Road*, 70–80.

12. Franklin, "To the People of Kentucky"; "To the Citizens of Fayette County," *Early American Imprints, Series 1: Evans, 1679–1800*, Charles Evans, Roger P. Bristol, contributors (Worcester, MA: American Antiquarian Society, 2002), http://infoweb.newsbank.com.proxy.library.nd.edu (accessed 2006).

13. Coward, *Kentucky*, 63–65; Daniel Drake, *Pioneer Life in Kentucky, 1785–1800* (New York: H. Schuman, 1948), 207–208.

14. Drake, *Pioneer Life*, 93; Lucas, *History of Blacks in Kentucky*, xi–xviii; Coleman, *Slavery Times*, 3–17; Eslinger, "Shape of Slavery," 2–4; Hudson, "Slavery in Louisville," 262–267; Aron, "Poor Men to Starve," 184–186.

15. Aron, *How the West Was Lost*, 92–99, pinpoints Henry Clay's marriage as the exact moment he went from being openly antislavery to a compromiser on slavery. John Donald Barnhart, *Valley of Democracy: The Frontier versus the Plantation in Ohio Valley, 1775–1818* (Bloomington: Indiana University Press, 1953), began the historiographical trend that emphasizes slavery as the reason why poor whites left Kentucky for Indiana. While historians give different effects of this migration, many still point to slavery as the original motivating factor. See Nicole Etcheson, *The Emerging Midwest: Upland Southerners and the Political Culture of the Old Northwest, 1787–1861* (Bloomington: Indiana University Press, 1996); Aron, *How the West Was Lost*; Eugene H. Berwanger, *The Frontier against Slavery: Western Anti-Negro Prejudice and the Slavery Extension Controversy* (Urbana: University of Illinois Press, 1967); Allen, "Debate over Slavery," 66. While slavery undoubtedly motivated some to leave Kentucky, the recent corrective that white migrants likely left searching for agriculturally similar lands and then developed antislavery views seems more plausible for the majority of immigrants. See Darrel E. Bigham, *Towns and Villages of the Lower Ohio*, Ohio River Valley Series (Lexington: University Press of Kentucky, 1998), 11–46; Kim M. Gruenwald, *River of Enterprise: The Commercial Origins of Regional Identity in the Ohio Valley, 1790–1850* (Bloomington: Indiana University Press, 2002), 3–38; John Craig Hammond, *Slavery, Freedom, and Expansion in the Early American West* (Charlottesville: University of Virginia Press, 2007).

16. John May, *Journal and Letters of Col. John May, of Boston Relative to Two Journeys to the Ohio Country in 1788 and 89* (Cincinnati: Robert Clarke & Co., 1873), as cited in Emily Foster, ed., *The Ohio Frontier: An Anthology of Early Writings* (Lexington: University Press of Kentucky, 1996), 77; Friend, "Work and Be Rich," 130–151; John D. Barnhart, "Sources of Southern Migration into the Old Northwest," *Mississippi Valley Historical Review* 22, no. 1 (1935): 49–62.

17. Lowell H. Harrison, "A Virginian Moves to Kentucky, 1793," *William and Mary Quarterly*, 3rd ser., 15, no. 2 (1958): 201–213, quote on 201; William Christian, letter, 12 December 1785, Hugh Blair Grigsby Papers, Virginia Historical Society, quoted in Eslinger, "Shape of Slavery," 11.

18. Friend, "Work and Be Rich," 128–129; "Some Particulars Relative to Kentucky," in Eugene Schwabb, ed., *Travels in the Old South*, vol. 1 (Lexington: University Press of Kentucky, 1973), 59, as cited in Friend, "Work and Be Rich," 130.

19. Friend, *Along the Maysville Road*, 105–128, makes the argument that in Kentucky all settlers wanted to become wealthy and provide for their families, but they differed in terms of means. Thus the conflict was not over fundamental principles, only over opportunity. I find this plausible and a way to understand the migration of whites across the border. They sought opportunity not to live an entirely separate life, and their ability to do so across the river stemmed the possibility of radical action in Kentucky. On Marietta, see Gruenwald, *River of Enterprise*, 14.

20. Philip Gatch, *Sketch of Rev. Philip Gatch Prepared by Hon. John M'Lean* (Cincinnati: Swormstedt & Poc, 1854), 6–59, as cited in John Wigger, "Ohio Gospel: Methodism in the Early Ohio Valley," in Andrew R. L. Cayton and Stuart D. Hobbs, eds., *Center of a Great Empire: The Ohio Country in the Early American Republic* (Athens: Ohio University Press, 2005), 62–80, quote on 62; Allen, "Debate over Slavery," 11–12; Michael Mangin, "Freemen in Theory: Race, Society and Politics in Ross County, Ohio, 1796–1850" (Ph.D. diss., University of California, San Diego, 2002), 48.

21. Allen, "Debate over Slavery," 67–68.

22. Over thirty years ago Davis, *Problem of Slavery*, 255–284, demonstrated how the Founding Fathers' belief in gradual progress made them both idealistic and unwilling to act quickly to end slavery. Don Fehrenbacher, *The Slaveholding Republic: An Account of the United States Government's Relations to Slavery* (New York: Oxford University Press, 2001), 246–248, picked up that theme and made the argument that political leaders were willing to end slavery north of the Ohio River because there was not a significant slave population at the time. While the ambivalence of the Founding Fathers plays a vital role in William Freehling, *The Road to Disunion* (New York: Oxford University Press, 1990), 138–141, in the case of the ordinance he makes the argument that inaction was actually significant because it left the decision up to the settlers.

23. George E. Greene, *History of Old Vincennes and Knox County, Indiana* (Chicago: S. J. Clarke, 1911), 323.

24. Deposition of Peter McNelly given before Judge George Turner, Knox County, Territory of the United States Northwest of the Ohio, 7 June 1794, William H. English Collection, Special Collections Research Center, University of Chicago, found in "The First American West: Ohio Valley 1750–1820"; Daniel K. Richter, *Facing East from Indian Country: A Native History of Early America* (Cambridge, MA: Harvard University Press, 2001), 6; Aron, *How the West Was Lost*, 6–7.

25. Deposition of Peter McNelly.

26. It is my argument that captive exchange and chattel slavery were distinct systems based on different principles. What is interesting in this case is how the two systems seem to have blended together, suggesting perhaps that captivity and servitude were anchors on a continuum of bondage. For a similar interpretation in the Southwest, see James Brooks, *Captives and Cousins: Slavery, Kinship, and Community in the Southwest Borderlands* (Chapel Hill: University of North Carolina Press, 2002). On captivity in North America, see Linda Colley, *Captives* (New York: Pantheon Books, 2002), 137–240; John Demos, *The Unredeemed Captive: A Family Story from Early America* (New York: Vintage Books, 1994). On the uniqueness of eighteenth-century plantation slavery in North America, see Robin Blackburn, *The Making of New World Slavery: From the Baroque to the Modern, 1492–1800* (New York: Verso, 1998), 307–370, 457–508.

27. On Turner and the laws he passed, including a law banning the sale of liquor to Indians and restricting the sale of it to soldiers, see *The Biographical Annals of Ohio*

1904–1905: A Handbook of the Government and Institutions of the State of Ohio, compiled under authority of the Act of 19 April 1904 by F. E. Scobey, Clerk of the Senate, and E. W. Doty, Clerk of the House (Springfield, OH: Springfield Publishing Company, State Printers, 1905), 137.

28. Deposition of Peter McNelly. On the Fugitive Slave Law and the fugitive slave clause of the U.S. Constitution, see Paul Finkelman, "Implementing the Proslavery Constitution: The Adoption of the Fugitive Slave Law of 1793," in Paul Finkelman, *Slavery and the Founders: Race and Liberty in the Age of Jefferson* (Armonk, NY: M. E. Sharpe, 1996), 81–104; Carol Wilson, *Freedom at Risk: The Kidnapping of Free Blacks in America, 1780–1865* (Lexington: University Press of Kentucky, 1994), 40–66; Fehrenbacher, *Slaveholding Republic*, 205–230.

29. Fortescue Cuming, *Sketches of a Tour to the Western Country, through the States of Ohio and Kentucky, a Voyage down the Ohio and Mississippi Rivers, and a Trip through the Mississippi Territory, and Part of West Florida* (Pittsburgh: Cramer, Spear & Eichbaum, 1810), in Reuben Gold Thwaites, *Early Western Travels, 1748–1846*, vol. 4 (Cleveland: A. H. Clark, 1904), 202. Oliver Smith wrote of sheriffs: "they seemed to have been selected as candidates on account of their fine voices to call jurors and witnesses from the woods, from the door of the court building, and their ability to run down and catch offenders," in Gayle Thornbrough and Dorothy Lois Riker, eds., *Readings in Indiana History* (Indianapolis: Indiana Historical Bureau, 1956), 165.

30. Deposition of Joseph Baird before Judge George Turner, Knox County, Territory of the United States Northwest of the Ohio, 14 June 1794; Deposition of Joseph LaMotte before Judge George Turner, Knox County, Territory of the United States Northwest of the Ohio, 8 June 1794; Deposition of Toussaint Dubois before Judge George Turner, Knox County, Territory of the United States Northwest of the Ohio, 11 August 1794; Deposition of Peter McNelly, "The First American West: Ohio Valley 1750–1820."

31. Deposition of Peter McNelly; Deposition of Joseph Baird; Deposition of Joseph LaMotte; Deposition of Toussaint Dubois.

32. Nathaniel Ewing headed west from Pennsylvania into Kentucky with his father at least as early as 1784 with hopes of acquiring a fortune through trade. See Elizabeth A. Perkins, *Border Life: Experience and Memory in the Revolutionary Ohio Valley* (Chapel Hill: University of North Carolina Press, 1998), 71.

33. On trade in the early Ohio Valley, see Gruenwald, *River of Enterprise*, 25–38; Andrew R. L. Cayton, *Frontier Indiana* (Bloomington: Indiana University Press, 1996), 167–195; Richard White, *The Middle Ground: Indians, Empires, and Republics in the Great Lakes, 1650–1815* (New York: Cambridge University Press, 1991), 413–433.

34. Joseph LaMotte deposed that he was hired to carry away the McNellys "because the said Peter had made application to the Territorial Judge for freedom for himself and wife"; see Deposition of Joseph LaMotte. Baird and Dubois both indicated that they knew about Peter McNelly's application as well; see Deposition of Joseph Baird; Deposition of Toussaint Dubois.

35. Deposition of Peter McNelly; Deposition of Joseph Baird. Moses Decker deposed that "disliking the sight," he untied Queen McNelly; see Deposition of Moses Decker before Judge George Turner, Knox County, Territory of the United States Northwest of the Ohio, 11 June 1794.

36. Deposition of Peter McNelly; Deposition of Joseph Baird. The 1810 census for the Indiana Territory lists five slaves in White River Township. See William Wesley Woolen, William Wesley, Daniel Wait Howe, and Jacob P. Dunn, eds., *Executive Journal of Indiana Territory, 1800–1816*, repr. with revisions (Indianapolis: Family History Section, Indiana Historical Society, 1985), 84–85.

37. Deposition of Peter McNelly. Deposition of Joseph Baird and Deposition of Moses Decker both mention Richard Levins as the purchaser of Queen McNelly.

38. Dubois deposed that he and Nathaniel Ewing promised to help Baird and LaMotte; see Deposition of Toussaint Dubois. LaMotte corroborated this in his deposition; see Deposition of Joseph LaMotte.

39. Deposition of Moses Decker; Deposition of Toussaint Dubois; Deposition of Luke Decker before Judge James Johnson, Knox County, Territory of the United States Northwest of the Ohio, 8 September 1795, "The First American West: Ohio Valley 1750–1820."

40. Examination of Henry Vanderburgh before Judge George Turner, Knox County, Territory of the United States Northwest of the Ohio, 30 September 1794, "The First American West: Ohio Valley 1750–1820"; Deposition of Christopher Wyant on the conduct of Judge George Turner, 1795, William H. English Collection, IHS. On the back of this writ Turner confirmed Peter McNelly's freedom, Writ of Habeas Corpus ad Subjiciendum for Henry Vanderburgh, and Peter and Queen McNelly for the appearance of Henry Vanderburgh, Peter and Queen McNelly, 23 August 1794, "The First American West: Ohio Valley 1750–1820."

41. Deposition of Christopher Wyant before Judge James Johnson, Knox County, Territory of the United States Northwest of the Ohio, 14 June 1794, "The First American West: Ohio Valley 1750–1820"; Deposition of Joseph Baird.

42. On the status of African Americans before the courts, see Juliet E. K. Walker, "The Legal Status of Free Blacks in Early Kentucky, 1792–1825," *Filson Club History Quarterly* 57, no. 4 (1983): 382–395; J. Blaine Hudson, "References to Slavery in the Public Records of Early Louisville and Jefferson County, 1780–1812," *Filson Club History Quarterly* 73, no. 4 (1999): 325–354. On Vanderburgh and slavery as the "custom of the country," see George W. Geib, "Jefferson, Harrison, and the West: An Essay on Territorial Slavery," in Darrel E. Bigham, ed., *Indiana Territory, 1800–2000: A Bicentennial Perspective* (Indianapolis: Indiana Historical Society, 2001), 99–125.

43. George Turner to Arthur St. Clair, August 1794, and Arthur St. Clair to George Turner, December 1794, in Thornbrough and Riker, *Readings in Indiana History*, 145, 146.

44. Writ of Habeas Corpus and Order for the Release of Henry Vanderburgh, 7 September 1795, "The First American West: Ohio Valley 1750–1820."

45. Petition for Turner's removal, *American State Papers, Misc.*, 1:151, 157; *St. Clair Papers*, 2:372, cited in Clarence Walworth Alvord, ed., *The Centennial History of Illinois*, vol. 1: *The Illinois Country 1673–1818* (Springfield: Illinois Centennial Commission, 1920), 405; Jacob Piatt Dunn, *Indiana: A Redemption from Slavery*, new and enlarged ed. (Boston: Houghton, Mifflin, 1916), 223–224.

46. Lee Soltow, "Inequality amidst Abundance: Land Ownership in Early Nineteenth Century Ohio," *Ohio History* 88, no. 2 (1979): 133–151; Jonathan Bean, "Marketing the Great American Commodity: Nathaniel Massie and Land Speculation on the Ohio Frontier, 1783–1813," *Ohio History* 103 (Summer–Autumn 1994): 152–169; Andrew Cayton, "Land, Power, and Reputation: The Cultural Dimension of Politics in the Ohio Country," *William and Mary Quarterly*, 3rd ser, 47, no. 2 (April 1990): 255–286; Mangin, "Freemen in Theory," 46.

47. Petition of John Edgar and William and Robert Morrison, 1796, in Jacob Piatt Dunn, *Slavery Petitions and Papers* (Indianapolis: Bowen-Merrill, 1894), 447–452.

48. Soltow, "Inequality amidst Abundance," 142; Mangin, "Freemen in Theory," 33; Cayton, "Land, Power and Reputation," 281; Dunn, *Indiana*, 288–289; Edward Tiffin to Thomas Worthington, 7 March 1798, Worthington Papers, OHS, as cited in Cayton, "Land, Power and Reputation," 281; *Register of Black, Mulatto and Poor Persons in Four Ohio Counties, 1791–1861* (Bowie, MD: Joan Turpin Heritage Books, 1985), typescript, OHS, 17; Marion Nelson, "Power in Motion: Western Success Stories of the Jeffersonian Republic" (Ph.D. diss., University of Pennsylvania, 2006).

49. Andrew R. L. Cayton, *Ohio: The History of a People* (Columbus: Ohio State University Press, 2002), 36; Stephen Middleton, *The Black Laws: Race and the Legal Process in Early Ohio* (Athens: Ohio University Press, 2005), 31.

50. Cayton, *Frontier Indiana*, 167–195; John D. Barnhart and Donald F. Carmony, *Indiana, from Frontier to Industrial Commonwealth* (New York: Lewis Historical Publishing Company, 1954), 101–103.

Chapter 3

1. Michael Mangin, "Freemen in Theory: Race, Society and Politics in Ross County, Ohio, 1796–1850" (Ph.D. diss., University of California, San Diego, 2002), 58; Andrew Cayton, *The Frontier Republic: Ideology and Politics in the Ohio Country, 1780–1825* (Kent, OH: Kent State University Press, 1986), 51–80; Andrew Cayton, "Land, Power, and Reputation: The Cultural Dimension of Politics in the Ohio Country," *William and Mary Quarterly* 47, no. 2 (1990): 266–286. Marion Nelson, "Power in Motion: Western Success Stories of the Jeffersonian Republic" (Ph.D. diss., University of Pennsylvania, 2006), 155–175, makes a strong case for the importance of making connections in Worthington's vision for the nation.

2. *Chillicothe Scioto Gazette*, 28 August 1802, 18 November 1802. On party spirit in frontier Ohio, see Donald J. Ratcliffe, *Party Spirit in a Frontier Republic: Democratic Politics in Ohio, 1793–1821* (Columbus: Ohio State University Press, 1998); Stephen

Middleton, *The Black Laws: Race and the Legal Process in Early Ohio*, Law, Society, and Politics in the Midwest (Athens: Ohio University Press, 2005), 18–41.

3. Census from University of Virginia Web site, http://fisher.lib.virginia.edu/col lections/stats/histcensus/index .html (accessed October 2012); Ellen Eslinger, "The Shape of Slavery on the Kentucky Frontier, 1775–1800," *Register of the Kentucky Historical Society* 92, no. 1 (1994): 1–23.

4. Historians have made much of white workers' resentment of slave labor as unfair competition, which was especially true in cities such as Lexington, where white and black workers labored side by side in rope-making factories; see Stephen Aron, "The Poor Men to Starve: The Lives and Times of Workingmen in Early Lexington," in Craig Thompson Friend, ed., *Buzzel about Kentuck: Settling the Promised Land* (Lexington: University Press of Kentucky, 1999), 175–193, in particular 184–186. However, outside the urban environment, competition for labor was less direct because labor demands were less specific, which made resentment less pronounced. For an example of the use of slaves as collateral for debts, see Frederick Ridgely to Gabriel Lewis, 20 January 1804, in "The First American West: Ohio Valley 1750–1820," Library of Congress (online), http://memory.loc.gov/ammem/award99/icuhtml/fawhome.html (accessed October 2012).

5. In a discussion of the Missouri Crisis, William J. Cooper, *Liberty and Slavery: Southern Politics to 1860* (Columbia: University of South Carolina Press, 2000), 136–138, argues that southerners had been committed to slavery at least since the Revolution because of its ties to their definition of liberty. Kentucky's transition from a western frontier to a slaveholding state and the insipient class antagonisms between settlers and the emerging elite are well-trod ground; see Craig Thompson Friend, *Kentucke's Frontiers* (Bloomington: Indiana University Press, 2010), 172–254; Craig Thompson Friend, *Along the Maysville Road: The Early American Republic in the Trans-Appalachian West* (Knoxville: University of Tennessee Press, 2005); Stephen Aron, *How the West Was Lost: The Transformation of Kentucky from Daniel Boone to Henry Clay* (Baltimore: Johns Hopkins University Press, 1996).

6. Articles of Agreement between Alexander Scott Bullitt and John Anthony Tarascon, 15 September 1807, 25 September 1809; Articles of Agreement between Bullitt and William Haywood, Bullitt Family Papers, Oxmoor Collection, FHS. Bullitt purchased a female slave, Molly, from Noel and Tarlton Goldsby for $350 on 4 June 1810, there are receipts for the purchase of several slaves in June 1810, and one bill of sale from 12 June shows that he purchased six slaves. On the influence of Bullitt, see J. Blaine Hudson, "Slavery in Early Louisville and Jefferson County, Kentucky, 1780–1812," *Filson Club History Quarterly* 73, no. 3 (July 1999): 249–283.

7. Elias Pym Fordham, *Personal Narrative of Travels in Virginia, Maryland, Pennsylvania, Ohio, Indiana, Kentucky; and of a Residence in the Illinois Territory: 1817–1818* (Cleveland: Arthur H. Clark Company, 1906), 16. On the association between slaveholding and opportunity more broadly, see James Oakes, *The Ruling Race: A History of American Slaveholders* (New York: Knopf, 1982).

8. George Corlis to John Corlis, 9 March 1816; Joseph Corlis to John and Susan Corlis, 25 February 1816; George Corlis to John Corlis, 24 March 1816, Corlis-Respess Family Papers, FHS.

9. George Corlis to John Corlis, 14 April 1816; John Corlis to George Corlis, April 1816, Corlis-Respess Family Papers, FHS.

10. George Corlis to John Corlis, 13 April 1816, 14 April 1816, 23 April 1816; numerous receipts for the hiring of slaves, for example for 18 December 1818, 11 November 1819, Corlis-Respess Family Papers, FHS.

11. Will (a negro) v. Thompson, 15 May 1805, from Lexis-Nexis, http://www.lexis nexis.com.proxy.library.nd.edu/us/lnacademic/sear ch (accessed 2006).

12. Jerrett v. Higbee, October 1827, and Ely v. Thompson, December 1820, in Helen Catterall, *Judicial Cases Concerning American Slavery and the Negro*, vol. 1 (Washington, DC: Carnegie Institution of Washington, 1926), 308, 295–296. For a case in which the judge stated that color presumed status, see Davis (a man of color) v. Curry, 1810, in Catterall, *Judicial Cases*, 286. On the slave code of 1798 and Kentucky law, see Juliet E. K. Walker, "The Legal Status of Free Blacks in Early Kentucky, 1792–1825," *Filson Club History Quarterly* 57, no. 4 (1983): 382–395; Marion B. Lucas, *A History of Blacks in Kentucky: From Slavery to Segregation, 1760–1861* (Frankfort: Kentucky Historical Society, 1992), 61.

13. Beall v. Joseph (a negro), March 1806, from Lexis-Nexis (accessed 2006); Rankin v. Lydia, October 1820, in Catterall, *Judicial Cases*, 294.

14. Cayton, *Frontier Republic*, 58. Slaves commonly accompanied white men on their trips of exploration; some famous examples include Daniel Boone, Lewis and Clarke. John Tipton surveyed boundaries in Indiana and brought a slave with him; see Tipton, *The John Tipton Papers*, 3 vols. (Indianapolis: Indiana Historical Bureau, 1942), 1: 266.

15. *Register of Black, Mulatto and Poor Persons in Four Ohio Counties, 1791–1861* (Bowie, MD: Joan Turpin Heritage Books, 1985), typescript, 17, OHS.

16. John Cleves Symmes to Charles Short, 9 April 1810, Short-Henry Papers, IHS.

17. Charles Wilkins Short to John Cleves Short, 17 August 1817, Charles Wilkins Short Papers, FHS. A series of letters in 1819 revealed Charles's dire situation in Kentucky; see Charles Wilkins Short to John Cleves Short, 12 April 1819, 13 June 1819, 26 September 1819, 19 December 1819, Charles Wilkins Short Papers, FHS.

18. Ellen Eslinger, "The Evolution of Racial Politics in Early Ohio," in Andrew R. L. Cayton and Stuart D. Hobbs, eds., *Center of a Great Empire: The Ohio Country in the Early American Republic* (Athens: Ohio University Press, 2005), 81–104, in particular 101.

19. Sarah Worthington King Peter, *The Private Memoir of Thomas Worthington* (Cincinnati, 1882), 29–31; Mangin, "Freemen in Theory," 33, 114–118; Andrew R. L. Cayton, *Ohio: The History of a People* (Columbus: Ohio State University Press, 2002), 35.

20. Middleton, *Black Laws*, 37.

21. *Register of Black, Mulatto and Poor Persons in Four Ohio Counties, 1791–1861*, 17, OHS.

22. John Craig Hammond, *Slavery, Freedom, and Expansion in the Early American West* (Charlottesville: University of Virginia Press, 2007), 78; Cayton, *Frontier Republic*, 54.

23. Adam Rothman, *Slave Country: American Expansion and the Origins of the Deep South* (Cambridge, MA: Harvard University Press, 2005); Peter S. Onuf, *Statehood and Union: A History of the Northwest Ordinance* (Indianapolis: Indiana University Press, 1987); David Brion Davis, "The Significance of Excluding Slavery from the Old Northwest in 1787," *Indiana Magazine of History* 84, no. 1 (1988): 75–89.

24. Emil Pocock, "Slavery and Freedom in the Early Republic: Robert Patterson's Slaves in Kentucky and Ohio 1804–1819," *Ohio Valley History* 6, no. 1 (Spring 2006): 3–25; Jeffrey Brooke Allen, "The Debate over Slavery and Race in Ante-Bellum Kentucky: 1792–1850" (Ph.D. diss., Northwestern University, 1973), 66.

25. Henry B. Fearon, *Sketches of America* (London: Printed for Longman, Hurst, Rees, Orme and Brown, 1818), 224; Eslinger, "Evolution of Racial Politics," 90.

26. John Craig Hammond makes the following distinction between freedom/slavery and antislavery: "Ohioans articulated not so much an incipient antislavery ideology, but rather a political culture that celebrated freedom from slavery as one of their society's foundational strengths"; see Hammond, *Slavery, Freedom, and Expansion*, 142.

27. Hon. William Henry Smith, "The First Fugitive Slave Case of Record in Ohio," from the Annual Report of the American Historical Association for 1893 (Washington, DC: Government Printing Office, 1894), 93–100, IHS.

28. Middleton, *Black Laws*, 42–73.

29. "Overseers of the Poor 1811–1847," Bates Papers, box 2, folder 12, CHS.

30. Historians of Ohio, and the Midwest at large, have a vexed relationship with the role of race in the development of the region. Their vexation stems from Ohioans' seemingly incongruous efforts to prove their antislavery principles while systematically attempting to remove African Americans from the landscape. Some historians claim that whites tried to keep slavery out of the state because they also wanted to keep blacks out of the state. These historians argue that upland southern migrants brought their racism with them when they crossed the river and that they somehow passed it down to their children; see, for example, Eugene H. Berwanger, *The Frontier against Slavery: Western Anti-Negro Prejudice and the Slavery Extension Controversy* (Urbana: University of Illinois Press, 1967), 7–29. Other historians argue that newly arrived migrants rejected slavery out of principle but held onto their belief that African Americans were inferior. Thus they crossed the river to escape from slavery, but their racial attitudes followed them. In this, more nuanced, explanation, Ohioans' views on slavery and on race are distinct. However, this explanation still relies on origins when invoking Ohioans' virulent racism; see Middleton, *Black Laws*, 42–73.

Barbara Fields persuasively argues that race, and its practice (racism), is an ideology derived from, and verified by, daily interactions. According to Fields, ideology is the "descriptive vocabulary of day-to-day existence, through which people make rough sense of the social reality that they live and create from day to day." It is not "a material entity, or a thing of any sort, that you can hand down like an old garment, pass on like a germ, spread like a rumour, or impose like a code of dress or etiquette." The only way that ideology continues is through the "ritual repetition of the appropriate social behavior." Thus, in its earliest form, midwestern racism was not simply the by-product of upland southern migration. Instead it was a language used to make sense of cross-border migration from a slave state to a free state. In addition, as Fields suggests, racial ideology assumed its greatest importance in free states because slavery and African Americans were minor exceptions to the radically defined liberty of nominally free states. See Barbara Fields, "Slavery, Race, and Ideology in the United States of America," *New Left Review* 181 (May-June 1990): 95–118.

31. *The Blacks of Pickaway County, Ohio in the Nineteenth Century,* compiled by James Buchanan (Bowie, MD: Heritage Books, 1988), OHS. An especially good analysis of the connection between race, dependence, and slavery is Francois Furstenberg, "Beyond Freedom and Slavery: Autonomy, Virtue, and Resistance in Early American Political Discourse," *Journal of American History* 89 (March 2003): 1295–1330.

32. *Register of Black, Mulatto and Poor Persons in Four Ohio Counties, 1791–1861,* 19, OHS. An in-depth discussion of this can be found in Middleton, *Black Laws,* 42–73.

33. *Register of Black, Mulatto and Poor Persons in Four Ohio Counties, 1791–1861,* in particular Highland County, 4–9; Friend, *Along the Maysville Road,* 128.

34. Fordham, *Personal Narrative,* 193.

35. John Melish, *Travels through the United States of America, in the Years 1806 & 1807, and 1809, 1810 & 1811, Including an Account of Passages betwixt America & Britain, and Travels through Various Parts of Britain, Ireland and Canada: With Corrections and Improvements Till 1815* (New York: Johnson Reprint Corp., 1970), 477.

36. Fordham, *Personal Narrative,* 168; Andrew R. L. Cayton, *Frontier Indiana* (Bloomington: Indiana University Press, 1996), 179. The Indiana Territory included all of present-day Indiana and Illinois, which in 1800 was mostly Indian territory. It was only sparsely settled by Euro-Americans, the majority of whom settled in what would become the state of Illinois. There were three primary areas of settlement within the future state of Indiana: Vincennes; Clark's grant along the Ohio River across the river from Louisville; and the Gore in eastern Indiana stretching up from the Ohio River. Most of the 929 persons in Clark's grant were Clark's soldiers, and most of the settlers in the Gore were squatters who had left Kentucky. The more than 1,500 persons in and around Vincennes made it the most populous area. The settlements were scattered across hundreds of miles of uninhabited forests and Indian territory and were therefore only loosely connected by trade routes and the Ohio River. See John D. Barnhart and Donald F. Carmony, *Indiana, from Frontier to Industrial Commonwealth* (New York: Lewis Historical Publishing Company, 1954), 97–100.

37. Melish, *Travels through the United States*, 382; William Wesley Woolen, Daniel Wait Howe, and Jacob P. Dunn, eds., *Executive Journal of Indiana Territory, 1800–1816* (Indianapolis: Family History Section, Indiana Historical Society, 1985).

38. Jacob Piatt Dunn, *Slavery Petitions and Papers* (Indianapolis: Bowen-Merrill, 1894). When Harrison arrived in Vincennes, Henry Vanderburgh told him that slaveholding was one of the "customs of the country" and urged him not to interfere with settlers' lives; see George W. Geib, "Jefferson, Harrison, and the West: An Essay on Territorial Slavery," in Darrel E. Bigham, ed., *Indiana Territory, 1800–2000: A Bicentennial Perspective* (Indianapolis: Indiana Historical Society, 2001), 99–125.

39. Fordham, *Personal Narrative*, 221, 125; Cayton, *Frontier Indiana*, 190.

40. Complaint filed by Elihu Stout against Peter Jones, April 1811 (emphasis mine), William H. English Collection, Special Collections Research Center, University of Chicago, in "The First American West: Ohio Valley 1750–1820"; Carl J. Ekberg, *French Roots in the Illinois Country: The Mississippi Frontier in Colonial Times* (Urbana: University of Illinois Press, 1998), 161–170.

41. Cayton, *Frontier Indiana*, 193; Emma Lou Thornbrough, *The Negro in Indiana: A Study of a Minority* (Indianapolis: Indiana Historical Bureau, 1957), 15; will of John Johnson, 1817, William H. English Collection, IHS; Silvia Parker v. Alexander B. Craig, July 1815, Clark County Circuit Court Civil Order Book, 1801–1817, microfilm, Family History Library, Salt Lake City, UT.

42. *Indiana Negro Registers, 1852–1865*, comp. Coy D. Robbins (Bowie, MD: Heritage Books, 1994), 58–60.

43. Thornbrough, *Negro in Indiana*, 12–13.

44. The document that stated the slaves escaped was the petition presented in the suit United States v. Benjamin Beekes, 9 September 1809, and the document indicating they were brought is a plea from the suit Peggy v. Simon Vannorsdall, September 1808; both documents are found in "The First American West: Ohio Valley 1750–1820." See also *1820 Federal Census for Indiana*, comp. Willard Heiss (Indianapolis: Genealogy Section of the Indiana Historical Society, 1966), 232.

45. Secondary sources do not clarify the issue; see Jacob Piatt Dunn, *Indiana: A Redemption from Slavery*, new and enlarged ed. (Boston: Houghton, Mifflin, 1916), 237–238, 314–315.

46. Woolen et al., *Executive Journal of Indiana Territory*, 123; Dunn, *Indiana*, 237.

47. Dunn, *Indiana*, 314–315.

48. Ibid., 238; petition presented in the suit United States v. Benjamin Beekes, in "The First American West: Ohio Valley 1750–1820."

49. Writ of habeas corpus for Hanah and Benjamin Beekes, 10 August 1808, in "The First American West: Ohio Valley 1750–1820."

50. Plea from the suit United States v. Simon Vannorsdall, April 1805; complaint and jury finding from the suit Peggy v. Simon Vannorsdall, September 1808, in "The First American West: Ohio Valley 1750–1820."

51. Petition presented in the suit United States v. Benjamin Beekes; *1820 Federal Census for Indiana*, 26.

52. Deposition of William Prince et al., December 1805, William H. English Collection, IHS.

53. Fordham, *Personal Narrative*, 125; Paul Finkelman, "Evading the Ordinance: The Persistence of Bondage in Indiana and Illinois," in Finkelman, *Slavery and the Founders: Race and Liberty in the Age of Jefferson* (New York: M. E. Sharpe, 2001), 58–80; Onuf, *Statehood and Union*.

54. Dunn, *Slavery Petitions and Papers*, 507, 517. Historians have emphasized how the slavery ban at the very least slowed the migration of slaveholders to the old Northwest. See Davis, "Significance of Excluding Slavery," 75–89; William W. Freehling, *The Road to Disunion* (New York: Oxford University Press, 1990), 138–141.

55. Dunn, *Slavery Petitions and Papers*, 517, 478.

56. William Henry Harrison to Thomas Worthington, 26 October 1803, in John D. Barnhart, ed., "Documents: Letters of William H. Harrison to Thomas Worthington, 1799–1813," *Indiana Magazine of History* 47, no. 1 (1951): 66–67.

57. Barnhart and Carmony, *Indiana*, 105. The Friends in North Carolina, hindered by state law in emancipating their slaves, saw nothing in Indiana law prohibiting the introduction of free African Americans. Friends acted as trustees for masters who wished to free their slaves, and they found means of transporting the slaves to free states. By 1814, 350 African Americans had been transferred, and by 1826 the Committee on the Subject of the People of Color had transferred 600. See Thornbrough, *Negro in Indiana*, 33.

58. Dunn, *Slavery Petitions and Papers*, 518–520. Deliberate indecisiveness probably best describes the strategy of Congress in response to the petitions from the Indiana Territory. Slavery was an extremely sensitive issue, even in the 1790s, and rather than confront the issue, Congress repeatedly avoided it. Congress prized national unity over everything and therefore followed a strict policy of silence and procrastination. The federal government's silence on the issue of slavery in the territories was not an indication that the issue lacked salience; the silence was deliberate. Congressional committees repeatedly denied the requests of petitioners. Even when a congressional committee agreed to suspend the Northwest Ordinance, the issue eventually died on the house floor. Federal noninterference created an ambiguous situation, but an ambiguous situation with limits. The absence of federal intervention left residents of the Ohio River Valley to determine their own fate. But federal silence also acted as a check on the power of local residents because they could not unconditionally adopt slavery. See William W. Freehling, *The Reintegration of American History: Slavery and the Civil War* (New York: Oxford University Press, 1994); Finkelman, *Slavery and the Founders*, 52.

59. Dunn, *Slavery Petitions and Papers*, 526. Citizen of Vincennes, "Citizens of Indiana," 1809, *Early American Imprints, Series 1: Evans, 1679–1800*, http://infoweb .newsbank.com.proxy.library.nd.edu (accessed 2007), reads, "I hope he does not wish

to colonize the territory with free negroes; and if they are to be slaves, why not call things by their proper names."

60. John Badollet to Albert Gallatin, 1 January 1806 and 16 December 1804, in Gayle Thornbrough, ed., *The Correspondence of John Badollet and Albert Gallatin, 1804–1836*, Indiana Historical Society Publications 5, no. 22 (Indianapolis: Indiana Historical Society, 1963), 62, 40. Nicole Etcheson, *The Emerging Midwest: Upland Southerners and the Political Culture of the Old Northwest, 1787–1861* (Bloomington: Indiana University Press, 1996), 15–26, argues that the battle for statehood was ideological, but the level of politicking in early Indiana suggests that while some were ideologically motivated, others were skilled politicians.

61. William Henry Harrison to Albert Gallatin, 29 August 1809, and John Badollet to Albert Gallatin, 13 November 1809, in Thornbrough, *Correspondence of Badollet and Gallatin*, 107–113, 116, 117, 126.

62. Thornbrough, *Correspondence of Badollet and Gallatin*, 345, 124, 339.

63. Cayton, *Frontier Indiana*, 244–248.

64. Daniel Walker Howe, *What Hath God Wrought: The Transformation of America, 1815–1848* (New York: Oxford University Press, 2007), 31–32; Fordham, *Personal Narrative*, 210; Cayton, *Frontier Indiana*, 250.

65. *1820 Federal Census for Indiana*, 129, 216. Ewing befriended John Badollet in the land office and apparently joined in the fight to end slavery in the state; see Thornbrough, *Correspondence of Badollet and Gallatin*, 102. Johnston authored the summary of petitions against the suspension of article six; see Dunn, *Slavery Petitions and Papers*, 523–526. On his defense of his reversal, see Dunn, *Indiana*, 370.

66. Thomas Posey to John Gibson, 13 March 1813, William H. English Collection, IHS; Gayle Thornbrough and Dorothy Lois Riker, *Readings in Indiana History* (Indianapolis: Indiana Historical Bureau, 1956), 147; Cayton, *Frontier Indiana*, 252–260.

67. David Thomas, *Travels through the Western Country in the Summer of 1816*, and Eneas Mackenzie, *An Historical, Topographical and Descriptive View of the United States of America, and of Upper and Lower Canada* [1820], in Harlow Lindley, ed., *Indiana as Seen by Early Travelers: A Collection of Reprint from Books of Travel, Letters and Diaries prior to 1830* (Indianapolis: Indiana Historical Commission, 1916), 85, 245.

68. Alexander Mitchell, *An Address to the Inhabitants of the Indiana Territory on the Subject of Slavery, by a Citizen of Ohio* (printed at the *Philanthropist* office, 1816), 22, 10, IHS. Mitchell's pamphlet contains the ideas that Eric Foner, *Free Soil, Free Labor, Free Men: The Ideology of the Republican Party before the Civil War* (New York: Oxford University Press, 1995) detailed in his description of the free-soil movement of the later 1840s and 1850s. However, it would not be fair to use this piece as evidence of the free-labor ideology, because Mitchell argues against both slavery and prejudice based on color. So while he sees slavery as an impediment to progress, he does not explicitly argue that free territory should be reserved for white families, a key element of the free-soil movement of later decades.

69. Silvia Parker v. Alexander B. Craig, July 1815, and Jack Green v. John Gibson, April 1815, "Clark County Circuit Court Civil Order Book, 1801–1817" microfilm, Family History Library, Salt Lake City, Utah; Thornbrough, *Negro in Indiana*, 25–26.

70. Thornbrough, *Negro in Indiana*, 28–30.

71. While Gordon S. Wood famously stated, "The founding fathers were unsettled and fearful not because the American Revolution had failed but because it had succeeded," he ultimately asserted that the principles of liberty and freedom espoused in the American Revolution led to the demise of slavery in the early nineteenth century; see Wood, *The Radicalism of the American Revolution* (New York: Knopf, 1991), 186–187. See also Bernard Bailyn, *The Ideological Origins of the American Revolution* (Cambridge, MA: Belknap Press of Harvard University Press, 1967), 230–246; Gary B. Nash, *Race and Revolution*, Merrill Jensen Lectures in Constitutional Studies (Madison, WI: Madison House, 1990). However, other works have suggested that African Americans developed their own understanding of freedom and liberty that they combined with the patriot ideas from the Revolution. African Americans worked for their emancipation against the currents of white social and political thought; on the limitations of revolutionary thought, see David Brion Davis, *The Problem of Slavery in the Age of Revolution, 1770–1823* (New York: Oxford University Press, 1999), 262–265, 314–342. On the efforts of African Americans, see Douglas Egerton, *Gabriel's Rebellion: The Virginia Slave Conspiracies of 1800 and 1802* (Chapel Hill: University of North Carolina Press, 1993); James Sidbury, *Ploughshares into Swords: Race, Rebellion and Identity in Gabriel's Virginia, 1730–1810* (New York: Cambridge University Press, 1997); Shane White, *Somewhat More Independent: The End of Slavery in New York City, 1770–1823* (Athens: University of Georgia Press, 1991); Joanne Pope Melish, *Disowning Slavery: Gradual Emancipation and "Race" in New England, 1780–1860* (Ithaca, NY: Cornell University Press, 1998); Ira Berlin, *Generations of Captivity: A History of African American Slaves* (Cambridge, MA: Harvard University Press, 2003), 99–111. In addition recent historiography has demonstrated that the spread of slavery to the then Southwest and the end of slavery in the then Northwest were the results of individual actions that often had nothing to do with the Revolution. See Rothman, *Slave Country*; Eva Sheppard Wolf, *Race and Liberty in the New Nation: Emancipation in Virginia from the Revolution to Nat Turner's Rebellion* (Baton Rouge: Louisiana State University Press, 2006); Hammond, *Slavery, Freedom, and Expansion*.

72. This interpretation of the multiple meanings of revolution and the influence of the Haitian revolution on Americans' understanding of their own revolution is heavily influenced by Lester D. Langley, *The Americas in the Age of Revolution 1750–1850* (New Haven, CT: Yale University Press, 1996), 1–10, 122–124, 285–287.

73. In many ways historians' efforts to define and characterize borderlands downplay the diversity of experience along the border in order to fit everything into an explanatory schema. While Stephen Aron leaves his definition of frontiers appropriately vague, his description of Missouri's transition from borderland to border state is perhaps a little too linear. Changes outpaced residents' understanding of those

changes, and often those changes became linear only after residents assigned meaning to the past. Thus, while identifying an important continuity in Missouri's history as a border area, Aron's application of his theoretical framework simplifies the chaos, unpredictability, and elusiveness of borders. See Stephen Aron, *American Confluence: The Missouri Frontier from Borderland to Border State* (Bloomington: Indiana University Press, 2006). I prefer instead to leave the definition of this borderland necessarily vague and open-ended, arguing that the region was a borderland precisely because there was a border. Residents assigned a variety of often contradictory meanings to the border, but the presence of the border remained constant. Even more important, the river was there before the creation of the border and would be there long after the border was destroyed.

Chapter 4

1. Elisha Winfield Green, *Life of the Rev. Elisha W. Green, One of the Founders of the Kentucky Normal and Theological Institute—Now the State University at Louisville . . . and Over Thirty Years Pastor of the Colored Baptist Churches of Maysville and Paris, Written by Himself* (Maysville, KY: Republican Printing Office, 1888), 14–15.

2. Seth Rockman, "The Unfree Origins of American Capitalism," in Cathy Matson, ed., *The Economy of Early America: Historical Perspectives and New Directions* (University Park: Pennsylvania State University Press, 2006), 335–362.

3. *1820 Federal Census for Indiana,* compiled by Willard Heiss (Indianapolis: Genealogy Section of the Indiana Historical Society, 1966), 232, 129; U.S. Census Bureau, "1830 Knox County, Indiana, Census," transcribed by Carol Johnson Hulen, contributed by Sue Montgomery, 1998, files.usgwarchives.net/in/knox/census/1830/1830cens.txt (accessed October 2012).

4. Gayle Thornbrough, ed., *The Diary of Calvin Fletcher,* vol. 1: *1817–1838* (Indianapolis: Indiana Historical Society, 1972), 103. Although critiquing it, Christine Stansell, *City of Women: Sex and Class in New York, 1789–1860* (Chicago: University of Illinois Press, 1982), 1–38, provides a great discussion of the importance of the household in early America.

5. *1820 Federal Census for Indiana,* 67, 162; U.S. Census Bureau, "1830 Knox County, Indiana, Census." This does not suggest that African Americans accepted the notion that residence within a white house gave them respectability. Instead they seemed to use residence within white households for protection. On the power of reputation in the early republic, see Andrew M. Shocket, "Thinking about Elites in the Early Republic," *Journal of the Early Republic* 25 (Winter 2005): 547–556; Christopher Clark, "Comment on the Symposium on Class in the Early Republic," *Journal of the Early Republic* 25 (Winter 2005): 557–564.

6. Out of a total of 270 households with African American members, 63 were figures of authority or members of the military, which is roughly 23 percent; see *1820 Federal Census for Indiana.* As an example of a local judge taking charge of a former indentured servant, Davis Floyd took charge of Silvia until she turned eighteen; see

Silvia Parker v. Alexander B. Craig, July 1815, Clark County Circuit Court Civil Order Book 1801–1817. In the case of Susan and Robert Stephens discussed above, Susan was living with Daniel Lane, a judge in the Indiana Circuit Court.

7. *Register of Black, Mulatto and Poor Persons in Four Ohio Counties, 1791–1861* (Bowie, MD: Joan Turpin Heritage Books, 1985), typescript, OHS, 4–9.

8. Exactly how deeply Americans questioned the emerging capitalist order continues to be a topic of debate among historians. Charles Sellers initiated both a historiographical trend and a critique with his interpretation of Americans' response to the Panic of 1819 and capitalism in general. Arguably, Sellers's interpretation of American democracy as a reaction to capitalism continues to hamstring the historiography, See Charles Sellers, *Market Revolution: Jacksonian America 1815–1846* (New York: Oxford University Press, 1991), 103–136; Melvin Stokes and Stephen Conway, eds., *The Market Revolution in America: Social, Political, and Religious Expressions, 1800–1880* (Charlottesville: University of Virginia Press, 1996); Daniel Feller, *The Jacksonian Promise: America, 1815–1840* (Baltimore: Johns Hopkins University Press, 1995); Sean Wilentz, *The Rise of American Democracy: Jefferson to Lincoln* (New York: W. W. Norton, 2005); Daniel Walker Howe, *What Hath God Wrought: The Transformation of America, 1815–1848* (New York: Oxford University Press, 2007); John Lauritz Larson, *The Market Revolution in America: Liberty, Ambition, and the Eclipse of the Common Good* (New York: Cambridge University Press, 2010). On the impact of the panic on Illinois, see Adam Rowe, "The Republican Rhetoric of a Frontier Controversy: Newspapers in the Illinois Slavery Debate," *Journal of the Early Republic* 31, no. 4 (Winter 2011): 671–699.

9. In the 1950s the journalist John Howard Griffin traveled to the South disguised as a black man to highlight the psychological barrier posed by race. Griffin stated that as a black man he was always aware of racial boundaries even when they were not explicitly stated. The looks he received from whites constantly reinforced the racial boundary between them. See John Howard Griffin, *Black Like Me* (Boston: Houghton Mifflin, 1961).

10. Derived from the historical census browser available on the University of Virginia Library Web site, http://fisher.lib.virginia.edu/collections/stats/histcensus/index .html (accessed October 2012). All census information hereafter also came from the historical census browser unless otherwise noted.

11. J. Blaine Hudson, *Fugitive Slaves and the Underground Railroad in the Kentucky Borderland* (Jefferson, NC: McFarland & Co., 2002), 14.

12. Nikki M. Taylor, *Frontiers of Freedom: Cincinnati's Black Community, 1802–1868* (Athens: Ohio University Press, 2005), 28–49.

13. Dorothy C. Rush, "Early Accounts of Travel to the Falls of the Ohio: A Bibliography with Selected Quotations, 1765–1833," *Filson Club History Quarterly* 68, no. 2 (1994): 232–266, quotations on 255, 262; Emma Lou Thornbrough, *The Negro in Indiana: A Study of a Minority* (Indianapolis: Indiana Historical Bureau, 1957), 31–54; Joe William Trotter, *River Jordan: African American Urban Life in the Ohio Valley,*

Ohio River Valley Series (Lexington: University Press of Kentucky, 1998), 3–51; Taylor, *Frontiers of Freedom*, 28–49; J. Blaine Hudson, "Slavery in Early Louisville and Jefferson County, Kentucky, 1780–1812," *Filson Club History Quarterly* 73, no. 3 (July 1999): 249–283; Andrew R. L. Cayton, "Artery and Border: The Ambiguous Development of the Ohio Valley in the Early Republic," *Ohio Valley History* 1, no. 1 (2001): 19–26; Kim M. Gruenwald, "Space and Place on the Early American Frontier: The Ohio Valley as Region, 1790–1850," *Ohio Valley History* 4, no. 3 (2004): 31–48; George H. Yater, *Two Hundred Years at the Falls of the Ohio: A History of Louisville and Jefferson County* (Louisville: Heritage Corp., 1979), 32–42; Paton Yoder, *Taverns and Travelers: Inns of the Early Midwest* (Bloomington: Indiana University Press, 1969).

14. The historian most responsible for turning our attention to the variations of American slavery is Ira Berlin; see Berlin, *Generations of Captivity: A History of African American Slaves* (Cambridge, MA: Harvard University Press, 2003); Berlin, *Many Thousands Gone: The First Two Centuries of Slavery in North America* (Cambridge, MA: Harvard University Press, 1998). Recent books have put Upper South slavery in the context of difference; see, for example, Diane Mutti Burke, *On Slavery's Borders: Missouri's Small-Slaveholding Households, 1815–1865* (Athens: University of Georgia Press, 2010).

15. Davis (a man of color) v. Curry, in Helen Catterall, *Judicial Cases Concerning American Slavery and the Negro*, vol. 1 (Washington, DC: Carnegie Institution of Washington, 1926), 238; Henry Scribner to the [Floyd County] Overseers of the Poor, 25 December 1827, John K. Graham Papers, IHS; Dorothy Riker and Gayle Thornbrough, eds., *Messages and Papers Relating to the Administration of James Brown Ray, Governor of Indiana 1825–1831* (Indianapolis: Indiana Historical Bureau, 1954), 470. On Kentucky's legal system generally, see Juliet E. K. Walker, "The Legal Status of Free Blacks in Early Kentucky, 1792–1825," *Filson Club History Quarterly* 57 (October 1983): 382–395.

16. *Proceedings of the Ohio Anti-Slavery Convention Held at Putnam on the 22, 23, and 24th of April, 1835* (Indianapolis: Beaumont and Wallace, printers, 1835), IHS; Darrel Bigham, *On Jordan's Banks: Emancipation and Its Aftermath in the Ohio River Valley*, Ohio River Valley Series (Lexington: University Press of Kentucky, 2006), 16–18; Darrel Bigham, *Towns and Villages of the Lower Ohio* (Lexington: University Press of Kentucky, 1998), 63; Marion Lucas, *A History of Blacks in Kentucky: From Slavery to Segregation, 1760–1861* (Frankfort: Kentucky Historical Society, 1992), 101–117; Trotter, *River Jordan*, 3–51; John Hope Franklin and Loren Schweninger, *Runaway Slaves: Rebels on the Plantation* (New York: Oxford University Press, 1999), 124–148; J. Blaine Hudson, "Crossing the 'Dark Line': Fugitive Slaves and the Underground Railroad in Louisville and North-Central Kentucky," *Filson Club History Quarterly* 75 (Winter 2001): 33–83.

17. Taylor, *Frontiers of Freedom*, 37–39, 54–55; Bigham, *On Jordan's Banks*, 34–36; Leonard Curry, *The Free Black in Urban America 1800–1850: The Shadow of the Dream* (Chicago: University of Chicago Press, 1981), 249–251.

18. Lyle Koehler, *Cincinnati's Black Peoples, A Chronology and Bibliography, 1787–1982*, prepared originally for the Cincinnati Arts Consortium through the Center for Neighborhood and Community Studies, University of Cincinnati, June 1986, 7, CHS; *Louisville Public Advertiser*, 5 February 1820, 30 November 1835.

19. Louisville Trustee Book, 15 September 1826 and 10 June 1825, FHS; *Louisville Public Advertiser*, 28 September 1825; John Blassingame, ed., *Slave Testimony: Two Centuries of Letters, Speeches, Interviews, and Autobiographies* (Baton Rouge: Louisiana State University Press, 1977), 432–433. In Nicholasville, Kentucky, the town trustees instituted a curfew and gave any white man the authority to arrest and whip any African American, free or slave, without a pass; see Nicholasville Minute Book of the Town Trustees, September 1824, 30 March 1826, 21 November 1828, FHS.

20. Eric Foner, "The Idea of Free Labor in the Nineteenth Century," new introductory essay in Foner, *Free Soil, Free Labor, Free Men: The Ideology of the Republican Party before the Civil War* (New York: Oxford University Press, 1995), ix–xlii; Walter Johnson, "The Pedestal and the Veil: Rethinking the Capitalism/Slavery Question," *Journal of the Early Republic* 24 (Summer 2004): 299–308; Gordon Wood, *The Radicalism of the American Revolution* (New York: Random House, 1991), 278–280.

21. Amy Dru Stanley, *Wage Labor, Marriage, and the Market in the Age of Slave Emancipation* (New York: Cambridge University Press, 1998), 1–59; Walter Johnson, *Soul by Soul: Life inside the Antebellum Slave Market* (Cambridge, MA: Harvard University Press, 1999), 117–134.

22. Jonathan D. Martin, *Divided Mastery: Slave Hiring in the American South* (Cambridge, MA: Harvard University Press, 2004), 39; Clement Eaton, "Slave-Hiring in the Upper South: A Step toward Freedom," *Mississippi Valley Historical Review* 46 (March 1960): 663–678; T. Stephen Whitman, *The Price of Freedom: Slavery and Manumission in Baltimore and Early National Maryland* (Lexington: University Press of Kentucky, 1997).

23. *Cincinnati Directory for the Year 1842*, comp. Charles Cist (Cincinnati: E. Morgan and Co., 1842); Lucas, *History of Blacks in Kentucky*, 101–117; Trotter, *River Jordan*, 3–51; Bigham, *On Jordan's Banks*, 5–55; Keith C. Barton, "Good Cooks and Washers: Slave-Hiring, Domestic Labor, and the Market in Bourbon County, Kentucky," *Journal of American History* 84 (September 1997): 436–460.

24. *Louisville Public Advertiser*, 1 June 1825; *Vincennes (IN) Western Sun*, 11 December 1824, 18 July 1820, 27 September 1827; Henry Bibb, *Narrative of the Life and Adventures of Henry Bibb, an American Slave, Written by Himself* (New York: The author, 1849), 86–87, http://docsouth.unc.edu/neh/bibb/bibb.html (accessed October 2012); Josiah Henson, *The Life of Josiah Henson, Formerly a Slave, Now an Inhabitant of Canada, as Narrated by Himself* (Boston: Arthur D. Phelps, 1849), 22–25, http://docsouth.unc.edu/neh/henson49/henson49.html (accessed October 2012).

25. Pamela Peters, *The Underground Railroad in Floyd County, Indiana* (Jefferson, NC: McFarland & Co., 2001), 61; Blassingame, *Slave Testimony*, 385–386.

26. John Malvin, *North into Freedom: The Autobiography of John Malvin, Free Negro, 1795–1880* (1879; Cleveland: Press of the Western Reserve University, 1966),

39; Brother James Harrison to Robert Smith, 7 November 1843, Robert Smith Papers, OHS; *Columbus Palladium of Liberty*, 22 February 1844.

27. *Louisville Public Advertiser*, 31 January 1821, 27 November 1824; *Vincennes (IN) Western Sun*, 11 December 1824, 18 July 1820, 27 September 1827.

28. Blassingame, *Slave Testimony*, 48; Joanne Pope Melish, "The 'Condition' Debate and Racial Discourse in the Antebellum North," and James Brewer Stewart, "Modernizing 'Difference': The Political Meaning of Color in the Free States, 1776–1840," in Michael A. Morrison and James Brewer Stewart, eds., *Race and the Early Republic: Racial Consciousness and Nation Building in the Early Republic* (Lanham, MD: Rowman and Littlefield, 2002), 75–94, 113–134; Leon F. Litwack, *North of Slavery: The Negro in the Free States, 1790–1860* (Chicago: University of Chicago Press, 1961), 30–186; Ira Berlin, *Slaves without Masters: The Free Negro in the Antebellum South* (New York: Pantheon Books, 1975), 182–249; Berlin, *Generations of Captivity*, 230–244; Joanne Pope Melish, *Disowning Slavery: Gradual Emancipation and "Race" in New England, 1780–1860* (Ithaca, NY: Cornell University Press, 1998), 261–274; Thornbrough, *Negro in Indiana*, 92–150.

29. *Vincennes (IN) Western Sun*, 7 June 1828, 1 May 1830; Thomas C. Buchanan, *Black Life on the Mississippi: Slaves, Free Blacks and the Western Steamboat World* (Chapel Hill: University of North Carolina Press, 2004), 53–80.

30. "The Diaries of Donald McDonald, 1824–1826," in *Indiana Historical Society Publications*, vol. 14 (Indianapolis: Indiana Historical Society, 1942), 241.

31. Travel journal, Benjamin Lundy Papers, OHS; Abraham Lincoln to Mary Speed, 27 September 1841, Speed Family Papers, FHS; Abraham Lincoln to Joshua Speed, 24 August 1855, in Abraham Lincoln, *Selected Speeches and Writings*, with an introduction by Gore Vidal (New York: Vintage Books, 1992), 103.

32. Numbers derived from the historical census browser available on the University of Virginia Library Web site http://mapserver.lib.virginia.edu (accessed October 2012); Feller, *Jacksonian Promise*, 22–25; Sellers, *Market Revolution*, 43–44; Lucas, *History of Blacks in Kentucky*, 96–100; Andrew R. L. Cayton, *Frontier Indiana* (Bloomington: Indiana University Press, 1996), 275; Darrel Bigham, "River of Opportunity: Economic Consequences of the Ohio," in Robert L. Reid, ed., *Always a River: The Ohio River and the American Experience* (Bloomington: Indiana University Press, 1991), 130–179; Adam Rothman, *Slave Country: American Expansion and the Origins of the Deep South* (Cambridge: Harvard University Press, 2005), 165–216; Michael Tadman, *Speculators and Slaves: Masters, Traders, and Slaves in the Old South* (Madison: University of Wisconsin Press, 1989), 301–302. Stephen Deyle, *Carry Me Back: The Domestic Slave Trade in American Life* (New York: Oxford University Press, 2005), makes the claim that most slave sales in the antebellum period were local.

33. *Louisville Public Advertiser*, 19 December 1829; J. G. Barclay and Company specialized in trading black females and began advertising in 1827, for example, *Louisville Public Advertiser*, 10 February 1827; the auctioneer Robert Ormsby requested "ten or fifteen negro boys and girls from eighteen to twenty-four," *Louisville Public Advertiser*, 26 September 1821; examples of advertisements for public slave sales: *Louisville*

Public Advertiser, 5 January 1820, 5 December 1821, 31 January 1821; examples of ads for the purchase of many slaves at once: *Louisville Public Advertiser*, 21 September 1821, 26 September 1821. On the slave trade in Louisville, see Hanford Dozier Stafford, "Slavery in a Border City: Louisville 1790–1860" (Ph.D. diss., University of Kentucky, 1982), 128–129; Lucas, *History of Blacks in Kentucky*, 84–100.

34. On commodification in American slavery, see David Brion Davis, *Inhuman Bondage: The Rise and Fall of Slavery in the New World* (New York: Oxford University Press, 2006), 35; Johnson, *Soul by Soul*; James Oakes, *Slavery and Freedom: An Interpretation of the Old South* (New York: Knopf, 1990); Stephanie Smallwood, "Commodified Freedom: Interrogating the Limits of Anti-Slavery Ideology in the Early Republic," *Journal of the Early Republic* 24 (Summer 2004): 292; Edward E. Baptist, " 'Cuffy, Fancy Maids, and One-Eyed Men': Rape, Commodification, and the Domestic Slave Trade in the United States," *American Historical Review* 106, no. 5 (2001): 1619–1650.

35. William Wells Brown, *Narrative of William W. Brown, an American Slave, Written by Himself* (London: C. Gilpin, 1849), 29–30 (emphasis mine), http://docsouth.unc.edu/brownw/brown.html (Accessed October 2012).

36. Benjamin Drew, *The Refugee: A North-Side View of Slavery*, in Robert W. Winks, ed., *Four Fugitive Slave Narratives* (1856; Reading, MA: Addison-Wesley, 1969), 241.

37. On Kentucky steamboat law, see Edwards v. Vail, April 1830, in Catterall, *Judicial Cases*, 315.

38. Mrs. Miller to her daughter, undated letters, Miller-Thum Family Papers, 1781–1962, FHS; Barton, "Good Cooks and Washers," 436–460.

39. Jerrett v. Higbee, October 1827, in Catterall, *Judicial Cases*, 308; Bosworth v. Brand, October 1833, in Catterall, *Judicial Cases*, 325.

40. Rush, "Early Accounts of Travel," 260; Tyson v. Ewing, January 1830, in Catterall, *Judicial Cases*, 314; Keith P. Griffler, *Front Line of Freedom: African Americans and the Forging of the Underground Railroad in the Ohio Valley* (Lexington: University Press of Kentucky, 2004).

41. Graham v. Strader, October 1844, in Catterall, *Judicial Cases*, 65–68; J. Winston Coleman Jr., *Slavery Times in Kentucky* (Chapel Hill: University of North Carolina Press, 1940), 100; Henson, *Life of Josiah Henson*, 28–29.

42. *Louisville Public Advertiser*, 10 October 1821; Jerrett v. Higbee, in Catterall, *Judicial Cases*, 305.

43. *Vincennes (IN) Western Sun*, 11 March 1820; *Louisville Public Advertiser*, 22 January 1820; *Indiana Gazette*, 7 May 1821; Franklin and Schweninger, *Runaway Slaves*, 211–212.

44. *Louisville Public Advertiser*, 28 August 1824; *Indiana Gazette*, 2 December 1820. Literacy remained a powerful tool that enslaved African Americans could use to gain their freedom. However, their very ability to do so made white Americans suspicious even of written proofs of freedom. The idea that literacy actually undermined the security of freedom sits awkwardly with Frederick Douglass's narrative of his transition from slavery to freedom. According to Douglass, the power of literacy kept him

from becoming a "brute" under slavery and helped him transform from a slave into a "man." Ironically the literacy of men such as Douglass increased the suspicion of whites, which limited the freedoms of African Americans. See Frederick Douglass, *My Bondage and My Freedom* (1855; New York: Arno Press, 1968).

45. William Buckner to Thomas Buckner, 29 April 1824, Buckner Family Papers, FHS; Coleman, *Slavery Times*, 175; Stanley Harrold, *Border War: Fighting over Slavery before the Civil War* (Chapel Hill: University of North Carolina Press, 2010), 17.

46. *Vincennes (IN) Western Sun*, 22 February 1823; Wilberforce Lyle to Mr. Charles Philips, 25 September 1830, ISL; Stephen Middleton, *The Black Laws: Race and the Legal Process in Early Ohio* (Athens, OH: Ohio University Press, 2005), 157–200; *(Madison) Indiana Republican*, 2 January 1819. On Ohio's black laws, see Paul Finkelman, "Ohio's Struggle for Equality before the Civil War," *Timeline* 23 (January–March 2006): 28–43.

47. *Minutes of the Committee of Indiana Yearly Meeting of Friends on the Concerns of the People of Colour*, 4–17, Friends Collection, Earlham College, Richmond, IN.

48. Rankin v. Lydia, in Catterall, *Judicial Cases*, 294.

49. On the importance of appearance in identity, see Kathleen Brown, *Good Wives, Nasty Wenches, and Anxious Patriarchs: Gender, Race and Power in Colonial Virginia* (Chapel Hill: University of North Carolina Press, 1996); Rhys Isaac, *The Transformation of Virginia, 1740–1790* (Chapel Hill: University of North Carolina Press, 1982), 34–42; Laurel Ulrich, *The Age of Homespun: Objects and Stories in the Creation of an American Myth* (New York: Knopf, 2001); David Waldstreicher, "Why Thomas Jefferson and African Americans Wore Their Politics on Their Sleeves," in Jeffrey L. Pasley, Andrew W. Robertson, and David Waldstreicher, eds., *Beyond the Founders: New Approaches to the Political History of the Early American Republic* (Chapel Hill: University of North Carolina Press, 2004), 79–106; Karen Halttunen, *Confidence Men and Painted Women: A Study of Middle-Class Culture in America, 1830–1870* (New Haven, CT: Yale University Press, 1982), 56–91.

50. *Louisville Public Advertiser*, 16 October 1819.

51. Stephanie Camp, *Closer to Freedom: Enslaved Women and Everyday Resistance in the Plantation South* (Chapel Hill: University of North Carolina Press, 2004), 78–87.

52. *Vincennes (IN) Western Sun*, 10 June 1820, 27 September 1827; *Louisville Public Advertiser*, 3 November 1824.

53. William Hendricks, *A Joint Resolution, Respecting the Graduate Emancipation of Slaves, and Colonization of People of Color within the United States*, 7 February 1825, http://www.gilderlehrman.org/collection/index.html (accessed October 2012); Taylor, *Frontiers of Freedom*, 56–57; Harold D. Tallant, *Evil Necessity: Slavery and Political Culture in Antebellum Kentucky* (Lexington: University Press of Kentucky, 2003).

54. Isaac Blackford, *An Address at the First State Meeting of the Indiana Colonization Society: Delivered at Indianapolis, in the Hall of Representatives by the Request of the Board of Managers, on the 14th Day of December 1829* (Indianapolis: Printed at the State Gazette Office, 1829); Lowell H. Harrison, *The Antislavery Movement in Kentucky*

(Lexington: University Press of Kentucky, 1978), 29–30; David Smith, *Brief Exposition of the Views of the Society for the Colonization of Free Persons of Colour in Africa; Published under the Direction of the Board of Managers of the Ohio State Colonization Society: Addressed to the Citizens of Ohio* (Columbus: Printed at the Office of the Ohio Monitor, 1827), 4; Rev. James Blythe, *A Speech Delivered at the Anniversary of the Indiana Colonization Society, on December 23, 1833* (Indianapolis: N. Bolton & Co., 1834), IHS.

55. Smith, *Brief Exposition*, 7. On the relationship between paranoid language and paranoid thought, see the classic article Gordon Wood, "Rhetoric and Reality in the American Revolution," *William and Mary Quarterly*, 3rd ser., 23, no. 1 (January 1966): 3–32.

56. For example, see *Louisville Public Advertiser*, 30 November 1835; Thomas C. Leonard, *News for All: America's Coming-of-Age with the Press* (New York: Oxford University Press, 1995), 6–12; Yoder, *Taverns and Travelers*.

57. Max Grivno, *Gleanings of Freedom: Free and Slave Labor along the Mason-Dixon Line, 1790–1860* (Urbana: University of Illinois Press, 2011), quote on 22. Another work that deals with slavery and freedom in urban Maryland is Seth Rockman, *Scraping By: Wage Labor, Slavery and Survival in Early Baltimore* (Baltimore: Johns Hopkins University Press, 2009).

58. Lewis Garrard Clarke and Milton Clarke, *Narratives of the Sufferings of Lewis and Milton Clarke, Sons of a Soldier of the Revolution, during a Captivity of More than Twenty Years among the Slaveholders of Kentucky, One of the So-Called Christian States of North America* (Boston: Bela Marsh, 1846), 98, http://docsouth.unc.edu/clarkes/clarkes.html (accessed October 2012).

Chapter 5

1. Richard White, *The Middle Ground: Indians, Empires, and Republics in the Great Lakes, 1650–1815* (New York: Cambridge University Press, 1991).

2. Thomas M. Wilson and Hastings Donnan, "Nation, State and Identity at International Borders," in Wilson and Donnan, eds., *Border Identities: Nation and State at International Frontiers* (New York: Cambridge University Press, 1998), 1–30; Gloria Anzaldua, *Borderlands/La Frontera: The New Mestiza* (San Francisco: Aunt Lute Books, 1987). For an excellent critique of Anzaldua, see David E. Johnson and Scott Michaelsen, "Border Secrets: An Introduction," in Scott Michaelsen and David E. Johnson, eds., *Border Theory: The Limits of Cultural Politics* (Minneapolis: University of Minnesota Press, 1997), 1–39.

3. Kim M. Gruenwald, *River of Enterprise: The Commercial Origins of Regional Identity in the Ohio Valley, 1790–1850* (Bloomington: Indiana University Press, 2002). The debate over slavery in Illinois was fierce, and as historians have demonstrated, the decision to ban slavery was by no means a foregone conclusion. My argument here is that because both Ohio and Indiana had banned slavery, it was more difficult to justify making slavery legal in Illinois. Counterfactually, if Ohio and Indiana had legalized

slavery in their state constitutions, article six of the Northwest Ordinance would have carried far less weight, and Illinoisans would have been more likely to follow the course charted by their eastern neighbors. On the Illinois debate, see James Simeone, *Democracy and Slavery in Frontier Illinois: The Bottomland Republic* (De Kalb: Northern Illinois University Press, 2000). William Freehling, *The Road to Disunion*, vol. 1: *Secessionists at Bay, 1776–1854* (New York: Oxford University Press, 1990), 138–141, articulates the basic principles of this argument; according to Freehling, it was far easier to ban slavery officially in an area where slavery had not yet been introduced on a large scale than it was to enact emancipation where slavery already existed (138–141).

4. *Indiana House Journal, 1816–1817*, 11, quoted in Emma Lou Thornbrough, "Indiana and Fugitive Slave Legislation," *Indiana Magazine of History* 50, no. 3 (1954): 203. This law was amended in 1819 to include a punishment of whipping from ten to one hundred lashes for the crime of "manstealing" (203–204).

5. Gabriel Slaughter to Jonathan Jennings, 14 September 1817, and Report of the Committee in the Indiana House of Representatives, in Logan Esarey, ed., *Messages and Papers of Jonathan Jennings, Ratcliff Boon, and William Hendricks, 1816–1825* (Indianapolis: Indiana Historical Commission, 1924), 48–49, 51–52.

6. Paul Finkelman, "Implementing the Proslavery Constitution: The Adoption of the Fugitive Slave Law of 1793," in Finkelman, *Slavery and the Founders: Race and Liberty in the Age of Jefferson* (Armonk, NY: M. E. Sharpe, 1996), 81–104; Emma Lou Thornbrough, "Indiana and Fugitive Slave Legislation," 201–228.

7. Squire Brooks referred to Davis Floyd as the "great emancipator," according to the testimony of General Bartholomew, State of Indiana v. John Williams and Russelton Coupton, Clark County Circuit Court Civil Order Book, 1817–1819, 370, 371, 372, 421, 428, 534. Strangely, a detailed description of this case appeared in the order book for 1821–1823, 107–110, but said that the trial took place in 1819.

8. In 1807 Davis Floyd was secretary of a meeting in Clark County that adopted an antislavery memorial to Congress; see Dunn Jacob Piatt Dunn, *Slavery Petitions and Papers* (Indianapolis: Bowen-Merrill, 1894), 518–520. Benjamin Parke participated in a newspaper debate about slavery with John Badolett in the *Western Sun* in 1809. Parke, writing under the pseudonym "Slim Simon," defended slavery as a profitable and progressive institution (*Vincennes [IN] Western Sun*, 4, 11 February 1809). Parke's authorship is indicated in a letter of Badollet's cited in Gayle Thornbrough, ed., *The Correspondence of John Badollet and Albert Gallatin, 1804–1836*, Indiana Historical Society Publications, 5, no. 22 (Indianapolis: Indiana Historical Society, 1963), 122, 123n.

9. Emma Lou Thornbrough, *The Negro in Indiana: A Study of a Minority* (Indianapolis: Indiana Historical Bureau, 1957), 95–96.

10. Narrative of the Stephens story based on letters and correspondence, in Esarey, ed., *Messages and Papers of Jennings, Boon, and Hendricks*, 48–223 passim.

11. Robert Stephens to John Tipton, 17 May 1818, and Richard Stephens to John Tipton, 26 July 1820, in Dorothy Riker and Nellie Robertson, eds., *The John Tipton*, 3 vols. (Indianapolis: Indiana Historical Bureau, 1942), 1: 146–147, 221–222.

12. John Tipton to Davis Floyd, in Riker and Robertson, eds., *Tipton Papers*, 1: 125–126. In 1813 Perry claimed he had been set free in 1813, but his former master, William Stith, was trying to bring him back into slavery. Judge Waller Taylor of the General Court gave Stith a certificate for the removal of Perry to Kentucky, but Perry escaped and returned to Harrison County.

13. Richard Stephens to John Tipton, 26 July 1820, and Robert Stephens to John Tipton, 7 January 1820, in Riker and Robertson, eds., *Tipton Papers*, 1: 221–222, 173.

14. While Jonathan Jennings never mentioned slavery in his personal correspondence with his family and friends, he wrote to John Quincy Adams on more than one occasion about his efforts to defend his state against a corrupt slave power, and he received praise from Adams for his hard work. This suggests that at the very least Jennings had a commitment to political antislavery. John Quincy Adams mentioned the contents of Jennings's letter in John Quincy Adams to Jonathan Jennings, 17 July 1820, in Worthington Chauncey Ford, ed., *The Writings of John Quincy Adams*, vol. 7 (New York: Macmillan, 1917), 52–54.

15. Perhaps because Mason placed special emphasis on the states of the old Northwest in his analysis, this duality of the Missouri Crisis characterizes the crisis in the Ohio River Valley; see Matthew Mason, *Slavery and Politics in the Early American Republic* (Chapel Hill: University of North Carolina Press, 2006), 177–212. See also Freehling, *Road to Disunion*, 121–161; Robert Pierce Forbes, *The Missouri Compromise and Its Aftermath: Slavery and the Meaning of America* (Chapel Hill: University of North Carolina Press, 2007); Don E. Fehrenbacher, *The Slaveholding Republic: An Account of the United States Government's Relations to Slavery* (New York: Oxford University Press, 2001); William J. Cooper, *Liberty and Slavery: Southern Politics to 1860* (Columbia: University of South Carolina Press, 2000).

16. Annals of Congress, 15th Congress, 1st Sess. (15 December 1817): 446–447, 514; (26 January–1 February 1818): 819, 825–831, 837–840; (10 April 1818): 1716–1717; 2nd Sess. (15 January 1819): 546–547.

17. Ibid., 2nd Sess. (16 February 1819): 1214–1215; (1 March 1819): 274.

18. Esarey, ed., *Messages and Papers of Jennings, Boon, and Hendricks*, 90–94; Annals of Congress, 16th Congress, 1st Sess. (2 March 1820): 1585–1588; (February 17): 427–428.

19. Jonathan Jennings to Gabriel Slaughter, 24 December 1819, and Jennings in special message to the state senate, 15 January 1820, in Esarey, ed., *Messages and Papers of Jennings, Boon, and Hendricks*, 100, 98–99. For all letters in the correspondence, see Esarey, ed., *Messages and Papers of Jennings, Boon, and Hendricks*, 98–108.

20. *Kentucky Reporter* (Lexington), 19 January 1820.

21. *Louisville Public Advertiser*, 9, 19, 23 February 1820; 22, 25 March 1820; 1, 5, 8 April 1820; 6 May 1820.

22. Ibid., 8 April 1820. Gruenwald, *River of Enterprise*, 123–158, persuasively argues that shifting economic interests led to the disintegration of the coherent vision of the "Western Country." However, in its place residents developed a new sense of

the region rooted in a stronger sense of unique state identities. While they celebrated their state's uniqueness, residents along the Ohio River also congratulated themselves on their ability to coexist peaceably with their sister states.

23. *Louisville Public Advertiser,* 22 March 1820, 19 February 1820.

24. Diary of John Brown, 4 March 1822, FHS; Thomas C. Leonard, *News for All: America's Coming-of-Age with the Press* (New York: Oxford University Press, 1995), 6–12; Paton Yoder, *Taverns and Travelers: Inns of the Early Midwest* (Bloomington: Indiana University Press, 1969); Jeffrey L. Pasley, *"The Tyranny of Printers": Newspaper Politics in the Early American Republic* (Charlottesville: University of Virginia Press, 2001); David Waldstreicher, *In the Midst of Perpetual Fetes: The Making of American Nationalism, 1776–1820* (Chapel Hill: University of North Carolina Press, 1997), 1–14, 269–293.

25. *Vincennes (IN) Western Sun,* 24 March 1821; *1820 Federal Census for Indiana,* comp. Willard Heiss (Indianapolis: Genealogy Section of the Indiana Historical Society, 1966), 454; Pamela Peters, *The Underground Railroad in Floyd County, Indiana* (Jefferson, NC: McFarland & Co., 2001), 27; L. A. Williams & Co., *History of the Ohio Falls Cities and Their Counties,* vol. 2 (Cleveland: L. A. Williams & Co., 1882), 87–90. Woodruff's home served as both a tavern and a courthouse until he helped erect the new courthouse in 1823.

26. *Vincennes (IN) Western Sun,* 24 March 1821.

27. *Louisville Public Advertiser,* 28 February 1821. The *Vincennes (IN) Western Sun* listed a New Albany newspaper as the source, the historian Pamela Peters cited a Cincinnati newspaper as her source, and the *Louisville Public Advertiser* printed the story. Stanley Harrold, *Border War: Fighting over Slavery before the Civil War* (Chapel Hill: University of North Carolina Press, 2010), 29, cites the Moses case as an example of the constant conflict between border states. However, Harrold uses only the newspapers as evidence and in so doing does not contextualize Seth Woodruff's actions. I argue that while conflicts such as this erupted fairly regularly, when they are put into context we can better understand the long periods of accommodation that accompanied the moments of conflict.

28. *1820 Federal Census for Indiana,* 263. Reputation provided a measure of coherence to what historians have described as white Americans' complicated and contradictory views on race. Historians point to white Americans' willingness to betray African Americans one minute and protect them the next as a contradiction; see Eugene H. Berwanger, *The Frontier against Slavery: Western Anti-Negro Prejudice and the Slavery Extension Controversy* (Urbana: University of Illinois Press, 1967), 7–59. However, reputation apparently relieved this contradiction. White Americans could be sympathetic to slavery, and perhaps even own a slave, but still protect someone whom they recognized as a free citizen. They could join a posse to round up an escaped slave and fight in a mob protecting a fugitive who had lived in the state for a number of years. They could petition the government to prevent African American immigration to the state but work alongside African Americans who already lived in

the state. They were not antislavery because they were antiblack; their views were complex enough to distinguish between African Americans whom they wished to protect and those they wished to see remain in slavery. See Emil Pocock, "Slavery and Freedom in the Early Republic: Robert Patterson's Slaves in Kentucky and Ohio 1804–1819," *Ohio Valley History* 6, no. 1 (Spring 2006): 3–25.

29. Emma Lou Thornbrough, "Indiana and Fugitive Slave Legislation," 212; *Indiana Gazette* (Corydon), 23 January 1819.

30. Historians look at political sources or court records and make the argument that residents along the Ohio River battled over the border between slavery and freedom; see John Craig Hammond, *Slavery, Freedom and Expansion in the Early American West* (Charlottesville: University of Virginia Press, 2007); Stephen Middleton, *The Black Laws: Race and the Legal Process in Early Ohio* (Athens: Ohio University Press, 2005), 7–73, 157–200. However, Hammond's use of political sources misrepresents the extent of the conflict, since politicians so often said one thing and did another. Middleton used court records to find instances of resistance against slavery and racial restrictions, but African Americans almost universally got the short end of the stick in these conflicts. This pattern suggests that white residents found ways to resolve their conflicts without much regard for the African Americans involved. This formulation is strongly influenced by the following works on political conflict in the early republic: Waldstreicher, *In the Midst*, 349–352; Andrew W. Robertson, " 'Look on This Picture . . . and on This!' Nationalism, Localism, and Partisan Images of Otherness in the United States, 1787–1820," *American Historical Review* 106, no. 4 (2001): 1263–1280.

31. Middleton, *Black Laws*, 41.

32. Cited in Nikki M. Taylor, *Frontiers of Freedom: Cincinnati's Black Community, 1802–1868* (Athens: Ohio University Press, 2005), 63.

33. Ibid., 80–105.

34. Gruenwald, *River of Enterprise*, 103–158; Andrew R. L. Cayton, *Ohio: The History of a People* (Columbus: Ohio State University Press, 2002), 45–56. On the promise and frustration of internal improvements generally, see Daniel Walker Howe, *What Hath God Wrought: The Transformation of America, 1815–1848* (New York: Oxford University Press, 2007), 142–147; John Lauritz Larson, *Internal Improvement: National Public Works and the Promise of Popular Government in the Early United States* (Chapel Hill: University of North Carolina Press, 2001).

35. Ohio Governor, 1832–1836 (Robert Lucas), in *Report No. 1, Annual Meeting of Governor Lucas, with Accompanying Documents, Dec. 6, 1836,* cited in Middleton, *Black Laws*, 164–165.

36. *Louisville Public Advertiser*, 19 March 1823; *Indiana Gazette* (Corydon), 10 September 1823; Berwanger, *Frontier against Slavery*, 12–29.

37. Emma Lou Thornbrough, "Indiana and Fugitive Slave Legislation," 215.

38. Dorothy Riker and Gayle Thornbrough, eds., *Messages and Papers Relating to the Administration of James Brown Ray, Governor of Indiana 1825–1831* (Indianapolis: Indiana Historical Bureau, 1954), 112, 119; Dorothy Riker, ed., *Executive Proceedings*

of the State of Indiana 1816–1836 (Indianapolis: Indiana Historical Bureau, 1947), 322, 326–327. Between 1824 and 1839 the Indiana government requested the extradition of more fugitives from Ohio (fourteen) than from Kentucky (ten) (Riker, *Executive Proceedings*, 294–302).

39. See 25–26 December 1829, in Gayle Thornbrough, ed., *Diary of Calvin Fletcher*, vol. 1: *1817–1838* (Indianapolis: Indiana Historical Society, 1972), 167–168.

40. *Indiana State Gazette* (Indianapolis), 26 February 1830; James Brown Ray to James Noble, 25 February 1830, in Riker and Thornbrough, *Messages and Papers Relating to the Administration of James Brown*, 529–530.

41. Ray's message to the General Assembly, 8 December 1829, and Ray's address to the General Assembly, 2 December 1828, in Riker and Thornbrough, *Messages and Papers Relating to the Administration of James Brown Ray*, 470–471, 374.

42. Emma Lou Thornbrough, *Negro in Indiana*, 39; "We believe the provisions of the act referred to, are unjust and oppressive, we direct that the subject be laid before the yearly meeting. There is a similar law in Ohio," *Minutes of the Committee of Indiana Yearly Meeting of Friends on the Concerns of the People of Colour*, Friends Collection, Earlham College Archives, Richmond, Indiana.

43. *Indiana, Journal* (Indianapolis), July 1831; *Indiana Palladium*, 4 December 1830; newspaper citations found in Dorothy Riker and Gayle Thornbrough, eds., *Messages and Papers Relating to the Administration of Noah Noble, Governor of Indiana, 1831–1837* (Indianapolis: Indiana Historical Bureau, 1958), 18.

44. Although written later, Daniel Drake's evaluation of the African American population in Ohio reveals the connections that white Ohioans drew between the presence of African Americans and slavery: "In former times free negroes were in demand as servants; but that demand has greatly diminished . . . they are and should be kept a distinct and subordinate caste"; see Drake, *Dr. Daniel Drake's Letters on Slavery to John C. Warren, of Boston*, repr. from the *National Intelligencer* (Washington, DC), 3, 5, 7 April 1851, with an introduction by Emmet Field Horine (New York: Schuman's, 1940), 31–32, 34.

45. Riker and Robertson, eds., *Tipton Papers*, 1: 266, 2: 609–610.

46. J. Blaine Hudson, *Fugitive Slaves and the Underground Railroad in the Kentucky Borderland* (Jefferson, NC: McFarland & Co., 2002), 14.

47. Harrold, *Border War*, 79–80.

48. James A. Ramage and Andrew S. Watkins, *Kentucky Rising: Democracy, Slavery and Culture from the Early Republic to the Civil War* (Lexington: University Press of Kentucky, 2011), 263–264.

49. Ibid., 259–270; Harold D. Tallant, *Evil Necessity: Slavery and Political Culture in Antebellum Kentucky* (Lexington: University Press of Kentucky, 2003), 95.

50. On the turning point of the 1830s, see John Ashworth, *Slavery, Capitalism and Politics in the Antebellum Republic*, vol. 1: *Commerce and Compromise, 1820–1850* (New York: Cambridge University Press, 1995), 125–139, 192–196; Freehling, *Road to Disunion*, 271–286. On planters in the Southwest, see James Oakes, *The Ruling Race:*

A History of American Slaveholders (New York: Knopf, 1982). On the ideology of Calhoun, see William W. Freehling, *The Reintegration of American History: Slavery and the Civil War* (New York: Oxford University Press, 1994), 105–137. On paternalism, see Eugene Genovese, *The Political Economy of Slavery: Studies in the Economy and Society of the Slave South* (New York: Pantheon Books, 1965); Stephanie McCurry, *Masters of Small Worlds: Yeomen Households, Gender Relations, and the Political Culture of the Antebellum South Carolina Low Country* (New York: Oxford University Press, 1995); Kenneth Greenberg, *Masters and Statesmen: The Political Culture of American Slavery* (Baltimore: Johns Hopkins University Press, 1985).

51. Peter S. Onuf, *Statehood and Union: A History of the Northwest Ordinance*, Midwestern History and Culture (Bloomington: Indiana University Press, 1987), 152; James Brewer Stewart, "The Emergence of Racial Modernity and the Rise of the White North, 1790–1840," *Journal of the Early Republic* 18 (Summer 1998): 181–217. The abolitionist attack on slavery and resulting proslavery defense may have marked a transition in white Americans' understanding of slavery and freedom in New England and the Deep South, but along the border white Americans developed a racially based understanding of slavery and freedom in response to social and political changes. This too was a transition, but one that increased racial solidarity across the Ohio River while highlighting the difference between freedom and slavery. On the difference between race relations in the Deep South and those in the upper South, see Ira Berlin, *Generations of Captivity: A History of African American Slaves* (Cambridge, MA: Harvard University Press, 2003), 159–244.

Chapter 6

1. John W. Blassingame, *Slave Testimony: Two Centuries of Letters, Speeches, Interviews, and Autobiographies* (Baton Rouge: Louisiana State University Press, 1977), 519–521.

2. Darrel E. Bigham, *On Jordan's Banks: Emancipation and Its Aftermath in the Ohio River Valley* (Lexington: University Press of Kentucky, 2006), 5–55; Joe William Trotter, *River Jordan: African American Urban Life in the Ohio Valley* (Lexington: University Press of Kentucky, 1998), 3–51; Marion B. Lucas, *A History of Blacks in Kentucky*, vol. 1: *From Slavery to Segregation, 1760–1861* (Frankfort: Kentucky Historical Society, 1992), 101–117; Hanford Dozier Stafford, "Slavery in a Border City: Louisville, 1790–1860" (Ph.D. diss., University of Kentucky, 1982), 112–128; Andrew Jackson, *Narrative and Writings of Andrew Jackson of Kentucky . . .* (Syracuse: Daily and Weekly Star Office, 1847), 13, http://docsouth.und.edu/neh/jacksona/jacksona.html (accessed October 2012). On the 1793 fugitive slave law, see Paul Finkelman, *Slavery and the Founders: Race and Liberty in the Age of Jefferson* (Armonk, NY: M. E. Sharpe, 1996), 81–104. On fugitive slaves as a national issue, see Don E. Fehrenbacher, *The Slaveholding Republic: An Account of the United States Government's Relations to Slavery* (New York: Oxford University Press, 2001), 205–251. On fugitive slaves in the upper

South, see Ira Berlin, *Generations of Captivity: A History of African American Slaves* (Cambridge, MA: Harvard University Press, 2003), 204–241. On the ways in which the legal systems of Kentucky, Ohio, and Indiana deprived African Americans of their rights, see Juliet E. K. Walker, "The Legal Status of Free Blacks in Early Kentucky, 1792–1825," *Filson Club History Quarterly* 57 (October 1983): 382–395; Stephen Middleton, *The Black Laws: Race and the Legal Process in Early Ohio* (Athens: Ohio University Press, 2005), 157–200; Emma Lou Thornbrough, *The Negro in Indiana: A Study of a Minority* (Indianapolis: Indiana Historical Bureau, 1957), 119–150.

3. Blassingame, *Slave Testimony*, 218–224; Davis (a man of color) v. Curry, 2 Bibb 238, Fall 1818, in Helen Catterall, ed., *Judicial Cases Concerning American Slavery and the Negro*, 5 vols. (Washington, DC: Carnegie Institution, 1926–1937), 1: 286. On Chase's legal efforts, see Middleton, *Black Laws*, 195–200; Paul Finkelman, *An Imperfect Union: Slavery, Federalism, and Comity* (Chapel Hill: University of North Carolina Press, 1981), 157–178. Examples of kidnapping and fugitive reclamation regularly appeared in the antislavery *Philanthropist* in the late 1830s and early 1840s. Although the paper publicized these incidents to gain public support for the repeal of Ohio's black laws, the many examples reveal how common kidnapping and fugitive reclamation were. See the *Cincinnati Philanthropist*, 8 October 1838, 24 March and 11 November 1840, 24 March and 12 May 1841. The most thorough examination of kidnapping is Carol Wilson, *Freedom at Risk: The Kidnapping of Free Blacks in America, 1780–1865* (Lexington: University Press of Kentucky, 1994).

4. Benjamin Drew, *The Refugee: A North-Side View of Slavery*, in Robert W. Winks, ed., *Four Fugitive Slave Narratives* (1856; Reading, MA: Addison-Wesley, 1969), 241; Blassingame, *Slave Testimony*, 385–386. In New Albany, Indiana, directly across the river from Louisville, two free African Americans, Joshua and Jessie Wilson, commanded their own fleet of steamers and were among the wealthiest men in Indiana; see Pamela Peters, *The Underground Railroad in Floyd County, Indiana* (Jefferson, NC: McFarland & Co., 2001), 61. The historiography well documents the circumscribed lives of free African Americans; see Leonard P. Curry, *The Free Black in Urban America 1800–1850: The Shadow of the Dream* (Chicago: University of Chicago Press, 1981), 249–251; Leon F. Litwack, *North of Slavery: The Negro in the Free States, 1790–1860* (Chicago: University of Chicago Press, 1961), 30–186; Ira Berlin, *Slaves without Masters: The Free Negro in the Antebellum South* (New York: Pantheon Books, 1975), 182–249; Berlin, *Generations of Captivity*, 230–244; Joanne Pope Melish, *Disowning Slavery: Gradual Emancipation and "Race" in New England, 1780–1860* (Ithaca, NY: Cornell University Press, 1998), 261–274; Eugene W. Berwanger, *The Frontier against Slavery: Western Anti-Negro Prejudice and the Slavery Extension Controversy* (Urbana: University of Illinois Press, 1967), 7–59; Middleton, *Black Laws*, 42–73; Bigham, *On Jordan's Banks*, 15; Thornbrough, *Negro in Indiana*, 92–150. Some recent works that revise the view of a wholly racist North include Keith P. Griffler, *Front Line of Freedom: African Americans and the Forging of the Underground Railroad in the Ohio Valley* (Lexington:

University Press of Kentucky, 2004); Nikki M. Taylor, *Frontiers of Freedom: Cincinnati's Black Community, 1802–1868* (Athens: Ohio University Press, 2005); Paul Finkelman, "Ohio's Struggle for Equality before the Civil War," *Timeline* 23 (January–March 2006): 28–43.

5. Blassingame, *Slave Testimony*, 444; Bigham, *On Jordan's Banks*, 16–18; Account Book, 1830–1860, James Rudd Papers, FHS; Lucas, *History of Blacks in Kentucky*, 101–117; Trotter, *River Jordan*, 3–51; Jonathan D. Martin, *Divided Mastery: Slave Hiring in the American South* (Cambridge, MA: Harvard University Press, 2004), 39; Clement Eaton, "Slave-Hiring in the Upper South: A Step toward Freedom," *Mississippi Valley Historical Review* 46 (March 1960): 663–678; Keith C. Barton, "Good Cooks and Washers: Slave-Hiring, Domestic Labor, and the Market in Bourbon County, Kentucky," *Journal of American History* 84 (September 1997): 436–460; Darrel E. Bigham, *Towns and Villages of the Lower Ohio* (Lexington: University Press of Kentucky, 1998), 63; John Hope Franklin and Loren Schweninger, *Runaway Slaves: Rebels on the Plantation* (New York: Oxford University Press, 1999), 124–148; J. Blaine Hudson, "Crossing the 'Dark Line': Fugitive Slaves and the Underground Railroad in Louisville and North-Central Kentucky," *Filson Club History Quarterly* 75 (Winter 2001): 33–83. Historians argue that hired slaves forced to pay their wages back to their owners desired their freedom that much more; see Franklin and Schweninger, *Runaway Slaves*, 33–35; Lucas, *History of Blacks in Kentucky*, 105. However, hired slaves' experiences in the market also raised their awareness of the way race limited their economic opportunities. Hired slaves, especially along the border, were well aware of the limits of freedom, and some remained at the same job even after emancipation; see Blassingame, *Slave Testimony*, 387.

6. Berlin, *Generations of Captivity*, 223; Frederick Douglass, *Life and Times of Frederick Douglass*, in Henry Louis Gates, ed., *Douglass: Autobiographies* (1881; New York: Library of America, 1994), 609–610.

7. Historians have placed too much emphasis on opportunity in their discussions of fugitive slaves; while opportunity played a vital role, it interacted with the personal beliefs and situations of slaves. The substantial literature on fugitive slaves has greatly influenced the interpretation offered herein. See Walter Johnson, *Soul by Soul: Life inside the Antebellum Slave Market* (Cambridge, MA: Harvard University Press, 1999), 31–32; James Oakes, *Slavery and Freedom: An Interpretation of the Old South* (New York: Knopf, 1990); John W. Blassingame, *The Slave Community: Plantation Life in the Antebellum South* (1972; New York: Oxford University Press, 1979), 192–222; Eugene D. Genovese, *Roll, Jordan, Roll: The World the Slaves Made* (New York: Pantheon Books, 1974), 657; J. Blaine Hudson, *Fugitive Slaves and the Underground Railroad in the Kentucky Borderland* (Jefferson, NC: McFarland and Co., 2002), 156; Griffler, *Front Line of Freedom*, 1–29. Two works that argue that a desire for freedom, while always present, was not necessarily enough to prompt escape are Larry Gara, *The Liberty Line: The Legend of the Underground Railroad* (1961; Lexington: University Press of Kentucky, 1967), 19; Steven Hahn, *A Nation under Our Feet: Black Political Struggles in the*

Rural South, from Slavery to the Great Migration (Cambridge, MA: Harvard University Press, 2003), 19, 485.

8. Franklin and Schweninger, *Runaway Slaves*, 19. The present consideration of the interplay of human conditions and resistance draws on Walter Johnson, "On Agency," *Journal of Social History* 37 (Fall 2003): 113–124. Borderland literature cited in the introduction influenced this interpretation. Mark Simpson, *Trafficking Subjects: The Politics of Mobility in Nineteenth-Century America* (Minneapolis: University of Minnesota Press, 2005), a work on the significance of policing mobility in antebellum America, also had a strong influence.

9. Drew, *Refugee*, 189; Blassingame, *Slave Testimony*, 53. Since Genovese's seminal work, *Roll, Jordan, Roll*, historians have generally characterized the master/slave relationship as a negotiation, though they disagree whether paternalism or the chattel principle more strongly influenced the relationship. In addition to Genovese's, the most influential studies include Johnson, *Soul by Soul*; James Oakes, *The Ruling Race: A History of American Slaveholders* (New York: Knopf, 1982); Oakes, *Slavery and Freedom*; Christopher Morris, "The Articulation of Two Worlds: The Master-Slave Relationship Reconsidered," *Journal of American History* 85 (December 1998): 982–1007.

10. Blassingame, *Slave Testimony*, 152–153. On slaves' deceptions of masters, see Gilbert Osofsky, "Introduction to Puttin' on Ole Massa: The Significance of Slave Narratives," in Osofsky, ed., *Puttin' on Ole Massa: The Slave Narratives of Henry Bibb, William Wells Brown, and Solomon Northup* (New York: Harper & Row, 1969), 9–44. For broader discussions of slave culture in the Deep South, including slaves' understanding of and desire for freedom, see Michael Gomez, *Exchanging Our Country Marks: The Transformation of African Identities in the Colonial and Antebellum South* (Chapel Hill: University of North Carolina Press, 1998); Sterling Stuckey, *Slave Culture: Nationalist Theory and the Foundations of Black America* (New York: Oxford University Press, 1987), 3–97; Lawrence Levine, *Black Culture and Black Consciousness: Afro-American Folk Thought from Slavery to Freedom* (New York: Oxford University Press, 1977), 3–135; Blassingame, *Slave Community*; Genovese, *Roll, Jordan, Roll*; Hahn, *Nation under Our Feet*, 14–61.

11. Lewis Garrard Clarke and Milton Clarke, *Narratives of the Sufferings of Lewis and Milton Clarke, Sons of a Soldier of the Revolution, during a Captivity of More Than Twenty Years among the Slaveholders of Kentucky, One of the So-Called Christian States of North America* (Boston: Bela Marsh, 1846), 33–34, http://docsouth.unc.edu/clarkes/clarkes.html (accessed October 2012).

12. Michael Tadman, *Speculators and Slaves: Masters, Traders, and Slaves in the Old South* (Madison: University of Wisconsin Press, 1989), 301–302; Hudson, *Fugitive Slaves*, 14; Robert H. Gudmestad, *A Troublesome Commerce: The Transformation of the Interstate Slave Trade* (Baton Rouge: Louisiana State University Press, 2003), 62–92; Stephen Deyle, *Carry Me Back: The Domestic Slave Trade in American Life* (New York: Oxford University Press, 2005); William W. Freehling, *The Road to Disunion*, vol. 1: *Secessionists at Bay, 1776–1854* (New York: Oxford University Press, 1990), 23–24; Berlin, *Generations of Captivity*, 161; Oakes, *Slavery and Freedom*, 151.

13. Harry Smith, *Fifty Years of Slavery in the United States of America* (Grand Rapids: West Michigan Printing Co., 1891), 15–16, http://docsouth.unc.edu/neh/smithhar/smithhar.html (accessed October 2012); Drew, *Refugee*, 126, 260; Harriet Beecher Stowe, *Uncle Tom's Cabin or Life among the Lowly* (1853; New York: Signet Classic, 1998), 56–60, 67–68. Historians have long understood sale to be a defining feature of life for border South slaves; see Berlin, *Generations of Captivity*, 167–175; Johnson, *Soul by Soul*, 19–44.

14. Franklin and Schweninger, *Runaway Slaves*, 17–74.

15. Blassingame, *Slave Testimony*, 390–391; Lucas, *History of Blacks in Kentucky*, 105–108; Eaton, "Slave-Hiring," 663–678. There are several examples of slaves who purchased their freedom and moved to Canada in Drew, *Refugee*, 131, 174, 189, 199. Still, the slaves who purchased their freedom and moved north represented only a small fraction of the more than two hundred thousand who remained enslaved in Kentucky. For the contrasting story of Maryland, see T. Stephen Whitman, *The Price of Freedom: Slavery and Manumission in Baltimore and Early National Maryland* (Lexington: University Press of Kentucky, 1997); Barbara Jeanne Fields, *Slavery and Freedom on the Middle Ground: Maryland during the Nineteenth Century* (New Haven, CT: Yale University Press, 1984); Christopher Phillips, *Freedom's Port: The African American Community of Baltimore, 1790–1860* (Urbana: University of Illinois Press, 1997).

16. Drew, *Refugee*, 189; *Proceedings of the Ohio Anti-Slavery Convention Held at Putnam on the 22, 23, and 24th of April,1835* (Cincinnati: Beaumont and Wallace, 1835), 30, 43. Such practices closely follow what Whitman has called "term slavery"; see Whitman, *Price of Freedom*, 98–101. Douglas Egerton has argued that enslaved African Americans' understanding of cash power opened their minds to new possibilities, which increased their likelihood to rebel. On the Ohio River borderland more hired slaves than field hands ran away, which fits with Egerton's model. However, Egerton's model does not adequately explain how market relations stabilized slavery at the periphery. In the city of Louisville, market relations penetrated the practice of slavery as deeply as in any other urban center. Yet in this city where nearly 30 percent of the enslaved population was hired out, many of whom traveled into free states, less than 2 percent escaped. See Douglas R. Egerton, "Slaves to the Marketplace: Economic Liberty and Black Rebelliousness in the Atlantic World," *Journal of the Early Republic* 26 (Winter 2006): 617–639.

17. Josiah Henson, *The Life of Josiah Henson, Formerly a Slave, Now an Inhabitant of Canada, as Narrated by Himself* (Boston: Arthur D. Phelps, 1849), 22–25, http://docsouth.unc.edu/neh/henson49/henson49.html (accessed October 2012). While self-purchase was a contract, slaves and owners viewed it in different ways. For a similar interpretation of the master/slave relationship, see Morris, "Articulation of Two Worlds," 982–1007.

18. Drew, *Refugee*, 106; Blassingame, *Slave Testimony*, 251–252.

19. Israel Campbell, *An Autobiography: Bond or Free; or Yearnings for Freedom, from My Green Brier House: Being the Story of My Life in Bondage, and My Life in*

Freedom (Philadelphia: The Author, 1861), 121–122, http://docsouth.unc.edu/neh/campbell/campbell.html (accessed October 2012). Hired slaves' desire for market freedom suggests that the shift in values associated with the market revolution influenced them and that those market values held more sway than the precapitalist moral economy explicated by Genovese and others. See Charles Sellers, "Capitalism and Democracy in American Historical Mythology," in Melvin Stokes and Stephen Conway, eds., *The Market Revolution America: Social, Political, and Religious Expressions, 1800–1880* (Charlottesville: University of Virginia Press, 1996), 311–329; Genovese, *Roll, Jordan, Roll*, 44–49, 587–598; Eugene D. Genovese, *From Rebellion to Revolution: Afro-American Slave Revolts in the Making of the Modern World* (Baton Rouge: Louisiana State University Press, 1979); James C. Scott, *The Moral Economy of the Peasant: Rebellion and Subsistence in Southeast Asia* (New Haven, CT: Yale University Press, 1976). The idea of "stealing" versus "earning" freedom is loosely drawn from Edward E. Baptist, "Stol and Fetched Here: Enslaved Migration, Ex-slave Narratives, and Vernacular History," in Baptist and Stephanie M. H. Camp, eds., *New Studies in the History of American Slavery* (Athens: University of Georgia Press, 2006), 243–274.

20. Lucas, *History of Blacks in Kentucky*, 84–86, 92, 99; Harold D. Tallant, *Evil Necessity: Slavery and Political Culture in Antebellum Kentucky* (Lexington: University Press of Kentucky, 2003), 141–143; Henson, *Life of Josiah Henson*, 40–41; Blassingame, *Slave Testimony*, 386, 89; Hudson, *Fugitive Slaves*, 32–33. Josiah Henson planned to purchase his freedom in the 1830s, negotiating a price of $450 with his owner. When his master backed out and raised the price to an unreachable and unreasonable $1,000, Henson despaired of ever raising enough money.

21. William Wells Brown, *Narrative of William W. Brown, an American Slave, Written by Himself* (London: C. Gilpin, 1849), 30, http://docsouth.unc.edu/brownw/brown.html (accessed October 2012). On the ways that family shaped slaves' motives for flight, see Franklin and Schweninger, *Runaway Slaves*, 50–53, 66; Hudson, *Fugitive Slaves*, 55–58; Berlin, *Generations of Captivity*, 190–195; Hahn, *Nation under Our Feet*, 19.

22. Blassingame, *Slave Testimony*, 389, 440; J. D. Green, *Narrative of the Life of J. D. Green, a Runaway Slave, from Kentucky, Containing an Account of His Three Escapes, in 1839, 1846, and 1848* (Huddersfield, UK: Henry Fielding, 1864), 22, http://docsouth.unc.edu/neh/greenjd/greenjd.html (accessed October 2012).

23. Drew, *Refugee*, 182, 197; Blassingame, *Slave Testimony*, 275–276.

24. Henry Bibb, *Narrative of the Life and Adventures of Henry Bibb, an American Slave, Written by Himself* (New York: The Author, 1849), 83, http://docsouth.unc.edu/neh/bibb/bibb.html (accessed October 2012).

25. Ibid., 189; Blassingame, *Slave Testimony*, 49. Bibb wrote, "Sometimes standing on the Ohio River bluff, looking over on a free State, and as far north as my eyes could see, I have eagerly gazed upon the blue sky of the free North, which at times constrained me to cry out from the depths of my soul." These words suggest that he viewed the Ohio River as a border between slavery and freedom. However, he added,

"Oh! Canada, sweet land of rest—Oh! when shall I get there? Oh, that I had the wings of a dove, that I might soar away to where there is no slavery"—language that indicates he viewed freedom in Canada as different than freedom in southern Ohio; see Bibb, *Narrative of the Life*, 29.

26. Barton, "Good Cooks and Washers," 447–448; Bigham, *On Jordan's Banks*, 16; Hudson, *Fugitive Slaves*, 36; Franklin and Schweninger, *Runaway Slaves*, 60–63; Stephanie M. H. Camp, *Closer to Freedom: Enslaved Women and Everyday Resistance in the Plantation South* (Chapel Hill: University of North Carolina Press, 2004).

27. Blassingame, *Slave Testimony*, 388–390; Berlin, *Generations of Captivity*, 215; Wilma A. Dunaway, *The African American Family in Slavery and Emancipation* (New York: Cambridge University Press, 2003), 51–114.

28. Jacqueline Jones, *Labor of Love, Labor of Sorrow: Black Women, Work, and the Family from Slavery to the Present* (New York: Vintage Books, 1995); Wilma A. Dunaway, *Slavery in the American Mountain South* (New York: Cambridge University Press, 2003), 193–197. On the impact of gender on truancy and escape, see Camp, *Closer to Freedom*, 33–47.

29. Edward E. Baptist, "'Cuffy, Fancy Maids, and One-Eyed Men': Rape, Commodification, and the Domestic Slave Trade in the United States," *American Historical Review* 106, no. 5 (2001): 1619–1650. Slaveholders and enslaved people recognized that control of the movement of enslaved bodies lay at the center of the slave regime and slave resistance; see Camp, *Closer to Freedom*, 12–34.

30. Hudson, *Fugitive Slaves*, 143–147; Middleton, *Black Laws*, 229–231.

31. Blassingame, *Slave Testimony*, 432–433; Lucas, *History of Blacks in Kentucky*, 121; Middleton, *Black Laws*, 31; Berlin, *Generations of Captivity*, 215; Hahn, *Nation under Our Feet*, 35, 42; Taylor, *Frontiers of Freedom*, 44; Gomez, *Exchanging Our Country Marks*, 186–243; Lyle Koehler, *Cincinnati's Black Peoples: A Chronology and Bibliography, 1787–1982* (Cincinnati: University of Cincinnati, 1986), 4; Xenia Cord, "Free Black Communities in Indiana: A Selected Annotated Bibliography," mss., iii–vi, IHS. Examples of works about enslaved black ministers who traveled extensively are Elisha Winfield Green, *Life of the Rev. Elisha W. Green, One of the Founders of the Kentucky Normal and Theological Institute—Now the State University at Louisville . . . and Over Thirty Years Pastor of the Colored Baptist Churches of Maysville and Paris, Written by Himself* (Maysville, KY: Republican Printing Office, 1888), 5–9; Henson, *Life of Josiah Henson*, 26–27.

32. Lucas, *History of Blacks in Kentucky*, 92–93; Taylor, *Frontiers of Freedom*, 138–160.

33. Drew, *Refugee*, 233. Historians agree about the importance of racial solidarity among the African American community in the Ohio River Valley. They argue that fugitive slaves turned to the black community for protection but fail to note how this relative security could reduce slaves' desire to escape north. See Hudson, "Crossing the 'Dark Line,'" 33–83; Hahn, *Nation under Our Feet*, 35, 42; Taylor, *Frontiers of Freedom*, 29; Berlin, *Generations of Captivity*, 43, 215; Griffler, *Front Line of Freedom*, 30–57.

34. Bibb, *Narrative of the Life*, 19; Drew, *Refugee*, 214; Blassingame, *Slave Testimony*, 391, 390; Philip S. Foner and George E. Walker, eds., *Proceedings of the Black State Conventions, 1840–1865*, vol. 1: *New York, Pennsylvania, Indiana, Michigan, Ohio* (Philadelphia: Temple University Press, 1979), 214–315.

35. Francis Fedric, *Slave Life in Virginia and Kentucky; or, Fifty Years of Slavery in the Southern States of America* (London: Wertheim, Macintosh, and Hunt, 1863), 75–76, http://docsouth.unc.edu/fedric/fedric.html (accessed October 2012); Blassingame, *Slave Testimony*, 152; Frederick Douglass, *My Bondage and My Freedom* (1855; New York: Arno Press, 1968), 170.

36. Charles Sellers, *The Market Revolution* (New York: Oxford University Press, 1991), 364–395; Daniel Feller, *The Jacksonian Promise: America, 1815–1840* (Baltimore: Johns Hopkins University Press, 1995), 14–32; Andrew R. L. Cayton, *Ohio: The History of a People* (Columbus: Ohio State University Press, 2002), 45–72; Andrew R. L. Cayton, *Frontier Indiana* (Bloomington: Indiana University Press, 1996), 261–300.

37. Clarke and Clarke, *Narratives of the Sufferings*, 33; Walter Johnson, "The Pedestal and the Veil: Rethinking the Capitalism/Slavery Question," *Journal of the Early Republic* 24 (Summer 2004): 299–308; Morris, "Articulation of Two Worlds," 984; Cathy Matson, ed., *The Economy of Early America: Historical Perspectives and New Directions* (University Park: Pennsylvania State University Press, 2006), 183–217, 335–361. Historians have begun to offer new ways to move beyond the hoary question of whether slavery was capitalist (or not) by examining how slavery, freedom, and capitalism were related.

38. Oakes, *Slavery and Freedom*, 155; Hahn, *Nation under Our Feet*, 19. On the chattel principle as the central contradiction of American slavery, see David Brion Davis, *Inhuman Bondage: The Rise and Fall of Slavery in the New World* (New York: Oxford University Press, 2006), 35; Johnson, *Soul by Soul*, 29, 188.

Chapter 7

1. Harriet Beecher Stowe, *Uncle Tom's Cabin or Life among the Lowly* (1853; New York: Signet Classic, 1998).

2. This interpretive link between informal actions and resistance is based on Robin Kelley, "'We Are Not What We Seem': Rethinking Black Working-Class Opposition in the Jim Crow South," *Journal of American History* 80, no. 1 (June 1993): 75–112.

3. Benjamin Drew, *The Refugee: A North-Side View of Slavery*, in Robert W. Winks, ed., *Four Fugitive Slave Narratives* (1856; Reading, MA: Addison-Wesley, 1969), 378.

4. Henry Bibb, *Narrative of the Life and Adventures of Henry Bibb, an American Slave, Written by Himself* (New York: Published by the author, 1849), 72, http://docsouth.unc.edu/neh/bibb/bibb.html (accessed October 2012).

5. The perfect example of this is Henry "Box" Brown, who shipped himself to freedom in a wooden crate; see Brown, *Narrative of the Life of Henry Box Brown Written by Himself* (Manchester: Lee and Glyn, 1851), http://docsouth.unc.edu/neh/brownbox/brownbox.html (accessed October 2012).

6. Peter Bruner, *A Slave's Adventures toward Freedom, Not Fiction but the True Story of a Struggle* (Oxford, OH, 1919), 12; John W. Blassingame, *Slave Testimony: Two Centuries of Letters, Speeches, Interviews, and Autobiographies* (Baton Rouge: Louisiana State University Press, 1977), 156. When Josiah Henson knocked over a white man in defense of his own master, the aggrieved man ambushed Henson the next day and broke his arms and shoulder blades. Josiah Henson wrote that his attacker wanted to teach him "what it was to strike a white man"; see Henson, *The Life of Josiah Henson, Formerly a Slave, Now an Inhabitant of Canada, as Narrated by Himself* (Boston: Arthur D. Phelps, 1849), 17, http://docsouth.unc.edu/neh/henson49/henson49.html (accessed October 2012).

7. Andrew Jackson, *Narrative and Writings of Andrew Jackson of Kentucky . . .* (Syracuse: Daily and Weekly Star Office, 1847), 14, http://docsouth.und.edu/neh/jacksona/jacksona.html (accessed October 2012); Lewis Clark, speech published in two parts in *National Antislavery Standard*, 20, 27 October 1842, and recorded by Lydia Maria Child, in Blassingame, *Slave Testimony*, 158.

8. William Wells Brown, *Narrative of William W. Brown, an American Slave, Written by Himself* (London: C. Gilpin, 1849), 94–95; *Cincinnati Philanthropist*, 14 September 1837; Bibb, *Narrative of the Life*, 91–92.

9. Bibb, *Narrative of the Life*, 91–92.

10. Blassingame, *Slave Testimony*, 190; J. D. Green, *A Runaway Slave from Kentucky . . .* (Huddersfield: Henry Fielding, Pack Horse Yard, 1864), 34, http://docsouth.unc.edu/neh/greenjd/greenjd.html (accessed October 2012).

11. *Cincinnati Philanthropist*, 19, 5 February 1845.

12. *Special Message of the Governor, Transmitting a Communication from Messrs. Morehead and Smith, Commissioners from Kentucky*, 3, OHS; Emma Lou Thornbrough, *The Negro in Indiana: A Study of a Minority* (Indianapolis: Indiana Historical Bureau, 1957), 446.

13. Derived from the historical census browser available on the University of Virginia Library Website, http://fisher.lib.virginia.edu/collections/stats/histcensus/index.html (accessed October 2012). In the Clark County census, African Americans were listed in clusters, which was significant because the census was organized by location and not alphabetically. Thus clusters of African Americans in the census suggest that new African American residents tended to settle near and among established black residents. See U.S. Census Bureau, "1850 Clark County, Indiana Census," transcribed by Renee Hill and proofread by Michelle R. Hill for the USGenWeb Census Project, us-census.org/pub/usgenweb/census/in/clark/1850 (accessed October 2012). Historians sometimes assume that African Americans moved to free states *because* of their freedom from slavery, but surely there were other motivating factors; see Keith P.

Griffler, *Front Line of Freedom: African Americans and the Forging of the Underground Railroad in the Ohio Valley* (Lexington: University Press of Kentucky, 2004), 30–57; Andrew R. L. Cayton, *Ohio: The History of a People* (Columbus: Ohio State University Press, 2002), 108–109.

14. *Cincinnati Philanthropist*, 8 May 1839. On the free black community and the underground railroad, see especially Griffler, *Front Line of Freedom*; Nikki M. Taylor, *Frontiers of Freedom: Cincinnati's Black Community, 1802–1868* (Athens: Ohio University Press, 2005); Paul Finkelman, "Ohio's Struggle for Equality before the Civil War," *Timeline* 23 (January–March 2006): 28–43; J. Blaine Hudson, "Crossing the 'Dark Line': Fugitive Slaves and the Underground Railroad in Louisville and North-Central Kentucky," *Filson Historical Quarterly* 75 (Winter 2001): 33–83.

15. William A. White to the *Liberator*, 22 September 1843, ISL.

16. This account of the 1841 riot is based on Taylor, *Frontiers of Freedom*, 50–79.

17. The historians Keith Griffler and Nikki Taylor depict border violence as clashes between the forces of freedom and slavery; see Griffler, *Front Line of Freedom*, 31, 84–85; Taylor, *Frontiers of Freedom*, 117–160. The fact that some African Americans stood up to the threat of violence and assisted fugitive slaves escape is remarkable, but most likely others sought to avoid conflict. The growth of the free black population in northern Ohio suggests that some tried to protect themselves by leaving the "battleground."

18. Stephen Middleton, *The Black Laws: Race and the Legal Process in Early Ohio* (Athens: Ohio University Press, 2005), 115–156; John R. McKivigan and Stanley Harrold, eds., *Antislavery Violence: Sectional, Racial and Cultural Conflict in Antebellum America* (Knoxville: University of Tennessee Press, 1999), 1–37; Stanley Harrold, *The Rise of Aggressive Abolitionism: Addresses to the Slaves* (Lexington: University Press of Kentucky, 2004).

19. Philip S. Foner and George E. Walker, eds., *Proceedings of the Black State Conventions, 1840–1865*, vol. 1: *New York, Pennsylvania, Indiana, Michigan, Ohio* (Philadelphia: Temple University Press, 1979), 228.

20. Drew, *Refugee*, 273. William Freehling argues that a determined minority can control majoritarian politics. This was how slaveholders manipulated the political system throughout the antebellum period. However, that determined minority first had to be on the inside of the political arena, which of course slaveholders were. See William Freehling, *The Reintegration of American History: Slavery and the Civil War* (New York: Oxford University Press, 1994), 176–219. African Americans, on the other hand, were complete outsiders, and they were working against a system that dictated against outsider influence. Thus they could do little no matter how determined members of this minority were. This was the hegemonic power of antebellum America's democratic system rooted in racial subordination. The greatest advocate of the power of the two-party system to control the issues is Michael Holt; see Holt, *The Rise and Fall of the American Whig Party: Jacksonian Politics and the Onset of the Civil War* (New York: Oxford University Press, 1999).

21. Cayton, *Ohio*, 15–17. Numbers were derived from the following census records: U.S. Census Bureau, "1850 Posey County, Indiana Census," transcribed by Betty Emery, and "1850 Daviess County, Kentucky Census," transcribed by Maria Troutman and proofread by Tim Troutman, USGenWeb Archives Census Project, http://www.usgenweb.org/census (accessed October 2012); "1850 United States Census, Lawrence County, Ohio," submitted by Henry Dillon and Shirley Reed, the Lawrence Register, http://www.lawrencecountyohio.com/census/1850/index1850.html (accessed October 2012); *The 1840 Newport City Directory*, http://www.rootsweb.ancestry.com/~kycchgs/1840Npt.html (accessed October 2012).

22. Kim M. Gruenwald, *River of Enterprise: The Commercial Origins of Regional Identity in the Ohio Valley, 1790–1850* (Bloomington: Indiana University Press, 2002), 124–138; John Garreston Clark, *The Grain Trade in the Old Northwest* (Urbana: University of Illinois Press, 1966); James H. Madison, *The Indiana Way: A State History* (Bloomington: Indiana University Press, 1986), 58–66. On the movement west, see Eugene H. Berwanger, *The Frontier against Slavery: Western Anti-Negro Prejudice and the Slavery Extension Controversy* (Urbana: University of Illinois Press, 1967), 30–122.

23. John Corlis to Susan Corlis, July 1831, Lloyd Halsey to John Corlis, 4 July 1836, Corlis-Respess Family Papers, FHS; U.S. Census Bureau, "1850 Census of Clark County, Indiana."

24. U.S. Census Bureau, "1850 Census of Wilkinson County, Mississippi," transcribed by Tina Hall and proofread by T. Hall for the USGenWeb Census Project; U.S. Census Bureau, "1850 Census of Warren County, Mississippi," transcribed by Larry Cooley and proofread by Carol Cooley for the USGenWeb Census Project. White northerners who moved south are seldom if ever discussed in most histories. Yet the arch villain of Harriet Beecher Stowe's *Uncle Tom's Cabin*, Simon Legree, was from New England.

25. The rise of abolitionism in the West differed from that in the East, where African Americans played a vital role in the conversion of abolitionist leaders in Boston and Philadelphia. The three leading western abolitionists all spent a considerable amount of time in the South, and this experience was the key in their conversion. Theirs was a practical conclusion based on the inefficacy of colonization. Key works that stress the role of African Americans in the abolition movement include Richard Newman, *The Transformation of American Abolitionism: Fighting Slavery in the Early Republic* (Chapel Hill: University of North Carolina Press, 2002), 86–106; Patrick Rael, *Black Identity and Protest in the Antebellum North* (Chapel Hill: University of North Carolina Press, 2002), 157–208; Paul Goodman, *Of One Blood: Abolitionism and the Origins of Racial Equality* (Berkeley: University of California Press, 1998), 23–44; David Brion Davis, *Inhuman Bondage: The Rise and Fall of Slavery in the New World* (New York: Oxford University Press, 2006), 255–260; Dickson D. Bruce, *The Origins of African American Literature, 1680–1865* (Charlottesville: University of Virginia Press, 2001), 175–210; Peter Ripley, ed., *Black Abolitionist Papers*, vol. 3: *The United States, 1830–1846* (Chapel Hill: University of North Carolina Press, 1985), 3–70.

26. Robert Azbug, *Passionate Liberator: Theodore Dwight Weld and the Dilemma of Reform* (New York: Oxford University Press, 1980), 83–87; Gilbert Hobbs Barnes and Dwight L. Dumond, eds., *Letters of Theodore Dwight Weld, Angelina Grimke and Sarah Grimke, 1822–1844* (New York: D. Appleton-Century, 1934), 95–98; John Rankin, *Letters on American Slavery* (Boston: Isaac Knapp, 1838), 21–22, 41–42; Dwight L. Dumond, ed., *Letters of James Gillespie Birney* (New York: D. Appleton-Century, 1938), 13, 27.

27. Dumond, *Letters of James Birney* (quotation), 89, 9–10, 27, 49, 51–52, 89–90, 261–263, 826–827.

28. Ibid., 241; David Grimsted, *American Mobbing, 1828–1861: Toward Civil War* (New York: Oxford University Press, 1998), 85–184.

29. Dumond, *Letters of James Birney*, 234.

30. Gilbert Hobbes Barnes, ed., *Letters of Theodore Dwight Weld, Angelina Grimke Weld and Sarah Grimke, 1822–1844* (New York: Appleton-Century Company, 1934), 266–267, 156–160. On the abolitionists' commitment to reform, see Robert Azbug, *Cosmos Crumbling: American Reform and the Religious Imagination* (New York: Oxford University Press, 1994), 129–162; Goodman, *Of One Blood*, 81–136; Ronald Walters, *The Antislavery Appeal: American Abolitionism after 1830* (Baltimore: Johns Hopkins University Press, 1976); James Brewer Stewart, *Holy Warriors: The Abolitionists and American Slavery* (New York: Hill and Wang, 1976), 51–96; R. Jackson Wilson, *Figures of Speech: American Writers and the Literary Marketplace, from Benjamin Franklin to Emily Dickinson* (New York: Knopf, 1989), 151–155.

31. Dumond, *Letters of James Birney*, 350; William Birney, *James G. Birney and His Times* (New York: D. Appleton and Co., 1890), 180–187; John C. Nerone, *Culture of the Press in the Early Republic: Cincinnati 1793–1848* (New York: Garland, 1989).

32. In truth, Birney had little choice but to remain in Ohio. If he could not print a paper in a free state, his only other option as an abolitionist reformer was to expatriate to Canada or England. But Birney refused to compromise and printed scathing editorials denouncing "gentlemen property and standing," which only angered his opponents. See Taylor, *Frontiers of Freedom*, 110–112.

33. Dumond, *Letters of James Birney*, 319. Abolitionists had an ambivalent relationship with violence: they feared it but also believed that it was beneficial to their cause (ibid., 128). The murder of Elijah Lovejoy is the most notable exception to the property-focused violence of antiabolitionist mobs in the North. Abolitionists held Lovejoy up as a martyr.

34. *Boston Liberator*, 15 August 1835, 26 December 1835, 26 September 1835. On Garrison, see Henry Mayer, *All on Fire: William Lloyd Garrison and the Abolition of Slavery* (New York: St. Martin's, 1998), 71–150.

35. *Proceedings of the Indiana Convention Assembled to Organize a State Anti-Slavery Society, Held in Milton, Wayne Co., September 12th, 1838* (Cincinnati: Sam'l A. Alley, Printer, 1838); Ripley, Ohio, Anti-Slavery Society Minute Book, 11 August 1836, 26, http://www.ohiomemory.org (accessed October 2012); *Cincinnati Philanthropist*, 18 December 1838, 19 October 1839, 30 June 1841.

36. Brother Andrew to Mrs. Bishop, 15 February 1841, Columbus, OHS; *Cincinnati Weekly Herald*, 18 February 1845; Ira Bean to A. G. Hoit, 8 November 1833, and Ira Bean to his father, 11 March 1848, Ira A. Bean Letters, CHS; Joshua Giddings, letter, 21 March 1842, OHS; Cayton, *Ohio*, 118–126.

37. Pamela Peters, *The Underground Railroad in Floyd County, Indiana* (Jefferson, NC: McFarland & Co., 2001), 26–38; Richard F. Nation, *At Home in the Hoosier Hills: Agriculture, Politics and Religion in Southern Indiana, 1810–1870* (Bloomington: Indiana University Press, 2005), 187–213. Most Indianans and Ohioans would have declared themselves antislavery, but few supported the apparent radicalism of abolitionists. Historians cite the origins of the settlers as the reason for the differences between antislavery in Indiana and antislavery in Ohio. See Nicole Etcheson, *Emerging Midwest: Upland Southerners and the Political Culture of the Old Northwest, 1787–1861* (Bloomington: Indiana University Press, 1996); John Barnhart, *Valley of Democracy: The Frontier Versus the Plantation in the Ohio Valley, 1775–1818* (Bloomington: Indiana University Press, 1953). However, the factors mentioned above also created a more receptive audience to abolitionism in Ohio.

38. Esther Hollowell to William Townsend, 10 November 1835, William Townsend Letters, 1835–1855, and James Butchey to Ann, 8 December 1848, Hubert Hawkins Misc. Papers, ISL; Joel S. Migdal, "Mental Maps and Virtual Checkpoints: Struggles to Construct and Maintain State and Social Boundaries," in Migdal, ed., *Boundaries and Belonging: State and Societies in the Struggle to Shape Identities and Local Practices* (New York: Cambridge University Press, 2004); Mark Simpson, *Trafficking Subjects: The Politics of Mobility in Nineteenth-Century America* (Minneapolis: University of Minnesota Press, 2005).

39. Augustus W(N?)attles writes about the situation; see his letter to Governor Mordecai Bartley, 16 August 1846, and executive order demanding that law and order be restored, 30 August 1846, Governor Papers, OHS.

40. Dorothy Riker and Gayle Thornbrough, eds., *Messages and Papers Relating to the Administration of Noah Noble, Governor of Indiana, 1831–1837* (Indianapolis: Indiana Historical Bureau, 1958), 600; Emma Lou Thornbrough, "Indiana and Fugitive Slave Legislation," *Indiana Magazine of History* 50, no. 3 (1954): 201–228, quote on 218; Stanley Harrold, *Border War: Fighting over Slavery before the Civil War* (Chapel Hill: University of North Carolina Press, 2010), 88–90.

41. Harold D. Tallant, *Evil Necessity: Slavery and Political Culture in Antebellum Kentucky* (Lexington: University Press of Kentucky, 2003).

42. *Columbus Statesman*, 27 February 1839, 28 September 1838.

43. Rachel Myers to Julia Myers, New Lisbon, 1848 or 1849, OHS; *Preamble and Resolution in Relation to Slaves Who Escape from Their Owners into the States of OH, IN and IL*, 3 February 1837, IHS; Lewis Garrard Clarke and Milton Clarke, *Narratives of the Sufferings of Lewis and Milton Clarke, Sons of a Soldier of the Revolution, during a Captivity of More Than Twenty Years among the Slaveholders of Kentucky, One of the So-Called Christian States of North America* (Boston: Bela Marsh, 1846), 92, http://docsouth.unc.edu/clarkes/clarkes.html (accessed October 2012).

44. Anne Norton, *Reflections on Political Identity*, Johns Hopkins Series in Constitutional Thought (Baltimore: Johns Hopkins University Press, 1988), 143–184.

45. Joshua Giddings [Pacificus], *The Rights and Privileges of the Several States in Regard to Slavery*, 1843, 3, OHS. I admire James Birney, but a prime example of Birney's condescension was when he questioned the authenticity of Henry Bibb's testimony and narrative. Bibb wrote, "you supposed I was an imposter and was kind a neugh to tell me for my own good" (Dumond, *Letters of James Birney*, 928).

46. *Columbus Statesman*, 27 February 1839, 28 September 1838. In October 1828 James Birney wrote to G. Bailey, "So far, I do not think you have made one tenth part enough out of the Mahan Case" (Dumond, *Letters of James Birney*, 475). Shortly thereafter Bailey devoted an entire issue to the Mahan case: *Cincinnati Philanthropist*, November 1838. See also Gruenwald, *River of Enterprise*, 148.

47. However, as Chase drew a sharp line between Ohio and Kentucky, the cases lent backhanded support to fugitive slaves but offered no legal support to the act of escape. On Chase's legal efforts, see Middleton, *Black Laws*, 195–200; Paul Finkelman, *An Imperfect Union: Slavery, Federalism, and Comity* (Chapel Hill: University of North Carolina Press, 1981), 157–178.

48. Both Union County's and Henderson County's enslaved populations increased by more than 32 percent. Jefferson County's enslaved population increased by better than 25 percent and topped ten thousand total by 1850. These examples suggest that slavery was rapidly expanding in certain areas along the Ohio River. These numbers were derived from the census database on the University of Virginia Web site, http://fisher.lib.virginia.edu/collections/stats/histcensus/index .html (accessed October 2012). Historians tend to emphasize the "whitening" of the upper South as the interstate slave trade drained slaves to the cotton plantations of the Southwest; see Freehling, *Reintegration of American History*; William Freehling, *The Road to Disunion: Secessionists at Bay, 1776–1854* (New York: Oxford University Press, 1991); Ira Berlin, *Generations of Captivity: A History of African-American Slaves* (Cambridge, MA: Belknap Press of Harvard University Press, 2003).

49. Account Book, 1830–1860, James Rudd Papers, FHS; James F. Hopkins, *A History of the Hemp Industry in Kentucky* (Lexington: University Press of Kentucky, 1998). Historians emphasize how tangential slavery was to the Kentucky economy, arguing that white Kentuckians never viewed slavery as essential to their well-being. However, the diversity of slavery in Kentucky was the source of its strength. For a similar argument about colonial slavery in the American colonies, see Robin Blackburn, *The Making of New World Slavery: From the Baroque to the Modern, 1492–1800* (New York: Verso, 1997), 457–508; David Waldstreicher, *Runaway America: Benjamin Franklin, Slavery and the American Revolution* (New York: Hill and Wang, 2004), 175–224.

50. John Green to Hector Green, 26 September 1833, Green Family Papers, FHS.

51. *Lexington Examiner*, 31 July 1847, 25 September 1847; Lowell H. Harrison, *The Antislavery Movement in Kentucky* (Lexington: University Press of Kentucky, 1978), 51–54.

Chapter 8

1. The historiography on Civil War causation is wonderfully rich and nuanced, and far too vast for me to do justice to it in an endnote. Any study of the 1850s should probably begin with David M. Potter's classic work, *The Impending Crisis, 1848–1861*, completed and edited by Don E. Fehrenbacher (New York: Harper & Row Perennial, 1976). The works of Michael Holt and William Gienapp are essential: Michael Holt, *Political Crisis of the 1850s* (New York: Wiley, 1978); Michael Holt, *The Fate of Their Country: Politicians, Slavery Extension and the Coming of the Civil War* (New York: Hill and Wang, 2004); William Gienapp, *The Origins of the Republican Party, 1852–1856* (New York: Oxford University Press, 1988). The works of William Freehling have helped untangle the complicated world of southern politics; see Freehling, *The Road to Disunion*, vol. 1: *Secessionists at Bay, 1776–1854* (New York: Oxford University Press, 1990); Freehling, *Road to Disunion*, vol. 2: *Secessionists Triumphant, 1854–1861* (New York: Oxford University Press, 2007). John Ashworth has linked sectional conflict with oppositional labor systems; see Ashworth, *Slavery, Capitalism, and Politics in the Antebellum Republic*, vols. 1–2 (New York: Cambridge University Press, 1995, 2008). Other historians have argued that the Civil War was an irrepressible conflict because the North and South were two different worlds by 1860: Eric Foner, *Free Soil, Free Labor, Free Men: The Ideology of the Republican Party before the Civil War* (New York: Oxford University Press, 1995); Bruce Levine, *Half Slave and Half Free: The Roots of the Civil War* (New York: Hill and Wang, 1992). James Huston has made an argument that economic self-interest had a powerful impact on southerners' desire to protect the institution of slavery; see Huston, *Calculating the Value of the Union: Slavery, Property Rights, and the Economic Origins of the Civil War* (Chapel Hill: University of North Carolina Press, 2003).

2. On the powerful appeal of unionism, see Peter B. Knupfer, *The Union as It Is: Constitutional Unionism and Sectional Compromise, 1787–1861* (Chapel Hill: University of North Carolina Press, 1991). Stanley Harrold, *Border War: Fighting over Slavery before the Civil War* (Chapel Hill: University of North Carolina Press, 2010), argues that constant violent conflict at the border drove the region apart. I agree with Harrold's assessment that conflict plagued borderland residents throughout the antebellum period. However, I believe that this tradition of conflict and resolution fostered a powerful commitment to the Union and allowed residents to promote a regional history rooted in compromise. Eric Hobbsbawm and Terrence Ranger, eds., *The Invention of Tradition* (New York: Cambridge University Press, 1992), makes the argument that invented traditions strongly influence the development of nationalism. These traditions give people a shared past and a sense of common origin, even if they are entirely apocryphal. In the case of national, and in this case regional, identity, perception often carries more weight than reality. White residents of the borderland looked at their ability to coexist for more than sixty years as evidence of a tradition of compromise and accommodation.

3. Holt, *Fate of Their Country*, 1–91.

4. Potter, *Impending Crisis*, 90–120.

5. Ibid., 209–211.

6. Holt, *Fate of Their Country*, 86–88.

7. Philip S. Foner and George E. Walker, eds., *Proceedings of the Black State Conventions, 1840–1865*, vol. 1: *New York, Pennsylvania, Indiana, Michigan, Ohio* (Philadelphia: Temple University Press, 1979), 277.

8. Ibid., 263. Black abolitionists radically departed from the more conservative turn in the white antislavery movement. African Americans became convinced that the boundary between slavery and freedom was *the* reason for racial prejudice.

9. Ronald Walters, *The Antislavery Appeal: American Abolitionism after 1830* (Baltimore: Johns Hopkins University Press, 1976), 133.

10. *Cincinnati Weekly Herald*, 27 March 1844; William Freehling, *The Reintegration of American History: Slavery and the Civil War* (New York: Oxford University Press, 1994), 235.

11. Stephen E. Maizlish, *Triumph of Sectionalism: The Transformation of Ohio Politics, 1844–1856* (Kent, OH: Kent State University Press, 1983), 121–146.

12. On the increasing radicalism of Ohioans, see Harrold, *Border War*, 138–158; Stephen Middleton, *The Black Laws: Race and the Legal Process in Early Ohio* (Athens: Ohio University Press, 2005), 201–240. On the political divisions of the state and the uniqueness of southwestern Ohio, see Maizlish, *Triumph of Sectionalism*.

13. Harrold, *Border War*, 180.

14. Middleton, *Black Laws*, 227–230.

15. Emma Lou Thornbrough, *The Negro in Indiana: A Study of a Minority* (Indianapolis: Indiana Historical Bureau, 1957), 55; *Congressional Globe*, 32nd Congress, 1st Sess., appendix, 1123–1124, cited in Charles B. Murphy, "Political Career of Jesse D. Bright," Indiana Historical Society Publications, 10, no. 3 (Indianapolis: Indiana Historical Society, 1931), 101–145; Richard Thompson, letter, 8 June 1847, Richard W. Thompson Correspondence and Papers, ISL.

16. Charles Kettlebrough, *Constitution Making in Indiana: A Sourcebook of Constitutional Documents, with Historical Introduction and Critical Notes*, vol. 1 (Indianapolis: Indiana Historical Commission, 1916), 290–294, 361–363; *Indiana Election Returns, 1816–1851*, comp. Dorothy Riker and Gayle Thornbrough (Indianapolis: Indiana Historical Bureau, 1960), 388–390.

17. Harrold, *Border War*, 182.

18. Information regarding the free black population was derived from the University of Virginia's census browser at http://mapserver.lib.virginia.edu (accessed October 2012).

19. Marion Lucas, *A History of Blacks in Kentucky: From Slavery to Segregation, 1760–1861* (Frankfort: Kentucky Historical Society, 1992), 84–86, 92, 99; Harold D. Tallant, *Evil Necessity: Slavery and Political Culture in Antebellum Kentucky* (Lexington: University Press of Kentucky, 2003), 141–143.

20. James A. Ramage and Andrea S. Watkins, *Kentucky Rising: Democracy, Slavery, and Culture from the Early Republic to the Civil War* (Lexington: University Press of Kentucky, 2011), 271–272.

21. Bullock to William Bodley, 29 January 1849, Bodley Papers, FHS; *Louisville Examiner*, 11 August 1849. William Freehling puts this argument forward in his works. Freehling cites the divisions within the South as the key to both secession and the demise of the Confederacy; see Freehling, *Road to Disunion*, vol. 2; Freehling, *The South vs. the South: How Anti-Confederate Southerners Shaped the Course of the Civil War* (New York: Oxford University Press, 2001). The unionist sentiment of Kentuckians was anything but a lack of commitment to slavery. On the contrary, their commitment to slavery was a foundational component of their unionist sentiment. The union was what gave slavery its vitality in Kentucky because it was so diverse.

22. My understanding of sectionalism as nationalism is strongly influenced by Edward L. Ayers, *All over the Map: Rethinking American Regions* (Baltimore: Johns Hopkins University Press, 1996).

23. Ramage and Watkins, *Kentucky Rising*, 274–275.

24. Brad Asher, *Cecelia and Fanny: The Remarkable Friendship between an Escaped Slave and Her Former Mistress* (Lexington: University Press of Kentucky, 2011), 102–103.

25. Ibid., 104–105.

26. Alexis de Tocqueville, *Democracy in America*, trans., ed., and with an introduction by Harvey C. Mansfield and Delba Winthrop (Chicago: University of Chicago Press, 2002), 331–332.

27. Mark Twain, *The Adventures of Huckleberry Finn* (New York: Bantam Books, 1981), 85.

28. The debate over the degree of difference between the antebellum North and South has a historiography dating back to the Civil War. Covering ideology, labor systems, social development, and politics, some of the most well-known works include, Foner, *Free Soil, Free Labor, Free Men*; Levine, *Half Slave and Half Free*; Huston, *Calculating the Value of the Union*; Ashworth, *Slavery, Capitalism, and Politics*, vols. 1–2; William J. Cooper, *Liberty and Slavery: Southern Politics to 1860* (Columbia: University of South Carolina Press, 2000). The above list is not exhaustive, but these works stress the inherent and irreconcilable differences between northern and southern societies. Recently Edward Ayers and William Thomas developed a close analysis of two counties, one in Virginia and the other in Pennsylvania. Through their analysis they discovered that slavery had led to distinctly different social and economic patterns in the southern county. However, the differences between the free and the slave counties represented different aspects of modernity, rather than a division between a modern society and a premodern society. In the current study I used some of the same points of comparison and methods as Ayers and Thomas did, but I had different results. Thomas and Ayers compared two counties they believed to be socially similar, but those counties did not border one another. In contrast, the results of my analysis

demonstrated striking cross-river similarities between counties bordering the Ohio River. I have argued for the importance of the Ohio River in the creation of these similarities. Therefore my work does not directly dispute the work of Ayers and Thomas but instead complicates it. The Ohio River played a vital role in the creation of the borderland and led to similar social and economic developments. The work and resources used by Ayers and Thomas can be found at http://valley.lib.virginia.edu (accessed October 2012).

29. I accessed all of the data analyzed in this chapter using the University of Virginia's online census browser, http://mapserver.lib.virginia.edu (accessed October 2012). To determine cash value per farm I divided the total cash value of farms by the total number of farms. To determine the value per acre I first totaled the acres of improved and unimproved land, and then I divided the total cash value of farms by the total acreage.

30. Historians have debated the economic differences between the North and the South for years. Without dispute, historians agree that the North's manufacturing production dwarfed that of the South. In addition the North developed a far more extensive railroad system than the South did. However, northern production dwarfed that of most European nations. Cotton was king in the South, and as Huston, *Calculating the Value of the Union*, has demonstrated, southerners invested heavily in slaves. In addition the South had an extensive river system to aid in transportation. Based on the historiography, it is my understanding that slavery did, in fact, have a powerful impact on the South's agricultural economy. In addition much work has been done revealing the links between the northern and southern economies, so discussing them as two separate entities may be misleading. Instead it seems that there was one national economy that had numerous working parts. A wonderful synthesis of the historiography on slavery and capitalism is Seth Rockman, "The Future of Civil War Era Studies: Slavery and Capitalism," *Journal of the Civil War Era* 2, no. 1 (March 2012), accessed at http://journalofthecivilwarera.com/forum-the-future-of-civil-war-era-studies/the-future-of-civil-war-era-studies-slavery-and-capitalism/#to-t he-future-of-civil-war-era-studies-slavery-and-capitalism-n-7 (accessed June 2012). Some works on the southern economy include Robert William Fogel and Stanley L. Engerman, *Time on the Cross: The Economics of American Negro Slavery* (Boston: Little, Brown, 1974); Gavin Wright, *Political Economy of the Cotton South: Households, Markets, and Wealth in the Nineteenth Century* (New York: W. W. Norton, 1978); Robert William Fogel, *Without Consent or Contract: The Rise and Fall of American Slavery* (New York: W. W. Norton, 1989); Tom Downey, *Planting a Capitalist South: Masters, Merchants, and Manufacturers in the Southern Interior, 1790–1860* (Baton Rouge: Louisiana State University Press, 2006); Aaron W. Marrs, *Railroads in the Old South: Pursuing Progress in a Slave Society* (Baltimore: Johns Hopkins University Press, 2009); Harry L. Watson, "Slavery and Development in a Dual Economy: The South and the Market Revolution," in Melvyn Stokes and Stephen Conway, eds., *The Market Revolution in America: Social, Political, and Religious Expressions, 1800–1880* (Charlottesville: University of Virginia Press, 1996), 43–73.

Manufacturing development along the Ohio River suggests the important link between transportation and development. Along the Ohio River, shipbuilding turned New Albany into a manufacturing center. The Ohio River encouraged the development of New Albany's economy, and New Albany in turn furthered the development of the larger Ohio River economy. But more provocatively, the absence of a major industrial center in Indiana reveals the coherence of the regional economy. With Cincinnati and Louisville there was no need for another major city, and thus one did not develop in southern Indiana. In this particular case Louisville, a slaveholding city, and Cincinnati, a nonslaveholding city, combined to feed the needs of the larger region. All of this is to suggest that the logic of the market economy in antebellum America did not necessarily heed sectional boundaries.

31. The breakdown of regional differences at the county level suggests that broad comparisons fail to do justice to the complexities of local economies and their place in the national economy. Recently Marc Egnal has made the argument that the economic factors caused the Civil War. He argues that, rather than slavery, oppositional economic development in the 1850s set the sections at odds. In particular the Great Lakes economy reoriented the larger northern economy, creating stronger east-west ties than north-south ties. Also the upper South became more closely tied to the northern economy. See Marc Egnal, *Clash of Extremes: Economic Origins of the Civil War* (New York: Hill and Wang, 2009). On the one hand, Egnal's argument for the disengagement of the northern and southern economies sits awkwardly with the coherence of Ohio River economy. On the other hand, given the combination of the Great Lakes economy with his argument for the upper South, the Ohio River Valley's economic coherence makes a lot of sense. How this region both undermines and supports Egnal's argument is suggestive of the inherent contradictions of the Ohio River borderland.

32. Potter, *Impending Crisis*, 405–447.

33. There are numerous places to get the results of the 1860 election by county, but oddly the most user-friendly version, because of its size and readability, is at http://en.wikipedia.org/wiki/United_States_presidential_ele ction,_1860 (accessed January 2012).

34. I determined the growth rates by subtracting the 1850 total from the 1860 total and then dividing the result by the 1850 total.

35. On the Republican Party, see Gienapp, *Origins of the Republican Party*; on the breakdown of the Whigs on a broad scale and the development of the political alignment in the 1850s, see Holt, *Political Crisis*.

36. *Indiana Daily State Sentinel*, 27 January 1860; Stephen I. Rockenbach, "'War upon Our Border'": War and Society in Two Ohio Valley Communities, 1861–1865" (Ph.D. diss., University of Cincinnati, 2005), 61, 17.

37. Anne E. Marshall, *Creating a Confederate Kentucky: The Lost Cause and Civil War Memory in a Border State* (Chapel Hill: University of North Carolina Press, 2010), 19; Asher, *Cecilia and Fanny*, 105.

38. Andrew R. L. Cayton, *Ohio: The History of a People* (Columbus: Ohio State University Press, 2002), 126–130; James Madison, *The Indiana Way: A State History*

(Bloomington: Indiana University Press, 1986), 197–198; Jennifer L. Weber, *Copperheads: The Rise and Fall of Lincoln's Opponents in the North* (New York: Oxford University Press, 2006).

39. James McPherson, *Battle Cry Freedom: The Civil War Era* (New York: Oxford University Press, 1988), 294–297; Ramage and Watkins, *Kentucky Rising*, 289–296; Asher, *Cecilia and Fanny*, 105–107.

40. Prior to the election, Union general Ambrose Burnside arrested Vallandigham for a speech denouncing the war and Lincoln. A military tribunal convicted Vallandigham and sentenced him to two years imprisonment, but Lincoln decided to exile him to the Confederacy. Finding Tennessee less than hospitable, Vallandigham exiled himself to Canada, where he ran his campaign. He lost the election thanks in large part to the votes of Ohio soldiers who viewed a vote for Vallandigham as a vote for a traitor.

41. Marshall, *Creating a Confederate Kentucky*, 20; Freehling, *Reintegration of American History*, 233–236.

42. The historians Darrell Bigham and Marion Lucas both make the persuasive argument that the movement of African Americans destroyed slavery in the state; see Bigham, *Jordan's Banks*, 78–79; Lucas, *History of Blacks*, 152–177.

43. Tony Horwitz, *Confederates in the Attic: Dispatches from the Unfinished Civil War* (New York: Vintage Books, 1999), 89–124; David Blight, *Race and Reunion: The Civil War in American Memory* (Cambridge, MA: Belknap Press of Harvard University Press, 2001), 132–237; Marshall, *Creating a Confederate Kentucky*. Not coincidentally, the Underground Railroad museum is in Cincinnati, perhaps the most southern of northern cities before the Civil War. Despite Kentucky's official neutrality, many Kentuckians have a deep attachment to the Confederacy. White residents celebrate their rebel heritage by advertising numerous antebellum homes and Civil War battlefields in tourism brochures. Yet in some ways the borderland remains. The landscape of southern Indiana more closely resembles Kentucky countryside than the cities to the north, and residents speak with a southern accent thicker than that of residents of Louisville, who call their environ Kentuckiana as an expression of their close ties with the cities of New Albany and Jeffersonville across the river.

INDEX

abolitionists: 14, 190–91, 199, 207–8, 219, 294 n.51, 304 n.25; impact on the border, 7, 203–4; James Birney's conversion to abolitionism, 199–201; Kentuckians' response, 227–28; mob violence, 190–91, 202–3, 233 n.32; proslavery reaction, 162–63. *See also* African Americans; mob violence

Adams, John Quincy, 149, 151, 290 n.14

African Americans: abolitionism, 7, 193–95, 218–19; free communities, 116–18, 153–54, 180–81, 192–94; labor, 11, 49, 72–73, 79–80, 86–87, 109–11, 118–19, 163, 172–73, 178–79, 238–41; migration, 52–53, 67, 78–79, 90–91, 92, 191–93; mobility, 6, 76–77, 114–15, 120–22, 126–28, 170, 173, 176–77, 188, 249; population growth, 49–50, 72, 105, 113–14, 161, 189–90, 191–93, 209, 220–21, 224–25, 227–28. *See also* antislavery movement; colonization of African Americans; commodification; convention movement; emancipation; fugitive slaves; indentured servitude; racism; slavery

American Colonization Society, 134. *See also* colonization of African Americans

American Revolution, 26–27, 280 n.71

antislavery movement, 185–86; African Americans and, 186, 193–95; Indiana, 98–106, 139–42, 149–50, 157–60, 204, 222–25; Kentucky, 45–51, 53–55, 161–63, 200–201, 210–11, 225–28; Ohio, 80–84, 154–55, 203–2, 206–9, 220–22. *See also* abolitionists

Aron, Steven, 2–3, 252–53 n.4, 280–81 n.73

Bacon's Rebellion, 52

Badolett, John, 100–101

Barrow, David, 54

Berlin, Ira, 5, 255 n.10

Bibb, Henry, 120, 122, 169, 177–78, 181–82, 187, 189, 190, 299–300 n.25, 307 n.45

Birney, James, 199–201, 202, 203, 207, 208, 219

borderland, definition of, 2–4, 12, 16–17, 21, 28, 29, 41–42, 106–9, 112, 137–38, 163–64, 165–66, 167–69, 213–14, 229–41, 244–46, 250

Breckenridge, John, 47, 49, 52, 70

Bright, Jesse, 249

Brown, John, 222, 217

Brown, William Wells, 125, 175, 189

Buffalo Trace, 30 (map), 55–56

Bullitt, Alexander Scott, 73–76

canals, 154, 197

captivity, 18–19, 33–34, 55–57

Chase, Salmon P., 166, 208–9, 217, 218, 220, 221

Cincinnati, Ohio, 42, 78, 107, 114, 116–18, 120, 126, 127, 129–30, 151–54, 173, 179–81, 185, 187, 189–90, 192–94, 197, 201–4, 208, 210, 220–21, 232, 236, 238, 243, 248, 312 n.30, 313 n.43. *See also* Hamilton County, Ohio

Civil War, 246–49

Clark, George Rogers, 26, 29, 34

Clark County, Indiana, 97, 98, 101, 104, 113, 140, 197, 244

Clarke, Lewis, 170, 182, 183, 184, 188, 189

Clarke, Milton, 136, 207

Clay, Cassius, 210–11, 225–26

Clay, Henry, 48, 49, 51, 73, 134, 145, 216–17, 226, 245

colonization of African Americans, 133–35, 162, 164, 199, 200. *See also* American Colonization Society

commodification, 7, 73, 75–76, 119, 124–25,
    186–87, 214, 225. *See also* slave trade
Compromise of 1850, 215, 216–17
Constitution, U.S., 35–37, 40
convention movement, 185, 194–95, 218–19
Corlis family, 74–75, 76
Covington, Kentucky, 115, 129, 189, 197, 213
Craik, Reverend James, 227
Crittenden, John, 247, 249
Crosby, Isaac, 141–42

Daly, Richard, 165–66
Decker, Luke, 35, 40–41, 60, 62
Decker, Moses, 60–62, 271 n.35
dependence, 47–49, 52, 84–86, 109–10, 117,
    163, 276 n.31
Douglass, Frederick, 168, 182, 193, 218–19,
    286 n.44

emancipation: African Americans, 86, 104–5,
    172–73, 186, 194–95, 218–19; Indiana,
    92–95, 97–106; Kentucky, 45–51, 55,
    210–11, 225–28, 249–50
Evansville, Indiana, 193, 238, 239, 243–44
Ewing, Nathaniel, 58–59, 62, 65, 102, 110

Falls of the Ohio, 17, 20, 26, 29, 32, 55, 65
Fee, John G., 227
Filson, John, 52
Fletcher, Calvin, 110, 157–58
Floyd, Davis, 141–42, 143–44, 281–82 n.6,
    289 n.7
Floyd County, Indiana, 113, 192, 224–25,
    239, 244. *See also* New Albany, Indiana
Foner, Eric, 8, 310 n.28
Fort Duquense (Fort Pitt), 23–44
Freehling, William, 9, 258 n.19
French Empire, 16, 19, 20–25, 28, 32–35,
    41–42
Fugitive Slave Law of 1793, 57, 76, 140, 141,
    156, 166
Fugitive Slave Law of 1850, 166, 218, 219
fugitive slaves: interstate conflict, 82–84,
    139–44, 146–51, 206–8, 220–23; methods
    of escape, 120, 126–28, 131–33, 188–89,
    193; rationale for escape, 167–70, 173–74,
    176–79, 182–83; reclamation, 58–64,
    93–95, 141, 156–57, 190–91, 205–6,
    220–22, 223; violence and, 149–50,
    189–90, 220–22, 223

Garner, Margaret, 179–80
Garrison, William Lloyd, 199, 202–3
Giddings, Joshua, 204, 208, 220
Grant, Ulysses S., 248
Green, Elisha, 108
Gruenwald, Kim, 154, 265 n.53, 290–91 n.22

Haitian Revolution, 106–7
Hamilton County, Ohio, 85, 191, 230–32,
    236, 237, 238, 240, 242, 243
Harrison, William Henry, 68, 88–91, 93, 95,
    97–98, 100, 101, 105, 146, 277 n.38
Harrold, Stanley, 9, 254 n.6, 257 n.16, 308
    n.2
hemp, 181, 210, 249
Henderson County, Kentucky, 192–93, 239,
    242, 244, 307 n.48
Henson, Josiah, 120, 127, 173, 299 n.20, 302
    n.6
Holt, Michael, 8, 216, 245

immigration restrictions, 205; Indiana law
    (1831), 151, 158–59; 1851 Indiana Consti-
    tution, 223; Kentucky state constitution,
    225–26; Ohio black codes, 83–85, 153–54
indentured servitude, 58, 60–61, 64, 67–68,
    70–78, 80–82, 86–87, 89–91, 93, 95,
    103–5, 110, 111, 118, 160
Indiana: constitutional convention 1816,
    103–4; constitutional convention 1851,
    222–23
Indiana Territory, 68, 88–104
Innes, Harry, 48, 49, 51
Iroquois, 19, 21, 23, 25

Jackson, Andrew, 166, 189
Jefferson, Thomas, 66, 70, 84, 100, 145
Jefferson County, Kentucky, 61, 73, 113–14,
    140, 191–92, 209, 227, 232, 236, 238, 239,
    243. *See also* Louisville, Kentucky
Jeffersonville, Indiana, 101, 141
Jennings, Jonathan, 101–2, 105, 139–40, 142,
    144, 146–47, 151
Johnston, General Washington, 102, 105

Kaskaskia, Illinois, 21, 33, 34
Kentucky, constitutional convention: 1792,
    45–46; 1799, 49; 1849, 225–27
kidnapping, 9, 82, 111, 124, 130–31, 139,
    148, 152, 154–55, 156, 166, 167, 181, 184,

185–86, 193, 195, 202, 206–8, 218,
    221–22, 224, 295 n.3
Know-Nothing Party, 243
Knox County, Indiana, 56, 63, 91, 97, 102,
    104–5, 140, 150

Land Act of 1800, 88
Lincoln, Abraham, 123; election of, 241–46
Locke, John, 22
Lord Dunmore, 25–26
Louisville, Kentucky, 11, 17, 42, 55, 63,
    113–14, 116–18, 120, 121, 124, 126–27,
    149–50, 151, 165, 171, 172, 175, 178, 181,
    186–87, 193, 197, 209–11, 223, 225, 232,
    236, 243, 246–49

Madison, Indiana, 193, 113, 126, 127, 130,
    151, 165, 177, 187
Madison, James, 138
Magoffin, Beriah, 248, 249
Mahan, John B., 208
Malvin, John, 121, 122
Mason-Dixon Line, 3–4, 107, 244
Massie, Nathaniel, 66–67, 71, 78, 80–81
McNelly, Peter, 55–64
migration: race and, 85–88, 116, 153,
    191–93; reasons for, 29–32, 40, 51–55, 67,
    81, 97–98, 194–98, 239–41
military bounty lands, 66
Missouri Compromise (1820), 144–46,
    148–49
mob violence, 9, 82–83, 149–50, 153–54,
    189–90, 193–94, 201–2, 205, 208, 220–23,
    243
Monroe, James, 142, 151
Morton, Oliver, 246–47

New Albany, Indiana, 113, 116, 126, 149–50,
    151, 187, 224, 246, 249, 312 n.30
Newport, Kentucky, 129, 196, 197, 213, 227
newspapers, 93, 122, 124, 128, 130, 135,
    147–50, 156, 161, 166, 200–203, 210, 218,
    224, 227, 246
Nicholas, George, 47
Noble, James, 146, 148
Noble, Noah, 159–60, 206
Non-Importation Act (1833), 152, 161–62,
    175, 225
Northwest Ordinance (1787), 29, 37; article
    six, 1, 4, 16, 35–42, 57, 64, 65, 82, 96–97,
    163–64, 265 n.53

Northwest Territory, 4, 6, 13, 37–41, 51–53,
    55–56, 64, 65, 68

Ohio Black Laws, 84–88, 220
Ohio constitutional convention, 70–72,
    80–81
Ohio River: border conflict, 34–35, 39–40,
    55–64, 82–84, 135–36, 139–44, 146–51,
    156–58, 163–64, 206–8, 211–14, 220–23,
    246–50; economic function of, 118–20,
    186–87, 192–93, 196–98, 209–10, 225,
    230–41; formation of, 16–17; slave trade
    and, 123–25, 162, 170–71, 175, 176, 179,
    186–88, 193, 210, 214, 225, 228; travel
    and, 21–22, 29–30, 114, 122–23
Overseers of the Poor, 84–85, 118, 153. *See
    also* dependence

Panic of 1819, 118–19, 161
Parke, Benjamin, 141, 156, 289 n.8
Patterson, Robert, 82–83
Pontiac's Rebellion, 24
population growth, 18–19, 30–32, 49–50,
    112–14, 196–97, 243; Indiana, 97–98, 113,
    191–92, 224–25; Kentucky, 72, 113–14,
    161, 192–93, 209–11, 227–28; Ohio, 114,
    191–92, 221–22
Proclamation of 1763, 25

Quakers (Society of Friends), 97–98, 130–31,
    159, 223
Quebec Act, 26, 28

racism, 6, 11, 48–49, 65–66, 76, 84–86,
    90–92, 106–7, 115–18, 128–30, 132–36,
    147–48, 153–54, 159–62, 163–64, 166–67,
    183–84, 189–90, 205–8, 220, 222–23,
    249–50
Rankin, John, 199
Ray, James B., 116, 157–59
Rice, David, 46, 47, 48, 51, 133, 266 n.3

Second Great Awakening, 199
Seven Years' War, 24
Shawnee, 19, 21, 23, 25–26
Sherman, William T., 248
Short, Charles, 79
Slaughter, Gabriel, 139, 142, 146–47
slavery: European empires and, 33–34,
    38–39; extension into Indiana, 35, 38–41,
    88–106; hiring out, 5, 11, 32, 50, 53,

slavery (*continued*)
    72–77, 80–81, 87, 116–18, 119–21, 159,
    167, 172–74, 176, 178–79, 209–10, 296
    n.5, 298 n.16, 299 n.19; necessary evil,
    defense, 7, 46, 73, 96, 162–63, 186;
    settlement of Kentucky, 45, 49–50, 52–53,
    72–73
slave trade, 34–35, 44, 56–57; domestic,
    123–25, 162, 170–71, 175, 176, 179,
    186–88, 193, 210, 214, 225, 228
Spradling, Washington, 121, 167
St. Clair, Arthur, 39–41, 55, 63–64, 70–71
steamboats: African Americans and, 12, 109,
    120, 123–25, 127, 130, 151, 167, 175, 179,
    181–82, 186–88, 189, 193, 223; impact on
    economy, 10, 112, 114, 122–23, 152, 227
Stephens, Robert, 142–49, 151
Stout, Elihu, 90
Stowe, Harriet Beecher, 1, 171, 185
Sumner, Charles, 217–18

Tarvideau, Bartholomew, 34, 39
Taylor, Waller, 103, 146, 290 n.12
Tiffin, Edward, 67–68, 71, 80–81
Tipton, John, 142–44, 151, 160, 245
tobacco cultivation, 39, 74–75, 107, 193, 239,
    249

Tocqueville, Alexis de, 229, 240
Turner, George, 57–58, 61–65, 68
Twain, Mark, 229

Underground Railroad, 193
unionism, 6–8, 211, 215–16, 219, 222,
    227–28, 241–50, 257 n.16

Vallandigham, Clement, 221, 228, 248, 313
    n.40
Vanderburgh, Henry, 56–64, 93–94, 102
Vanderburgh County, Indiana, 238, 239, 243,
    244. *See also* Evansville, Indiana
Vannorsdall, Simon, 93–95
Vincennes, Indiana, 32–35, 39–41, 55–61,
    63, 68, 88–89, 91–95, 97, 100, 101, 102,
    150, 264 n.39, 276 n.36

Washington, George, 24, 38, 41, 57
Weld, Theodore Dwight, 199, 201, 202, 219
Western Confederacy, 26–27, 31
White, Richard, 137
Wilmot Proviso, 216, 220. *See also*
    Compromise of 1850
Woodruff, Seth, 149–50, 291 n.25
Worthington, Thomas, 67–68, 70–71, 80–81,
    97, 106–7

ACKNOWLEDGMENTS

This book is the product of many years of reflection and guidance, making it impossible to truly list everyone who contributed to the final project. These acknowledgments, then, much like the book itself, cannot be truly comprehensive. I have been the beneficiary of supportive scholars, colleagues, friends, and family, and for that I consider myself lucky.

Robert Lockhart at the University of Pennsylvania Press has helped with the sometimes mysterious process of transforming my manuscript into a book. My readers provided thoughtful and challenging critiques to the manuscript. In particular I want to thank Andrew Cayton for his reminder to take my own advice and "listen to the river."

Before it was a book, this project began as my attempt to write a researchable article. Several colleagues convinced me that I had, in fact, stumbled onto something much more significant. When working through the project, Thomas Slaughter significantly shaped and improved each chapter with his straightforward and insightful comments. His quiet guidance helped make me the scholar I am today. I am only now realizing just how much wisdom he passed on to me. Jon Coleman had a way of asking ostensibly simple questions that challenged my assumptions and improved my arguments. Linda Przybyszewski and Richard Pierce challenged me to realize and articulate the significance of the project. David Waldstreicher provided trenchant and illuminating criticisms that made this a far better project. He has generously provided comments at all stages, including the final polishing revisions. David's unflagging support has helped me develop from a diffident researcher to a confident scholar.

Without the help of archivists and staff members at various institutions I could never have found so much wonderful material. When I first started the project, Thomas Hamm at Earlham College helpfully pulled several items I had no idea were even in the collections. At the Indiana Historical Society, Wilma Moore pointed me in the direction of numerous articles and gems from the archives. The staffs of the Indiana State Library, the Cincinnati Historical Society, and the Ohio Historical Society skillfully found any items I requested. I spent a week as a Fellow at the Filson Historical Society, and during that time staff members helped me discover more material in their archives than I could have possibly imagined. The conversations were also rewarding. All in all, it was a very fruitful week of research.

I am indebted to numerous scholars, many of whom have no idea of my indebtedness. William Freehling's work combining social and political history, Ira Berlin's work on the variations within slavery, and borderland scholars such as Stephen Aron have provided inspiration and frameworks for building my narrative. I have presented much of the material in this book at conferences, and the comments by chairs and commentators continuously helped me refine my arguments. Glenn Crothers at the Filson Historical Society also deserves special recognition. Glenn saw enough promise in an article that I submitted to *Ohio Valley History* to see it through significant revisions and put it into print. The article went on to win the Richard Wade Award, thanks in large part to Glenn's efforts.

While at Notre Dame I benefited from numerous engaging and challenging discussions with colleagues. In particular, I enjoyed conversations with my cadre of fellow early Americanists, Bryan Smith, Chris Osborne, and Erin Miller. Teaching at North Dakota State University has been a challenging and rewarding experience. In particular, teaching writing improved my own ability to formulate and articulate an argument. For that, I would like to thank all of my students from my various writing classes.

Without the financial support I received, this project would not exist. The Filson Historical Society, the Society of Indiana Pioneers, and the University of Notre Dame provided travel grants that allowed me to complete my archival research.

I would also like to thank my family. My brother, brother-in-law, sister, and sister-in-law have all expressed interest in my book. They may not know it, but simple questions of interest always meant a lot to me. Bill and Sherrie Blodgett (Dad and Mom B.) have been both loving and supportive throughout the process. My parents, Bill and Nancy Salafia, have supported me through every stage of my life. They continue to provide guidance both in their words and in their example. Thanks to my dogs, Lenny and Steve, writing this book has never been a solitary process. Their not-so-subtle reminders to stop work and their perfectly timed licks to my face kept me both sane and happy.

Last and most important, I would like to thank my wife, Elizabeth Blodgett Salafia. I cannot possibly put into words just how much I owe her. Her love and understanding gave me the strength to carry on, even when I did not want to do so. I am thankful for every day I have with her and will be forever.